Metareasoning

Metareasoning

Thinking about Thinking

edited by Michael T. Cox and Anita Raja

foreword by Eric Horvitz

The MIT Press
Cambridge, Massachusetts
London, England

This book was set in Stone Sans and Stone Serif by Toppan Best-set Premedia Limited.

Library of Congress Cataloging-in-Publication Data

Metareasoning: thinking about thinking / edited by Michael T. Cox and Anita Raja ; foreword by Eric Horvitz.
p. cm.
Inculdes bibliographical references and index.
ISBN 978-0-262-01480-9 (hardcover : alk. paper), 978-0-262-53875-6 (pb.)
1. Artificialintelligence. 2. Reasoning (Psychology). 3. Intellect. I. Cox, Michael .,T 1955 – II. Raja, Anita, 1975 – .
Q335.M3987 2011
006.3—dc22

2010015787

Contents

Foreword

By its very nature, the evolving field of artificial intelligence is fundamentally a discipline of reasoning about reasoning, or *metareasoning*. The passionate pursuit of insights about the computational mechanisms underlying thought and intelligent behavior starts with a spark of curiosity about the nature of reasoning processes—when the future AI scientist first turns the spotlight of his or her attention on reasoning as the *object* of analysis. For a great deal of the history of reflection about the nature of intelligence, AI scientists have played the role of metareasoner. However, in several waves of effort, extending back to the earliest days of AI research, scientists have explored opportunities for endowing computational systems with an autonomous ability to reflect about and to guide their processes of perception, inference, and action. Research on metareasoning has led to new insights about principles of intelligence—and has yielded concrete machinery that limited agents can employ to enhance their performance amid the varying and uncertain challenges they face in the open world.

This interesting collection of essays captures a spectrum of approaches to metareasoning, stemming from reports by researchers who gathered at a workshop entitled "Metareasoning: Thinking about Thinking," held in Chicago in July 2008. Readers will find in the collection a tapestry of intriguing ideas that includes diverse perspectives on metareasoning that draw from the rich intellectual traditions of philosophy, cognitive psychology, and computer science. The chapters communicate the depth and promise of research on imbuing computational systems with an ability to reflect about themselves, and about the worlds in which they are immersed.

Eric Horvitz
October 2009

I Basic Themes

1 Metareasoning: An Introduction

Michael T. Cox and Anita Raja

Philosophers and cognitive scientists of many persuasions have long wondered what is unique to human intelligence. Although many ideas have been proposed, a common differentiator appears to be a pervasive capacity for thinking about ourselves in terms of who we are, how others see us, and in terms of where we have been and where we want to go. As humans, we continually think about ourselves and our strengths and weaknesses in order to manage both the private and public worlds within which we exist. But the artificial intelligence (AI) community has not only wondered about these phenomena; it has attempted to implement actual machines that mimic, simulate, and perhaps even replicate this same type of reasoning called *metareasoning*.

The term is an overloaded one, and no consensus exists as to its definition. Some have described metareasoning computationally in terms of specific programs and algorithms, whereas others have analyzed metacognition and focused on data from human experience and behavior. Indeed, Ann Brown (1987) described research into metacognition as a "many-headed monster of obscure parentage." Many of the technical terms used in research on metareasoning and related areas are quite confusing. Often, authors use different terms for the same concept (e.g., introspection and reflection), and sometimes the same terms are used in different ways (e.g., metareasoning has been cast as both process and object). The literature contains many related topics such as metaknowledge, metamemory, self-adaptation, and self-awareness. The index in the back of this book demonstrates the complexity of the subject by its length. So the main goal of this book is to assemble some measure of consistency and soundness in the topic.

To attempt to achieve progress toward this goal we have written a very brief summary of some existing research and put forth a simple, abstract model of metareasoning. We then asked numerous scientific researchers on the subject to address our "manifesto" by describing the relationship between their research and this model. The task is to compare and contrast separate theories and implementations to this sketch of what lies at the core of metareasoning. This model certainly has some weaknesses. The method of abstraction leaves out various details that may prove critical to a more in-depth understanding of the mechanisms behind the process. We also recognize that metareasoning is a much larger umbrella under which many related topics such as metaknowledge lie. Yet by going through this exercise, we hope that the reader and the researcher will both gain a deeper insight into the knowledge structures and computation involved.

Metareasoning: A Manifesto

The twenty-first century is experiencing a renewed interest in an old idea within artificial intelligence that goes to the heart of what it means to be both human and intelligent. This idea is that much can be gained by thinking about one's own thinking. Traditionally within cognitive science and artificial intelligence, thinking or *reasoning* has been cast as a decision cycle within an action-perception loop similar to that shown in figure 1.1. An intelligent agent perceives some stimuli from the environment and behaves rationally to achieve its goals by selecting some action from its set of competencies. The result of these actions at the ground level is subsequently perceived at the object level, and the cycle continues. *Metareasoning* is the process of reasoning about this reasoning cycle. It consists of both the metalevel control of computational activities and the introspective monitoring of reasoning (see figure 1.2). This cyclical arrangement represents a higher-level reflection of the standard action-perception cycle, and as such, it represents the perception of reasoning and its control.

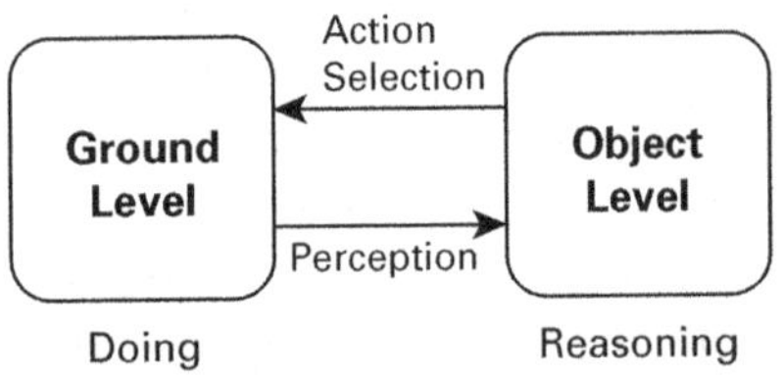

Figure 1.1
The action-perception cycle.

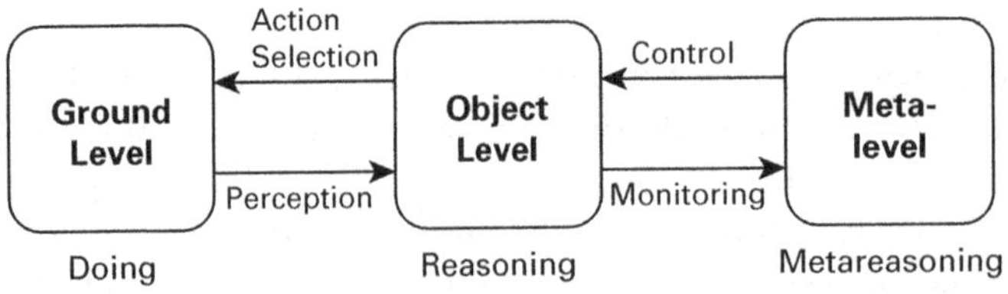

Figure 1.2
Duality in reasoning and acting.

The goal of *metalevel control* is to improve the quality of its decisions by spending some effort to decide what and how much reasoning to do as opposed to what actions to do. It balances resources between object-level actions (computations) and ground-level actions (behaviors). But while metalevel control allows agents to dynamically adapt their object-level computation, it could interfere with ground-level performance. Thus identifying the decision points that require metalevel control is of importance to the performance of agents operating in resource-bounded environments.

Introspective monitoring is necessary to gather sufficient information with which to make effective metalevel control decisions. Monitoring may involve the gathering of computational performance data so as to build a profile of various decision algorithms. It could involve generating explanations for object-level choices and their effect on ground-level performance. When reasoning fails at some task, it may involve the explanation of the causal contributions of failure and the diagnosis of the object-level reasoning process.

Under the banner of *distributed metareasoning*, significant research questions also exist concerning the extent to which metalevel control and monitoring affects multiagent activity. In multiagent systems, where the quality of joint decisions affects individual outcomes, the value obtained by an agent exploring some portion of its decision space can be dependent on the degree to which other agents are exploring complementary parts of their spaces. The problem of coordinated metalevel control refers to this question of how agents should coordinate their strategies to maximize the value of their joint actions.

Finally, any complete cognitive system that reasons about itself and its actions in the world will necessarily combine many aspects of metareasoning. A truly intelligent agent will have some conception of self that controls its reasoning choices, represents the products of monitoring, and coordinates the self in social contexts. Hence, a comprehensive approach will include *models of self* in support of metareasoning and integrated cognition.

Metalevel Control

A significant research history exists with respect to metareasoning (Anderson & Oates, 2007; Cox, 2005), and much of it is driven by the problems of limited rationality. That is because given the size of the problem space, the limitations on resources, and the amount of uncertainty in the environment, finite agents can often obtain only approximate solutions. So, for example, with an anytime algorithm that incrementally refines plans, an agent must choose between executing the current plan or further deliberation with the hope of improving the plan. When making this choice, the agent is reasoning about its own reasoning (i.e., planning) as well as its potential actions in the world (i.e., the plan). As such this represents the problem of explicit control of reasoning.

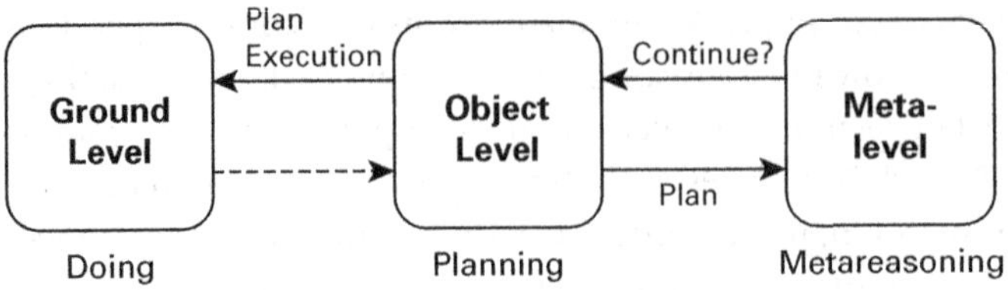

Figure 1.3
Classical metareasoning (from Russell & Wefald, 1991).

Figure 1.2, along its upper portion, illustrates the control side of reasoning. Reasoning controls action at the ground level in the environment; whereas metareasoning controls the reasoning at the object level. For an anytime controller, metareasoning decides when reasoning is sufficient and thus action can proceed. Although other themes exist within the metareasoning tradition (e.g., Leake, 1996), this characterization is a common one (e.g., Raja & Lesser, 2007; Hansen & Zilberstein, 2001; Russell & Wefald, 1991).

Now consider figure 1.3. The most basic decision in classical metareasoning is whether an agent should act or continue to reason. For example, the anytime planner always has a current best plan produced by the object-level reasoning. Given that the passage of time itself has a cost, the metareasoner must decide whether the expected benefit gained by planning further outweighs the cost of doing nothing. If so, it produces another plan; otherwise, it executes the actions in the plan it already has. Note that this simple decision can be performed without reference to any perception of the ground level. Of course, many more sophisticated metalevel control policies exist that include feedback.

Introspective Monitoring

The complementary side of metareasoning is less well studied. The introspective monitoring of reasoning about performance requires an agent to maintain some kind of internal feedback in addition to perception, so that it can perform effectively and can evaluate the results of metareasoning. For instance, Zilberstein (Zilberstein & Russell, 1996) maintains statistical profiles of past metareasoning choices and the associated performance and uses them to mediate the subsequent control and dynamic composition of reasoning processes.

But introspective monitoring can be even more explicit. If the reasoning that is performed at the object level (and not just its results) is represented in a declarative knowledge structure that captures the mental states and decision-making sequence, then these knowledge structures can themselves be passed to the metalevel for monitoring. For example, the Meta-AQUA system (Cox & Ram, 1999) keeps a trace of its

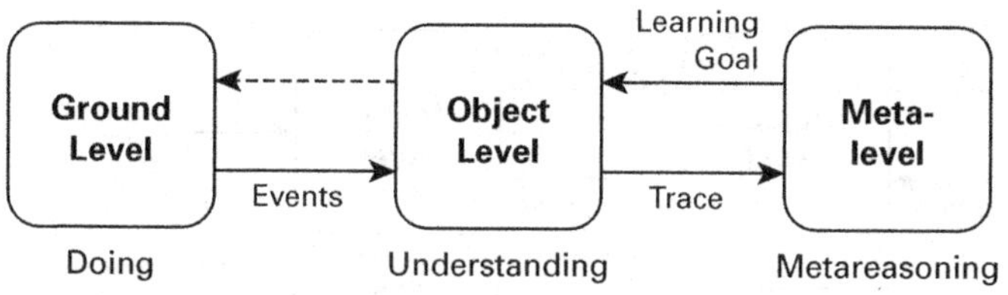

Figure 1.4
Introspective monitoring in Meta-AQUA.

story understanding decisions in structures called a *trace meta-explanation pattern* (TMXP). Here the object-level story understanding task is to explain anomalous or unusual events in a ground-level story perceived by the system (see figure 1.4).[1] Then, if this explanation process fails, Meta-AQUA passes the TMXP and the current story representation to a learning subsystem. The learner performs an introspection of the trace to obtain an explanation of the explanation failure called an *introspective meta-explanation pattern* (IMXP). The IMXPs are used to generate a set of learning goals that are passed back to control the object-level learning and hence improve subsequent understanding. TMXPs explain *how* reasoning occurs; IMXPs explain *why* reasoning fails.

Note that the object-level process described above is a story-understanding task that makes no reference to the execution of personal actions at the ground level. The emphasis here is on the perception and monitoring side of the model; that is, the understanding or comprehension processes in the model are equally as important as the action and control processes were in figure 1.3, and indeed they can be treated independently. However, most systems, especially agent-based systems, combine both in various fashions.

Distributed Metareasoning

In a multiagent context, if two or more agents need to coordinate their actions, the agents' metacontrol components must be on the same page. The agents must reason about the same problem and may need to be at the same stage of the problem-solving process. For example, suppose one agent decides to devote little time to communication/negotiation (Alexander et al., 2007) before moving to other deliberative decisions, while another agent sets aside a large portion of deliberation time for negotiation; the latter agent would waste time trying to negotiate with an unwilling partner.

We define an agent's problem-solving context as the information required for deliberative-level decision making, including the agent's current goals, action choices,

1. Meta-AQUA performs no action at the ground level. Rather, it perceives events representing characters in the story performing actions.

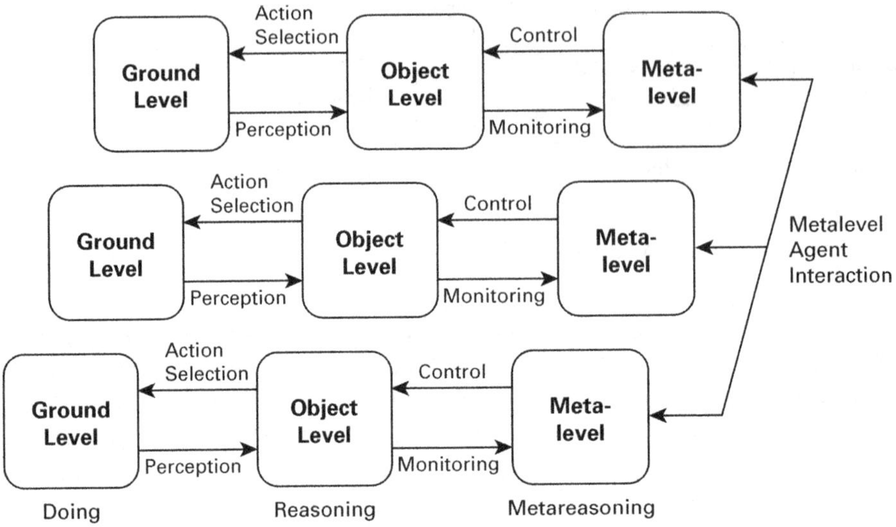

Figure 1.5
Metalevel reasoning among multiple agents.

its past and current performance, resource usage, dependence on other agents, and so on. Suppose the agent's context when it is in the midst of execution is called the *current context,* and a *pending context* is one where an agent deliberates about various "what-if" scenarios related to coordination with other agents. Distributed metareasoning can also be viewed as a coordination of problem-solving contexts. One metalevel control issue would be to decide when to complete deliberation in a pending context and when to replace the current context with the pending context. Thus, if an agent changes the problem-solving context on which it is focused, it must notify other agents with which it may interact. This suggests that the metacontrol component of each agent should have a multiagent policy where the content and timing of deliberations are choreographed carefully and include branches to account for what could happen as deliberation (and execution) plays out. Figure 1.5 describes the interaction among the metalevel control components of multiple agents.

Another metacontrol question when there are multiple pending contexts is to determine which pending context should be allocated resources for deliberation. In all of these examples, the metareasoning issues are a superset of single agent cases.

Models of Self

For a cognitive agent to behave intelligently in a physical and social environment with complex, dynamic interactions, many if not all of the features necessary for an integrated human-level model of intelligence are required. For it to succeed in such

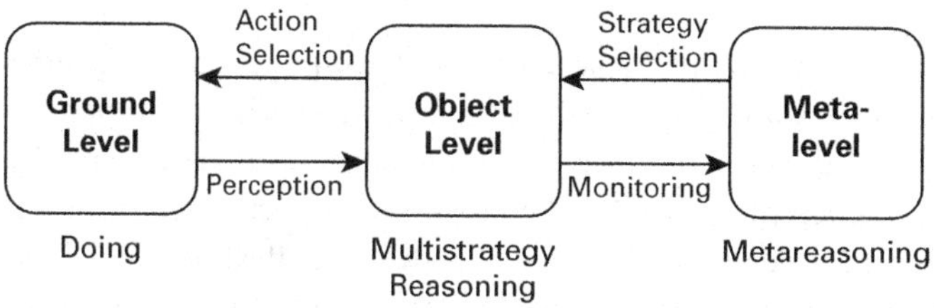

Figure 1.6
An integrated model of self.

an environment, an agent must perceive and interpret events in the world, including actions of other agents, and it must perform complex actions and interact in a social context. These constitute the minimal object-level requirements. At the metalevel, an agent must have a model of itself to represent the products of experience and to mediate the choices effectively at the object level. Facing novel situations, the successful agent must learn from experience and create new strategies based on its self-perceived strengths and weaknesses. Consider figure 1.6.

Monitoring at the metalevel can determine the kinds of mental actions at which the agent excels and those at which it fails. Using such introspective information allows the agent to choose reasoning strategies that best fit future intellectual demands, like the agent that selects actions based on past task performance. In more complicated approaches, the agent may actually construct a complex reasoning strategy rather than simply choose an atomic one. In either case, the basis for such metareasoning comes from a picture of itself, its capacities (both physical and mental), and its relationships to other agents with which it must interact to recognize and solve problems.

Many theorists have speculated as to the interactions between levels of representation and process (i.e., the architecture), but few researchers have attempted to implement the full spectrum of computation implied in a comprehensive model of self (see Singh, 2005, for one such attempt). We challenge the AI community to consider seriously the problems of metareasoning in this larger context. How would an agent best understand itself and use such insight to construct a deliberate knowledge-level reasoning policy? Can an agent know enough about itself and its colleagues' self-knowledge to communicate its metalevel needs for coordination? Can it estimate the time it might take to negotiate a coordination policy with its fellow agents and hence negotiate the time and length of a negotiation session? Finally, could an intelligent soccer agent decide that it is good at planning but getting weak at passing, and so aspire to becoming a coach? We claim that the model of acting, reasoning, and metareasoning put forth in this chapter can help maintain clarity if this challenge is to be embraced and questions like these pursued.

Discussion

This manifesto has tried to present in plain language and simple diagrams a brief description of a model of metareasoning that mirrors the action-selection and perception cycle in first-order reasoning. Many theories and implementations are covered by this model, including those concerning metalevel control, introspective monitoring, distributed metareasoning, and models of self. We claim that it is flexible enough to include all of these metacognitive activities, yet simple enough to be quite parsimonious. Figures 1.3 through 1.6 and their accompanying examples suggest some variations on the potential implementations rather than dictate an agenda. We offer the model as a framework to which the community can compare and contrast individual theories, but most of all, we hope that this model can clarify our thinking about thinking about thinking.

Overview

Each chapter considers this model at some level of detail. Starting with this chapter, Part I sets the stage by providing some of the fundamental themes within this book. Don Perlis (chapter 2) notes the ubiquity of self-reference within the metareasoning literature (e.g., the previous sentence) and argues that reference in general has at its core a concept that is at the heart of what it means for an object to refer to itself. Shlomo Zilberstein (chapter 3) examines several approaches to building rational agents and the extent to which they rely on metareasoning. He demonstrates the application of an optimal metareasoning approach using anytime algorithms and discusses its relationships with other approaches to bounded rationality. The rest of the book follows the structure of the manifesto and is divided into four parts: Part II is on metalevel control; Part III is on introspective monitoring; Part IV is on distributed metareasoning; and Part V is on models of self.

In examining metalevel control in Part II, Susan L. Epstein and Smiljana Petrovic (chapter 4) employ metareasoning to manage large bodies of heuristics and to learn to make decisions more effectively. Their approach gauges the program's skill within a class of problems and determines when learning for a class is complete and whether it has to be restarted. George Alexander, Anita Raja, and David Musliner (chapter 5) discuss their efforts to add metalevel control to a Markov decision process–based deliberative agent. The agent uses heuristic guidance to incrementally expand its considered state space and solve the resulting MDP. Jihie Kim, Karen Meyers, Melinda Gervasio, and Yolanda Gil (chapter 6) describe a metalevel framework for coordinating different agents using explicit learning goals. By supporting both top-down and bottom-up control strategies, the framework enables flexible interaction among learners and is shown to be effective for coordinating learning agents to acquire complex process knowledge for a medical logistics domain. Paul Robertson and Robert Laddaga (chapter 7) discuss metareasoning in an image-interpretation architecture called GRAVA where the goal is to produce good image interpretations under a wide range of environmental conditions. The section concludes with Vincent Conitzer's (chapter 8) discussion on how to formulate variants of the metareasoning problem as formal computational problems. He also presents the implications of the computational complexity of these problems.

In exploring introspective monitoring in Part III, Michael T. Cox (chapter 9) examines the role of self-modifying code, self-knowledge, self-understanding, and self-explanation as aspects of self from a computational stance. Ashok K. Goel and Joshua Jones (chapter 10) describe the use of metaknowledge for structural credit assignment in a classification hierarchy when the classifier makes an incorrect prediction. They present a scheme in which the semantics of the intermediate abstractions in the classification hierarchy are grounded in percepts in the world and show that this scheme enables self-diagnosis and self-repair of knowledge content at intermediate nodes in the hierarchy. Josep Lluís Arcos, Oğuz Mülâyim, and David B. Leake (chapter 11) present an introspective model for autonomously improving the performance of CBR systems. To achieve this goal, the model reasons about problem-solving failures by monitoring the reasoning process, determining the causes of the failures, and performing actions that will improve future reasoning processes. Matthew D. Schmill and colleagues (chapter 12) describe the metacognitive loop (MCL), a human-inspired metacognitive approach to dealing with failures in automated systems behavior. MCL attempts to improve robustness in cognitive systems in a domain-general way by offering a plug-in reasoning component that will help decrease the brittleness of AI systems.

In Part IV on distributed metareasoning, Anita Raja and colleagues (chapter 13) present a generalized metalevel control framework for multiagent systems and discuss the issues involved in extending single-agent metalevel control to a team of cooperative agents requiring coordination. They present a methodology for constructing a class of MDPs that can model the interactions necessary for coordinating metalevel control among multiple agents. Zachary Rubinstein, Stephen S. Smith, and Terry Zimmerman (chapter 14) consider the role of metareasoning in achieving effective coordination among multiple agents that maintain and execute joint plans in an uncertain environment. They identify several degrees of freedom in configuring the agent's core computational components, each of which affects the proportion of computational cycles given to local scheduling and interagent coordination processes. They also motivate the need for online reasoning by considering how aspects of the current control state affect the utility of different configurations. Catriona M. Kennedy (chapter 15) presents a distributed metareasoning architecture for a single cognitive agent where the metalevel and object-level components form a nonhierarchical network in which the metalevels mutually monitor and protect each other. She argues that coordination among metalevels can also allow the agent to explain itself in a coherent way. Brett J. Borghetti and Maria Gini (chapter 16) present a metareasoning system that relies on a prediction performance measurement and propose a novel model performance measurement called weighted prediction divergence that fulfills this need.

In Part V, several approaches to building models of self are presented. Fabrizio Morbini and Lenhart Schubert (chapter 17) highlight the importance of metareasoning for self-aware agents and discuss some key requirements of human-like self-awareness including using a highly expressive representation language for the formalization of metalevel axioms. Justin Hart and Brian Scassellati (chapter 18) discuss an approach to building rich models of the sensory and kinematic structure of robots and examine tasks to which such models may be applied. Here the task is for a robot to recognize itself in a mirror. Andrew S. Gordon, Jerry R. Hobbs, and Michael T. Cox (chapter 19) describe anthropomorphic self-models as an alternative approach to current approaches. They argue that developing integrated, broad-coverage, reusable self-models for metareasoning can be achieved by formalizing the commonsense theories that people have about their own human psychology.

In the concluding chapter, Aaron Sloman (chapter 20) surveys varieties of metacognition and draws our attention to some types that appear to play a role in intelligent biological individuals (e.g., humans) and which could also help with practical engineering goals.

Conclusion

As with many collections on technical subjects, this book raises as many questions as it answers. We have avoided an overly restrictive definition of metareasoning and have left it open to some variation in interpretation, as many of the chapters have done. Some generalities can be stated, however. In a sense, the metareasoning task is easier than that of object-level perception, because theoretically, no hidden state exists. In practice, many of the case studies described in this volume abstract the mental states and processes represented at the object level to make metareasoning tractable, and thus it is not possible to inspect all details at the object level. In fact, in some cases metareasoning can be modeled using the same techniques as object-level reasoning, but it is at a higher level of abstraction and has a nonmyopic view. In another sense, reasoning at the metalevel is more difficult than reasoning at the object level. This is because metareasoning is never performed in the absence of object-level reasoning. Consequently, metareasoning adds to the computational overhead of the object-level task, making the search space larger and the computational burden greater. Identifying the characteristics of problem domains where metareasoning is easier than object-level reasoning and vice versa is an area yet to be explored.

Another open issue is the relationship between metareasoning and learning. Although many of the chapters discuss learning, it is not clear how to formally map one to the other or even whether learning belongs to the object level or the metalevel. The AI literature describes many learning systems without reference to metareasoning; yet a number of chapters link learning strongly to a metareasoning framework (see chapters 4, 6, 10, and 11, for example). If one considers learning to be a change in the agent that improves its overall performance, then an agent's reasoning about itself should lead toward that goal.[2] But in much of the current machine learning research, the algorithmic focus is on data disembodied from any agent, or, at best, is on the agent's actions at the ground level.

The goal of this book is to present a comprehensive narrative that incorporates an integrated set of chapters on various themes pertaining to metareasoning from both artificial intelligence and cognitive science perspectives. It includes concepts from research on multiagent systems, planning and scheduling technology, learning, case-based reasoning, control theory, logic programming, autonomic computing, self-adaptive systems, and cognitive psychology. We hope the reader will find that the model described in the manifesto operates as a central theme that supports a larger narrative. The manifesto is intended to be a shared organizational framework to which each author compares and contrasts his or her theory, results, and implementational details. For the most part, the authors have found this to be a useful abstraction. We hope that the reader will as well.

Acknowledgments

The views, opinions, and findings contained in this essay are those of the authors and should not be interpreted as representing the official views or policies, either expressed or implied, of the Defense Advanced Research Projects Agency or the Department of Defense. This document has been approved for public release by DARPA for unlimited distribution.

References

Alexander, G., Raja, A., Durfee, E., & Musliner, D. (2007). Design paradigms for meta-control in multi-agent systems. In A. Raja & M. T. Cox (Eds.), *Proceedings of the First International Workshop on Metareasoning in Agent-based Systems* (pp. 92–103).

2. In some respects this is the implied perspective of Russell & Norvig, 2003, given the way they cast a learning agent (see Russell & Norvig, 2003, p. 53, fig. 2.15). The learning element (at the metalevel) receives knowledge from and makes changes to the performance element (at the object level).

Anderson, M. L., & Oates, T. (2007). A review of recent research in metareasoning and metalearning. *AI Magazine, 28*(1), 7–16.

Brown, A. (1987). Metacognition, executive control, self-regulation, and other more mysterious mechanisms. In F. E. Weinert & R. H. Kluwe (Eds.), *Metacognition, motivation, and understanding* (pp. 65–116). Hillsdale, NJ: Lawrence Erlbaum.

Cox, M. T. (2005). Metacognition in computation: A selected research review. *Artificial Intelligence, 169*(2), 104–141.

Cox, M. T., & Ram, A. (1999). Introspective multistrategy learning: On the construction of learning strategies. *Artificial Intelligence, 112,* 1–55.

Hansen, E., & Zilberstein, S. (2001). Monitoring and control of anytime algorithms: A dynamic programming approach. *Artificial Intelligence, 126*(1–2), 139–157.

Leake, D. B. (1996). Experience, introspection, and expertise: Learning to refine the case-based reasoning process. *Journal of Experimental & Theoretical Artificial Intelligence, 8*(3), 319–339.

Raja, A., & Lesser, V. (2007). A framework for meta-level control in multi-agent systems. *Autonomous Agents and Multi-Agent Systems, 15*(2), 147–196.

Russell, S. J., & Norvig, P. (2003). *Artificial intelligence: A modern approach* (2nd ed.). Upper Saddle River, NJ: Prentice Hall.

Russell, S. J., & Wefald, E. (1991). Principles of metareasoning. *Artificial Intelligence, 49,* 361–395.

Singh, P. (2005). *EM-ONE: An architecture for reflective commonsense thinking.* Unpublished doctoral dissertation, Massachusetts Institute of Technology, Department of Electrical Engineering and Computer Science, Cambridge, Massachusetts.

Zilberstein, S., & Russell, S. J. (1996). Optimal composition of real-time systems. *Artificial Intelligence, 82*(1–2), 181–213.

2 There's No "Me" in "Meta"—Or Is There?

Don Perlis

Metareasoning is one of the many notions of the form meta-*X*. In this chapter I first explore meta-*X* in general, and observe that the role of metareasoning in commonsense reasoning is a kind of self-reference fundamental to most of these notions. From there I take up the theme of reference in general, informal and formal, and suggest that a suitable, but as yet foggy, notion of self appears poised to play a major role in future work in commonsense reasoning.

Meta-this or meta-that carry the sense of an *X* (a this or a that) which is being examined from a vantage point that allows *X* to be taken in as a whole—or at least in large chunks that can be used in characterizing general properties of *X*.

- *Metalanguage* is the mode of expression used in examination of a mode of expression, that is, of (possibly another) language, for example, in asking questions such as: What does that word mean? What language are they speaking? Is that a valid expression? How is that spelled? Can you repeat that?
- *Metamathematics* is an examination of mathematics (or a portion thereof). It confronts questions such as: Is it consistent? What rules govern it? and so on.
- *Metacognition* is the examining of (one's own) cognition. One comes to characterize some of one's mental processes: My memory failed me; I am no good at arithmetic; I easily remember faces; I have a good sense of direction.

Several themes percolate through these examples, just below the surface. One is that meta-*X* involves a person—a reasoner—who is doing the examining of *X*. Another is that *X* itself is a kind of reasoning people do: we do math, we cognize, we use language. Yet another is that in doing meta-*X*, we are examining something about ourselves, namely, our doing of *X*. And a fourth is that one takes a step back from performing *X* in order to examine *X*, that is, to perform meta-*X*.[1]

1. Metaphysics does not quite fit this description; instead of being an examination of the practice of finding laws of nature, it examines (among other things) why there are laws of nature at all, what are "reality" and "existence." But for that reason, metaphysics is not a case of meta-*X* at all. In fact, the term seems to have originated in reference to the topic in Aristotle's writings that came after his writings on physics, thus effectively eliminating metaphysics from our concern here. My thanks to Aaron Sloman for calling this to my attention.

So it would appear that in performing meta-X we are stepping back from our X-performance in order to examine it; we stop doing X so we can look at it. This resonates with the familiar dictum: we cannot catch ourselves in the act—but only in the aftermath of ceasing that act.

To quote William James (1892) at some length, both for context and for the pure joy of Jamesian prose:

> When we take a general view of the wonderful stream of our consciousness, what strikes us first is the different pace of its parts. Like a bird's life, it seems to be an alternation of flights and perchings. The rhythm of language expresses this, where every thought is expressed in a sentence, and every sentence closed by a period. The resting-places are usually occupied by sensorial imaginations of some sort, whose peculiarity is that they can be held before the mind for an indefinite time, and contemplated without changing; the places of flight are filled with thoughts of relations, static or dynamic, that for the most part obtain between the matters contemplated in the periods of comparative rest.
>
> Let us call the resting-places the 'substantive parts,' and the places of flight the 'transitive parts,' of the stream of thought. . . . And we may say that the main use of the transitive parts is to lead us from one substantive conclusion to another.
>
> Now it is very difficult, introspectively, to see the transitive parts for what they really are. If they are but flights to a conclusion, stopping them to look at them before the conclusion is reached is really annihilating them. Whilst if we wait till the conclusion be reached, it so exceeds them in vigor and stability that it quite eclipses and swallows them up in its glare. Let anyone try to cut a thought across in the middle and get a look at its section, and he will see how difficult the introspective observation of the transitive tracts is. The rush of the thought is so headlong that it almost always brings us up at the conclusion before we can rest it.

Yet in metamathematics it turns out that (for example via Gödel numbering) a good deal of the meta-X (X being mathematics) is itself part of X. To be sure, the concerns or aims of meta-X are not quite the same as those of X; but there is a large overlap of the two, at least in this case. And the typical metalanguage for a natural language—say, English—is English itself.

So, here is the theme/poser of this essay: when we examine our performance of a cognitive activity X, must that examining (itself an activity) effectively halt our X-performance, or at least so change it that it no longer is what we were attempting to examine? And if so, can it then be examined in pristine form only from without, by a highly distinct process? Or can one perform a mental activity that continues full-blast ("in a headlong rush," to borrow from James) even while being looked at from within—perhaps even an activity that is that very looking at its own performance of itself? Answers tend to involve one of two notions, which we may refer to as *hierarchical* (looker is separate from lookee) or *loopy* (looker and lookee can be intertwined and even one and the same). These terms will be further explained as we proceed.

However, it seems clear that the notion of a self, or a me, is near and dear to the theme at hand. And now I hope the meaning of the title is somewhat clearer as well.

Consideration of our theme will lead us to a number of traditionally far-flung topics: informal (natural-language based) self-reference; formal self-reference in mathematical logic; the problem of reference in general; consciousness; commonsense reasoning; and mistakes. We will now take these up in turn.

Informal Self-Reference

Perhaps the most famous example of a self-referential utterance is the so-called *Liar*:

L: This sentence is false.

The Liar, or L for short, has two curious features: (i) it appears to refer to itself, and (ii) it appears to contradict itself. The latter feature is the one that has received most attention, but we will focus instead on the former. At this early stage let us simply note that there is an issue as to what, if anything, can guarantee that the word "This" in L succeeds in referring to L itself, as opposed (say) to some other sentence that may have recently been uttered or pointed to. Presumably it is our agreement that it so refer; but then there is personal agency involved.

Consider these two sentences that directly speak to personal agency:

I am using the letter "L" to refer to the sentence to the right of that letter.

The above sentence calls attention specifically to how an expression is to be taken as referring, according to the agent-speaker.

Here I am speaking in English in Chicago as I scratch my head, wondering how I will complete this sentence that I will complete . . . now.

In this sentence there is no explicit mention of reference or meaning, but words such as "Here" and "I" must be understood as referring to the present time and to the speaker. Moreover, surely this sentence is true—or was true when it was uttered—and surely in uttering it I referred to myself and to that very sentence-uttering process as it was occurring. The process refers to itself, wearing, so to speak, its meaning on its sleeve, and it achieves that in virtue of my decision to make it do that and of your understanding that this is what I am doing.

Perhaps more precisely, I am referring to my uttering activity as it occurs, and that referring action is simply that very uttering activity itself. The uttering activity is a self-referring process. Not the sentence, but the activity. What activity? Not mere production of words. Uttering in this context is supposed to mean something like: attempting to convey something to someone, and the self-referential uttering activity is one that is (or involves) an attempt to convey itself—that is, its own self-conveyingness—to someone.

But this then rests on a clear reference for "I," presumably once again an agent with referential intentions, a matter seemingly far removed from the usual concerns in discussions of the Liar.

This is pretty weird stuff. Self-referring entities tend to be suspect; yet instead of being accidental oddities that creep in because the expressive power of our languages (formal or otherwise) is too lax, they are essential. In fact, the very possibility of reference of any kind supervenes on a special kind of self-reference, which I have called *strong self-reference* (Perlis, 1997).

Indeed, as Grice (1957) has urged, every utterance is implicitly of this sort, a self-commenting or self-meta-self, as if it were of the form:

With this utterance I am attempting to convey the meaning of this utterance to you.

Well, that might not work; it is not clear it has a lot of meaning. But the Chicago utterance-process above has a clear meaning. It is also clear that it is an attempt to convey something, and that that something is that very process itself.

One natural-enough reaction to the above circumstances is to suppose that some sentences (such as the Liar) are, after all, neither true nor false, indeed neither true nor not true. This may seem to play fast and loose with the word "not"; after all, "not" simply asserts the failure of what follows it. But perhaps there is something hidden here. In order to be a candidate for failure in the matter of its truth, any sentence must first have a potential truth that can fail, that is, it must have a clear enough meaning that can be measured against some criterion of truth. How does a sentence acquire a meaning? This is the subject of much dispute, and we will return to it a bit later on.

Formal Self-Reference

The examples we have considered so far are informal, based largely on commonsense notions. However, it is not hard to capture similar behaviors in more formal dress. A key component of the formalization is the *Diagonal Lemma*, which asserts that in any reasonably expressive formal theory F, for each unary well-formed formula (wff) $P(x)$ there is a sentence p such that in F it is provable that $p \Leftrightarrow \neg P(`p')$ where $`p'$ names (rather than asserts) the sentence p. Given the Diagonal Lemma, various formal results along the lines of the Liar follow.

With more work (Gödel's famous Incompleteness Theorem) one can devise a wff Thm(x) of F such that, for all sentences s, Thm('s') is provable in F if and only if s is provable in F; that is, Thm is a provability-predicate for F.

Now from the Diagonal Lemma, there is a sentence g (a so-called Gödel sentence) such that in F it is provable that $g \Leftrightarrow \neg$Thm('g'), that is, that g is equivalent to its own unprovability in *F*. It follows that if *g* is provable, then so is ¬Thm('g'), and hence we get Gödel's Theorem: either *g* is unprovable in *F* and thus true, in the sense that what it "asserts" (its own unprovability) holds, or *F* is inconsistent (since if *g* is provable then so are both Thm('g') and ¬Thm('g').

But such formal results are purely syntactic, and reference (let alone self-reference) plays no real role. For example, that L refers to anything is irrelevant to the proof that the formal version of the Liar is inconsistent. And the Gödel sentence *g* does not really refer to anything at all, let alone to its own unprovability.

And who cares? Isn't self-reference just a curiosity, an accident arising as a side effect of an overexpressive language, with surprisingly useful but equally accidental application in formal logic, and of no deep significance in itself? Can we not then simply ignore the bad (contradictory) cases and welcome the good? As it turns out, we cannot: self-reference, far from being an unimportant side effect, is central to reference, hence to meaning, and arguably to meta-*X* as well. This leads us to set out two highly dissimilar approaches to meaning assignment.

Hierarchical or Loopy?

Since the above formal results are just that, formal (syntactic) and not dependent on semantics, it might be possible to keep the advantages of certain "seeming" self-reference (as in Gödel's Theorem) without the disadvantages of the Liar (such as inconsistency). Tarski (1983) showed how to do this by means of a restriction on how languages refer. He posited a hierarchy of languages L_1, L_2, . . . where each L_{j+1} has expressions that refer only to objects in a previously defined language L_j. There is then no expression that can refer to itself. This approach simply banishes self-reference from expression altogether, while leaving intact the syntactic vestiges needed for the Diagonal Lemma (and useful formal results).

On the other hand, this hierarchal approach seems to banish too much. There are perfectly innocuous but semantically based cases of self-reference, such as:

This sentence has five words.

Yet this is not expressible in the Tarski Hierarchy. Nor is the following pair of straightforward sentences, each referring to the other (one happens to be false):

The sentence below has seven words.

The sentence above has six words.

Yet if these are clear enough, if a sentence can clearly refer to another specific sentence, above or below itself, then why not to itself, as in:

The sentence right at this spot is in English.

For that matter, in referring to something above itself, a sentence implicitly refers to its own position to give meaning to "above" or "below." Since the meanings of some sentences are not captured hierarchically, we will borrow a phrase of Hofstadter's (2007), and say they have *loopy semantics*: their meanings do not (entirely) lie outside the sentences but rather turn back to the sentences themselves.

How does meta-*X* bear on hierarchical or loopy semantics? The hierarchical case is simple enough: each language L_{j+1} is a metalanguage for the previous one; it takes a step back, provides the vantage point, for commenting on other sentences. There is no "me" in these sentences, since they always refer to another domain, never to the one where they sit.

Loopy semantics, on the other hand, is precisely that of sentences that self-refer, whether directly, or indirectly, via (a loop through) other sentences such as in the pair above. But is this then not also simple, straightforward? Yes and no; here is where we start to see some complexities in the concept of meaning.

The problem, at its core, is that the hierarchical semantics does not really address reference at all. In postulating that language L_{j+1} is "about" objects (e.g., sentences) in L_j, one is simply making a stipulation, not explicating what it is for a sentence to mean anything, or refer. It is only by means of an agreement among whichever logicians happen to be participating in the discussion that an expression refers to anything at all.

The deictic "this" of natural language (as in "This sentence is false") has been bypassed altogether in formal treatments. Indeed, reference (or semantics) of any kind is traditionally placed outside a formal language, as a function defined on expressions in the language, mapping to an external domain. The language in question does not typically have an expression that stands in for this function; and even if it did, what would determine that standing-in relation? It is as if meaning, or truth, is always one step removed, leaning on some agreement lying outside whatever language is used.

So, as far as the hierarchical approach goes, a map between symbols and referents is arbitrary, relying on a decision to use that map, and not some other, by an agent who intends to use that map. Contrary to what Putnam (1975) has claimed, meaning is (at least partly, and very significantly) in the head (of the agent using that meaning). Only when this issue is faced head on do we encounter genuine cases of reference and the possibility of genuinely self-referring expressions. And these turn out to be precisely the loopy cases.

General Reference

A lesson we draw is that self-reference proper has largely been left untouched by the very large literature purportedly on that subject. This is because reference has largely been left untouched, or rather pushed to the sidelines, via Gödel numbering or a similar artificial mechanism that relies on external agreements to bring reference in at all. Attention has focused, rather, on formal counterparts of self-reference that do, to be sure, carry with them a substantial potential for contradictoriness, in close analogy to their informal—but more genuinely self-referential—sources. But while this attention has produced much of great importance, it has left much out as well. First and foremost is this problem: Can there be representation (meaning, reference) without an agent who chooses to so represent? And secondarily, what is the relation between reference in general and self-reference? Third, what can be said about "genuine" informal self-referential expressions, in light of answers to the former questions? Space does not permit a detailed discussion, but my answers are: No representation without intentional stipulative agency; reference supervenes on self-reference; and genuine or "strong" self-reference is a special "loopy" agency bordering on consciousness.

Consciousness

Wait a minute! Consciousness? Aren't we aimed at understanding meta-*X* here?

Well, a "me," a self, arguably is the essence of consciousness (however, this is incredibly controversial). But if so, and if a me or a self is part of meta, then meta involves consciousness. But we have seen two versions of meta: hierarchical and loopy. The former is little more than a sequence; the latter is mysterious. Hierarchical meta-*X* presumably is akin to a Tarskian pair of levels, the object-level *X* and the monitoring-level meta-*X*. There seems little more to be said about it, except that someone sets up a map by which the expressions at the meta-*X* level refer to items at the *X* level. But then whoever sets up this map is really the determiner of meanings, without whom there is no particular designated map, and *X* and supposed meta-*X* have no particular relationship. And meaning determiners, as far as we know, are always people, or at least agents with intentions.

We are faced, then, once again with agents: agents that perform activities and also refer to those activities (some of which are self-referring).

Consider again that English is its own metalanguage. We typically talk about English in English, and for the most part do not need a special set of meta-English terms to do this, beyond ones such as "word" and "means" and "spell" and "sentence." But even here, such terms refer to bits of English only because at least one human has taken them to so refer.

What is it, then, for an agent to "take" one thing to "refer" to another? Consider a primitive case: coining an expression, explicitly linking a symbol *s* to a referent *r*. This would seem to be no more nor less than an intention to use *s* as a stand-in for *r* in certain contexts. Following this trail, we now ask what it is to intend something, and we are smack-dab in the middle of both philosophy of language and philosophy of mind. And to reinvoke Grice, every utterance is a case not merely of intending, but also of intending listeners to understand that the utterer intends that intending. Can all this happen in the absence of a fairly sophisticated (and quite possibly conscious) cognitive engine? Moreover, the natural languages that we use for expression of intentions are—as noted—their own metalanguages, allowing loopy self-reference made possible by our intentions to so refer: We speak of ourselves, not just past or future, but our immediate present self and present activity including the activity of noting that activity.

So, once again, does meta have a me? If meta involves reference, and if reference involves agency with intentions, including intentional self-referring activity, and if that in turn is at least a hint of a self, then yes.

Thus a bare-bones agent self-reference may be the most basic kind of reference. What is bare-bones self-reference like? Imagine yourself stripped little by little of this sensation, that thought, until all that is left is your own grasp of being there, a bare loopiness without—for the moment—any further trappings: no personal history, no connections with or knowledge of entities in the world other than the one thing: you-as-bare-awareness.

Such a minimal subjective state—if there is such a thing—I have dubbed the "ur-quale": the most primitive sensation or feeling possible, namely, that of simply being a being, an entity whose one activity is self-monitoringness (Perlis, 1997, 2000).[2]

Let us step back a little from such tenuous speculations to more of an engineering perspective, following an idea of John Perry (1979). He describes pushing his shopping cart along in an attempt to find the shopper whose cart is leaving a trail of sugar on the floor, only later to realize that he is that shopper. But what is it that he learns? Perry explores this question at some length, for although on the one hand it seems obvious, on the other it is devilishly hard to say what it is. Still, it seems to matter, and not only for egocentric reasons. Our everyday actions seem tied to it.

Commonsense Reasoning

We can ask a related question about robot design. Consider a robot that can decide that *it* is the robot who is leaking oil, upon hearing that robot 17 is leaking oil. What is it for robot 17 to know that it, itself, is that robot? How does this affect its behavior? Presumably it is quite important to have such a capability, for example, for survival. See Anderson and Perlis (2005) for more elaborate discussion of this idea.

2. I should point out that there has been a tremendous amount of work done on paradoxes of self-reference, formal and informal. For example, Gilmore (1974) and Kripke (1975) in particular have formulated two closely related approaches that not only defuse the paradoxical (contradictory) aspects but also retain (much of) the self-referential aspects. The focus of such work in general has been on clarifying the notion of truth, which is slightly tangential to our concerns here.

It is worth stopping to ask what good such a thing might be (whether full-blast or loopy). One answer seems easy to come by: the self-examining that consciousness appears to provide has survival value. And in fact, much of recent work in AI has been aimed at providing useful self-examining capacities to automated systems, including commonsense reasoners. Indeed, that is presumably what this book is about. I turn then to an approach central to my own work, which not only seems to promise some usefulness for AI systems, but also bears a bit on some of the other issues we have been exploring. Namely, I will briefly discuss active logic.

Active logic is a type of "commonsense formal inference engine"; that is, it consists of a language and rules of inference, but with a twist: the rules are sensitive to the actual physical passage of time. Thus the inference of Q from P and $P \Leftrightarrow Q$ is sanctioned only if that inference occurs at a time $t+1$ when both P and $P \Leftrightarrow Q$ had been inferred at time t. In effect, time values are part of the language; but that in itself is no news: temporal logics have such as well. Active logic, however, ties time values to actual physical time-passage, by keeping track of the evolving current time. The active logic sentence 'Now(t)' has the obvious meaning. But what is striking is the so-called *clock rule*: from 'Now(t)' infer 'Now(t+1)'. So we have a sentence that, if believed, leads to its own disbelief. The reason, of course, is that such a belief is time sensitive, and as time passes the belief becomes outdated. But it has major consequences for what active logic can do. For just one example, it facilitates a smooth handling of contradictions. On the other hand, semantics becomes much more complex; see Anderson et al. (2008).

I bring this up because active logic also provides a useful way to talk about differences, or the lack of differences, between metareasoning and object reasoning since the two are not distinguished at all in active logic. Each inference step involves looking back at the previous step to see what was inferred then, and on that basis drawing inferences at the new current step. Whether such an inference is modus ponens, based on the presence of P and $P \Leftrightarrow Q$ at the previous step, or instead is based on the presence of P and $\neg P$ and yields Contradiction(t) (recording the fact that there was a direct contradiction at the previous step), makes no difference at all to the machinery. It is only to us that these inferences seem to exist at different levels, and then only if we are sensitized to X versus meta-X as a hierarchical distinction from a young age in a formal logic class.

There is much more to be said, but we shall leave it and turn instead to the practical matter of mistakes.

Meta and Mistakes

As a technical branch of AI, commonsense reasoning is the subject of a great deal of study. Yet (as with many such things) there is no general agreement as to what it is, at least in sharp definitional terms.

Here is my own definition, offered as a kind of hypothesis:

Commonsense reasoning (CSR) is the form of metareasoning that monitors an activity for mistakes and then deals with them, sparing the main activity the embarrassment of making a fool of (or destroying) itself.

More specifically:

1. CSR consists of a module that *notes* mismatches between observation and expectation in a system's performance, *assesses* any such, and *guides* a response into place.
2. This is the essence of human common sense. We have expectations, note deviations from them, and decide on a response.[3]
3. Such a CSR module need not know much at all about the system in question, other than having access to at least some of the system's pre- and postconditions (expectations) for its actions and at least some of its observations (e.g., sensor readings).
4. This module can be fairly simple, based on a core set of general kinds of things that can go wrong and general kinds of fixes for them. For instance: Noise can interfere with sensor readings, in which case one can use another sensor or take repeated readings, or replace the sensor; data can be contradictory, and one can distrust one or more of the contradictands, seek corroborating evidence for them, change one's expectations, give up and work on another problem, ask for help, and so on.
5. The actual carrying out of such a response is not the CSR module's job; it merely recommends, and the system must then be equipped for the repair.
6. One particularly interesting case is that of a failure due to lack of some skill, so that training is needed. Training then can be recommended by the CSR module, and if training commences, the module monitors that, assesses its progress, and recommends when to stop training (whether due to its not working, or to its having succeeded).
7. If such a module were to be built and put to use with a given AI system, that system would become far less brittle, and vastly better at dealing with anomalies, than any AI systems at present.
8. Such a module could be general purpose, not built for any specific system or domain. This is because humans are not specific in that sense. We manage to muddle through in a wide variety of unanticipated changes within, and even to, arenas of action.

3. A reviewer points out that expectation-driven reasoning and learning from failed expectations is present in other work, such as that by Schank and Owens (1987) and Cox and Ram (1991). What is new here is the idea that a modest core set of such tools may be sufficient for not only a very general form of metareasoning but also for much of commonsense reasoning overall.

We are in fact hard at work designing just such a module—as an outgrowth of active logic—which we call the *metacognitive loop*; see Anderson et al. (2006). This module resides at the metalevel, monitoring and guiding the system of which it is a part.

Conclusion

What then can we say about our poser: Is there or is there not a *me* in meta? Well, to the extent that common, garden-variety so-called self-monitoring systems are "meta," with one distinct level monitoring another, the answer seems to be no. If one part of a system monitors another without any self-reference at all, the two parts are in effect distinct systems, passing information between them. On the other hand, if that information includes aspects bearing on both levels, we may see a kind of loopiness embedded within a traditional hierarchical form of meta.

In the case of active logic's form of meta-*X*, for example, there is (so far) no sharp notion of me or self. Still, an active logic sentence might refer to itself by invoking a description of itself (e.g., *the first sentence inferred at time t*). And there can be loops, with one sentence referring to a later one yet to come, which in turn may refer back to it.

But note that reasoning about a past or future or even present, does not in itself constitute an activity that reasons about its very self. And even in the case of the sentence italicized above, the self-description is akin to Perry's describing himself in a third-person manner as "the person who . . ." without having the special form of self-knowledge indicated by use of the pronoun "me."

Also, the metacognitive loop (MCL) in the form presented above does not appear to embrace anything close to self-reference. On the other hand, if MCL itself were to make mistakes and need to catch them, things might get more self-referentially interesting, especially if the mistake-noting were in some sense part of the mistake. That might nudge MCL (or active logic) toward more explicit (strong) self-reference.

How can such a thing be, and what could it possibly mean? Consider this:

This activity is taking too long; it must be stopped, including this very reasoning about it, so that other things get done.

We have not yet managed (or even tried very hard) to produce an automated version of such behavior. But it does seem that there is a computational advantage to it: Such a system would be able not only to peer in on other processes and reason about and control them; it would also be able to do so regarding the very same peering process that it is performing at the moment, so that it can get out of its own way, so to speak, deciding to stop what it is doing—including that very deciding—and move on to something else.

It is time to move on—and so with this sentence I end my chapter.

Acknowledgments

This essay was originally given as a talk at AAAI-08, the annual conference of the Association for Advancement of Artificial Intelligence, Chicago 2008, as part of the Workshop on Metareasoning; work supported by AFOSR, NSF, ONR.

References

Anderson, M., Gomaa, W., Grant, J., & Perlis, D. (2008). Active logic semantics for a single agent in a static world. *Artificial Intelligence, 172,* 1045–1063.

Anderson, M., Oates, T., Chong, W., & Perlis, D. (2006). The metacognitive loop I: Enhancing reinforcement learning with metacognitive monitoring and control for improved perturbation tolerance. *Journal of Experimental & Theoretical Artificial Intelligence, 18*(3), 387–411.

Anderson, M., & Perlis, D. (2005). The roots of self-awareness. *Phenomenology and the Cognitive Sciences, 4*(3), 297–333.

Cox, M., & Ram, A. (1991). Using introspective reasoning to select learning strategies. In R. S. Michalski & G. Tecuci (Eds.), *Proceedings of the First International Workshop on Multistrategy Learning* (pp. 217–230). Washington, D.C.: George Mason University, Center for Artificial Intelligence.

Gilmore, P. (1974). The consistency of partial set theory without extensionality. In T. Jech (Ed.), *Axiomatic set theory* (pp. 147–153). Providence, RI: American Mathematical Society.

Grice, P. (1957). Meaning. *Philosophical Review, 66,* 377–388.

Hofstadter, D. (2007). *I am a strange loop.* New York: Basic Books.

James, W. (1892). The stream of consciousness. In *Psychology* (chap. XI). New York: World Publishing.

Kripke, S. (1975). Outline of a theory of truth. *Journal of Philosophy, 72,* 690–716.

Perlis, D. (1997). Consciousness as self-function. *Journal of Consciousness Studies, 4,* 509–525. (Reprinted in Gallagher & Shear [Eds.], *Models of the self,* Imprint Academic, 1999.)

Perlis, D. (2000). What does it take to refer? *Journal of Consciousness Studies, 7*(5), 67–69.

Perry, J. (1979). The problem of the essential indexical. *Noûs, 13,* 3–21.

Putnam, H. (1975). The meaning of "meaning." In *Mind, language, and reality* (pp. 215–271). New York: Cambridge University Press.

Schank, R. C., & Owens, C. C. (1987). Understanding by explaining expectation failures. In R. G. Reilly (Ed.), *Communication failure in dialogue and discourse.* New York: Elsevier Science.

Tarski, A. (1983). The concept of truth in formalized languages. (English translation of original 1936 paper in German.) In J. Corcoran (Ed.), *Logic, semantics, metamathematics, papers from 1923 to 1938.* Indianapolis: Hackett.

3 Metareasoning and Bounded Rationality

Shlomo Zilberstein

This chapter explores the relationship between computational models of rational behavior and metareasoning. Metareasoning is generally considered a crucial component of human intelligence, but its role in computational models of intelligence is less prominent. We describe several approaches to building rational agents and examine the extent to which they rely on metareasoning. While metareasoning is a central component of some approaches, it is not required in others. Despite these differences, we point out an interesting way to reinterpret and unify two of the approaches.

In the pursuit of building decision-making machines or agents, artificial intelligence (AI) researchers often turn to theories of "rationality" in philosophy, decision theory, and economics. According to these theories, an agent is rational when it chooses actions that maximize its performance, given what it currently knows. Rationality is a desired property of intelligent agents since it provides well-defined normative evaluation criteria and since it establishes formal frameworks to analyze agents (Doyle, 1990; Russell & Wefald, 1991).

An agent is said to be perfectly rational if it chooses optimal actions that maximize its expected performance. Perfect rationality defines the actions that should be taken, but it tells nothing about the reasoning process that leads to selecting these actions. The reasoning process can be as simple as a table lookup that specifies which action should be taken in every situation, or it may involve a complex analysis of the situation and planning. In that sense, perfect rationality does not explicitly require metareasoning. In fact, it may require no reasoning at all.

Ignoring the reasoning process used to select actions—and its associated costs—is a significant drawback of perfect rationality. As early as 1947, Herbert Simon observed that optimal decision making mandated by perfect rationality is impractical in complex domains since it requires one to perform intractable computations within a limited amount of time (Simon, 1947, 1982). Moreover, the vast computational resources required to select optimal actions often reduce the utility of the result. Simon concludes that "a theory of rationality that does not give an account of problem solving in the face of complexity is sadly incomplete. It is worse than incomplete; it can be seriously misleading by providing 'solutions' that are without operational significance." Simon suggests that some criterion must be used to determine that an adequate, or satisfactory, decision has been found. He uses the Scottish word "satisficing," which means satisfying, to denote decision making that searches until an alternative is found that is satisfactory by the agent's aspiration-level criterion.

Simon's notion of satisficing has inspired much work within the social sciences and within AI in the areas of problem solving, planning, and search. In the social sciences, much of the work has focused on developing descriptive theories of human decision making (Gigerenzer, 2000). These theories attempt to explain how people make decisions in the real world, coping with complex situations, uncertainty, and limited amounts of time. The answer is often based on a variety of heuristic methods that are used by people to operate effectively in these situations (Gigerenzer et al., 1999). Work within the AI community has produced a variety of computational models that can take into account the computational cost of decision making (Dean & Boddy, 1988; Horvitz, 1987; Russell, Subramanian, & Parr, 1993; Wellman, 1990; Zilberstein, 1993). The idea that the cost of decision making must be taken into account was introduced by Simon and later by the statistician Irving Good who used the term *type II rationality* to describe it (Good, 1971). Good says, "when the expected time and effort taken to think and do calculations is allowed for in the costs, then one is using the principle of rationality of type II." But neither Simon nor Good presents any effective computational framework to implement "satisficing" or "type II rationality."

It is by now widely accepted that in most cases the ideal decision-theoretic notion of perfect rationality is beyond our reach. However, the concept of satisficing offers only a vague design principle that needs a good deal of formalization before it can be used in practice. In particular, one must define the required properties of a satisficing criterion and the quality of behavior that is expected when these properties are achieved. AI researchers have introduced over the years a variety of computational models that can be seen as forms of bounded rationality. We examine these models, divide them into four broad classes, and identify the role of metareasoning in each class.

Computational Approaches to Bounded Rationality

There has been a vast amount of work on bounded rationality in the social sciences, decision theory, and AI. This chapter focuses on computational approaches developed by the AI community. What is common to all these approaches is that they perform some form of approximate reasoning. They differ in the way the approximate solution is produced and evaluated.

Regardless of the form of approximation, approximate reasoning techniques can be complemented by some form of explicit or implicit metareasoning. Metareasoning in this context is a mechanism to make certain runtime decisions by reasoning about the problem solving–or object-level–reasoning process. This can be done either explicitly, by introducing another level of reasoning as shown in figure 1.2 in Cox and Raja's introduction, or implicitly, by precompiling metareasoning decisions into the object-level reasoning process at design time. For example, metareasoning has been used to develop search control strategies—both explicitly and implicitly. Thus, metareasoning could play a useful role in certain forms of approximate reasoning, but it is not by definition a required component. In the rest of this section, we examine several approaches to bounded rationality and divide them into four broad classes: heuristic search, approximate modeling, optimal metareasoning, and bounded optimality. We start by describing these classes and the role of metareasoning in each.

Heuristic Search

One of the early computational approaches to bounded rationality has been based on heuristic search. In fact, Simon had initially identified satisficing with a particular form of heuristic search. In this context, heuristic search represents a form of approximate reasoning. It uses some domain knowledge to guide the search process, which continues until a satisfactory solution is found. This should be distinguished from optimal search algorithms that use admissible heuristic techniques such as A*. Search processes that terminate only when they find an optimal solution are an important part of AI, but they have little to do with bounded rationality. When the search process focuses on optimal, rather than satisfying, solutions the role of heuristics is simply to accelerate the search process by pruning certain parts of the search space from consideration. Simon refers to another type of heuristic function in which heuristics are used to select "adequate" solutions. Such heuristic functions are rarely admissible, and the corresponding search processes are not optimal in any formal sense. Systems based on nonadmissible heuristic functions are often harder to evaluate, especially when optimal decisions are not available. Formal analysis is hard since nonadmissible heuristics do not always have well-defined properties.

Approximate reasoning using heuristic search is a general paradigm, not a specific framework for problem solving. Therefore, it is hard to pinpoint the role of metareasoning. What is clear is that some instances of this paradigm rely on some forms of metareasoning, for example, in order to select the appropriate heuristic for the situation, decide whether the heuristic solution found so far is of sufficient quality, or fine-tune search parameters to try to maximize solution quality within some deadline (Hansen, Zilberstein, & Danilchenko, 1997). Other instances of this general paradigm do not rely on metareasoning. Overall, metareasoning is not an essential component of every heuristic search approach.

Approximate Modeling

When it is not feasible to fully model a problem and solve it optimally, an important aspect of the approximation process is embedded in the creation of a suitable model. The challenge is to create a model that retains the main features of the original problem, but is computationally tractable. The hope is that an exact or approximate solution to the simplified problem would still be of similar quality when applied to the original domain. The process of reasoning about the representation of the given problem and choosing a suitable model is a form of metareasoning. Although there has been significant interest in automating this process, it is often handled by the designer of the system using forms of metareasoning that are not yet well understood. One example of such a process is when deterministic action models are used in planning, ignoring the uncertainty about action failures. Combined with suitable run-time execution monitoring, such an approach could be beneficial. In fact, the winner of the International Probabilistic Planning Competition in 2004 was a planner (FF-rePlan) based on these principles. Consequently, the general approach has gained significant attention, and some researchers have been tempted to conclude that probabilistic planning is just too complex. But the important principle that was demonstrated is the benefit of changing models—not specifically eliminating uncertainty. In fact, in other contexts it might be equally beneficial to introduce uncertainty in order to create a compact model of an otherwise very large deterministic problem.

Treating problem reformulation as a formal reasoning process was started long ago (Amarel, 1968). More recently, there have been some successful examples of treating it efficiently as a metareasoning process, particularly when the space of models being searched is restricted. For example, it has been shown that intelligent reformulation or restructuring of a belief network can greatly increase the efficiency of inference. A metareasoning process can be used to optimize the trade-off between the time dedicated to reformulating the network and the time applied to the implementation of a solution (Breese & Horvitz, 1990).

Approximate modeling is therefore an important component of bounded rationality, but the ability to formalize and automate this process is still quite limited. The forms of metareasoning that can be used in approximate modeling are very rich, but they are not yet efficiently encodable in algorithmic forms.

Optimal Metareasoning

If one adopts the view that metareasoning is a process that monitors and controls the object-level reasoning process—as shown in Cox and Raja's figure 1.2—one could pose the question of whether the metareasoning process itself is optimal. Optimality here is with respect to the overall agent performance, given its fixed object-level deliberation capabilities. This is a well-defined question that sometimes has a simple answer. For example, metareasoning may focus on the single question of when to stop deliberation and take action. Depending on how the base-level component is structured, the answer may or may not be straightforward. Optimal metareasoning has been also referred to as *rational metareasoning* (Horvitz, 1989) and *metalevel rationality* (Russell, 1995) to distinguish it from perfect rationality. This offers one precise form of bounded rationality that is relatively easy to achieve. We will further examine this approach in the following sections. Besides being well defined and, in some cases, easily implementable, this approach to bounded rationality has some methodological benefits. It helps decompose the overall problem of bounded rationality into two orthogonal questions: how to design good problem-solving components and how to manage the operation of these components. Improving object-level competence can be a long-term objective, but at any given time it makes sense for agents to try to use their existing capabilities optimally.

It should be noted, however, that optimal metareasoning can result in arbitrarily poor agent performance. This is true because we do not impose up front any constraints on the object-level deliberation process in terms of its efficiency or correctness. Nevertheless, we will see that this presents an attractive framework for bounded rationality and that performance guarantees can be established once additional constraints are imposed on the overall architecture.

Bounded Optimality

Bounded optimality techniques seek to restore a stronger notion of optimality in decision making in the face of computational complexity and limited resources. That is, instead of building systems that can find "sufficiently good" answers, the goal is to find a maximally successful program that can compute these answers. Optimality is defined with respect to a particular space of possible implementations of these programs (Russell, 1995; Russell & Wefald, 1991).

Russell and Wefald (1991) say that an agent exhibits bounded optimality "if its program is a solution to the constraint optimization problem presented by its architecture." This approach marks a shift from optimization over actions to optimization over programs. The program is *bounded optimal* for a given computational device for a given environment, if the expected utility of the program running on the device in the environment is at least as high as that of all other programs for the device. When the space of programs is finite, one can certainly argue that a bounded optimal solution exists. Finding it, however, could be very hard.

Russell, Subramanian, and Parr (1993) give an efficient construction algorithm that generates a bounded optimal program for a particular restricted class of agent architectures, in which a program consists of a sequence of decision procedures. The decision procedures are represented using condition-action rules. The authors admit that bounded optimality as defined above may be hard to achieve for most problems. Thus they propose a weaker notion of asymptotic bounded optimality as a more practical alternative. The latter case requires that the program perform as well as the best possible program on any problem instance, provided that its computational device is faster by a constant factor.

To establish bounded optimality, the designer of the system—not the agent itself—is responsible to identify the agent's reasoning architecture and to prove that the program satisfies the optimality conditions. In that sense, metareasoning does not play any significant role in this framework. Certainly there is no requirement that the agent itself be engaged in any form of metareasoning. As long as the agent's program is shown to satisfy the optimality conditions, the agent is deemed bounded optimal.

One criticism of bounded optimality is that although the bounded rationality criterion is well defined, it is very difficult to achieve in practice. In fact, there are very few examples in the literature of bounded optimal agents. Bounded optimality may well be the most precise formal approach to bounded rationality, but without further refinement, it is hard to use in practice.

Bounded Rationality as Optimal Metareasoning

We have considered four basic approaches to achieve bounded rationality: heuristic search, approximate modeling, optimal metareasoning, and bounded optimality. The latter two approaches represent specific, well-defined solutions, whereas the former two represent general principles that fall under the broad category of approximate reasoning. From a formal perspective, the first approach is underconstrained, essentially allowing any form of approximate reasoning to count as a solution. The second approach is yet to be fully formalized and effectively automated. The last approach appears to be overconstrained, being difficult to achieve in practice. This leaves us with optimal metareasoning as the most promising approach for further examination.

According to this approach, metareasoning is a process that manages the object-level reasoning process. We consider an agent to be bounded rational when its metareasoning component is optimal. That is, given a particular object-level deliberation model, we look for the best possible way to control it so as to optimize the expected ground-level performance of the agent. The metareasoning task can take many different forms and can present decisions of various complexities. We identify below the key questions that affect the form and complexity of the metareasoning problem.

1. What object-level decision-making architecture is employed? Is it complete? Is it sound? What trade-offs does it offer between computational resources and quality of results?
2. How does the metareasoning component model the object-level reasoning process? What kind of prior knowledge is available about the efficiency and correctness of the object-level component?

3. What run-time information about the state of the object-level reasoning process is being monitored? What is known about the external environment?
4. What control decisions are being made by the metalevel reasoning process? How do these decisions affect the object-level component?
5. When and how does execution switch between the object level and the metalevel?
6. How much time is consumed by the metalevel reasoning process? How much of the metareasoning strategy is precomputed off-line? What is the online overhead?
7. Is metareasoning optimal? What assumptions are needed to establish optimality?
8. What can be said about the overall performance of the agent? Can a bound be established on how close it is to an ideal perfectly rational agent?

Since the 1980s, several decision-making frameworks have been developed that match this form of bounded rationality. In the next section, we describe some of the frameworks and examine the answers to the above questions in these particular contexts. We then mention briefly a number of additional examples of this general paradigm.

Example: Optimal Metareasoning with Anytime Algorithms

One general approach to bounded rationality is based on composition and monitoring of anytime algorithms. Methodologically, problem solving with anytime algorithms is based on dividing the overall problem into four key subproblems: elementary algorithm construction, performance measurement and prediction, composability, and metalevel control of computation.

Elementary algorithm construction covers the problem of introducing useful trade-offs between computational resources and output quality in decision making. This fundamental problem has been studied by the AI community, resulting in a variety of "anytime algorithms" (Dean & Boddy, 1988) or "flexible computation" methods (Horvitz, 1987) whose quality of results improves gradually as computation time increases. The same problem has been studied within the systems community in the area of "imprecise computation" (Liu et al., 1991). Although iterative refinement techniques have been widely used in computer science, the construction of "well-behaved" anytime algorithms is not obvious. To serve as useful components of a resource-bounded reasoning system, such algorithms should have certain properties: measurable objective output quality, monotonicity and consistency of quality improvement, and marginal decrease in the rate of quality improvement over time. Constructing good, reusable anytime algorithms is an important, active research area. There are now many existing anytime algorithms for standard heuristic search and planning and reasoning tasks.

Performance measurement and prediction covers the problem of capturing the trade-off offered by each system component using a "performance profile." A good performance profile is a compact probabilistic description of the behavior of the component. A typical representation is a mapping from run time to expected output quality. It has been shown that conditioning performance profiles on input quality and other observable features of the algorithm can improve the precision of run-time quality prediction.

Composability covers the problem of building modular resource-bounded reasoning systems with anytime algorithms as their components. The fundamental issue is that composition destroys interruptibility—the basic property that defines anytime algorithms. A two-step solution to this problem has been developed that makes a distinction between "interruptible" and "contract" algorithms (Zilberstein, 1993). Contract algorithms offer a trade-off between output quality and computation time, provided that the amount of computation time is determined prior to their activation. The idea is to first compose the best possible contract algorithm and then make it interruptible with only a small, constant penalty (Zilberstein & Russell, 1996).

Finally, metalevel control covers the problem of run-time allocation of computational resources (sometimes referred to as "deliberation scheduling" Dean & Boddy, 1988) so as to maximize the overall performance of the system. In general, metalevel control involves modeling both the internal problem-solving process and the external environment and managing computational resources accordingly. In domains characterized by high predictability of utility change over time, the monitoring problem can be solved efficiently using contract algorithms and a variety of strategies for contract adjustment. In domains characterized by rapid change and a high level of uncertainty, monitoring must be based on the use of interruptible algorithms. An early approach to monitoring anytime algorithms has been based on estimating the marginal "value of computation" (Russell & Wefald, 1991). A more recent monitoring approach is sensitive to both the cost of monitoring and to how well the quality of the currently available solution can be estimated by the run-time monitor. The technique is based on modeling anytime algorithms as Markov processes and constructing an off-line monitoring policy based on a stochastic model of quality improvement (Hansen & Zilberstein, 1996). We use the basic form of this approach as an example and discuss the details below.

1. What object-level decision-making architecture is employed?

The basic assumption about the object level is that it is an anytime algorithm, normally an interruptible one. Some anytime algorithms, such as anytime A* (Hansen, Zilberstein, and Danilchenko, 1997), guarantee convergence on the optimal solution, but this is not generally required. If the anytime algorithm produces a result of quality q at time t, the value of that result is described by a time-dependent utility function, $U(q,t)$.

2. How does the metareasoning component model the object-level reasoning process?

Some form of a performance profile is normally used as prior knowledge. It characterizes the trade-off between run time and quality of results. Both deterministic and probabilistic models have been developed. A deterministic performance profile specifies a fixed solution quality per time allocation. A probabilistic performance profile, $\Pr(q_j \mid t)$, specifies the probability of getting solution quality q_j by running the algorithm for t time units. A more informative modeling tool is the dynamic performance profile, $\Pr(q_j \mid q_i, \Delta t)$, which specifies the probability of getting a solution of quality q_j by continuing the algorithm for time interval Δt when the currently available solution has quality q_i. This latter model revises the prediction of future quality based on the progress in problem solving made so far.

3. What run-time information about the state of the object-level reasoning process is being monitored?

One approach is to assume that the anytime algorithm used as the object-level reasoning process is a "black box" that does not provide any run-time indications of solution quality. When the quality of the current solution is available, that information together with running time can be used by the metareasoning process. In some cases, the quality of the current solution can only be estimated using certain features of the solution. In that case, the metareasoning component must estimate the quality of the solution using the available features (Hansen & Zilberstein, 2001). In our example, we assume that solution quality is observable and that a dynamic performance profile is available.

4. What control decisions are being made by the metalevel reasoning process?

The most basic metareasoning decision is when to stop the anytime algorithm and return the current solution.

One approach is based on the myopic estimate of the expected value of continuing the computation for a period Δt, which is defined as follows:

$$\mathrm{MEVC}(\Delta t) = \sum_j \Pr(q_j \mid q_i, \Delta t) U(q_j, t + \Delta t) - U(q_i, t)$$

where q_i is the current quality and t the current time. The myopic monitoring approach is to continue the computation as long as $\mathrm{MEVC}(\Delta t) > 0$.

A more general stopping policy can be found by optimizing the following value function (Hansen & Zilberstein, 2001):

$$V(q_i, t) = \max_d \begin{cases} U(q_i, t) & \text{if } d\text{=stop} \\ \sum_j \Pr(q_j \mid q_i, \Delta t) V(q_j, t + \Delta t) & \text{if } d\text{=continue} \end{cases}$$

to determine the following policy,

$$\pi(q_i, t) = \arg\max_d \begin{cases} U(q_i, t) & \text{if } d\text{=stop} \\ \sum_j \Pr(q_j \mid q_i, \Delta t) V(q_j, t + \Delta t) & \text{if } d\text{=continue} \end{cases}$$

where Δt represents a single time step and d is a binary variable that represents the decision to either stop or continue the algorithm.

When each activation of the metareasoning component takes a nonnegligible amount of computation time that slows down the object-level reasoning process, the decision could also include the frequency of monitoring (Hansen & Zilberstein, 2001). An even more complex situation could arise when the metareasoning component uses a variety of features that characterize the state of the environment and the state of the computation. Some of these features could be more costly to compute than others. In that case, the metareasoning decision is what to monitor, at what frequency, and when to stop the entire process.

5. When and how does execution switch between the object level and the metalevel?

In most cases, monitoring of anytime algorithms is done periodically at fixed intervals, say, every Δt time units. When we assume that monitoring itself incurs negligible overhead, the frequency of monitoring can be high with no negative consequences.

6. How much time is consumed by the metalevel reasoning process?

Work on anytime algorithms often relies on precomputed control strategies that are generated off-line using the performance profile of the algorithm and the overall time-dependent utility function. For example, the above value function and associated control policy can be computed off-line, resulting in a very fast reactive metareasoning component. Simple control strategies, such as the above myopic approach, that stop the computation when the marginal value of computation becomes negative can be computed online with little overhead. When solution quality or the state of the environment must be estimated at run time using nontrivial computations, this could introduce a significant overhead. However, extending the above monitoring technique to factor in this overhead is relatively straightforward (Hansen & Zilberstein, 2001).

7. Is metareasoning optimal?

Optimal metareasoning has been introduced for a wide range of scenarios involving anytime algorithms using certain assumptions about the performance profile and the utility function. One common assumption is that metareasoning incurs negligible overhead. The myopic stopping criteria can be shown to be optimal when the expected marginal increase in the intrinsic value of a solution is a nonincreasing function of quality and the marginal cost of time is a nondecreasing function of time. The monitoring policy computed by optimizing the above value function is optimal and does not require the latter assumptions. A range of situations in which optimal metareasoning can be established is described by Hansen and Zilberstein (2001) and Zilberstein (1996).

8. What can be said about the overall performance of the agent?

Even when metareasoning is optimal—and satisfies our definition of bounded optimality—not much can be said about the overall performance of the agents and how close it may be to a perfectly rational agent in the same situation. Generally, no performance bound exists because the anytime algorithm being monitored is not subject to any constraints in terms of its efficiency or correctness. But when the quality measure of the anytime algorithm provides an error bound on how close the result is to the optimal answer, a worst-case bound with respect to a perfectly rational agent can be established.

To summarize, there are many instances of optimal metareasoning involving anytime algorithms as an object-level deliberation method. There are also examples of optimal metareasoning with respect to other object-level components such as algorithm portfolios (Petrik & Zilberstein, 2006) and contract algorithms (Zilberstein, Charpillet, & Chassaing, 2003). These examples illustrate that this well-defined model of bounded rationality can be implemented in many domains.

Discussion and Conclusion

We examined several different computational approaches to bounded rationality. One approach—based on optimal metareasoning—seems particularly attractive because it is both relatively easy to implement and provides some formal guarantees about the behavior of the agent. We examined several instantiations of this approach using anytime algorithms and provided a characterization of the relationship between the object-level and metareasoning components. These examples show that metareasoning plays an important role in this particular approach to bounded rationality.

Although bounded optimality seems to be a very different approach, under some assumptions it can be unified with optimal metareasoning. If the architecture of the bounded-optimal agent specifies the object-level computations of Cox and Raja's figure 1.2, then the metareasoning problem can be seen as finding the best way to compose the object-level computations and create the most effective agent. In that case, the bounded-optimal program is a solution of the optimal metareasoning problem. One example is the problem of sequencing contract algorithms in order to produce the best possible interruptible anytime algorithm. Contract algorithms offer a trade-off between computation time and solution quality, but the run time must be determined when they are activated. Once activated, no solution is available before the end of the contract. Some reasoning and search methods produce useful contract algorithms. To use such algorithms when the available time is not known in advance, one could run them as a sequence of increasing contracts until the deadline. It has been shown that the best possible way to create such a sequence (in terms of the resulting performance profile) is to use a geometric series of contracts, doubling execution time in each step (Zilberstein & Russell, 1996; Zilberstein, Charpillet, and Chassaing, 2003). If the task of the metareasoning component is to determine the run time of each contract, then the optimal sequence provides a solution to the optimal metareasoning problem. At the same time, if we consider an architecture in which programs are composed of sequences of contracts, then the optimal sequence is also a solution of the bounded optimality problem. Hence, under certain assumptions the two approaches can be unified, yielding the same solution.

One interesting research challenge is to establish mechanisms to bound the performance difference between the more practical approach based on optimal metareasoning with a given object-level component and a bounded-optimal agent, using the same architecture. Creating a bounded-optimal agent is hard, but bounding the performance gap might be possible.

Another challenge is to develop models of bounded rationality suitable for multiple decision makers in either cooperative or competitive settings. When agents operate independently and cannot be controlled in a centralized manner, their metareasoning components need to coordinate as well. A simple example is a collaborative setting in which one agent decides to stop thinking and take action, but the other may see a need to continue deliberation. There has been little work so far on coordination between the metareasoning components of collaborative agents. The situation is even more complicated in competitive settings when agents need to monitor or reason about the deliberation processes of other agents, about which they may have little information or prior knowledge.

Acknowledgments

This work was supported in part by the National Science Foundation under Grants no. IIS-0535061 and IIS-0812149 and by the Air Force Office of Scientific Research under Grant no. FA9550-08-1-0181.

References

Amarel, S. (1968). On representations of problems of reasoning about actions. *Machine Intelligence, 3*, 131–171.

Breese, J., & Horvitz, E. (1990). Ideal reformulation of belief networks. In *Proceedings of Sixth Conference on Uncertainty in Artificial Intelligence* (pp. 64–72). Boston: Morgan Kaufmann.

Dean, T., & Boddy, M. (1988). An analysis of time-dependent planning. In *Proceedings of the Seventh National Conference on Artificial Intelligence* (pp. 49–54). Cambridge, MA: MIT Press.

Doyle, J. (1990). Rationality and its roles in reasoning. In *Proceedings of the Eighth National Conference on Artificial Intelligence* (pp. 1093–1100). Cambridge, MA: MIT Press.

Gigerenzer, G. (2000). *Adaptive thinking: Rationality in the real world.* Oxford: Oxford University Press.

Gigerenzer, G., Todd, P. M., & ABC Research Group. (1999). *Simple heuristics that make us smart.* Oxford: Oxford University Press.

Good, I. J. (1971). Twenty-seven principles of rationality. In V. P. Godambe & D. A. Sprott (Eds.), *Foundations of statistical inference* (pp. 108–141). Toronto: Holt, Rinehart, Winston.

Hansen, E. A., & Zilberstein, S. (1996). Monitoring the progress of anytime problem solving. In *Proceedings of the Thirteenth National Conference on Artificial Intelligence* (pp. 1229–1234). Menlo Park, CA: AAAI Press.

Hansen, E. A., & Zilberstein, S. (2001). Monitoring and control of anytime algorithms: A dynamic programming approach. *Artificial Intelligence, 126*(1–2), 139–157.

Hansen, E. A., Zilberstein, S., & Danilchenko, V. A. (1997). *Anytime heuristic search: First results.* Technical Report 97-50, Computer Science Department, University of Massachusetts, Amherst.

Horvitz, E. J. (1987). Reasoning about beliefs and actions under computational resource constraints. In *Proceedings of the 1987 Workshop on Uncertainty in Artificial Intelligence.* New York: Elsevier.

Horvitz, E. J. (1989). Rational metareasoning and compilation for optimizing decisions under bounded resources. In *Proceedings of the International Symposium on Computational Intelligence* (pp. 205–216). New York: North Holland.

Liu, J. W. S., Lin, K. J., Shih, W. K., Yu, A. C., Chung, J. Y., & Zhao, W. (1991). Algorithms for scheduling imprecise computations. *IEEE Computer, 24,* 58–68.

Petrik, M., & Zilberstein, S. (2006). Learning parallel portfolios of algorithms. *Annals of Mathematics and Artificial Intelligence, 48*(1–2), 85–106.

Russell, S. J. (1995). Rationality and intelligence. In *Proceedings of the Fourteenth International Joint Conference on Artificial Intelligence* (pp. 950–957). Menlo Park, CA: International Joint Conferences on Artificial Intelligence.

Russell, S. J., Subramanian, D., & Parr, R. (1993). Provably bounded optimal agents. In *Proceedings of the Thirteenth International Joint Conference on Artificial Intelligence* (pp. 338–344). Menlo Park, CA: International Joint Conferences on Artificial Intelligence.

Russell, S. J., & Wefald, E. H. (1991). *Do the right thing: Studies in limited rationality.* Cambridge, MA: MIT Press.

Simon, H. A. (1947). *Administrative behavior.* New York: Macmillan.

Simon, H. A. (1982). *Models of bounded rationality* (vol. 2). Cambridge, MA: MIT Press.

Wellman, M. P. (1990). *Formulation of tradeoffs in planning under uncertainty*. London: Pitman.

Zilberstein, S. (1993). *Operational rationality through compilation of anytime algorithms*. Ph.D. dissertation, Computer Science Division, University of California, Berkeley.

Zilberstein, S. (1996). The use of anytime algorithms in intelligent systems. *AI Magazine, 17*(3), 73–83.

Zilberstein, S., Charpillet, F., & Chassaing, P. (2003). Optimal sequencing of contract algorithms. *Annals of Mathematics and Artificial Intelligence, 39*(1–2), 1–18.

Zilberstein, S., & Russell, S. J. (1996). Optimal composition of real-time systems. *Artificial Intelligence, 82*, 181–213.

II Metalevel Control

4 Learning Expertise with Bounded Rationality and Self-Awareness

Susan L. Epstein and Smiljana Petrovic

When people provide only rudimentary knowledge about a problem domain, a *self-adaptive* system must learn its own expertise, that is, become better and faster at its task than the rest of us (D'Andrade, 1991). Essential to that development are *bounded rationality* (imposed resource limitations) and *self-awareness*, the ability to monitor one's own problem-solving behavior and reasoning. From this perspective, *metareasoning* examines and reflects upon the components of decision making and how they are controlled, rather than merely upon the decisions themselves. *Learning with metareasoning* occurs when the system seeks to improve its performance by the application of metareasoning to modify its behavior. A system with this capacity could, for example, decide to ignore some of its experience, to prefer some procedures to others, or even to stop learning because it is satisfied with what it has accomplished. Under the aegis of an architecture that supports learning with metareasoning, the three ambitious programs described here develop considerable expertise from experience with relatively few problems.

Despite the computational difficulties discussed by Conitzer (this vol., chap. 8), metareasoning often successfully enhances object-level reasoning. For example, Arcos, Mülâyim, and Leake (this vol., chap. 11) describe how introspective reasoning can improve a case-based system, and Alexander, Raja, and Musliner (this vol., chap. 5) describe how metalevel reasoning can successfully limit the resources for scheduling based on a Markov decision process. Zilberstein (this vol., chap. 3) examines the relationship between optimal metareasoning and bounded rationality on the object level. This chapter describes how an architecture enhanced by metareasoning assesses expertise, manages large bodies of heuristics, and learns to think more effectively.

The Architecture and the Problems

FORR (FOr the Right Reasons) is a learning and problem-solving architecture that models the development of expertise with bounded rationality and self-awareness (Epstein, 1994a). Figure 4.1 describes FORR as an elaboration on the fundamental

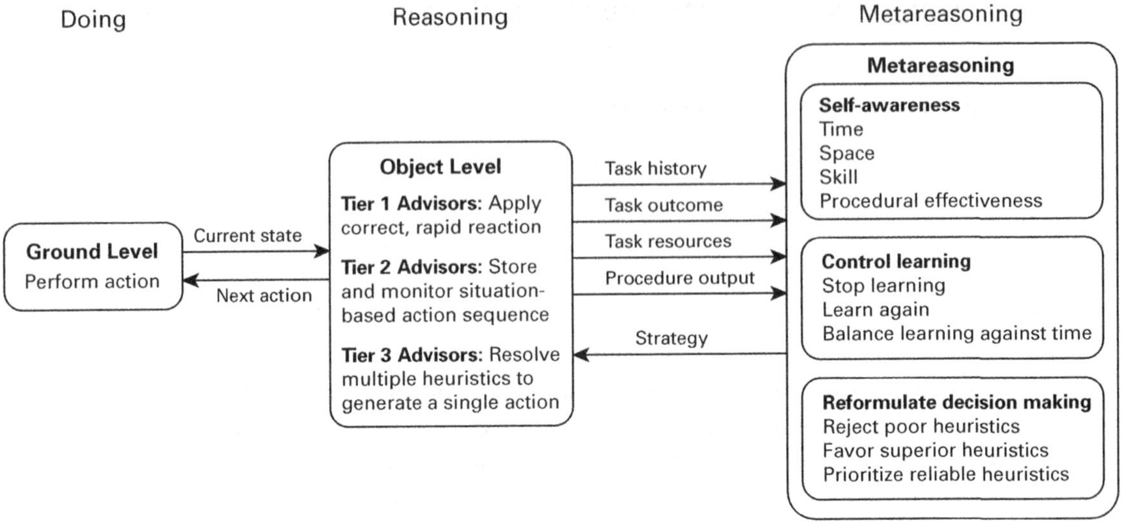

Figure 4.1
FORR in the context of chapter 1.

metareasoning diagram in figure 1.2 of chapter 1 of this volume. At the domain-dependent ground level, FORR describes each world state as it appears during search for a solution, and executes actions to move from one state to the next. At the object level, FORR re-represents the current state and reasons about it to select the next action in a sequence of decisions that addresses a single task. Here, decision makers are reactive procedures, opportunistic planners, or heuristics. After each task, the object-level forwards to the metareasoning level the history and outcome of the task, the computational resources consumed, and the contribution of each heuristic to each decision.

FORR addresses a *problem class* (a set of similar problems). Metareasoning assesses the program's skill within that class and the effectiveness of each procedure there. Metareasoning also determines whether to continue learning about the class, to stop, or to restart the entire learning process. Most dramatically, for a given class, metareasoning can reformulate the object level to eliminate ineffective procedures and favor superior ones. This chapter draws on three very different challenges addressed by FORR-based programs, each of which can be solved with a sequence of actions: game playing, path finding, and constraint satisfaction.

Hoyle learns to play 19 two-person, perfect-information, finite-board games (Epstein, 2001). Here a problem class is a game (e.g., tic-tac-toe), and a problem is a single contest whose actions are legal moves. A solution is a move sequence that achieves an *ideal outcome* (a win or a tie, as defined by the game tree). Given the rules, Hoyle plays against itself or an external opponent. Some games in Hoyle's repertoire have game trees of several billion nodes. The expert programs crafted as opponents required considerable game-specific knowledge and skill.

Ariadne learns to find paths in a two-dimensional grid maze (Epstein, 1998). Here a problem class is a maze, and a problem is a trip from an initial location to a goal. (The initial location and the goal vary from one problem to the next.) Ariadne has no map, only the coordinates of the robot and the goal, plus a view restricted to the grid positions between the robot and the nearest obstruction in four orthogonal directions. An action moves the robot in a straight line to a currently visible location. A solution is an action sequence that reaches the goal. Represented as a (cyclic) graph, a moderately challenging 20×20 maze would have 280 nodes and about 1,485 edges.

ACE (the Adaptive Constraint Engine) learns to solve constraint satisfaction problems (*CSPs*) (Epstein, Freuder, & Wallace, 2005). Here, a problem is a (binary) CSP: a set of variables, each with an associated set of values (*domain*), and a set of constraints that restrict how pairs of variables can be bound to values simultaneously. A CSP can be represented as a *constraint graph* with a vertex for each variable and an edge for each constraint. A problem class is a set of CSPs with the same descriptive characterization (e.g., number of variables and maximum domain size). Each action in ACE either selects a variable or assigns a value to a selected variable from its associated domain. After each assignment, *propagation* infers the impact on the domains of the as-yet-unassigned variables. If any variable then has no values consistent with the current assignments (*wipeout*), the most recent assignments are retracted chronologically until every variable has some possible value. A solution is an assignment sequence that satisfies all constraints and assigns every variable a value. (Although traditionally a CSP solution is merely an acceptable assignment to all the variables, some assignment sequences are more efficient than others, in terms of the inference they require. Expertise here values efficiency as well as the ability to find a valid assignment.) CSPs model many of the NP-hard problems addressed by AI systems, including graph coloring, propositional satisfiability, and scheduling.

Structured CSPs are more similar to real-world problems than simple random ones. Structured problems' pockets of densely connected variables with very tight constraints often present particular challenges for traditional solvers. Indeed, the opposites of traditional heuristics often fare better on them than the originals. We report here on a composed class (Aardal et al., 2003) with 30 variables and domain size 6 (7^{30} search nodes) and a geometric class (Johnson et al., 1989) with 50 variables and domain size 10 (11^{50} nodes). Problems from both classes often stumped the best solvers at a recent competition.

Foundation Assumptions

The following premises dictate FORR's general structure and behavior:

• *Good reasons underlie intelligent actions.* A good reason is a justification for a decision. Domain-specific good reasons are called *Advisors*. Input to any Advisor is the current problem state and the available legal actions. Output from any Advisor is *advice* about some number of actions. For example, *Material* advises Hoyle to capture an opponent's piece.
• *A domain has many such good reasons.* Human experts typically rely on a host of domain-specific Advisors. ACE, for example, has more than 100 Advisors drawn from the constraint literature.
• *Some good reasons are always correct.* These *tier-1 Advisors* take priority during decision making. Their fast, accurate guidance mandates an action or eliminates it from further consideration. For example, Ariadne's *Victory* always moves directly to a visible goal.
• *Some good decisions include several actions.* These *tier-2 Advisors* identify and address a subproblem with a *plan*, a (possibly ordered) set of actions. For example, Ariadne's *Roundabout* circumnavigates an obstruction that lies directly between the robot and the goal. At most one plan is active at a time. The tier-1 Advisor *Enforcer* appropriately supports the execution of an active plan or terminates it.
• *Most good reasons are fallible heuristics.* These *tier-3 Advisors* express preferences for choices numerically, as *strengths*. For example, Ariadne's *Giant Step* assigns greater strengths to longer steps. The object level in figure 4.1 coordinates all three tiers of Advisors to make a decision. It progresses to the next tier only if the current one does not produce a decision.
• *Good reasons make different contributions on different problem classes.* FORR evaluates each tier-3 Advisor on each new problem class. The more constructive are *class-appropriate*; the others are *class-inappropriate*. ACE's heuristics, for example, are provided in *dual pairs* (one to maximize and the other to minimize the same metric); ACE sorts out whether either is appropriate. Lines 1 and 2 in table 4.1 show that duals may perform differently on different problem classes.
• *A combination of good reasons offers substantial benefits.* There is evidence for this both in people's reliance on multiple heuristics (Biswas et al., 1995; Crowley & Siegler, 1993; Ratterman & Epstein, 1995; Schraagen, 1993) and in programs that integrate multiple rationales to their advantage (Keim et al., 1999). Table 4.1 (lines 3–5) shows how a pair of heuristics, one for variable selection and the other for value selection, may outperform individual heuristics (lines 1–2).
• *Good combinations of reasons vary with the problem class.* Table 4.1 (lines 3 and 5) shows that pairs of Advisors successful on one problem class may do less well on another.

Table 4.1

A heuristic's appropriateness varies with the problem class, and multiple heuristics outperform individual ones in CSP search. Variable-ordering metric *ddd* is the ratio of a variable's dynamic domain size to the number of its unassigned neighbors in the constraint graph. v_1 *and* v_2 are value-ordering heuristics. After propagation, v_1 prefers values that produce the smallest domain size, and v_2 prefers values that produce the largest product of domain sizes. Space is nodes searched; elapsed time is in CPU seconds. Fifty problems were tested in each class.

		Geometric			Composed		
	Heuristics	Space	Time	Solved	Space	Time	Solved
1	Min *ddd*	258.1	3.1	98%	996.7	2.0	82%
2	Max *ddd*	4722.7	32.3	6%	529.9	1.0	90%
3	Min *ddd*+v_1	199.7	3.6	98%	924.2	3.0	84%
4	Min *ddd*+v_2	171.6	3.3	98%	431.1	1.5	92%
5	Max *ddd*+v_2	3826.8	53.7	30%	430.6	1.4	92%
6	ACE mixture	146.8	5.1	100%	31.4	0.6	100%

• *A program can* learn *to become an expert.* In the *learning phase,* FORR addresses a sequence of problems, and all of figure 4.1 is active. Metareasoning examines the data from the object level after each learning-phase problem, and may reformulate its strategy. Then, in the *testing phase,* FORR turns learning off and evaluates its performance on a second set of problems. No further directives from the metareasoning module occur during testing. Because decisions may be nondeterministic, FORR evaluates performance over a set of such runs (an *experiment*). Relatively few learning problems should suffice. For example, ACE learns to solve each problem class well after learning on only 30 problems. Table 4.1 (line 6) shows how the mixture of heuristics that ACE learned for each of them outperformed both individual heuristics and pairs of them.

• *Multiple representations enhance reasoning.* Each Advisor has access to every representation of events and states from the ground level and the object level. These representations are shared and computed at the object level only on demand. For example, ACE has dozens of CSP descriptions, including many that identify different kinds of subproblems and relationships among variables.

Other systems that rely on a mixture of heuristics combine them in a variety of ways. More complex heuristics may be reserved for the harder problems (Borrett, Tsang, & Walsh, 1996). Heuristics from a *portfolio* may be selected to compete in parallel until one solves the problem, or may be used in turn on the same problem (Gagliolo & Schmidhuber, 2006; Gomes & Selman, 2001; Streeter, Golovin, & Smith, 2007). A system may also label its heuristics individually for their appropriateness with learned *weights*. Heuristics can be ranked by weight and consulted one at a time (Minton et al., 1995; Nareyek, 2003) or they can *vote*, combining advice from each of them on every decision (Fukunaga, 2002). In FORR, tier-1 and tier-2 Advisors are consulted in some prespecified, class-independent order; in tier 3, Advisors vote.

Learning with Bounded Rationality

Despite a fixed characterization, a random problem generator may not create a uniformly difficult problem class. For example, the difficulty a fixed algorithm experiences within a class of putatively similar, randomly generated CSPs may decrease according to a power law (Gomes et al., 2000). As a result, there are many far more difficult problems within the same class.

Bounded rationality sets an arbitrary performance standard. One might, for example, learn only from solutions achieved within bounded resources. This presumes that a fast solution or one that visits fewer search states is better. Setting such bounds is problematic, however. Under bounds too low for typical problems in the class, only the easiest are solved, solutions are fewer, and the learned behavior is untrustworthy because it arose from problems where most any decision would do. If bounds are set too high, however, long but successful searches provide traces of not-so-expert behavior. For example, figure 4.2 shows the impact on ACE of a limit on *search nodes* (partial assignments) while it learns to solve the geometric problems. A run was *successful* if it solved at least 80 percent of its 50 testing problems within the node limit. Observe how higher node limits during learning produced fewer successful runs and incurred a higher search cost than did lower limits.

Metareasoning can monitor overall skill and use it to control the learner. A coarse but significant measure of success is the frequency of solved problems during learning. FORR introduces *full restart*, the ability to reinitialize all heuristics' weights to some small value and begin again, on different problems from the same class (Petrovic & Epstein, 2006a). (This is different from restart on a problem, which tries to diversify search for its solution [Gomes & Sellman, 2004]). When problems frequently go unsolved during a learning phase, full restart begins the entire phase again. This abandons a run on an unusually difficult sample of problems, or one where solutions to very easy problems introduce misinformation. The resource limit is crucial here, as figure 4.2 indicates. As one would expect, higher resource bounds incur a higher learning cost, but under a high node limit, full restart considerably modulates that effect.

Modeling Expertise

Modeling expertise requires some standard: an oracle, perhaps, or an expert opponent. Such guidance, although important, may not offer enough variety to develop a robust

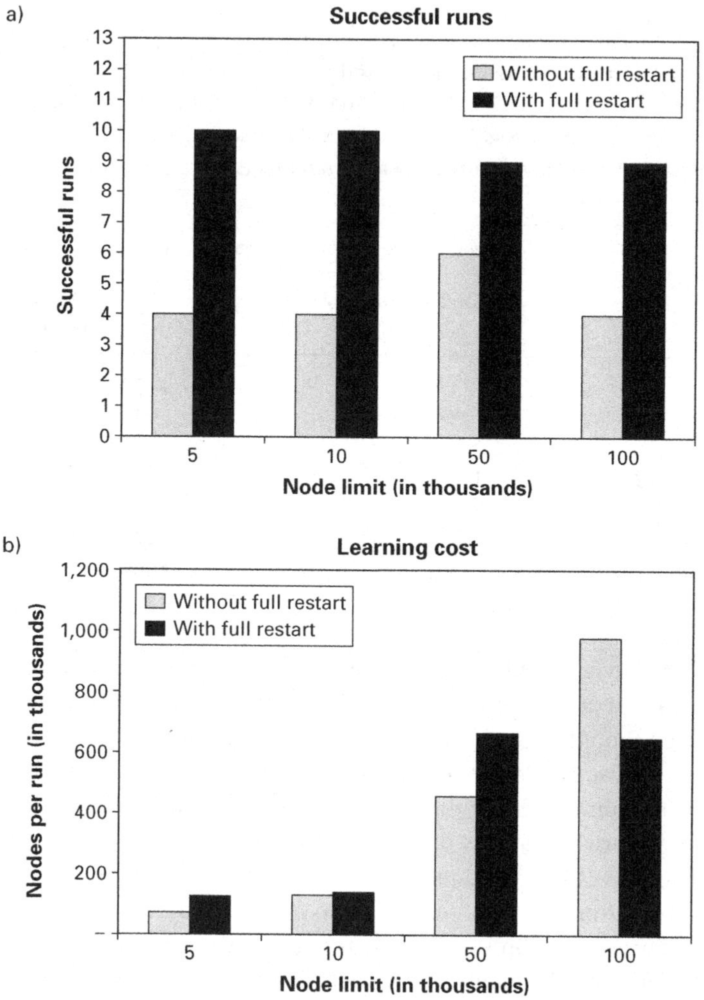

Figure 4.2
The impact of resource bounds on 10 runs for the geometric problems. (a) More runs in an experiment are successful with full restart (darker bars) and (b) fewer nodes are expanded.

Table 4.2
Skill after learning against different playing expertise (Epstein, 1995). For competition against opponents of different strengths at this draw game, lesson and practice training was better preparation than training against a perfect player. Hoyle played 100 testing contests against each of 4 opponents: one moved perfectly, the others had some percentage of random moves among otherwise perfect play: 10 percent random (expert), 70 percent random (novice), and 100 percent (random).

	Percentage of contests played correctly	
Outcomes	After learning against a perfect player	After lesson and practice training
Wins against an expert	12%	18%
Wins against a novice	59%	63%
Wins against random play	80%	85%
Wins or draws against perfect play	100%	100%
Wins or draws against an expert	93%	98%
Wins or draws against a novice	80%	97%
Wins or draws against random play	88%	100%

learner. Experiments with Hoyle in table 4.2, for example, found competition against a *perfect player* (a program that makes only optimal moves) too narrow (Epstein, 1994b). An expert player should succeed against opponents of any strength. After training against a perfect player, Hoyle lost testing contests to opponents with far less prowess—it was repeatedly flummoxed by their errors. Although some percentage of random decisions in an otherwise flawless opponent drives the learner's experience outside perfect play, such moves lack good rationales and are therefore often of poor quality—not the kind of decisions Hoyle should learn to make. If Hoyle learned only against itself, it did not always develop sufficiently strong expertise either. The most effective approach, *lesson and practice training*, had Hoyle alternately play two contests against a perfect player and then practice in seven contests against itself.

Without an external standard of expertise, a system can take traces of its own successes as a model. Neither Ariadne nor ACE has an external model; each learns alone and can only judge the correctness of its actions from its ability to solve problems. When the robot finds the goal, metareasoning excises any closed loops from a trace of the robot's path, and takes the remainder as a model. Similarly, when ACE solves a problem, metareasoning excises any decisions that have no alternative or are subsequently retracted and takes the remaining ones as a model. Nonetheless, neither a loop-free path nor a retraction-free search is likely to be ideal—there may have been a better way to solve the problem.

Learning about Advisors

Metareasoning permits a system to assess the performance of its individual components. Because most Advisors lie in tier 3, class-appropriateness, represented as a weight for each tier-3 Advisor, is an obvious learning target. FORR learns such weights and then uses them in tier 3's voting. Support for choice c is based on both the strength $s(A_j, c, C)$ that each Advisor A_j expresses for that choice among available choices C and the weight w_j of the Advisor. The choice with the highest support is selected:

$$\arg\max_{c \in C} \sum_{A_j \in Advisors} w_j s(A_j, c, C)$$

FORR's metareasoning extracts training instances from the (likely imperfect) trace of each solved problem during learning. A *training instance* is a problem state, the available choices there, and the decision made by the model of expertise. A *positive* training instance selects a correct action; a *negative* training instance does not. Weight learning judges the performance of Advisors on training instances.

Of course, training instances are not all equally important. They may be drawn from problems of inherently different difficulty, or be of different kinds. For example, in CSP search, a decision selects either a variable to consider or a value to assign it. Clever variable selection makes propagation particularly effective, and therefore makes value selection both easier and less significant.

To judge the correctness of advice labeled with numerical strengths, FORR has two options: top-rated strategies and relative support strategies. Under *top-rated*, an Advisor is considered correct on a positive training instance only if it gives the decision a strength at least as high (for negative training instances, as low) as any other it assigned there. Alternatively, the *relative support* $rs(A, c, C)$ of Advisor A for choice c in available choices C is the normalized difference between the strength A assigned to c and the average of the strengths A assigned across all of C:

$$rs(A,c,C) = \frac{s(A,c,C) - avg(A,C)}{avg(A,C)} \text{ where } avg(A,C) = \frac{\sum_{e \in C} s(A,e,C)}{|C|}$$

Under relative support, which attends more carefully to the nuances of variation in an Advisor's output, A is considered correct on decision $c \in C$ if and only if $rs(A, c, C)$ is positive.

FORR reinforces an Advisor's weight with a *reward* (increment) or a *penalty* (decrement) based on its correctness on each training instance. FORR tracks the number of training instances on which each tier-3 Advisor gives the correct advice. A tally is not enough because some Advisors (e.g., Hoyle's fork detector) produce crucial advice, but rarely. The fraction of times that an Advisor's advice has been correct is a somewhat better measure. ACE, however, has required the considerably more sophisticated metareasoning of *DWL* (Digression-based Weight Learning) and *RSWL* (Relative Support Weight Learning).

DWL judges correctness with top-rated. It calculates reinforcements in proportion to problem difficulty, as gauged by the resources consumed to solve it, relative to those required to solve problems earlier in the same learning phase (Epstein, Freuder, & Wallace, 2005). On training instances from shorter solutions, DWL assigns variable-selection Advisors larger rewards but assigns value-selection Advisors smaller rewards. DWL also reinforces behavior on a negative training instance in proportion to the size of the *digression* (eventually abandoned search tree) it began.

RSWL judges correctness with relative support (Petrovic & Epstein, 2006b). Under RSWL, reinforcements are directly proportional to relative support, but penalties are also inversely proportional to the number of choices. Two variations on RSWL modify rewards and penalties based on different estimates of training instance difficulty. RSWL-κ uses *constrainedness* (a measure of a CSP class difficulty (Gent, Prosser, & Walsh, 1996) to estimate the difficulty of each search state dynamically. RSWL-d is computationally less expensive; it uses search tree depth and assumes that decisions are more difficult at the top of the search tree. RSWL-d is based on the premise that, with respect to a given algorithm, every CSP has a *backdoor*, a set of variables after whose consistent assignment with the constraints search becomes extremely easy (Williams, Gomes, & Selman, 2003).

Learning on a sequence of problems applies knowledge from one successful search to subsequent searches. The first success increases the weights of those Advisors that contributed to its decisions. It may, however, be quite expensive to solve any first problem at all, particularly when the problems are hard, there are many Advisors, and they disagree with one another. On occasion a run fails because the learner has solved no problems at all, and therefore changed no weights. Otherwise, only the easiest problems in a class may be solved, which produces relatively few training instances, all from relatively easy situations. FORR's metareasoning therefore includes the ability to work with *random subsets* of Advisors (Petrovic & Epstein, 2008). For each problem in the learning phase, this method chooses a fresh subset of tier-3 Advisors to consult; if search solves that problem, FORR learns weights from it only for that subset. The expectation is that eventually the subset chosen for some problem will be dominated by class-appropriate heuristics, the problem will be solved, the class-appropriate weights in the subset will increase, and whenever any of those Advisors appears in a subsequent subset it will be more likely to influence search, making further successes more likely. Subset size is crucial, however: it must be large enough to select Advisors frequently, yet small enough to speed processing and to give an otherwise minority voice the opportunity to dominate decisions. Table 4.3 shows how performance improves using random subsets: It reduces the number of problems addressed during learning and speeds computation time on each decision. It even functions well when

Table 4.3

Random subsets of 30 percent improve ACE's learning performance on the geometric problems with full restart under a 5,000-node limit, with no statistically significant change in testing performance. An early failure is an unsolved problem before any solved one.

	Learning	
	Without random subsets	With random subsets
Number of learning problems	44.8	36.1
Number of learning failures	13.7	6.4
Number of early (learning) failures	7.1	0.9
Number of successful runs (of 10)	10	10
Seconds per learning decision	0.0161	0.0106
Seconds per learning run	1651.6	593.6
Average number of nodes in testing	192.7	195.9
Percentage of solved testing problems	98.6%	96.4%

we deliberately skew the initial Advisor pool with many more class-inappropriate than class-appropriate Advisors.

Finally, a self-aware system can monitor the rate at which its performance improves and stop learning once it is no longer learning anything new. FORR's metareasoning includes such *learning to stability* (Epstein, Freuder, & Wallace, 2005). Under this option, FORR monitors its Advisors' weights across a recent time window (e.g., the last 20 problems) and terminates a learning phase when the standard deviation of changes in the Advisors' weights across the window are less than ε. Learning to stability assumes that stable weights will remain stable; our experience over far longer learning phases confirms this. Making a learner more responsive to its own learning experience this way has proved successful in all three domains: there is no change in performance, only a reduction in the resources that would have been devoted to learning after the system found no way to improve its weights further. For example, Hoyle recognizes that it has learned all it can on simple games after 12 contests; more difficult games require as many as 120.

Learning to Reason Less

Metareasoning can monitor the traces from individual problems to reduce computation in a variety of ways, thereby restructuring the reasoning process itself. Unless errors can prove fatal, more thinking is not always better. Of course, such economy should be evaluated against the risks error presents and the cost required to recover from it.

Ideally, decision making uses only the best Advisors and emphasizes those that offer better advice. The metalevel can instruct the object level to omit from computation any Advisors that produce no advice during learning (e.g., Material in tic-tac-toe). Moreover, once weights are learned, FORR uses *benchmark Advisors*, which produce random advice, to identify class-appropriate Advisors. A benchmark Advisor does not vote, but it does receive a learned weight. After the learning phase, metareasoning eliminates from participation any Advisor whose weight is lower than its benchmark's. Moreover, any representation referenced only by eliminated Advisors will no longer be computed. Filtering the Advisors in these ways speeds decisions after learning, without decreasing performance. In ACE, for example, the average testing decision is accelerated by about 30 percent.

Although a tier-3 Advisor with a particularly high weight could be promoted to tier 1, our experience in all three domains has found this a dangerous practice. Instead, FORR partitions tier-3 Advisors retained after weight learning into groups of uneven size, based on their weights. Under this *prioritization*, tier-3 Advisors with the highest weights vote first; only under a tie do subsequent groups of Advisors have an opportunity to comment on the best tied actions. Fewer resources are consumed this way, since ties are relatively rare after the first group or two. With too many groups, prioritization effectively produces a ranked list. (Ranking underperforms a weighted mixture in all three of our domains, for every problem class we have investigated.) Partitions of three to seven subsets produce the best results, but the number of subsets depends on the problem class. We have rarely experienced more than a 10 percent speedup with prioritization. Although fewer Advisors make more mistakes, most representations are still computed, particularly the computationally intensive ones on which class-appropriate Advisors often rely.

Metareasoning can identify portions of the solution process where different behavior is warranted. In some domains, the last part of problem solving is more formulaic. Game players, for example, may have an endgame library and play there by lookup. ACE estimates the last part of CSP search as that after the maximum search depth at which it has experienced a wipeout within the problem class. Below this depth and only during testing, ACE's tier-1 Advisor *Pusher* consults the single highest-weighted tier-3 variable-selection Advisor as if it were in tier 1, bypassing tiers 2 and tier 3 entirely (Epstein, Freuder, & Wallace, 2005). Pushing generally reduces computation time by about 8 percent. ACE does not, however, push value selection. Experiments indicate that one can think less about where to search after the backdoor but not about the values to assign there.

Fast and frugal reasoning is a form of human metareasoning that favors recognized choices and then breaks ties among a random pair of them with one heuristic (Gigerenzer, Todd, & Group, 1999). For ACE, a recognized choice is one made earlier in search (and subsequently retracted) on the same problem. On problems where retractions are common, reusing prior decisions with the highest weighted Advisor to break ties accelerated decision time, despite increased errors (Epstein & Ligorio, 2004).

Conclusions

On difficult problems, errors in a model of expertise may be inevitable, and training instances from the same model may vary in their quality and significance. Nonetheless, a self-aware system can recognize its own prowess or lack thereof, and respond accordingly. Moreover, as we have shown here, a self-aware system can evaluate and reorganize its components to improve its performance.

Constraint solving is a paradigm for many kinds of AI problems. ACE learns to solve problems in many difficult classes, where problems stymie off-the-shelf solvers that cannot monitor and modify their own behavior. Hoyle and Ariadne each learn how to search a single space, a game tree or a maze, from which all the problems in a class are drawn. ACE learns about how to search a *set* of spaces, all of which are supposedly alike, a considerably more difficult task.

Metareasoning is essential in FORR's ability to learn to solve problems within a given class. As it learns to manage heuristics, FORR uses metareasoning to decide when to abandon an unpromising learning attempt, when to stop learning, how to select heuristics during learning, and how to prioritize heuristics. FORR also reasons about its performance on previous problems, its previous decisions, and the relative discriminatory power of its heuristics. Thinking about thinking makes FORR-based applications more incisive and more successful.

Acknowledgments

This work was supported in part by the National Science Foundation under IIS-0811437 and IIS-0739122. ACE is an ongoing joint project with Eugene Freuder and Richard Wallace of The Cork Constraint Computation Centre.

References

Aardal, K. I., van Hoesel, S. P. M., Koster, A. M. C. A., Mannino, C., &and Sassano, A. (2003). Models and solution techniques for frequency assignment problems. *4OR: A Quarterly Journal of Operations Research*, 1(4), 261–317.

Biswas, G., Goldman, S., Fisher, D., Bhuva, B., & Glewwe, G. (1995). Assessing design activity in complex CMOS circuit design. In P. Nichols, S. Chipman, & R. Brennan (Eds.), *Cognitively diagnostic assessment* (pp. 167–188). Hillsdale, NJ: Lawrence Erlbaum.

Borrett, J. E., Tsang, E. P. K., &and Walsh, N. R. (1996). Adaptive constraint satisfaction: The quickest first principle. In W. Wahlster (Ed.), *Proceedings of the 12th European Conference on Artificial Intelligence* (pp. 160–164). Chichester: Wiley.

Crowley, K., & Siegler, R. S. (1993). Flexible strategy use in young children's tic-tac-toe. *Cognitive Science, 17*(4), 531–561.

D'Andrade, R. G. (1991). Culturally based reasoning. In A. Gellatly & D. Rogers (Eds.), *Cognition and social worlds* (pp. 795–830). Oxford: Clarendon.

Epstein, S. L. (1994a). For the right reasons: The FORR architecture for learning in a skill domain. *Cognitive Science, 18*(3), 479–511.

Epstein, S. L. (1994b). Toward an ideal trainer. *Machine Learning, 15*(3), 251–277.

Epstein, S. L. (1995). Learning in the right places. *Journal of the Learning Sciences, 4*(3), 281–319.

Epstein, S. L. (1998). Pragmatic navigation: Reactivity, heuristics, and search. *Artificial Intelligence, 100*(1–2), 275–322.

Epstein, S. L. (2001). Learning to play expertly: A tutorial on Hoyle. In J. Fürnkranz & M. Kubat (Eds.), *Machines that learn to play games* (pp. 153–178). Huntington, NY: Nova Science.

Epstein, S. L., Freuder, E. C., & Wallace, R. J. (2005). Learning to support constraint programmers. *Computational Intelligence, 21*(4), 337–371.

Epstein, S. L., & Ligorio, T. (2004). Fast and frugal reasoning enhances a solver for really hard problems. In K. Forbus, D. Gentner & T. Regier (Eds.), *Proceedings of the 26th Annual Conference of the Cognitive Science Society* (pp. 351–356). Mahwah, NJ: Lawrence Erlbaum.

Fukunaga, A. S. (2002). Automated discovery of composite SAT variable-selection heuristics. In *Proceedings of the Eighteenth National Conference on Artificial Intelligence* (pp. 641–648). Menlo Park, CA: AAAI Press.

Gagliolo, M., & Schmidhuber, J. (2006). Dynamic algorithm portfolios. In *Proceedings of the Ninth International Symposium on Artificial Intelligence and Mathematics.* Fort Lauderdale, FL. Available at http://anytime.cs.umass.edu/aimath06.

Gent, I. P., Prosser, P., Walsh, T. (1996). The constrainedness of search. AAAI/IAAI, *1*, 246–252.

Gigerenzer, G., Todd, P. M., & Group, A. R. (1999). *Simple heuristics that make us smart.* New York: Oxford University Press.

Gomes, C. P., & Sellman, M. (2004). Streamlined constraint reasoning. In M. Wallace (Ed.), *Principles and practice of constraint programming CP-2004* (vol. LNCS 3258, pp. 274–287). Berlin: Springer Verlag.

Gomes, C. P., & Selman, B. (2001). Algorithm portfolios. *Artificial Intelligence, 126*(1–2), 43–62.

Gomes, C. P., Selman, B., Crato, N., & Kautz, H. (2000). Heavy-tailed phenomena in satisfiability and constraint satisfaction problems. *Journal of Automated Reasoning, 24*, 67–100.

Johnson, D. S., Aragon, C. R., McGeoch, L. A., & Schevon, C. (1989). Optimization by simulated annealing: An experimental evaluation; Part I, Graph Partitioning. *Operations Research, 37*, 865–892.

Keim, G. A., Shazeer, N. M., Littman, M. L., Agarwal, S., Cheves, C. M., Fitzgerald, J., et al. (1999). PROVERB: The probabilistic cruciverbalist. In *Proceedings of the Sixteenth National Conference on Artificial Intelligence* (pp. 710–717). Menlo Park, CA: AAAI Press.

Minton, S., Allen, J. A., Wolfe, S., & Philpot, A. (1994). An overview of learning in the Multi-TAC system. In M. L. Ginsberg (Ed.), *Proceedings of the First International Joint Workshop on Artificial Intelligence and Operations Research*. Technical report AFOSR-96-0394.

Nareyek, A. (2003). Choosing search heuristics by non-stationary reinforcement learning. In M. G. C. Resende & J. P. deSousa (Eds.), *Metaheuristics: Computer Decision-Making* (pp. 523–544). Boston: Kluwer.

Petrovic, S., & Epstein, S. L. (2006a). Full restart speeds learning. In *Proceedings of the 19th International FLAIRS Conference (FLAIRS-06)* (pp. 104–109). Menlo Park, CA: AAAI Press.

Petrovic, S., & Epstein, S. L. (2006b). Relative support weight learning for constraint solving. In W. Ruml & F. Hutter (Eds.), *Proceedings of the Workshop on Learning for Search at AAAI-06* (pp. 115–122). Menlo Park, CA: AAAI Press.

Petrovic, S., & Epstein, S. L. (2008). Random subsets support learning a mixture of heuristics. *International Journal of Artificial Intelligence Tools, 17*(3), 501–520.

Ratterman, M. J., & Epstein, S. L. (1995). Skilled like a person: A comparison of human and computer game playing. In J. D. Moore & J. F. Lehman (Eds.), *Proceedings of the Seventeenth Annual Conference of the Cognitive Science Society* (pp. 709–714). Hillsdale, NJ: Lawrence Erlbaum.

Schraagen, J. M. (1993). How experts solve a novel problem in experimental design. *Cognitive Science, 17*(2), 285–309.

Streeter, M., Golovin, D., & Smith, S. F. (2007). Combining multiple heuristics online. In *Proceedings of the Twenty-Second Conference on Artificial Intelligence (AAAI-07)* (pp. 1197–1203). Menlo Park, CA: AAAI Press.

Williams, R., Gomes, C., & Selman, B. (2003). On the connections between backdoors, restarts, and heavy-tails in combinatorial search. Paper presented at the Sixth International Conference on Theory and Applications of Satisfiability Testing (SAT03).

5 Controlling Deliberation in Coordinators

George Alexander, Anita Raja, and David Musliner

Intelligent agents often must make effective use of limited resources (such as time, computational power, or physical resources) in order to achieve their goals. Deliberative activities such as planning, scheduling, and negotiating are used to manage these resources. However, an agent may have limited time to devote to deliberation and may not be able to reach globally optimal decisions in the time available. Thus it becomes important to maximize the effective use of limited deliberative resources. Metalevel control is the process of reasoning about and controlling the agent's deliberative actions (figure 1.2, this vol., ch. 1). Examples of metalevel control questions are how to divide available deliberation time among the different deliberative actions available to the agent and what algorithms, parameters, and protocols the agent should use for deliberation if multiple options are available. This chapter describes efforts to add metalevel control capabilities to the Informed Unroller agent (IU-agent) (Musliner et al., 2007), a scheduling agent based on the Markov decision process (MDP) formalism designed to operate in a cooperative multiagent environment. Although the IU-agent can perform deliberative actions and domain actions simultaneously, the agent's tasks involve temporal constraints that necessitate intelligent management of deliberation. The goals of the research are to implement a metalevel control scheme to maximize the effectiveness of the IU-agent's deliberations and to identify characteristics of domains in which metalevel control of the IU-agent proves advantageous. For the IU-agent, the metalevel controller primarily determines when the agent should update its MDP policy, trying to ensure that the agent stays "on policy" (in the explored regions of the dynamically expanding MDP) for as long as possible.

The rest of the chapter is laid out as follows: We first discuss related work in metalevel control, especially in the area of performance profiling. We then discuss background information on Markov decision processes and the TAEMS modeling language (a derivative of which was used to represent the IU-agent's tasks) along with a description of the IU-agent. This is followed with a description of the implemented metalevel control approach and experimental results indicating its advantages for the IU-agent. The chapter concludes with a discussion of lessons learned over the course of implementing metalevel control for the IU-agent and a discussion of open issues for future work in metalevel control.

Related Work

There has been important previous work in metalevel control (Cox, 2005). For example, Russell and Wefald (1989) describe an expected utility-based approach to decide whether to continue deliberation or to stop it and choose the current best external action. They introduce myopic schemes such as metagreedy algorithms, single-step, and other adaptive assumptions to bound the analysis of computations. Raja and Lesser (2007) present a decision-theoretic approach that leverages an abstract representation of the agent's state to bound the cost of metalevel decision making in a complex multiagent environment. Dean and Boddy (1988) describe a decision-theoretic approach to scheduling deliberative actions implemented by anytime algorithms. These algorithms are guaranteed to return a result at any time they are interrupted, and it is assumed that their solution quality increases as they are given more computational time. Their approach uses performance profiles, which provide a measure of how the solution quality changes over time. Hansen and Zilberstein (2001) present a formal approach to metalevel control of anytime algorithms that reasons explicitly about monitoring costs. More recently, Larson and Sandholm (2004) have studied performance profile trees that stochastically model the *path* the solution takes. Online metalevel control of an adaptive real-time agent is investigated by Musliner, Goldman, and Krebsbach (2005). The metalevel control scheme described in this chapter uses the simplified representation of a performance profile as a curve and adds a multilevel decision-making strategy. The performance profiles are not assumed a priori, but are induced experimentally and maintained through periodic updates. The CMU agent (see chapter 14 of this volume) also views metalevel control as dynamic management of control parameters; that research identifies parameters that are most effective in boosting quality by balancing between local scheduling and explicit coordination with other agents.

Background

Markov Decision Processes

A Markov decision process (MDP) is a probabilistic model of a sequential decision problem, where states can be perceived exactly, and the current state and action selected determine a probability distribution on future states (Sutton & Barto, 1998). Specifically, the outcome of applying an action to a state depends only on the current action and state (and not on preceding actions or states). Formally, an MDP is defined via the 4-tuple <S, A, P, R>: a state set *S*, an action set *A*, a transition probability function $P: S \times A \times S \rightarrow [0, 1]$, and a reward function $R: S \times A \times S \rightarrow \Re$. On executing action a in state s, the probability of transitioning to state s' is denoted $P^a_{ss'}$ and the expected reward associated with that transition is denoted $R^a_{ss'}$. A rule for choosing actions is called a *policy*. Formally, it is a mapping $\Pi: S \times A \rightarrow [0, 1]$ (if the policy is deterministic, we may simplify this as $\Pi: S \rightarrow A$). If an agent follows a fixed policy, then over many trials, it will receive an average total reward known as the *value* of the policy. In addition to computing the value of a policy averaged over all trials, we can also compute the value of a policy when it is executed starting in a particular state s. This is denoted $V^{\Pi}(s)$ and it is the expected cumulative reward of executing policy Π starting in state s. This can be written as

$$V^{\pi}(s) = E\left[\gamma_{t+1} + \gamma_{t+2} + \ldots \middle| s_t = s, \pi\right]$$

where r_t is the reward received at time t, s_t is the state at time t, and the expectation is taken over the stochastic results of the agent's actions.

For any MDP, there exists a set of one or more optimal policies, which we will denote by Π^*, that maximize the expected value of the policy. All of these policies share the same optimal value function, written as V^*. The optimal value function satisfies the Bellman equations (Bertsekas & Tsitsiklis, 1996).

TAEMS Modeling Language

TAEMS models (Horling et al., 1999) are hierarchical abstractions of multiagent problem-solving processes that describe alternative ways of accomplishing a desired goal; they represent major problems, decision points, and interactions between problems. Nonleaf nodes in the hierarchy are called *tasks* (tasks may have one or more subtasks), while nodes at the lowest level are called *methods* and represent the domain-level actions available to an agent. Methods are characterized by discrete probability distributions along three dimensions: quality, duration, and cost. Quality accumulation functions (QAFs) define how quality propagates from a child node to its parent. Example QAFs are *q_sum*, indicating the parent is assigned the sum of qualities from its children, *q_max*, indicating the parent is assigned the maximum quality of any of its children, and *q_min*, indicating the parent is assigned the minimum quality of any of its children. In addition, temporal constraints may be represented by assigning earliest start times and deadlines to nodes; these constraints limit the time period available to achieve quality for the node. Temporal constraints propagate downward through the hierarchy. Finally, task interrelationships may be represented by linking nodes using nonlocal effects (NLEs). Example NLEs include hard constraints, such as *enables* (the enabled tasks cannot accrue quality until the enabling task has achieved nonzero quality), as well as soft constraints, such as *facilitates* (the facilitated task will accrue more quality if it is executed after the facilitating task has achieved nonzero quality). An example TAEMS structure is given in figure 5.1.

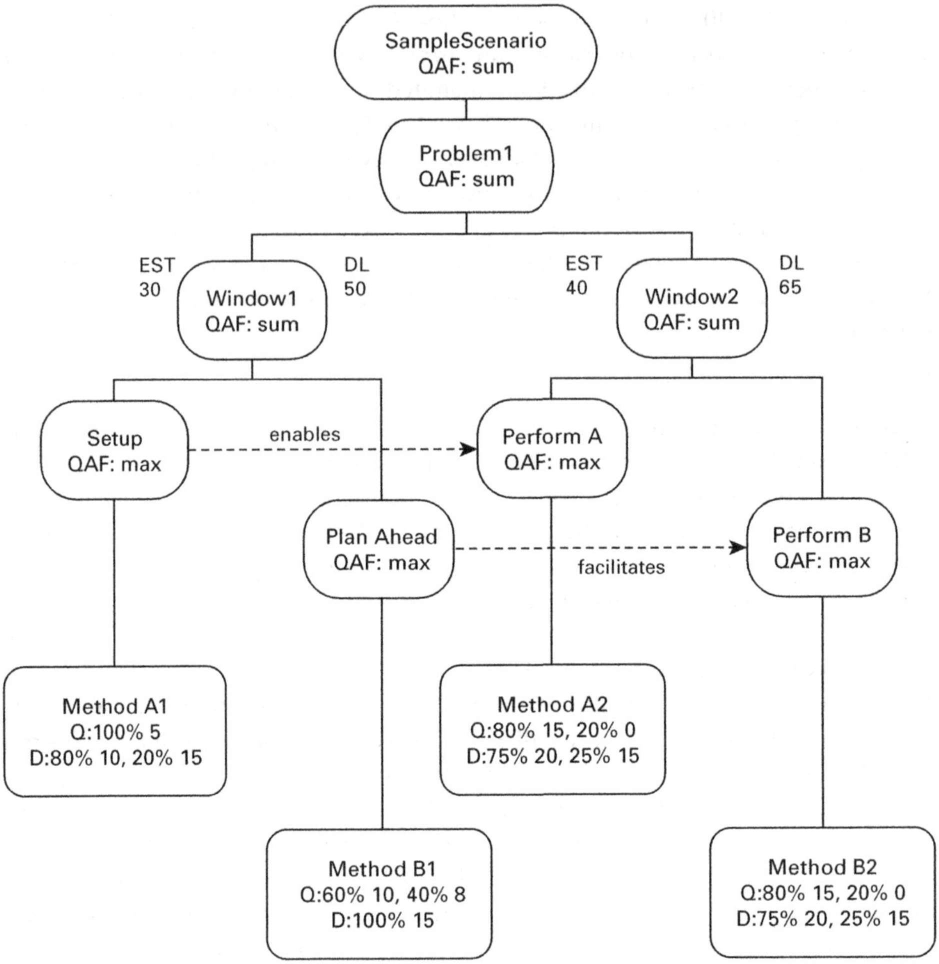

Figure 5.1
An example TAEMS structure.

A TAEMS model can be converted into an equivalent MDP and solved to obtain an optimal policy (Wu & Durfee, 2007). In fact, due to the deadline constraints in the TAEMS model, the conversion will produce a finite-horizon MDP. Starting from the initial state, successor states are generated based on all the actions available to the agent in a state and all possible outcomes of those actions. For example, if the agent could choose between two actions and these actions had no uncertainty in quality, cost, or duration, then two successor states would be generated. In general, if n actions are available in a given state, each having q possible quality values, c possible costs, and d possible duration values, then $n*q*c*d$ immediate successor states would be generated. In practice, even for fairly small TAEMS models, if there is a lot of flexibility in action choices and many possible outcomes of each action, the MDP may be too large for the agent to completely enumerate. The IU-agent thus performs this conversion incrementally and continually, alongside domain-level task execution. Although the IU-agent derives its MDP from a TAEMS model, our metalevel control approach does not depend on TAEMS per se, just the incremental unrolling process.

IU-agent

The IU-agent (Musliner et al., 2007; Wu & Durfee, 2007) translates its task model into an MDP beginning with the earliest states and expanding toward the problem horizon. This unrolling process must be periodically paused in order to derive a partial policy based on the currently expanded states. The unrolling process continues until the entire MDP is unrolled, the scenario deadline is reached, or the agent arrives in an unknown state and cannot remain on policy. States that have not yet been expanded are maintained in a queue called the *open list*.

If unrolling proceeds naively in a breadth-first manner, then the agent may only be able to expand states representing the near future and will consequently perform poorly. If the agent cannot unroll enough of the state space, or more specifically, an adequately far-sighted view of the state space, the resulting policy may be suboptimal. As more states are unrolled and the (partial) MDP becomes more forward-looking, the agent's partial policy approaches the optimal policy for the complete MDP. Thus it is natural to try to discover heuristics that guide the unrolling process in a way that maximizes the expected quality of the agent's policy given limited computational time.

The process of unrolling the metalevel control without such heuristic guidance is called *uninformed unrolling*. In contrast, the IU-agent uses a method called *informed unrolling*, from which it derives its name. Informed unrolling is based on the principle that the agent should not spend much time unrolling states that will probably never be reached; thus the IU-agent prioritizes unexpanded states in the open list according to the probability of reaching those states when following an optimal policy. Policy execution occurs alongside unrolling; hence as the actual outcome of actions becomes known, the probability of reaching a state changes and some states become unreachable. Therefore the IU-agent periodically removes or prunes unreachable states from the MDP and the open list.[1] Pruning may be triggered by the agent making an action choice (eliminating the states representing the action[s] not chosen) or by the completion of a method (eliminating the states representing those possible outcomes that did not in fact occur). In addition, the open list is periodically sorted so that states with the highest probability of being reached are placed toward the front of the queue. After sorting the open list, the IU-agent solves the current MDP to obtain a new partial policy. Meanwhile, the unrolling process remains paused until the sorting/policy derivation is complete. Policy derivation is not computationally cheap (in fact, it is polynomial); thus metalevel control is needed to balance the time spent unrolling versus the time spent sorting the open list and deriving a policy. The metalevel controller initiates the process by instructing the agent to perform an open list sort, which in turn triggers the policy derivation function. Since this sequence is opaque to the metalevel controller, we will refer to the entire procedure as a *deliberative action* that is triggered by an open list sort. Also, if a possible prune is detected while the agent is in the middle of the sorting process, the sort will be aborted and the prune processed, and then a new sort is begun using the pruned open list. Obviously, interrupting many sorts over the course of the agent's execution becomes expensive, wasting the computational time already spent before the sorts are aborted. Therefore, the agent requires adaptive control to schedule open list sorts at the most appropriate times. Since the unrolling process occurs alongside execution of domain actions, the agent may enter an unknown state or a state not considered in the agent's current partial policy. In this event, the agent abandons its MDP-based reasoning for a myopic greedy action selection method that is based on one-step lookahead.

Metalevel Control Approach

The metalevel control component for the IU-agent is designed with a number of goals in mind. The most basic motivation is the trade-off between keeping the agent's MDP policy current (by taking frequent deliberative actions) and maintaining a more forward-looking MDP (by unrolling more states). In addition to this consideration, it is desirable to reduce the amount of deliberation time wasted by the agent on sorts that are interrupted by prunes before completion, since these sorts-in-progress are thrown out and the wasted time could have been spent unrolling more MDP states. The third goal is to ensure that the agent stays on policy for as long as possible, rather than falling back on a greedy myopic deliberation method.

1. Only states that are intrinsically unreachable are removed (e.g., states corresponding to an earlier time period. States that could not be reached by the current policy are retained, since the policy may change as more of the state space is explored.

The agent can fall off policy in two different ways: off the end or off the side. When the agent reaches an area of the state space that has not yet been unrolled, the agent has fallen off the end of its policy. If the agent reaches a state that has been unrolled but not yet incorporated into its policy (that is, no action has been chosen for the state), it has fallen off the side of the policy. Falling off the end of the policy can be avoided by maximizing the number of MDP states unrolled, for example, by reducing aborted sorts and limiting the amount of time spent in deliberation. On the other hand, falling off the side of the policy can be avoided by maintaining an up-to-date policy, that is, by increasing the frequency of deliberative actions. Thus the metalevel component has to balance competing goals.

The metalevel control approach consists of building performance profiles for the agent's deliberative action and using a number of heuristics to determine whether to initiate a sort (triggering deliberation) or continue unrolling.

Performance Profiles

Initial data confirmed that the time required to reorder the open list as well as the time required for policy derivation (collectively, the deliberation time) scales with the number of reachable states in the agent's MDP; thus we collected from the agent's logs the deliberation time and reachable state count for all the deliberative actions taken across a number of domains and used these data with Gnuplot's built-in curve-fitting feature based on the Marquardt–Levenburg algorithm (Marquardt, 1963) to create a deliberation time estimator function. For this research, the correlation between reachable states and deliberation time was treated as domain independent (in other words, the performance of open list sorting and policy derivation depends just on the number of reachable states and not the particular topology of the MDP). Example deliberation time data are shown in figure 5.2 with the estimation function overlaid. Notice that the data follow a roughly linear trend until about 60,000 reachable states, when the sort times sharply increase. To account for this, the data are fitted with the following piece-wise function:

$$f(x)=\begin{cases} a_1x+a_0,\ x<60000 \\ b_a x^a+b_2x^2+b_1x+b_0,\ x\geq 60000 \end{cases}$$

Investigations suggested that the sharp increase in deliberation times was caused by garbage collection issues. After some memory optimizations were performed on the IU-agent's unrolling algorithm, the data followed a smoother curve. Timing data collected after these modifications were made is shown in figure 5.3 along with a retuned estimation function. The curve-fitting procedure had to be periodically rerun using the latest data as other changes were made to the agent; however, the overall trend of the data remained the same. These events hint at the possible interactions even at the coding level between metalevel control and deliberative control.

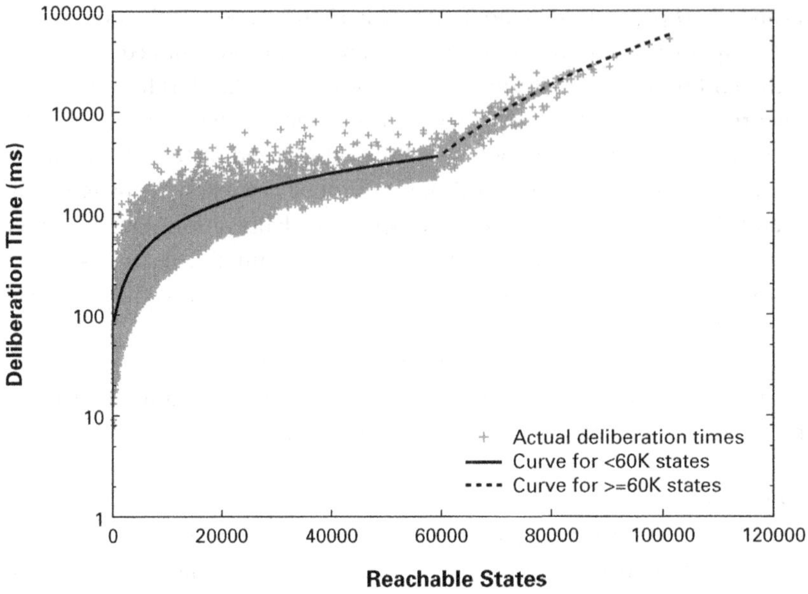

Figure 5.2
Deliberation time data before memory optimizations.

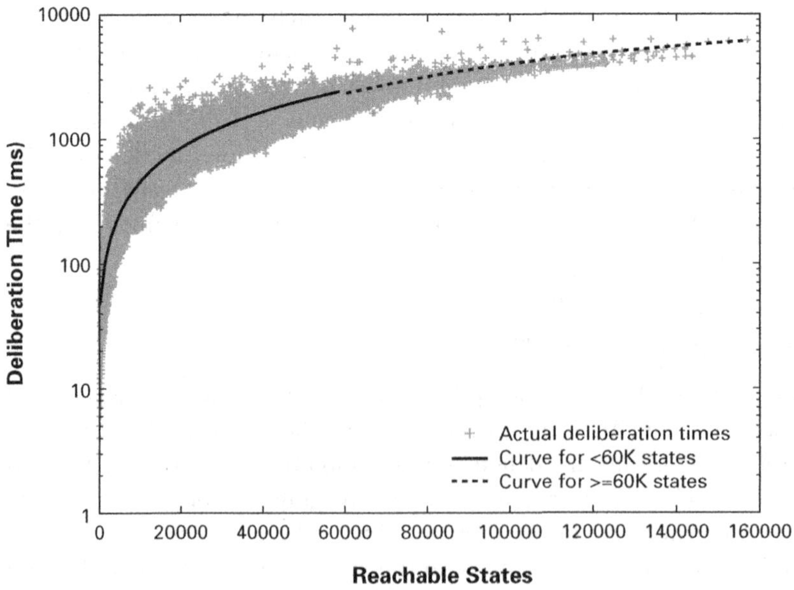

Figure 5.3
After memory optimizations, the trend in deliberation time data is much smoother.

Note that the true number of reachable states is unknown to the agent until after policy derivation is completed. For input to the deliberation time function, this number was estimated by the sum of the previous reachable state count, the number of states added to the open list, and the number of true terminal states added to the MDP.[2]

The general algorithm is summarized in Procedure 5.1. Each time a state is expanded from the open list, the IU-agent makes a decision about whether to pause unrolling, resort the open list, and derive a new partial policy, or just to continue unrolling. A single primary heuristic is tested first. If the primary heuristic does not return *true*, then one or more secondary heuristics are tested sequentially. If none of the heuristics returns *true*, then the IU-agent continues unrolling the MDP.

Procedure 5.1 Metalevel Control Loop

loop
    expand a state from the open list
    if *primaryHeuristic* **then**
        call openList sort and derive policy
    else if $secondaryHeuristic_1$ **then**
        call openList sort and derive policy
...
    else if $secondaryHeuristic_N$ **then**
        call openList sort and derive policy
    end if
end loop

Time-to-Sort Heuristics

The estimated deliberation time was used as input to several heuristic functions that determine whether the agent should stop unrolling and trigger an open list sort at a given point in time. These heuristics are divided into two categories: *primary* heuristics and *secondary* heuristics. Primary heuristics represent rules for when to initiate a sort under normal conditions. They are responsible for the periodic policy derivation that is necessary without any special considerations. Secondary heuristics represent rules for sorting in certain special cases; they allow the agent to react opportunistically when deriving an updated MDP policy is particularly desirable.

Primary Heuristics

The IU-agent uses a single primary heuristic that does not change over the course of a scenario. We considered a number of possible heuristics:

2. True terminal states are actual terminal states of the complete MDP, as distinguished from states that are merely at the edge of the partially unrolled MDP.

n-pops-and-growth This rule triggers an open list sort with associated policy derivation to be performed whenever N states have been popped off the open list and expanded and the MDP has grown by M states. Formally:

popped ← number of states popped off open list
growth ← number of states added to MDP
if $(popped > N) \wedge (growth > M)$ **then**
return true
else return false

One of the challenges in effectively applying this rule is deciding on appropriate values of N and M such that sorting occurs regularly but not too frequently.

process-openlist-n-percent This rule is invoked whenever N percent of the states from the open list have been expanded. Intuitively, the rule causes more frequent sorting (thus a more focused MDP explored depth-first along the choices made by the policy so far) during the beginning of a scenario with less frequent sorting (thus more breadth-first exploration) after the MDP becomes larger. Formally:

prevSize ← number of open list states after last sort
popped ← number of states popped off open list
if $popped > N/100 * prevSize$ **then**
return true
else return false

sort-budget This rule times sorts so that roughly a certain fraction of the agent's time is spent on deliberative actions versus unrolling. Let b be the budget amount (i.e., the fraction of the time relative to unrolling time that we wish to spend deliberating), then formally:

unrollTime ← time since last sort
delibDuration ← estimated deliberation time
deliberationRatio ← *delibDuration/unrollTime*
if $deliberationRatio \leq b$ **then**
return true
else return false

To prevent time lost to aborted sorts, these primary heuristics are constrained by an additional condition (given in Procedure 5.2) that the triggered deliberative action will not run over a method start time or possible method completion time (which would cause some states to be marked unreachable, hence aborting the sort-in-progress when these states are subsequently pruned from the MDP). A sort is triggered by the primary heuristic returning *true* only if Procedure 5.2 returns *true* as well.

Procedure 5.2 Not-too-close-to-next-possible-prune
delibDuration ← estimated deliberation time
nextEST ← next earliest start of a method
nextFinish ← next possible completion time of the currently executing method
nextPossPrune ← *min*(*nextEST*, *nextFinish*)
if *currentTime* + *delibDuration* ≤ *nextPossPrune* **then**
return true
else return false

Our experiments suggested that the *sort-budget* rule performed best in the domains of interest. We hypothesized that the best choice of primary heuristic may depend on characteristics of the domain, but no clear trends in this regard were discovered over the course of the experiments.

Secondary Heuristics

In addition to the primary heuristic used to determine when to perform routine open list sorting/policy derivation, the IU-agent uses multiple secondary heuristics to decide whether to take an opportunistic deliberative action should certain conditions occur.

perfect-time-to-sort This condition is triggered when the next deliberation is estimated to complete within a small time window before the IU-agent's next action-choice time. The purpose of this rule is to try to ensure that the MDP policy is always as up-to-date as possible whenever a domain-level decision is made. Formally:

Δ ← the size of the desired time window
delibDuration ← estimated deliberation time
timeAvail ← time left until next earliest start of a method
if 0 ≤ *timeAvail* – *delibDuration* ≤ Δ **then**
return true
else return false

need-actions-for-near-term-states This heuristic examines the reachable nonedge MDP states that correspond to times within a small window of the agent's current time. If any of these states do not have actions associated with them in the MDP policy, the rule triggers an open list sort. The reasoning behind this rule is that if the agent enters a state for which the policy has no associated action, then the agent will fall off the policy and use a myopic deliberative method for the duration of the scenario. Let Π be the agent's MDP policy, with Π(s) denoting the action associated with state s, and let time_s denote the time of state s. Furthermore, let Δ be the size of our desired time window, and let NearTerm = $\{s \in \text{ReachableStates}: \text{time}_s \leq \text{currentTime} + \Delta\}$. Then this rule is given formally as:

```
for all s ∈ NearTerm do
if s ∉ EdgeStates ^ Π(s) == NULL then
    return true
end for
return false
```

These secondary heuristics may trigger a sort at a time when it would normally be interrupted by a prune; however, since in the IU-agent's domain of interest the special conditions represented by these rules are considered more important than the benefits of processing prunes, sorts triggered by secondary heuristics are programmatically defined to be uninterruptible.

Experimental Results

The IU-agent was tested with and without metalevel control on a total of 169 domains, divided among eight groups. In the tests with metalevel control disabled, the agent used only the *n-pops-and-growth* rule with no secondary heuristics. The domains in Groups 1–3 and 7–8 were designed by external teams. Unfortunately, because of the size and complexity of the TAEMS models, it is difficult to give a succinct general description of these domains without knowledge of the motivations behind their design. However, the domains in Groups 4–6 were designed specifically to capitalize on the strengths of the metalevel control approach, focusing on two of the main intended benefits to the agent: increased number of unrolled states to avoid falling off the end of the policy and monitoring to prevent falling off the side of the policy. These domains are summarized as follows:

- *Group 4* An assortment of domains, mostly consisting of small chains of enabling NLEs along with scattered single NLEs. The design strategy is to give the agent many action choices and to require the agent to reason nonmyopically.
- *Group 5* Small domains consisting of long chains of enabling NLEs. Quality in these domains is essentially binary. If the agent cannot unroll the complete state space in time, then it will achieve 0 quality; otherwise, the agent gets a small amount of quality.
- *Group 6* Domains containing sets of low-quality actions that enable high-quality actions, with a single very high-quality action. The agent has to maximize the number of unrolled states in order to see the very high-quality state.

The results (see table 5.1) show a statistically significant increase in mean quality achieved for the IU-agent with metalevel control in Groups 4–5 in particular and for all groups regarded as a whole (overall mean quality increase ~ 12.6 percent). On many of the individual domains comprising Groups 2, 3, and 7, the agent was not able to achieve quality with or without metalevel control, and further investigation suggested

Table 5.1
Mean quality comparison

Group	Mean Qual. (MLC Off)	Mean Qual. (MLC On)	*N*	Sig. (1-tail paired *t*)
1	1188.82	1185.74	25	0.147
2	29.74	41.37	25	0.218
3	18.73	15.23	25	0.275
4	573.75	613.91	25	0.001
5	0.00	2.33	18	<0.001
6	155.56	178.17	7	0.079
7	6.44	6.44	25	—
8	184.85	463.04	19	0.066
All	297.73	335.23	169	0.030

that these domains may require communication capabilities more advanced than those implemented in the IU-agent at the time of the experiments. However, log information for runs of Groups 2 and 3 reveals that the agent was able to stay on policy longer with metalevel control enabled (figures 5.4 and 5.5 respectively).

Additionally, metalevel control was able to greatly reduce the number of open list sorts that were aborted and restarted. Figures 5.6 and 5.7 show the time wasted on aborted sorts over a run of all the domains in Group 4. The line $y = x$ is shown for illustration: Points near the line indicate that the deliberation was almost completed when it was interrupted. With metalevel control enabled, the IU-agent had about 12.7 percent of the aborted sorts of the agent lacking metalevel control.

Discussion

Metalevel control is not a panacea (Conitzer & Sandholm, 2003). In our experiments, we found several situations in which the agent performed just as well with metalevel control disabled. However, certain domain characteristics favored sophisticated metalevel control:

• High amounts of uncertainty or many options for domain actions require the IU-agent to unroll its MDP in a more breadth-first manner in order to avoid falling off the side of the policy (that is, if there are many [almost] equally likely outcomes for an action choice, then the agent must unroll several subtrees instead of focusing on a single high-probability subtree). Metalevel control's advantage in this case is in the increased number of states unrolled compared with the metalevel control-disabled IU-agent.

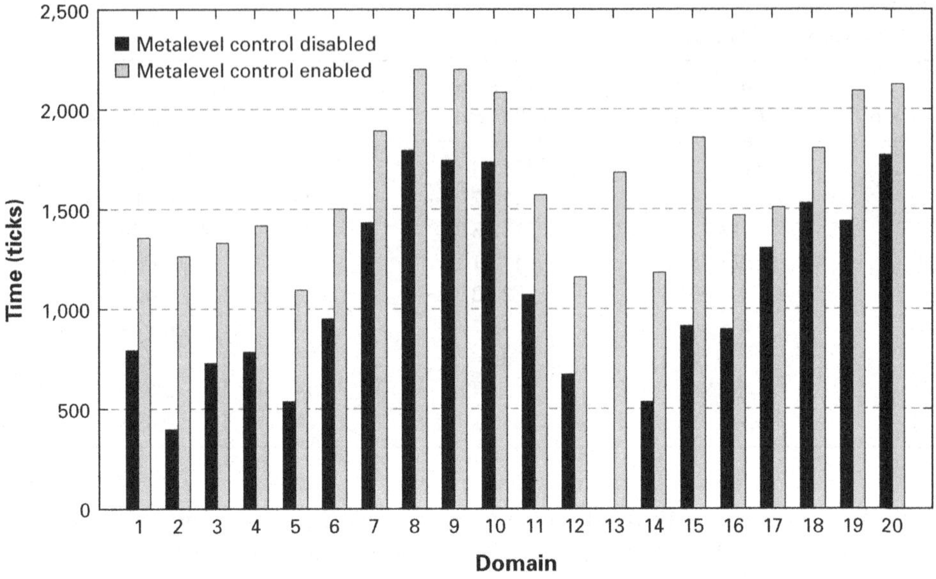

Figure 5.4
Time spent on policy. Metalevel control allows the agent to remain on policy longer.

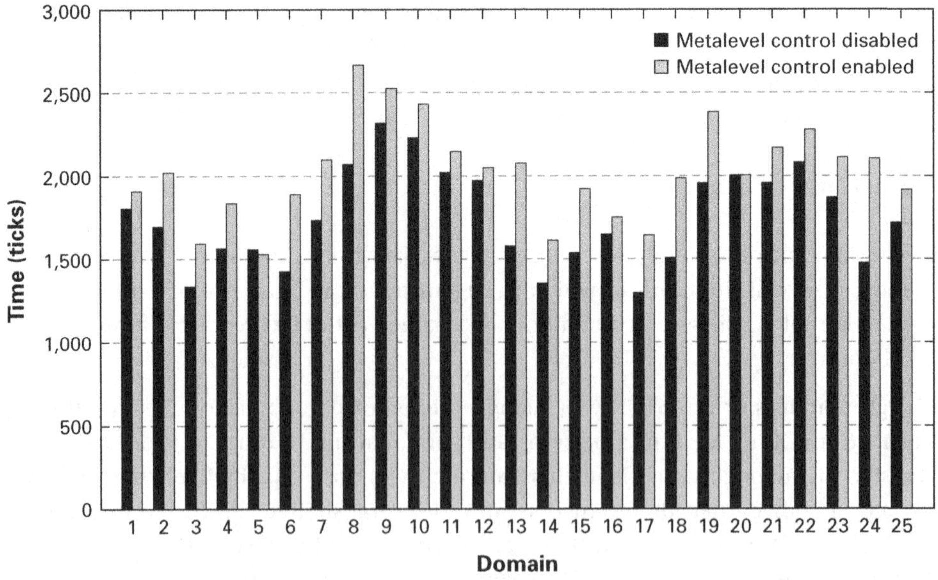

Figure 5.5
Time spent on policy. Metalevel control allows the agent to remain on policy longer.

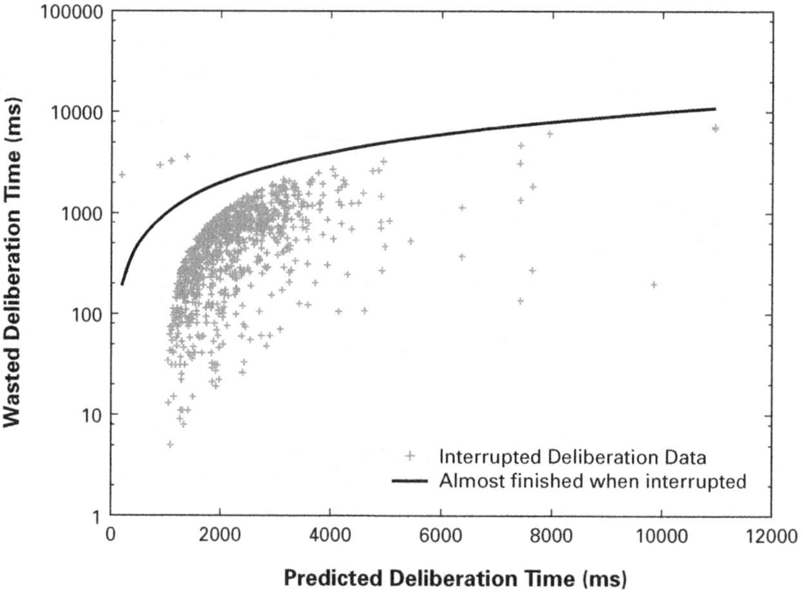

Figure 5.6
Time wasted on interrupted sorts (Group 4 domains). With the metalevel control features disabled, the agent estimated deliberation time by multiplying the time spent on the previous deliberative action by a constant ratio.

• Long chains of *enables* NLEs or time constraints that necessitate smart scheduling (e.g., actions with short time windows between their release times and deadlines) require the IU-agent to think far ahead. If the IU-agent's myopic fallback deliberation performs well in a domain, then much of the advantage of MDP-based deliberation would be lost.

Conversely, certain domain characteristics reduce or eliminate the advantages of metalevel control for the IU-agent:

• In domains that are very loosely constrained (e.g., no nonlocal effects, plenty of slack in the agent's schedule), a greedy approach may perform well. If such a ceiling effect eliminates the advantages of the IU-agent's reasoning capabilities, then of course metalevel control would not give it much added advantage.
• In domains that are too tightly constrained (e.g., very complex interdependencies among agents and very little slack time in an agent's schedule) it may be very difficult for even a highly sophisticated agent to perform well. Metalevel control may help in these domains, but it will not guarantee success if success is impossible.

In short, the described metalevel control scheme enhanced the existing reasoning capabilities of the IU-agent. One major lesson learned over the course of our research

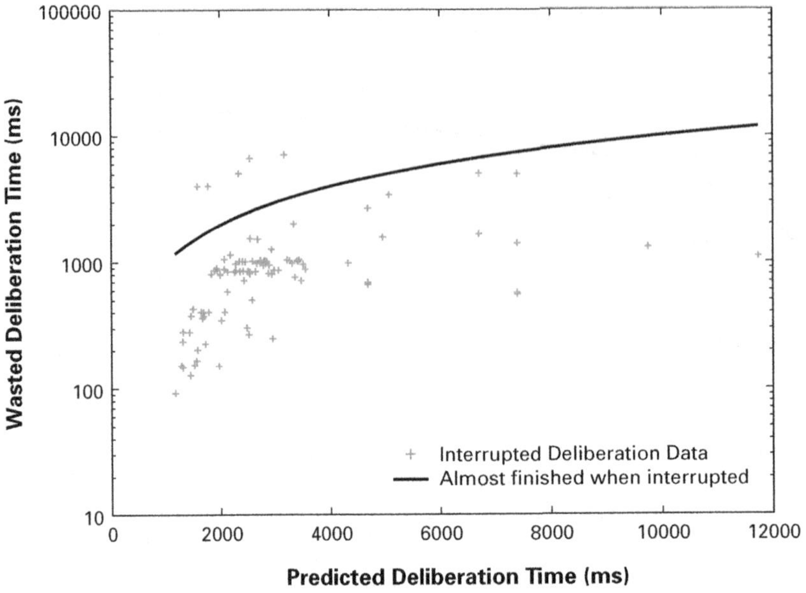

Figure 5.7
Metalevel control is enabled resulting in fewer interrupted sorts (Group 4 domains).

is that metalevel control should be considered from the beginning and should be developed alongside deliberation, since they affect each other. Changes in deliberation can require metalevel control changes; for example, on several occasions we noticed that the IU-agent performed as well without metalevel control on certain domains where metalevel control had formerly proven advantageous, and we had to adjust the parameters of our metalevel control to regain the advantage. Conversely, observations made while implementing the metalevel control strategy, such as gathering performance profile data, suggested areas for improving the deliberation of the agent.

Conclusion and Future Work

We have described an approach to controlling deliberation in an MDP-based scheduling agent. The approach consists of collecting performance profile information from the agent empirically and using these profiles in a multilevel heuristic decision-making strategy. Experimental results were presented that suggest the advantages of metalevel control for the agent in a subset of test domains. There are many open opportunities in metalevel control, especially in multiagent systems (Alexander et al., 2007; this vol., chaps. 13, 14, 15). In particular, in chapter 13 of this volume we discuss our work on extending isolated metalevel control of individual agents to distributed metalevel control of groups of cooperative agents. This involves many of the same issues as deliberative control of multiple agents, such as the need for coordination and negotiation.

Acknowledgments

This work is published with permission of IFAAMAS. This essay was originally published in the *Proceedings of the Seventh International Conference of Autonomous Agents and Multi-agent Systems.*

References

Alexander, G., Raja, A., Durfee, E., & Musliner, D. (2007). Design paradigms for meta-control in multi-agent systems. In A. Raja & M. T. Cox (Eds.), *Proceedings of the First International Workshop on Metareasoning in Agent-based Systems* (pp. 92–103), Richland, SC: IFAAMAS.

Bertsekas, D., & Tsitsiklis, J. (1996). *Neuro-dynamic programming.* Belmont, MA: Athena Scientific.

Boddy, M., & Dean, T. (1993). Decision-theoretic deliberation scheduling for problem solving in time-constrained environments. *Artificial Intelligence, 67*(2), 245–286.

Conitzer, V., & Sandholm, T. (2003). Definition and complexity of some basic metareasoning problems. In G. Gottlob & T. Walsh (Eds.), *Proceedings of the 18th International Joint Conference on Artificial Intelligence* (pp. 1099–1106). San Francisco: Morgan Kaufmann.

Cox, M. T. (2005). Metacognition in computation: A selected research review. *Artificial Intelligence, 169*(2), 104–141.

Dean, T., & Boddy, M. (1988). An analysis of time-dependent planning. In *Proceedings of the Seventh National Conference on Artificial Intelligence* (pp. 49–54). Menlo Park, CA: AAAI Press.

Hansen, E., & Zilberstein, S. (2001). Monitoring and control of anytime algorithms: A dynamic programming approach. *Artificial Intelligence, 126*(1–2), 139–157.

Horling, B., Lesser, V., Vincent, R., Wagner, T., Raja, A., Zhang, S., et al. (1999). The TAEMS White Paper. Unpublished Document, University of Massachusetts, Amherst.

Larson, K., & Sandholm, T. (2004). Using performance profile trees to improve deliberation control. In D. McGuinness & G. Ferguson (Eds.), *Proceedings of the Nineteenth National Conference on Artificial Intelligence* (pp. 73–79). Menlo Park, CA: AAAI Press.

Marquardt, D. (1963). An algorithm for least-squares estimation of nonlinear parameters. *Journal of the Society for Industrial and Applied Mathematics, 11*(2), 431–441.

Musliner, D., Goldman, R., Durfee, E., Wu, J., Dolgov, D., & Boddy, M. (2007). Coordination of highly contingent plans. In *Proceedings of the International Conference on Integration of Knowledge*

Intensive Multi-Agent Systems (pp. 418–422). IEEE Computer Society. http://www.musliner.com/david/papers/ksco07.pdf.

Musliner, D., Goldman, R., & Krebsbach, K. (2005). Deliberation scheduling strategies for adaptive mission planning in real-time environments. In M. Anderson & T. Oates (Eds.), *Working Notes of the 2005 AAAI Spring Symposium on Metacognition in Computation* (pp. 98–105). Technical Report SS-05-04. Menlo Park, CA: AAAI Press.

Raja, A., & Lesser, V. (2007). A framework for meta-level control in multi-agent systems. *Autonomous Agents and Multi-Agent Systems, 15*(2), 147–196.

Russell, S., & Wefald, E. (1989). Principles of metareasoning. In *Proceedings of the First International Conference on Principles of Knowledge Representation and Reasoning* (pp. 400–411). San Francisco: Morgan Kaufmann.

Sutton, R., & Barto, A. (1998). *Reinforcement learning*. Cambridge, MA: MIT Press.

Wu, J., & Durfee, E. (2007). Solving large TAEMS problems efficiently by selective exploration and decomposition. In E. Durfee, M. Yokoo, M. Huhns, & O. Shehory (Eds.), *Proceedings of the Sixth International Joint Conference on Autonomous Agents and Multi-Agent Systems* (pp. 291–298). Richland, SC: IFAAMAS.

6 Goal-Directed Metacontrol for Integrated Procedure Learning

Jihie Kim, Karen Myers, Melinda Gervasio, and Yolanda Gil

Developing systems that learn how to perform complex tasks presents a significant challenge to the artificial intelligence (AI) community. As the knowledge to be learned becomes complex, with diverse procedural constructs and uncertainties to be validated, the system needs to integrate a wide range of learning and reasoning methods with different focuses and strengths. For example, one learning method may be used to generalize from user demonstrations, another to learn by practice and exploration, and another to test hypotheses with experiments. The POIROT system pursues such a multistrategy learning methodology that employs multiple integrated learners and knowledge validation modules to acquire complex procedural knowledge for a medical logistics domain (Burstein et al., 2008).

For a learning system of such complexity, activities of participating agents must be coordinated to ensure that their collective activities produce the desired procedural knowledge. This kind of control is inherently *metalevel* (Anderson & Oates, 2007; Cox & Raja, this vol., chap. 1) in that it requires the system to reflect on what it is doing and why, to monitor its progress, and to make adjustments to its behavior when performance falls short of expectations. Without such introspection, effective coordination and prioritization of the base-level learning and reasoning components would not be possible. This type of introspection corresponds to a form of metareasoning centered on "stepping back" from the system to analyze its behavior, as discussed by Perlis (this vol., chap. 2). As such, it contrasts with the majority of work to date on metareasoning, which has focused on the problem of bounded rationality, as described by Zilberstein (this vol., chap. 3).

Developing a metalevel reasoner for such a complex, integrated learning system poses several challenges, including

- Assessing the progress of learning over time;
- Systematically addressing conflicts and failures that arise during learning;
- Addressing gaps and shortcomings of the individual and aggregate learning results; and

• Supporting flexible interactions among agents that pursue different learning strategies.

We describe a metalevel framework for coordinating the activities of a community of learners to create an integrated learning system. The metalevel framework is organized around *learning goals*, which are formulated through introspective reasoning to identify problems and requirements for the ongoing learning process. These learning goals are posted to a shared blackboard to direct the other components in the system. Goals can be either *process* or *knowledge* oriented.

Process goals define specific tasks to be performed as part of the learning process and are used to coordinate the activities of the various learning and reasoning components. Examples of process goals for task learning include hypothesis creation, hypothesis merging, explanation of observations, and hypothesis validation through experimentation.

Knowledge goals provide the means for a component to convey the need for additional information to further the learning process. In particular, the quality of learned knowledge could be compromised by missing critical information and the efficiency of learning may be impaired by ambiguity arising from insufficient knowledge.

In the succeeding sections of this chapter, we describe the modules within our metalevel framework that are responsible for addressing process (Maven) and knowledge (QUAIL) goals.

Maven (moderating activities of integrated learners) formulates and achieves metalevel process goals to support integrated learning. Maven's design is based on our prior work on metalevel goals and reasoning for interactive knowledge capture (Kim & Gil, 2007; Gil & Kim, 2002). Maven explicitly represents plans for achieving learning goals along with high-level strategies to prioritize learning goals. By generating assessment annotations on learned knowledge, Maven keeps track of learning progress and makes decisions on learning goals to pursue (Kim & Gil, 2008).

QUAIL (question asking to inform learning) addresses knowledge goals by managing a process of selecting and posing questions to a human expert to fill identified knowledge gaps (Gervasio & Myers, 2008; Gervasio et al., 2009). Question selection trades off the utility of missing knowledge with the cost of obtaining it.

Figure 6.1 shows how our goal-oriented metalevel framework for integrated learning maps onto a more general model of metareasoning described by Cox and Raja (this vol., chap. 1). The base-level actions correspond to the performance tasks for which procedural knowledge is being learned. Learning occurs at the reasoning level, while the metalevel supports control of learning through two essential mechanisms: metalevel process management (realized by Maven) and metalevel management of learned knowledge (realized by QUAIL). The metalevel influences the components at the reasoning level by posting appropriate learning goals and information to direct their activities.

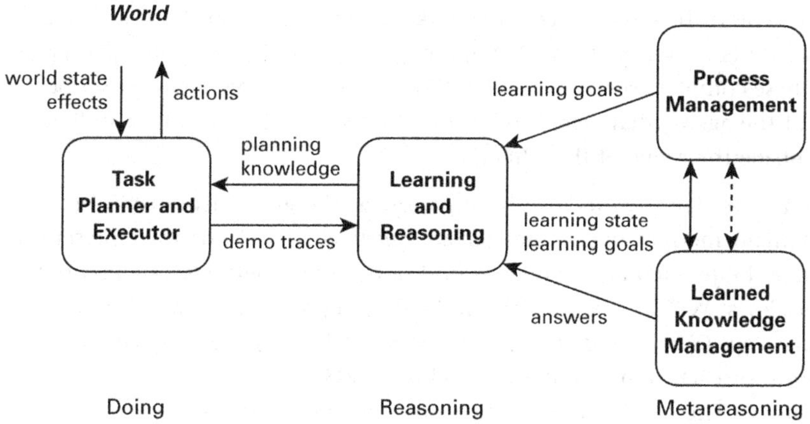

Figure 6.1
Metareasoning for integrated learning.

Metalevel process management tracks progress toward current learning goals by monitoring the performance of base-level components and their results; it also initiates additional goals to drive the system toward achieving overall learning objectives. Metalevel management of learned knowledge identifies knowledge gaps by introspection over the current state of the learned knowledge, takes actions to eliminate gaps by posing questions to the human demonstrator, and then provides information back to the base-level learners and reasoners to address unresolved knowledge goals. Although not yet supported in QUAIL, conceptually it could also coordinate with the metalevel process-management module to initiate additional activity by the base level as a means of addressing knowledge gaps (as opposed to relying solely on the human demonstrator to provide answers).

Background: A Multiagent Learning System

The POIROT system is designed to learn complex process models for a medical logistics domain. Users invoke web services to plan the evacuation of a set of patients, expressed as a *workflow*. Given a sequence of expert demonstration steps (called a *trace*) that shows how to create evacuation plans for moving patients from existing locations to desired hospitals, the POIROT system attempts to learn a general workflow that can solve similar evacuation problems. Each step in the trace is either a web service invocation (e.g., look up patient requirement, find an airport) or object selection action (e.g., select a flight from a proposed flight list).

The learning process constructs *domain methods* that contain step orderings, branches, loops, preconditions, task decompositions, and object-selection criteria, adopting the style of hierarchical-task network methods (Ghallab, Nau, & Traverso, 2004). Several different types of learning approaches (embodied as *agents*) participate in learning these complex workflows in POIROT. In the following list, we describe the capabilities of the agents that were modeled in our system. The details of individual agents are outside the scope of this chapter.

- Trace generalizers: These generalize information in the given demonstration trace and build domain method hypotheses (*domain methods*, for short) for representing step sequences, loops, branches, and preconditions. Such methods can be used in creating workflows. WIT uses a grammar induction approach to create a finite state model of trace steps (Yaman and Oates, 2007). DISTILL learns general procedure loops and conditions for each step (Winner and Veloso, 2003).
- Trace explainers: These build domain methods that explain the given top-level task goal against the given demo trace. XPLAIN/Meta-AQUA uses a set of explanation patterns for building such domain methods (Cox, this vol., chap. 9; Cox & Burstein, 2008).
- Hypothesis integrators: These integrate domain methods created by different learners and detect potential conflicts or ambiguity in the domain methods. Stitcher provides this capability (Burstein et al., 2008).
- Workflow constructors: For a given problem goal and an initial state, these create a workflow from a set of domain methods and primitive action definitions. SHOP2 provides this planning capability (Nau et al., 2005).
- Workflow executors: These test the constructed workflows by execution. SHOPPER provides this capability (Burstein et al., 2008).
- Knowledge validation by experiments: Test alternative hypotheses by designing and performing experiments. CMAX (Morrison & Cohen, 2007) provides this capability.

Individual agents, which are described in Burstein et al., 2008, communicate through a shared blackboard.

The learning problem given to POIROT consists of a single demonstration trace and a problem description (a top-level task goal and an initial state). The system currently has limited background knowledge, primarily web service definitions for primitive actions. To learn complex workflows from such input, the system needs to coordinate the learning agents effectively.

Managing Process Goals: Maven

Maven has explicit representations of process-oriented learning goals and a set of plans to prioritize and accomplish those goals. Maven follows the general BDI (belief, desire, and intention) agent model (Rao & Georgeff, 1995). In a BDI architecture, *beliefs* represent what the agent believes to be true about the current state of the world, *desires* consist of the agent's goals, *intentions* are what the agent has chosen to do, and *plans* describe how to achieve intentions. The BDI reasoner matches goals with plans that decompose them into subgoals, and turns those subgoals into desires. It then decides which goals to intend based on other plans. The BDI reasoner checks the external state with sensing actions, and may suspend intended goals or replan its behavior accordingly. This framework supports both reactive and goal-oriented behavior.

External State

As shown in figure 6.2, the shared knowledge base (a blackboard) where all the agents post results forms an external state for Maven. Maven monitors the results of the participating agents, including issues in generating procedural knowledge. From what it monitors, it forms models of the current workflow knowledge and reasons about what to do next, that is, what learning goals to generate. Maven *intend*s some of them using a set of goal-selection strategies. As an effect, Maven posts intended learning goals that can be achieved by the agents and initiates *AgentTasks*. The results from AgentTasks including new learned knowledge are stored in the shared knowledge base.

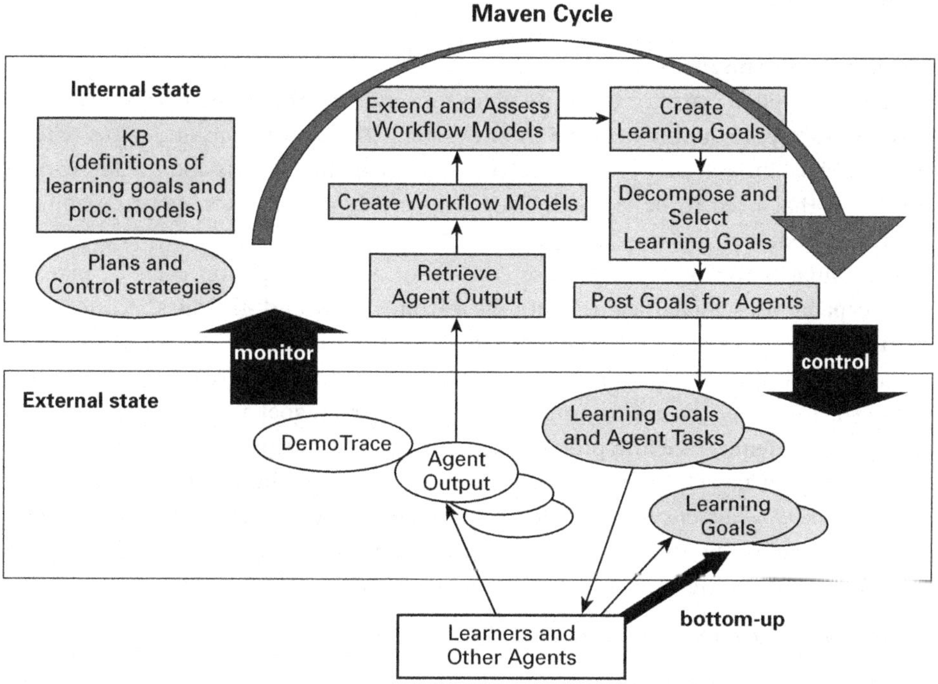

Figure 6.2
Maven's interaction with other agents.

If issues such as ambiguity or conflicts are found, they are also reported by the agents as a part of the results. The new result can lead to further learning goals.

Bottom-up control can result when learning agents create new learning goals themselves and post the goals as shared learning goals. The agents can pursue the goals asynchronously without Maven's intervention. Maven responds to the goals created by the agents as well as goals that Maven itself initiated.

Workflow Models

Maven keeps track of hypotheses from the participating agents as *workflow models*. Workflow models represent procedural knowledge formed or changed by the agents during generation of domain methods including alternative method hypotheses and their constructs such as step orderings.

Maven creates assessment annotations on individual workflow models with respect to issues found (e.g., unknown conditions for a branch), coverage (e.g., covered medical evacuation scenarios), and validation status (e.g., whether the model was validated with simulation). Maven also relates workflow models using superseding relations (i.e., one model supersedes another) and competing relations (i.e., a set of models for alternatives).

Learning Goals and Plans

Maven uses explicit learning goals and plans for achieving them. Table 6.1 shows some of the process goals and plans used by the system. The set of goals and plans reflects both the capabilities that are supported by the participating agents and the knowledge constructs that need to be learned. They can be extended as new agent capabilities are introduced.

The initial Maven knowledge base consists of a set of learning goals *G*, plans *P*, agent capabilities *C* for achieving primitive learning goals, and strategies *S* for selecting learning goals and progress assessment: $<P, G, C, S>$.

Each learning goal $g \in G$ can have a set of parameters $param_g$ that describes desired goals. For example, the LearnWorkflowFromDemoTrace goal is posted/desired with respect to the demo trace and problem description, and the given background knowledge. Each plan has (1) *trigger conditions* for determining when to execute the plan, (2) *achievement conditions* for detecting achievement of related learning goals, and (3) substeps for achieving the goal. The substeps in the plan are described in terms of the parameters and the subgoals involved in achieving the goal:

$$<tc_g(param_g), ac_g(param_g), substeps_g(param_g)>$$

A learning goal is *desired* when its trigger conditions are satisfied. We introduced the achievement condition in order to keep track of goal achievement while supporting bottom-up control. Maven relies on a set of *sensors* that keep track of trigger conditions

Table 6.1
Example Maven learning goals and plans

(a) Sample Learning Goal Types	**Knowledge Creation** GeneralizeTrace ExplainTrace CreateWorkflowWithDomainMethods **Issue Identification** IdentifyOrderingAmbiguity IdentifyUnexplainedSteps **Issue Resolution** ResolveAmbiguousStepOrderingHypotheses ResolveUnknownBranches **Knowledge Validation** ValidateWorkflowKnowledge EnsureWorkflowGeneratability EnsureTraceReproducibility ValidateKnowledgeWithExperiments
(b) Sample Maven Plans for Achieving Learning Goals	
Plan:LearnWorkflowFromDemoTrace (DemoTrace&ProblemDesc *tr*, BackgroundKnowlege *k*) —trigger condition: a new demonstration trace and a problem description (with the top-level task goal and initial state) given —substeps: GeneralizeTrace (*tr*, *k*) and/or ExplainTrace (*tr*, *k*), to create domain methods ms, and then CreateWorkflowWithDomainMethods (*tr*, *ms*) —Achievement condition: No remaining issue on created workflow **Plan:GeneralizeTrace** (DemoTrace&ProblemDesc *tr*, BackgroundKnowlege *k*) —trigger condition: No generalized domain methods for trace. —substeps: create an AgentTask for trace-generalizers (WIT & DISTILL) with the current trace information —Achievement condition: A set of domain methods for the trace is successfully created by the trace-generalizers **Plan:IntegrateKnowledge** (DomainMethods *m1*, DomainMethods *m2*) —trigger condition: more than one domain method hypotheses exist for the same trace steps. —substeps: create an AgentTask for trace-integrators with the alternative methods —Achievement condition: The methods are successfully integrated	**Plan:ValidateCausalHypotheses** (DemoTrace&ProblemDesc tr, StepOrderings orderings) —trigger condition: notices step sequence ambiguity —substeps: achieve subgoals in sequence DesignExperimentForCausalHypotheses (tr, orderings) to produce experiment packages{pkg} SelectExperimentsToRun ({pkg}, tr) to select pkgi RunDesignedExperiments (pkgi, tr) FindAppropriateStepOrderingHypos to confirm or modify orderings, or suggest more experiment —Achievement condition: Step orderings modified or confirmed **Plan:CreateWorkflowWithLearned Methods** (DomakinMethods *ms*, DemoProblemDesc *pr*) —trigger condition: new domain methods for achieving the top-level task goal created and there are no unresolved issues for the domain methods to use ... **Plan:EnsureTraceReproducibility** (Workflow *w*, DemoTrace&ProblemDesc *tr*) —trigger condition: a workflow can be generated from learned knowledge ...

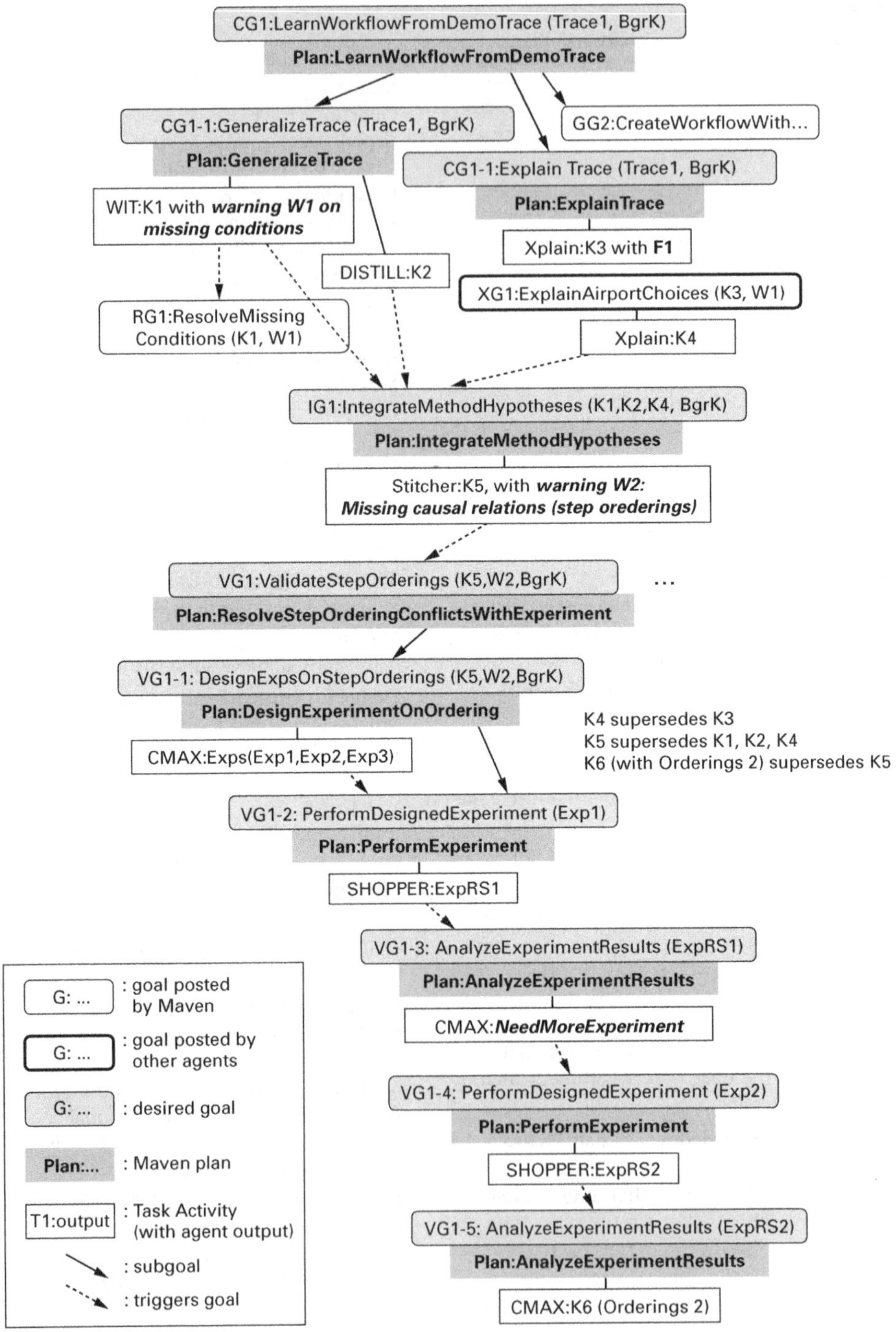
CG1:LearnWorkflowFromDemoTrace (Trace1, BgrK)
Plan:LearnWorkflowFromDemoTrace
CG1-1:GeneralizeTrace (Trace1, BgrK)
GG2:CreateWorkflowWith...
Plan:GeneralizeTrace
CG1-1:Explain Trace (Trace1, BgrK)
Plan:ExplainTrace
WIT:K1 with warning W1 on missing conditions
Xplain:K3 with F1
DISTILL:K2
XG1:ExplainAirportChoices (K3, W1)
RG1:ResolveMissing Conditions (K1, W1)
Xplain:K4
IG1:IntegrateMethodHypotheses (K1,K2,K4, BgrK)
Plan:IntegrateMethodHypotheses
Stitcher:K5, with warning W2: Missing causal relations (step orederings)
VG1:ValidateStepOrderings (K5,W2,BgrK)
...
Plan:ResolveStepOrderingConflictsWithExperiment
VG1-1: DesignExpsOnStepOrderings (K5,W2,BgrK)
Plan:DesignExperimentOnOrdering
K4 supersedes K3
K5 supersedes K1, K2, K4
K6 (with Orderings 2) supersedes K5
CMAX:Exps(Exp1,Exp2,Exp3)
VG1-2: PerformDesignedExperiment (Exp1)
Plan:PerformExperiment
SHOPPER:ExpRS1
VG1-3: AnalyzeExperimentResults (ExpRS1)
Plan:AnalyzeExperimentResults
CMAX:NeedMoreExperiment
VG1-4: PerformDesignedExperiment (Exp2)
Plan:PerformExperiment
SHOPPER:ExpRS2
VG1-5: AnalyzeExperimentResults (ExpRS2)
Plan:AnalyzeExperimentResults
CMAX:K6 (Orderings 2)
G: ... : goal posted by Maven
G: ... : goal posted by other agents
G: ... : desired goal
Plan:... : Maven plan
T1:output : Task Activity (with agent output)
: subgoal
: triggers goal

of all the learning goals and achievement conditions of desired learning goals. Goals can be achieved serendipitously or goals may fail unexpectedly even after associated plans are executed.

When an intended goal is decomposed into subgoals, its subgoals are desired as defined by the Maven plan. For example, in the initial phase of learning, when a new expert demonstration trace is detected by the Maven sensor, the goal of LearnWorkflowFromDemoTrace will be desired for the trace. The LearnWorkflowFromDemoTrace goal can be intended and decomposed into its subgoals, GeneralizeTrace, ExplainTrace, and GenerateWorkflow from learned domain methods. The top portion of figure 6.3 (history of desired goals) illustrates how the goals are related. For GeneralizeTrace, Maven will create an AgentTask for invoking trace-generalizers (a set of learning agents that create step orderings, branches, and loops from a given demonstration trace). When all the subgoals are achieved and the achievement condition is satisfied (i.e., a workflow is successfully generated from the learned domain methods and there are no issues), the original goal to LearnWorkflowFromDemoTrace becomes achieved.

Some kinds of learning goals can be iteratively desired when their trigger conditions are satisfied. For example, goals for validation experiments can be desired more than once until the experiment results provide enough information to confirm or disconfirm the tested hypotheses. The details of other goals in figure 6.3 are described below.

Control Strategies for Learning

In following the top-down control cycle, Maven can adopt different goal-prioritization strategies in selecting which goals to intend/pursue in the current situation. For example, Maven may choose to first create more knowledge and then validate the created knowledge. The strategies include:

- In the initial phase of learning, prefer domain-method-creation goals to issue-resolution goals;
- For a given piece of knowledge, prefer issue-resolution goals to knowledge-validation goals;
- When there are multiple issue-resolution goals, prefer those for more frequently used knowledge; and
- Prefer finishing subgoals of existing plans instead of intending new goals.

Additional criteria, such as confidence in the knowledge created and competence in solving related problems with learned knowledge, can be introduced to drive the learning process (Kim & Gil, 2007; Kim & Gil, 2003; Gil & Kim, 2002). That is, the

◀ **Figure 6.3**
A goal/plan decomposition of desired and intended learning goals.

selection of which learning goals to pursue can be decided based on expected confidence and competence changes by achieving goals or subgoals.

Depending on the strategies employed, the system may present different behavior such as an eager learner that generates more hypotheses first versus a cautious learner that tests learned knowledge from the beginning and produces more validation goals early on.

Learning Goal Life Cycle

The top-down and bottom-up control cycles imply that learning goals can take several different paths in their life cycle. This is shown in figure 6.4. A goal can be desired from a trigger condition of the goal or created by other agents, such as an agent posting a goal to resolve a gap. Some of the desired goals can be selected by Maven and intended. Such goals are achieved according to Maven plans. As described above, agents can pursue the goals themselves without Maven intervention. Some of the desired learning goals may never be intended by Maven, and agents do not follow up on them.

Belief Knowledge Base

The belief knowledge base (KB) in the blackboard (BB) represents the shared beliefs of the participating agents. The BB contains the given problem description (a demonstration trace, a top-level task goal and an initial state) and hypotheses that reflect learned knowledge so far. Hypotheses are represented as workflow models and can be annotated including how they *supersede* other hypotheses. For example, the analysis of experiment results may tell us that some step orderings supersede others.

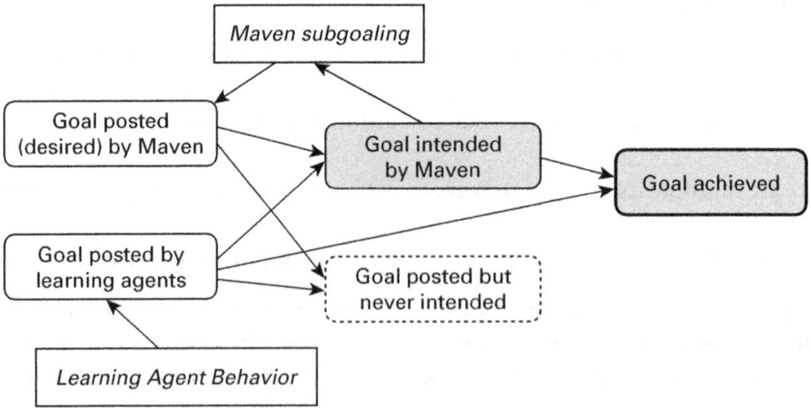

Figure 6.4
Learning goal life cycle.

Maven Reasoner

The Maven reasoner is responsible for keeping track of sensors for goal trigger conditions and achievement conditions, desired learning goals, and selecting learning goals according to the learning control strategies. The assessment of the overall learning status is performed using goals desired and achieved over time as follows.

```
Maven procedure <P, G, C, S>
While (not done) {
  retrieve_new-results (BB, learning_ history)
  cs ← update_workflow_models()
  ∀ g ∈G
    if tc_g(cs) = true, create_desired_goal (g, cs)
  ∀ a ∈ desired_goals ()
    if ac_a(cs) = true, set_achieved (a)
  if (desired_goals () = {} or significant_goals_achieved ())
    done ← true
  p ← prioritize&select (desired_goals(), S, cs)
  if (primitive_goal (p)) create_AgentTask (p, C)
  else // subgoals desired and intended in following iterations
    follow the substeps in plan_p, and update belief KB
}
```

In the above procedure, retrieve_new_results (*BB*, *learning_history*) accesses the results using the sensors employed in *BB*. Maven then updates the learning state by creating and updating workflow models. create_desired_goal (*g*, *learning_state*) creates a desired goal for *g* with respect to its parameters $param_g$. desired_goals () finds the current desired goals that are not achieved, and create_AgentTask (*p*, *agent-capabilities*) creates tasks for agents having capabilities to achieve *p*. prioritize&select (*goals*, *S*, *learning_state*) prioritizes desired goals and intend a goal according to the strategies *S* and *learning_state*. significant_goals_achieved () checks whether knowledge-creation goals have been achieved and there are no unresolved gaps or conflicts.

The selection of which learning goals and AgentTasks to perform depends on which learning control strategies *S* that are employed. Following the strategies described above, Maven can pursue knowledge-creation goals in the initial phase of learning, and select goals in a coherent manner by following existing plans where possible. Issue-resolution goals are prioritized based on the domain methods involved, including how they are related with other domain methods (e.g., superseding relations, how methods are used as submethods).

Coordinating Activities of Learning Agents: Examples

In this section, we provide a walkthrough of Maven behavior using examples from the POIROT system.

Initiate Learning

When a demonstration sequence Trace1 for a medical evacuation task is posted on the blackboard, Maven detects it as the trigger condition of the goal LearnWorkflow-FromDemoTrace. As shown in figure 6.3, Maven creates a desired goal CG1 with Trace1 and associated evacuation problem descriptions, including the initial state W0 and the task goal PSG1 (move patients before their latest arrival times). CG1 is then intended by Maven and its subgoals (GeneralizeTrace and ExplainTrace) will be desired. Maven then intends the subgoals and creates AgentTasks for them. The following shows how the learning agents accomplish these tasks in POIROT.

Example of Bottom-Up Behavior

WIT and DISTILL perform the task GeneralizeTrace. Maven monitors BB and recognizes that CG1-1 is achieved. In the meantime, additional learning goals are desired to address additional learning requirements. In particular, the WIT algorithm finds loops and branches but does not identify conditions for branches. Maven does not intend such goals yet since Maven control strategies provide higher priority for the knowledge-creation goals during the initial phase of learning. It also recognizes that the current workflow model does not yet cover the whole demonstration trace.

At that point, XPLAIN creates a set of domain methods but produces a failure in explaining some of the steps, including why the expert did not choose the closest airport (K3). XPLAIN has the capability to generate its own learning goals and share them with other agents. It can pursue the generated learning goal XG1 and resolve it by learning new knowledge K4 for explaining the steps. This type of activity illustrates the bottom-up asynchronous control of the learning process. Note that the shared learning goals are accessible by any agents in the system, and agents can proactively pursue learning goals.

Note that K4 supersedes K3 in that K4 resolves issues in K3. Maven keeps track of such superseding relations among the learned knowledge in workflow models. Maven uses them in prioritizing learning goals. For example, learning goals on validating superseded domain methods are less important than the goals for superseding domain methods.

Example of Top-Down Behavior

Maven notices that multiple alternative domain methods (i.e., competing workflow models) are created for the same trace steps, and triggers a goal for integrating created domain methods. When the knowledge-integration goal (IG1) is intended, Stitcher can perform the associated task.

The domain methods (workflow models) created by WIT, DISTILL, and XPLAIN complement each other. For example, DISTILL produces conditions for branches that are missing in WIT output. On the other hand, DISTILL ignores steps without effect. Stitcher recognizes such gaps and integrates the original methods (K1, K2, K4) into a new domain method set (K5). K5 supersedes K1, K2, and K4. Any learning goals for superseded workflow models are given lower priorities.

Learning Phases: Validation by Experiment

Both WIT and DISTILL rely on consumer–producer relations among the trace steps (which step produces an effect and which step uses the result) in deciding step orderings, and some of the causal relations may not be captured. For example, when a LookUpFlight web service call for a patient does not return any result, it may cause the expert to find available planes. Maven can initiate validation goals for potential missing causal or step-ordering relations.

CMAX has several experiment design strategies for testing different step orderings. Note that depending on the experiment execution result, CMAX may decide either to revise/confirm the orderings or perform further tests. This may involve the same type of goals triggered multiple times to perform tests and analyze the test results. Modified or confirmed orderings supersede existing knowledge. We have also developed a cost–benefit model deciding which experiment to perform.

Assessing Progress of Learning and Determining Completion

Once the detected issues are resolved, the system creates a workflow using learned domain methods that are not superseded by other alternative domain methods. SHOP2's planning mechanism is adopted in creating a workflow that achieves the given problem solving goal PSG1, given the initial state W0. If the planner cannot produce a complete workflow, then it will post an appropriate learning goal to address the source of the problem.

When a full workflow is generated, further validation can be done by executing the workflow with the given problem description and comparing the execution results with the provided demo trace. When no further issues are found, no more learning goals will be desired.

Maven can assess the status of learning by keeping track of (a) what goals were desired and achieved and (b) workflow models representing knowledge that is created and modified over time. For example, when all the significant intended goals are achieved, Maven can announce that learning is "done."

Question Asking for Knowledge Goals

We formulate the question-asking process in terms of three separate activities: *question nomination, question selection,* and *question posing.*

Question nomination refers to the generation of questions that can potentially provide value to the learning process. Within the POIROT framework, question generation is performed by the individual hypothesis formers and evaluators, as they are best positioned to determine their information needs.

Question selection is the process of choosing from among nominated questions those that should be posed to the user. The creation of appropriate selection strategies lies at the heart of our work and is discussed further below.

Question posing refers to the interactions with the user to obtain answers. Relevant issues include modality (not addressed in this chapter) and timing (discussed below).

Question Catalog

We have defined a catalog of questions to inform the learning-by-demonstration process, details of which can be found in Gervasio & Myers, 2008. The catalog covers areas such as the function and causality of elements in the demonstration trace, abstraction, alternatives and justifications, limitations on learned knowledge, and the process of learning. The question catalog was derived from an analysis of the general task-learning process. We identified the different types of generalizations required to induce a general set of problem-solving methods from the trace of a successful execution of a plan for a specific problem and then systematically analyzed the demonstration trace and the generated hypotheses to identify the relevant portions about which questions may arise.

Question Selection Strategies

Question-selection strategies must balance the need for information to further the learning process with the following considerations.

A. Individual questions contribute different levels of value to the learning process.
B. Answering questions imposes a burden on the user.
C. The role of question asking is to inform learning, rather than to replace it by a knowledge-acquisition process.

These considerations lead naturally to the formulation of the question-selection problem in terms of a cost–benefit analysis, drawing on models of *utility* and *cost* for individual questions.

Utility Model for Questions

The *base utility* of a question is determined by the component that nominates the question. The factors that affect base utility are highly dependent on the specifics of the nominating component. For example, learning components might measure utility in terms of the expected change in the theoretical lower bound on the number of examples needed to learn the target concept. Components faced with ambiguity might factor in the expected reduction in the number of valid alternative hypotheses.

Since our framework involves a community of learners, factors beyond base utility must be considered to determine overall question utility. First, base utility estimates must be normalized to make them comparable across components. Second, the relative importance of contributions from different components must be considered. Finally, multiple learners may benefit from the answer to a given question.

Given these considerations, we propose to model overall question utility relative to a set L of learners as follows:

$$Utility\ (q) = \Sigma_{l \in L}\ w_l \times Utility(q,l)$$

$$Utility\ (q,l) = w_B \times BaseUtility(q,l) + w_{LG} \times LearningGoalUtility(q,l)$$

The utility of a question for an individual learner l, denoted by $Utility\ (q,l)$, is defined to be a weighted sum of the base utility $BaseUtility(q,l)$ assigned by the learner and the utility $LearningGoalUtility(q,l)$ of the associated learning goal that motivated the question by the learner. Here, $BaseUtility(q,l) \in [0,1]$ while $w_B + w_{LG} = 1$. The overall utility for question q, denoted by $Utility\ (q)$, is a weighted sum of the utilities assigned by the individual learners, with the w_l encoding the relative weightings assigned to the individual learners subject to the constraint that $\Sigma_{l \in L} w_l = 1$.

Cost Model for Questions

Prior work on mixed-initiative systems has identified five cost factors for consideration by an agent when deciding whether to interact with a user (Cohen, Cheng, & Fleming, 2005):

1. Inherent difficulty of the question
2. Level of disruption given the user's current focus of attention
3. User's willingness to interact with the system
4. Timing of the interaction
5. Appropriateness of the question

Within a learning-by-demonstration setting, the user would be expected to focus on interacting with the system and be tolerant of questions that may seem ill motivated or have obvious answers. As such, we can disregard factors (2)–(5) above, focusing instead on the inherent difficulty of the question as the basis for the cost model.

With this perspective, the cost model should measure the cognitive burden incurred by the expert in answering the question. This can be an arbitrarily complex quantity to measure, involving not only readily observable factors such as time to answer and brevity of answer but also potentially more complex metrics such as difficulty in understanding a question. However, we can use certain heuristics to approximate cognitive burden. Typically, certain question formats will be easier to answer than others. For example, yes/no questions usually will be less costly to answer than multiple-choice questions, which in turn would be less costly than open-ended questions.[1] Similarly, a question grounded in the demonstration trace most likely will be easier to answer than the same question asked about a hypothetical situation.

With these observations in mind, we define the cost of a question by

$$Cost(q) = w_F \times FormatCost(q) + w_G \times GroundednessCost(q)$$

where $FormatCost(q)$ denotes the cost associated with the format of q, and $GroundednessCost(q)$ is either $C_{concrete}$ or C_{hypo}, depending on whether the question relates to concrete elements in the demonstration trace or a hypothetical situation. Both $FormatCost(q)$ and $GroundednessCost(q)$ are constrained to lie in the interval [0,1]. The weights w_F and w_G allow relative weighting of the two cost factors, subject to the constraint that $w_F + w_G = 1$.

Control Strategies for Question Posing

We consider two types of control for managing when to pose questions: *asynchronous* and *synchronous*.

Asynchronous Control An asynchronous control strategy lets questions be asked continuously during the learning process. Asynchronous strategies could possibly lead to faster learning as they would enable early elimination of incorrect or irrelevant hypotheses, leading to a more focused search. For example, questions to resolve substantial ambiguity during learning may better be asked as they arise, rather than waiting until a complete initial hypothesis has been formed.

However, asynchronous control complicates the management of question asking, since the decision of whether or not a question is worth asking has to be made without knowledge of any other questions and possibly even without a hypothesis space against which the value of a component's contribution can be measured. Management of continuous questioning has been considered previously. Techniques to address this problem generally can be categorized as *backward* or *forward looking*.

1. Question format and cognitive load are not perfectly correlated (e.g., the halting problem constitutes a particularly difficult yes/no question). Our question catalog has been designed to enforce this correlation, with simple question formats used only for questions with low expected cognitive load.

Backward-looking approaches incorporate historical information about previous interactions into their cost models, as a way to prevent question overload. For example, Cohen, Cheng, and Fleming (2005) use cost–benefit analysis to determine when the expected utility increase for asking a question outweighs the associated costs. The cost model includes both the associated *base bother cost* for a question and an *accumulation bother cost* derived by summing over costs associated with prior question initiations, scaled by a decay factor that takes into account the temporal distance from prior questions to the present.

In contrast, forward-looking approaches use Markov decision processes (MDPs) to reason about future expected costs and reward in order to determine when to initiate interactions. Forward-looking approaches have been used to support questions about both action-selection strategy (e.g., Scerri, Pynadath, & Tambe, 2002) and learning user preference models (e.g., Boutilier, 2002).

Forward-looking approaches require detailed models of the likelihood and utility of expected question outcomes, which will be difficult to obtain in practice. For this reason, a backward-looking approach has greater appeal for our question-asking framework.

Synchronous Control A synchronous control strategy lets questions be asked only at a fixed point during the learning process. Synchronous control may sacrifice some learning efficiency as components may not be able to get critical clarifications as early as desired. But it could lead to better use of the resources for question asking as the questions could be considered in groups, all pertaining to some stable state of the hypothesis space.

The synchronous question-selection problem can be formulated as follows. We assume the following functions defined for a collection of questions Q.

$Cost(Q) = \Sigma_{q \in Q} Cost(q)$

$Utility(Q) = \Sigma_{q \in Q} Utility(q)$

As noted above, question selection imposes a burden on the demonstrator. Furthermore, our goal is to provide question asking in *support of learning*, rather than devolving into a knowledge-acquisition process that obtains extensive procedure knowledge through system-initiated interactions. For these reasons, we impose a budget on question asking to restrict access to the user.

Definition (Synchronous Question Selection) Given a collection of questions $Q = \{q_1 \dots q_n\}$ and a budget B, determine a subset $Q' \subseteq Q$ with $Cost(Q') \leq B$ such that there is no Q'' $\subset Q$ for which $Cost(Q'') \leq B$ and $Utility(Q'') > Utility(Q')$.[2]

2. This formulation of the problem assumes that the questions in Q are independent of each other, i.e., obtaining the answer to one question does not affect the utility of answering the others.

This framing of synchronous question selection maps directly to the *knapsack* problem (Kellerer, Pferschy, & Pisinger, 2005). Although the knapsack problem is NP-complete, dynamic programming algorithms can generate solutions that run in time $O(nB)$. Given a reasonable number of nominated questions and budget, we anticipate acceptable performance.

Synchronous question selection could be applied at the end of the learning process, thus enabling individual learners to refine their initial hypotheses prior to generation of the final learning output. Another possibility is to support a fixed number of synchronous question-selection sessions during the learning process, thus enabling the effects of the answers to be propagated through the system. The available budget for question asking would be distributed across the different sessions, in a manner that provides the most benefit to the learning process. This *multiphase synchronous question selection* provides some of the benefits of asynchronous question selection but with simpler control and better-understood selection methods.

Current Status

Initial prototype versions of Maven and QUAIL have been designed and implemented to support metalevel control of integrated learning for the POIROT system.

The initial prototype of Maven was developed with explicit hierarchical relations among goals and subgoals in ontologies of goal trees using OWL (OWL, 2009). Maven (1) assesses learning status using workflow models that keep track of knowledge generated from agents, (2) triggers learning goals based on the assessment, (3) selects learning goals by applying several control strategies, and (4) pursues selected learning goals using metalevel plans. Whenever new results are posted on the blackboard by the agents, Maven follows these steps and creates new tasks for the agents. The prototype supports a simulation of various agent activities during workflow learning including hypothesis generation, hypothesis integration, and hypothesis validation through experiment. We plan to investigate different learning behaviors using simulation results.

Our initial QUAIL prototype implements a synchronous strategy for question selection. We are using this prototype to understand better how to model question utility and costs, how to distribute resources across multiple-phase synchronous question asking, and how learning performance (speed, quality) can be improved through appropriate question asking. Our initial focus has been on instantiating the question-asking framework for a particular type of learner, specifically a lexicographic preference learner (Yaman et al., 2008). Experimental results show that, generally speaking, judicious question asking can improve learning performance (Gervasio et al., 2009). However, the results make clear the importance of understanding the value of different types of information for learning in different contexts.

Related Work

In models of cognitive systems (both models of human cognition and artificial intelligence systems), memories play a critical role in learning and problem solving (Tulving 1983). Especially, metacognitive strategies that promote reflection and self-assessment are known to increase the effectiveness of learning. We are adopting some of these strategies for coordinating the activities of integrated learners.

Goal-driven approaches for learning systems (Ram & Leake, 1995) include Meta-AQUA (Cox & Ram, 1999), Pagoda (desJardins, 1995), and Ivy (Hunter, 1990). Whereas most of these systems focus on a uniform learning method, our work supports a wider range of learning methods with different strengths.

Ram and Hunter (1992) introduce the notion of explicit knowledge goals to capture gaps in the system's knowledge, defining knowledge goals as comprising both the specification of the missing knowledge and the task enabled by it. In addition, they propose augmenting knowledge goals with a utility measure to help drive the inference process.

Ensemble methods have been used in classification tasks for combining results from multiple learners (Dietterich, 2000). These methods show improved accuracy. However, learning complex "procedural" knowledge requires more diverse capabilities from different agents and more general strategies for exploiting their capabilities.

Recently, there has been increasing interest in control of computation and metareasoning in intelligent systems (Anderson & Oates, 2007; Cox, 2005; Raja & Cox, 2007). Some of the agent-control approaches involve development of utility models or deliberation policies that determine actions taken by agents in an open environment (Russell & Wefald, 1991; Schut & Wooldridge, 2001). We expect that similar utility models can be developed based on several criteria such as confidence in the knowledge being built and cost of agent tasks, and be used in combination with our existing learning control strategies.

Unlike in other metacontrol approaches that control learning with a set of performance measures (as described by Epstein and Petrovic in this vol., chap. 4), in our framework, the learning is driven by learning goals that represent gaps and issues in generating complex workflow knowledge. The goals are mapped to various capabilities that participating agents can support.

Summary and Lessons Learned

We introduced a goal-oriented approach for metalevel coordination of learning agents designed to acquire complex procedural knowledge. This framework employs a BDI model to support flexible top-down and bottom-up control. Based on the capabilities of participating learning agents and the characteristics of the knowledge to be learned, explicit learning goals and plans for achieving the goals are defined. The history of desired learning goals allows the system to keep track of progress while learning. The system employs a set of high-level learning control strategies for prioritizing learning goals. Question-asking capabilities enable knowledge goals to be addressed by exploiting the knowledge of the domain expert in order to fill gaps in learned knowledge.

The metareasoning that we employ for coordinating base-level reasoning and learning components is a form of introspection designed to enable a system to analyze and then adapt its behavior at execution time in order to improve overall performance. Our experience in this effort has validated our belief that this kind of introspective metareasoning is essential for effective problem solving in complex systems, and that more research is required to understand how to manage this kind of control process effectively. The focus for most work on metareasoning to date, by contrast, has emphasized the related but distinct problem of bounded rationality.

Our goal-directed approach combines selection from among predefined problem-solving strategies (for process goals) with question asking managed by cost–benefit analysis (for knowledge goals). While our work has shown that these approaches can be effective for metalevel control of a complex system, it proved more difficult than anticipated to formulate the domain-specific background models necessary to support these methods, namely, the control logic for process selection and the utilities for question asking. One important direction for future work is to enable development of these models in a more flexible and less time-consuming manner. For example, the control logic for process selection could be derived from high-level principles, rather than being explicitly hardwired. Such principles would be grounded in objectives for learning procedural knowledge, such as coverage, coherence, and confidence; general-purpose strategies would define approaches for achieving and trading off these objectives that could be tailored to specific procedure-learning situations. Utility models for question asking could be learned via experimentation that would assess the effectiveness of different questions in different contexts.

Another area for future work is to generalize the notion of processing for knowledge goals to support mechanisms other than posing questions to the expert user. In particular, the experimentation performed by CMAX could be applied to address knowledge gaps, as could the invocation of other learning mechanisms.

Currently, annotations on workflow models are limited to supersede and compete relations. Learning agents can provide more information including how methods are derived, such as the producer–consumer relations used in creating step orderings or assumptions made in finding loops. We plan to investigate how such intermediate results can be shared and facilitate further interaction among agents.

We expect that our metacontrol framework can be useful for capturing procedural knowledge or workflow knowledge in other applications. For example, interactive acquisition of process models requires reasoning about user-provided process information. To provide useful guidance, the system needs to keep track of issues and gaps in the knowledge being built (Kim, Gil, & Spraragen, 2009). Some of our learning goals, both process and knowledge goals, can be mapped to the issues that arise during such an acquisition process, and our metacontrol approaches may be useful in driving the interaction with the user.

Acknowledgments

This work was supported by the Defense Advanced Research Projects Agency and the United States Air Force through BBN Technologies Corp. on contract number FA8650-06-C-7606.

References

Anderson, M., & Oates, T. (2007). A review of recent research in metareasoning and metalearning. *AI Magazine, 28*(1), 12–16.

Boutilier, C. (2002). A POMDP formulation of preference elicitation problems. In *Proceedings of the 18th National Conference on Artificial Intelligence* (pp. 239–246). Menlo Park, CA: AAAI Press.

Burstein, M. H., Laddaga, R., McDonald, D., Cox, M. T., Benyo, B., Robertson, P., et al. (2008). POIROT—Integrated learning of web service procedures. In *Proceedings of the 23rd National Conference on Artificial Intelligence* (pp. 1274–1279). Menlo Park, CA: AAAI Press.

Cohen, R., Cheng, M., & Fleming, M. W. (2005). Why bother about bother: Is it worth it to ask the user? In *Proceedings of the AAAI Fall Symposium on Mixed-Initiative Problem-Solving Assistants* (pp. 26–31). Menlo Park, CA: AAAI Press.

Cox, M. T. (2005). Metacognition in computation: A selected research review. *Artificial Intelligence, 169*(2), 104–141.

Cox, M. T., & Burstein, M. H. (2008). Case-based explanations and the integrated learning of demonstrations. *Künstliche Intelligenz (Artificial Intelligence), 22*(2), 35–38.

Cox, M. T., & Ram, A. (1999). Introspective multistrategy learning: On the construction of learning strategies. *Artificial Intelligence, 112*(1–2), 1–55.

desJardins, M. (1995). Goal-directed learning: A decision-theoretic model for deciding what to learn next. In A. Ram & D. Leake (Eds.), *Goal-driven learning* (pp. 241–249). Cambridge, MA: MIT Press.

Dietterich, T. G. (2000). Ensemble methods in machine learning. In *Proceedings of the Third International Workshop on Multiple Classifier Systems* (pp. 1–15). New York: Springer Verlag.

Gervasio, M., & Myers, K. (2008). Question asking to inform procedure learning. In M. T. Cox & A. Raja (Eds.), *Proceedings of the AAAI Workshop Metareasoning: Thinking about Thinking* (pp. 68–75). Technical Report WS-08-07. Menlo Park, CA: AAAI Press.

Gervasio, M., Myers, K., desJardins, M., & Yaman, F. (2009). Question asking for preference learning: A case study. In *Proceedings of the AAAI Spring Symposium on Agents that Learn from Human Teachers* (pp. 56–62). Menlo Park, CA: AAAI Press.

Ghallab, M., Nau, D., & Traverso, P. (2004). *Hierarchical task network planning: Automated planning: Theory and practice*. San Francisco: Morgan Kaufmann.

Gil, Y., & Kim, J. (2002). Interactive knowledge acquisition tools: A tutoring perspective. In *Proceedings of the Annual Conference of the Cognitive Science Society* (pp. 357–362). Mahwah, NJ: Lawrence Erlbaum.

Hunter, L. E. (1990). Planning to learn. In *Proceedings of the Twelfth Annual Conference of the Cognitive Science Society* (pp. 261–276). Hillsdale, NJ: Lawrence Erlbaum.

Kellerer, H., Pferschy, U., & Pisinger, D. (2005). *Knapsack problems*. Berlin: Springer Verlag.

Kim, J., Gil, Y., & Spraragen, M. (2009). Principles for interactive acquisition and validation of workflows. *Journal of Experimental and Theoretical Artificial Intelligence, 22*, 103–134. http://www.informaworld.com/10.1080/09528130902823698.

Kim, J., & Gil, Y. (2008). Developing a meta-level problem solver for integrated learners. In M. T. Cox & A. Raja (Eds.), *Proceedings of the AAAI Workshop, Metareasoning: Thinking about Thinking* (pp. 136–142). Technical Report WS-08-07. Menlo Park, CA: AAAI Press.

Kim, J., & Gil, Y. (2007). Incorporating tutoring principles into interactive knowledge acquisition. *International Journal of Human-Computer Studies, 65*(10), 852–872.

Kim, J., & Gil, Y. (2003). Proactive acquisition from tutoring and learning principles. In *Proceedings of the International Conference on Artificial Intelligence in Education* (pp. 175–182). Amsterdam: IOS Press.

Morrison, C., & Cohen, P. (2007). Designing experiments to test planning knowledge about plan-step order constraints. In *Proceedings of the ICAPS Workshop on Intelligent Planning and Learning* (pp. 39–44). Menlo Park, CA: AAAI Press.

Nau, D., Au, T., Ilghami, O., Kuter, U., Munoz-Avila, H., Murdock, J., et al. (2005). Applications of SHOP and SHOP2. *IEEE Intelligent Systems, 20*(2), 34–41.

OWL (2009). Web Ontology Language. http://www.w3.org/TR/owl-features.

Raja, A., & Cox, M. (Eds.) (2007). *Proceedings of the First International Workshop on Metareasoning in Agent-Based Systems*. Collocated with AAMAS-07. Columbia, SC: IFAAMAS.

Ram, A., & Hunter, L. (1992). The use of explicit goals for knowledge to guide inference and learning. *Journal of Applied Intelligence, 2*(1), 47–73.

Ram, A., & Leake, D. (Eds.) (1995). *Goal-driven learning*. Cambridge, MA: MIT Press.

Rao, A., & Georgeff, M. (1995). BDI-agents: from theory to practice. In *Proceedings of the First International Conference on Multiagent Systems*. San Francisco.

Russell, S., & Wefald, E. (1991). Principles of metareasoning. *Artificial Intelligence, 49*(1–3), 361–395.

Scerri, P., Pynadath, D., & Tambe, M. (2002). Towards adjustable autonomy for the real world. *Journal of Artificial Intelligence Research, 17,* 171–228.

Schut, M., & Wooldridge, M. (2001). Principles of intention reconsideration. In *Proceedings of the International Conference on Autonomous Agents and Multiagent Systems* (pp. 340–347). New York: ACM Press.

Tulving, E. (1983). *Elements of episodic memory*. New York: Oxford University Press.

Winner, E., & Veloso, M. (2003). DISTILL: Learning domain-specific planners by example. In *Proceedings of the International Conference on Machine Learning* (pp. 800–807). Menlo Park, CA: AAAI Press.

Yaman, F., Walsh, T. J., Littman, M. L., & desJardins, M. (2008). Democratic approximation of lexicographic preference models. In *Proceedings of the International Conference on Machine Learning* (pp. 1200–1207). Menlo Park, CA: AAAI Press.

Yaman, F., & Oates, T. (2007). Workflow inference: What to do with one example and no semantics. In *Proceedings of the AAAI Workshop on Acquiring Planning Knowledge via Demonstration* (pp. 46–51). Menlo Park, CA: AAAI Press.

7 Metareasoning for Multispectral Satellite Image Interpretation

Paul Robertson and Robert Laddaga

In this chapter we discuss metareasoning in an image interpretation architecture called GRAVA: Grounded Reflective Adaptive Vision Architecture. We further discuss the role metareasoning plays in GRAVA: producing good image interpretations under a wide range of environmental conditions.

In chapter 1 of this volume ("Metareasoning: A Manifesto"), the authors, Cox and Raja, discuss introspective monitoring, and consider it to be an essential attribute of any system that operates in an uncertain environment. Online monitoring makes a number of online program repairs possible: replacing of failed approaches by alternatives, applying available contingent plans, or invoking failover procedures. However, such recovery mechanisms are fruitless when the failure suggests that the entire approach has been invalidated. Metareasoning is essential for reasoning about the validity of the current approach and to avoid having the program fruitlessly apply contingent methods in an environment where they will have no beneficial effect and indeed may lead to disastrous results.

Nowhere is this need more apparent than in computer vision applications, where changes in illumination, image context, and a host of other environmental factors can demand a completely different approach to the image-understanding process. Most successful computer vision programs operate in situations where conditions can be carefully controlled. In contrast, computer vision systems on mobile robots forces vision into uncontrollable environments, and we argue that metareasoning is the cleanest path to reliable systems in this domain. The real world is complex, and attempting to build static vision programs with hardwired logic to deal with every possibility is naive. The world in which we live exposes the eye, and camera, to an enormous diversity of visual variety. When faced with complexity, it is often a good strategy to "divide and conquer." We divide by *contexts*, and conquer each context with an individually tailored program configuration.

Our approach draws on observations by Lesser and colleagues (Erman et al., 1980) on the Hearsay II project but is implemented in an architecture that is self-adaptive

(Robertson, 2002). Metareasoning in our approach takes the form of reasoning about the *performance* of a subordinate computational process. Performance measurements can come from two sources: specific failures invoked by the subordinate process and poor performance in comparison to learned performance models. We utilize description length as one important component of learned performance models. Metareasoning in our system operates on *contexts* that are learned with the help of a clustering algorithm (Robertson & Laddaga, 2002a, 2003).

We consider a program, or a system of programs, that interprets a sequence of satellite images formed from the passage of the satellite as it traverses its orbit. The sequence of images thus created will depict the changing landscape visible from the directed camera of the satellite. These landscape changes we will treat as one component of the environment of the satellite image-interpretation program. Other components of the environment include the type of camera or sensor and the weather and atmospheric conditions.

Consider a collection of programs that specialize in interpreting different scene types and some way of switching between programs as necessary. Not only would such an approach make the complexity seem more manageable, but the constraints of the scene would allow better interpretations to be generated. The correct identification of objects in a scene may not be uniquely discernible from the pixels in the image, but the ambiguities might be resolvable from the context in which they appear. For example, a program that has to deal with ocean scenes is likely to correctly interpret large tankers as ships, whereas similarly appearing structures in an industrial scene would be interpreted as, say, a warehouse.

GRAVA employs a self-adaptive approach toward achieving reliable interpretations in complex and changing environments. Self-adaptive software is concerned with the problem of automatically adapting program *structure* in response to environmental changes in order to provide robust performance despite those changes (Laddaga, 2001). Self-adaptation encapsulates the idea that a running program may be viewed as a collection of context-dependent programs that are automatically selected in sequence as context changes are detected. The selected program is assumed to have the property that it is a good match for the environment at the time of the adaptation, but this assumption is continuously checked.

Even if we could know all the different states that the environment could be in, we would not know a priori what state the environment would be in at any particular time. Consequently, in order to achieve robust performance, image-understanding programs should determine the state of the environment at run time and adapt accordingly. Self-adaptive software constantly evaluates its own performance, and when that performance is below criteria, it changes its behavior. To accomplish this, the run-time code includes the following things not currently included in shipped software:

descriptions of software intentions (i.e., goals and designs);
descriptions of program structure;
descriptions of the environment of the running program, both computational and (for embedded software) physical; and
a collection of alternative implementations and algorithms (a reuse asset base).

Thus, self-adaptation is a model-based approach to building robust systems. The environment, the program's goal, and the program's computational structure are modeled, and constitute the system's model of itself. In principle, the idea is simple. The environment model and the program goal model support continuous evaluation of the performance of the program. When program performance deteriorates, the program goal model and the computation model together support modification of the program structure. In this way, the program structure evolves as the environment changes so that the components of the program are always well suited to the environment in which they are running. Robust performance results from having all components operating within their effective range.

GRAVA employs metareasoning because it provides the mechanisms necessary to support two of the core problems of self-adaptive software—a mechanism for reasoning about the state of the computational system and a mechanism for making changes to it. These are what Cox and Raja (this vol., chap. 1) call introspective monitoring and metalevel control, respectively.

While the focus of this chapter is on the application of metareasoning in producing reliable image descriptions in the satellite image-understanding program, a brief overview of the approach taken by the program in interpreting visual scenes is helpful. The satellite image-interpretation program described in this chapter segments, labels, and parses aerial images so as to generate a rich structural description of the image contents for each image in the sequence. Figure 7.1 shows a schematic summary of the GRAVA architecture focusing on the module-supporting dependencies. For example, the patchwork parser module and the self-adaptive architecture each directly support the image segmentation and labeling program. Each are also directly supported by the statistical MDL (minimum description length) theorem prover module.

To produce an image interpretation, several tools are brought into play. Tools vary in terms of both the goals they are intended to achieve and the methods they use. Each particular goal may be satisfied by many different algorithms or implementations. The selection of the right tools ultimately determines the quality of the resulting interpretation. First, the image is processed to extract features such as texture by applying tools appropriate to the image at hand. Next, a segmentation algorithm is employed to produce regions with outlines whose contents are homogeneous with respect to content as determined by the chosen texture and feature tools. The segmentation algorithm also depends on tools that select seed points that initialize the segmenta-

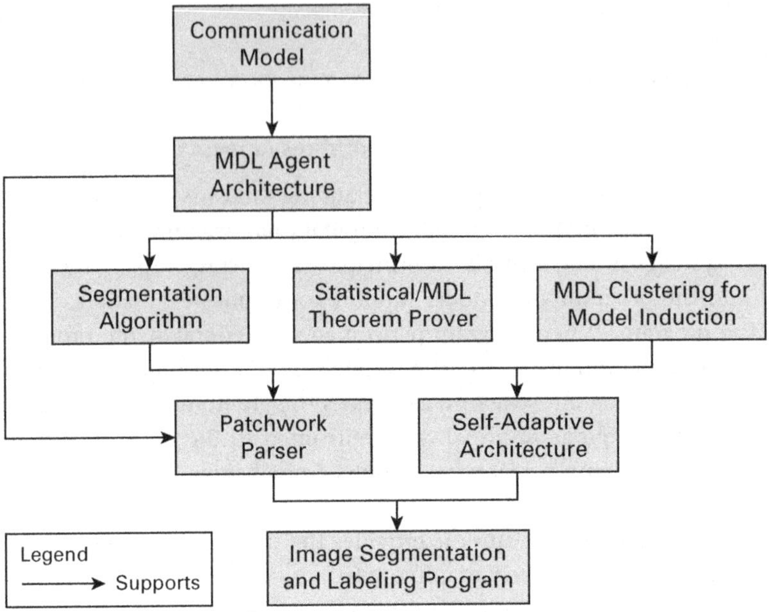

Figure 7.1
The GRAVA architecture with module dependencies.

tion. The choice of tools to initiate the segmentation determines what kind of segmentation will be produced. Next, the regions of the image are labeled based on their contents. Finally, the image is statistically parsed using a 2D picture grammar.

At any point, a bad choice of tool—for initial feature extraction, seed point identification, region identification, or parse rule—can lead to a poor image interpretation. The earlier the error occurs, the worse the resulting interpretation is likely to be. For example, a poor choice of tools for extracting textures from the image may result in a poor segmentation. The poor segmentation will likely result in poor region content analysis and a potentially disastrous parse of the image. The resulting interpretation can be very bad indeed. The challenge for a self-adaptive approach is to determine how the program formed from the collection of tools described above can be organized so that when a poor interpretation is produced, the program self-adapts into a program that does a better job.

Metareasoning

Before presenting the details of metareasoning in GRAVA, we begin with a general explanation and motivation for metareasoning. Metareasoning involves reasoning about the reasoning process. Metareasoning is just like reasoning, but it is applied to the reasoning engine rather than to the problem domain. Similar results could usually be achieved by adding further logic to the reasoning system, but several advantages accrue by having the metareasoning be structured as a separate layer of the reasoning process:

Code cleanliness Mixing metareasoning in with the reasoning logic is bad modularity. It makes the reasoning code hard to read, maintain, and debug.

Synchronization Metareasoning may need to be invoked at different times to the base reasoner. Putting them together makes this very difficult.

Representational efficiency By reasoning at the metalevel, we can handle a whole class of issues in one place that would have to be repeated for each member of the class at the reasoning level.

For metareasoning to take place, the base reasoner is instrumented to allow the state of reasoning to be reasoned about. For metareasoning to influence the reasoning process, the results of metareasoning must be available to the reasoning process. This can be accomplished by representing the results of metareasoning as data structures that are used by the reasoner or by interrupting the reasoning process and restarting it with new structures. Metareasoning in GRAVA not only reasons about the reasoning process, it can also interrupt the reasoning process and redirect it (as will be demonstrated below).

Metalevels in GRAVA

The GRAVA architecture was designed to support image-interpretation programs that take advantage of self-adaptation in order to effectively handle a changing environment. Self-adaptation results from a metareasoning event (also known as reflection). In GRAVA, an application is structured as a hierarchy of processing levels. GRAVA's base level incorporates not only image-processing elements ("doers" in the sense of chapter 1), but image-interpretation elements ("reasoners" in the sense of chapter 1). GRAVA base-level reasoners reason about the image that they are attempting to interpret. Metareasoning can occur in any of the levels above a base reasoner. To understand how metareasoning in GRAVA works, we begin by giving a brief overview of salient aspects of the GRAVA architecture.

Figure 7.2 shows two levels of a GRAVA program. Each layer of a GRAVA program contains a *description* that specifies the goal for the layer. The implementation of that description is a program consisting of a collection of agents (the tools) that is fixed at the top level but which is synthesized by the parent layer for all lower layers. The lowest level interprets the image by applying the agents that make up the interpreter. The parent layer of each layer contains a compiler whose purpose it is to synthesize

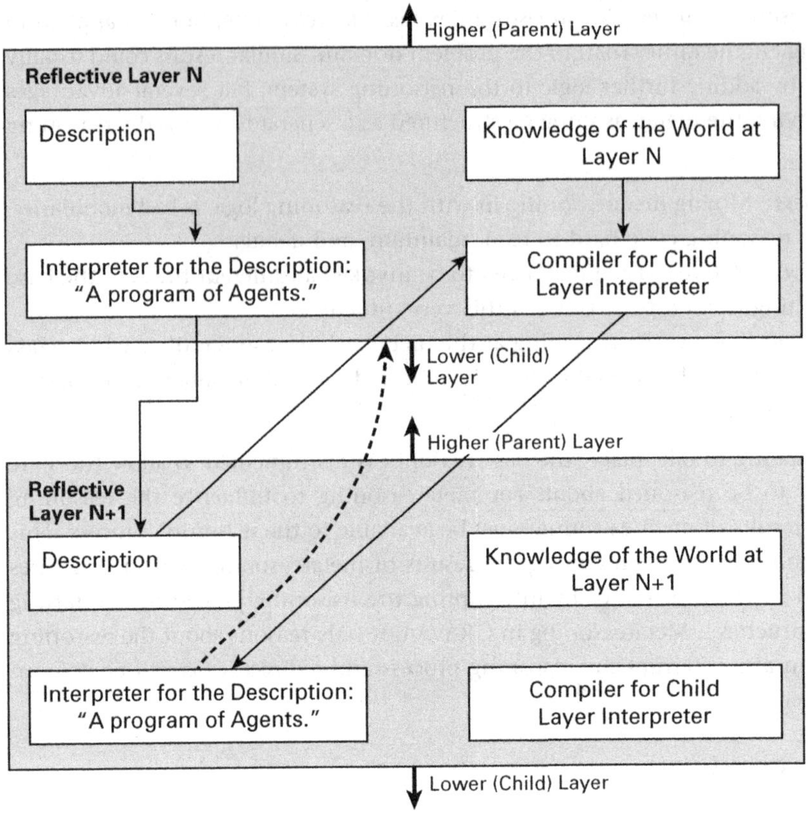

Figure 7.2
Relationship of interpreter levels in GRAVA.

the interpreter for the layer below by considering two sources of information:

The description for the child layer.
The knowledge of the world as collected by the child layer.

The "knowledge of the world" is the result of reasoning about the child layer and the product of the child layer. Since the knowledge of the world is an input to the compiler of the child interpreter, it indirectly affects the reasoning of the child process.

Reasoning in GRAVA

GRAVA reasons about image contents by fitting models to parts of the image. This process is achieved as part of a bidding process among competing agents each of which attempts to explain image parts. The winner is selected by a Monte Carlo selection mechanism that uses description length of the competing representations to bias the selection. If some area (x) of an image fits the agent "airport" and is selected by the Monte Carlo selection, this means that the reasoner has executed the rule:

area(x) & airportAgent $\rightarrow$ airport(x)

Layers of Interpretation

The satellite image interpretation program has three layers, as follows.

Layer 1 The bottom layer interprets the pixels of the image as nonoverlapping regions. The regions are obtained by a semantic segmentation algorithm (Robertson, 2002).
Layer 2 The segments are labeled with semantic markers.
Layer 3 The labeled segments are parsed using a picture grammar (Robertson, 2002).

The parse tree produced by layer 3 has segments as its leaves, which in turn have labels indicating their interpretation as objects in the scene. The layers are not simply applied sequentially. Instead, Monte Carlo sampling occurs across all layers so that segmentation, labeling, and parsing choices are made so as to achieve the final parsed image with a minimal description length (MDL). The Monte Carlo sampling employed to achieve this result is an anytime algorithm, so after a single iteration an image description is available, but much of the description will likely be incorrect. After multiple iterations the best MDL description emerges.

Model Learning and Contexts

Image interpretation with GRAVA is a two-phase process. The first, off-line, process learns models from hand-annotated training data or ground truth. These models include:

Grammar rules that model the 2D picture structures found in the annotated images;
Labeling models that map region contents to the named labels annotated by the human annotator and used in the grammatical rules as terminal symbols; and
Region content models that determine the features used to drive the segmenter.

These models correspond to the three layers of the aerial image-interpretation program described above. The training images are clustered to produce model groups that correspond to different contexts. GRAVA uses a clustering algorithm based on minimal description length and *principle component decomposition*; see Robertson and Laddaga (2002a). This is done for each of the levels.

The resulting clusters may distinguish different imaging contexts. For example, in our training set, images from different multispectral bands were provided. At the label layer, images are clustered based on different labels present in the images, and at the grammar layer images are clustered based on the grammatical forms present in the images. Though the contexts may not correspond to simple English descriptions they do represent different imaging features that require different tool sets. Selecting a context thus constrains how the image will be interpreted by determining the tool set.

Figure 7.3 shows four images that were clustered together into the same context by virtue of their similar label sets. One of the four images (bottom left) clearly comes from a different multispectral camera, so these images would not have been clustered together at the lower layer that clusters on the basis of optical information content. Clusters, of course, are not given names and may not even be obviously related. These images, however, all appear to be good examples of sea towns. Selecting agents based

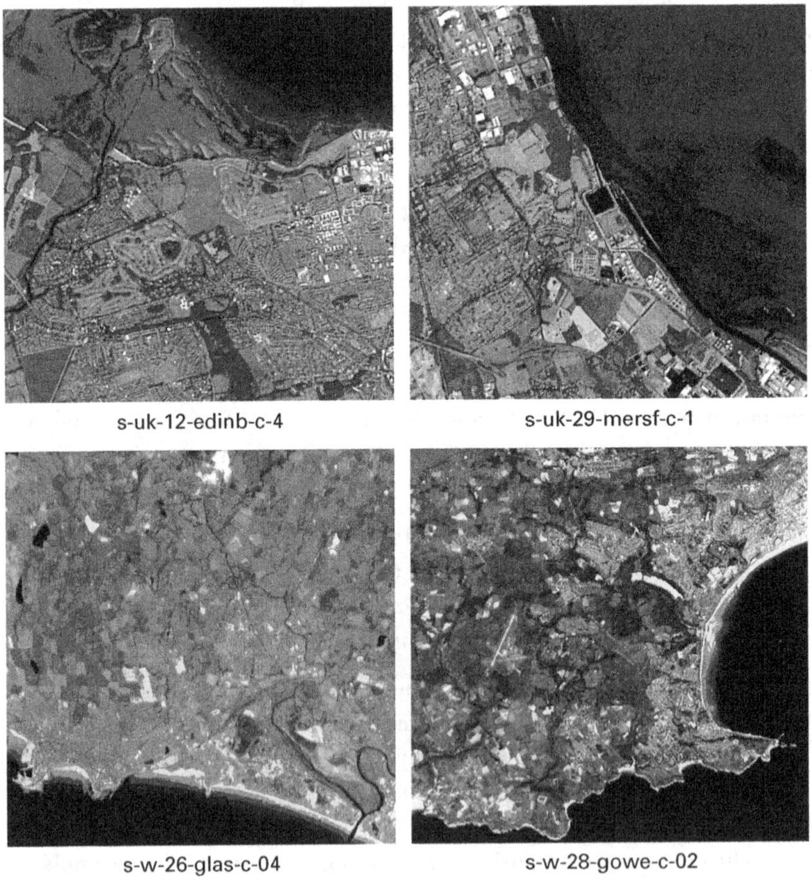

Figure 7.3
Four images from the same context.

on the correct context dramatically improves the likelihood that the resulting image interpretation will be accurate.

Each of the contexts in each of the categories comes with estimated *prior* probabilities based on their frequency in the training set. In the absence of any other information these priors allow the contexts at each layer to be sorted in order of decreasing likelihood. The contexts at each layer are used by the compiler to drive the selection of agents for each corresponding level of the program.

The Role of Contexts in Self-Adaptation

Metareasoning monitors the operation of the reasoner and estimates the most likely context based on the current state of knowledge about the world and the child layer's process state. When it determines that the currently selected context is not the most likely it resynthesizes the program operating at the level beneath it to utilize agents appropriate to the newly selected context. At the parsing level this may mean that a set of grammatical rules is replaced by another, more appropriate, set of rules. For example, if the grammar set was for a class of "rural landscape" images and collected world knowledge suggests that "seaport town" images represent a more appropriate context, the agents (grammatical rules) for a seaport town will be used in place of those for rural landscape. This will enable the seaport town to be properly parsed where a correct parse would have been impossible with a rule set dedicated to rural landscapes.

It is difficult to overstate the importance of context in image-understanding programs. Most vision programs can ignore the problem by being useful in only a single context. Interpretation of aerial surveillance images is an activity generally undertaken by experts, and as can be seen in figure 7.3, these images are not open to simple intuitive interpretation. For that reason, face recognition perhaps provides a more intuitive subject in which to consider the importance of context. Facial images vary in terms of: *pose, size, obscuration, race, gender, age, lighting, noise, color,* and *view.*

Most face-identification and recognition systems work by measuring a small number of facial features given a canonical pose and matching them against a database of known faces. Thus, typical face-recognition systems can only deal with well-lighted frontal views. In practical applications, however, few frames show a full frontal face. Furthermore, lighting may vary significantly. These factors frustrate attempts to identify a face. Many applications have much more relaxed recognition goals. If the goal is to track people as they move throughout a monitored space, the task may be to identify the individual from a relatively small set of people. For face profiles, different models involving ear, eye, and nose may prove successful. By building a face recognizer that can seamlessly switch between different contexts such as pose and lighting, we can construct a recognizer that is robust to normal changes in the natural environment (Robertson & Laddaga, 2002b). This permits a much wider application of face-recognition technology.

Figure 7.4
Context in face recognition.

In figure 7.4, we see four different images of faces,[1] showing four pose contexts: "profile," "oblique," "off-center," and "frontal." In GRAVA, the profile view is supported by agents that measure points along the profile of the face, the corner of the eye, and the lips. The oblique view with ear supports measurements of the ear and measurements of the position of the ear, eye, and nose. The triangle formed by the eye, ear, and nose help to determine the angle of the face to the camera, which allows measurements to be normalized before recognition. The off-center view permits measurements of points on the eyes, nose, and mouth. The shape of the nose can be measured but the width of the base of the nose cannot, due to self-occlusion. The frontal view allows nose width to be measured, but not the nose shape. There are other contexts that include or exclude ears. The different contexts control, among other things, what models can be used for matching, what features can be detected, and what transformations must be made to normalize the measurements prior to matching. This example shows contexts for pose, but there are also contexts for lighting, race, gender, and age.

1. In addition to aerial image interpretation, GRAVA handles other interpretation problems such as gesture recognition and face recognition.

Reasoning and Metareasoning about Context

Though the above sketch shows, for the satellite image interpretation domain, how a useful form of self-adaptation can be cast in terms of context switches, it does not explain how we arrive at the decision to change contexts. To understand this aspect of the problem we consider the relationship that $level_n$ has with $level_{n-1}$.

As we have seen above, each level has two relationships with its parent level. First, the child level's program is synthesized by its parent level by (a) using the child level's description as a specification for the child's program, (b) considering the known state of the child's process as represented in the parent-level knowledge base, and (c) by considering the set of available contexts that were learned for that level. The child level's description is the result of task decomposition of the parent level's description. The child level's relationship to its parent is therefore one of "task decomposition." The parent level also created the child level as the result of its reasoning about contexts, the child specification, and the state of knowledge. That relationship, which consists in the rationale for the decisions about the child's structure, is a metarelationship. The parent level thus encapsulates four pieces of knowledge about the child: (1) a more abstract representation of the child's structure; (2) knowledge about why the child was constructed the way it was—and what agents were ultimately chosen in its construction; (3) knowledge about the world collected by the child; and (4) how well the child has been doing at its task. Of the above, (1) and (2) relate to the construction of the child before the child had a chance to run, while (3) and (4) relate to knowledge and metaknowledge, respectively, of the child's execution history. We explain where (4) comes from in the next section.

In this application, we chose to use contexts to drive the child process structure; however, in a different application another approach might have been taken. The use of contexts in this application represents an off-line compilation of alternative self-adaptive choices. Whatever approach is taken, the parent level is *related* to the child level by two forms of knowledge located in the parent level. The child level is a program tailored to implement the specification of the task-decomposed goal of its parent. The child has no apparatus to reason about why it does what it does or how it might do differently if things do not work out well in the current environment—but the parent level does. The parent represents the knowledge that the child is using the agents chosen for it precisely because, at the time it was constructed, those agents were most suitable for performing the tasks decomposed from the parent's specification.

Knowing How Well the Child Layer Is Doing

The execution of any level results in an interpretation of the image chosen so as to produce the MDL representation. The description length is, in part, a measure of the goodness of the interpretation. The program can produce an interpretation of a blank image as an "urban scene" because of smoothing,[2] but the description length will be large. When a context begins to change, such as when the image in the sequence begins to transition from a rural landscape to a suburban one, more parts of the image will suffer from being alien to the context. That alienation from the context results in the use of a more smoothed rule and the inevitable growth in description length for the image. Description length of an image interpretation by a level is governed by two factors: (1) the complexity of the image being interpreted, and (2) the goodness of fit of the context used to create the level. Factor (1) tends to be dominated by the ground area covered by the image. When the contexts were established (off-line) the defining set of images that formed the cluster had interpretations whose description length was known. From that set of images' description lengths, a model of the typical description length of an image is established as Gaussian. Since the goodness of fit of the context dominates the changes in description length, serious deviations from the mean (outliers) indicate a change in context.

In figure 7.5, we see a description of the operation on GRAVA of a response to an evaluation requiring an inference about a change in context and the resulting change in the configuration of the child layer. That is, the child layer is operating using a previously compiled program, assuming a specific context. The child layer can either output an interpretation of an image, or *reflectUp* the problem and some assessment of the insufficiency of the results. That action causes the parent layer to reassess the context and compile a new child layer program. In GRAVA, assessing the performance of the child is a form of *model-based diagnosis* (Hamscher, Console & deKleer, 1992; Shrobe, 2002.) We said before that self-adaptive software will include descriptions of:

software intentions (i.e., goals and designs);
program structure; and
the environment of the running program.

Each of these descriptions will generally be in the form of a model. That is, the descriptions must involve a significant functional abstraction, so as to support operations on the descriptions that can in turn affect the functional behaviors of the things described. So, for example, we must be able to recompute subgoals of a goal in light of new contextual information. Also, we will want to use the models of program structure to diagnose problems and support reconfiguration of the program. Finally, models of the physical environment will be used to:

diagnose program failures and performance problems;
provide contextual basis for subgoaling and reconfiguring; and
provide a basis for choosing new strategies for the computation.

2. Smoothing is a method whereby rules are created to ensure the success of an operation (such as a grammatical rule). Rules generated by smoothing ensure success but entail a large description length.

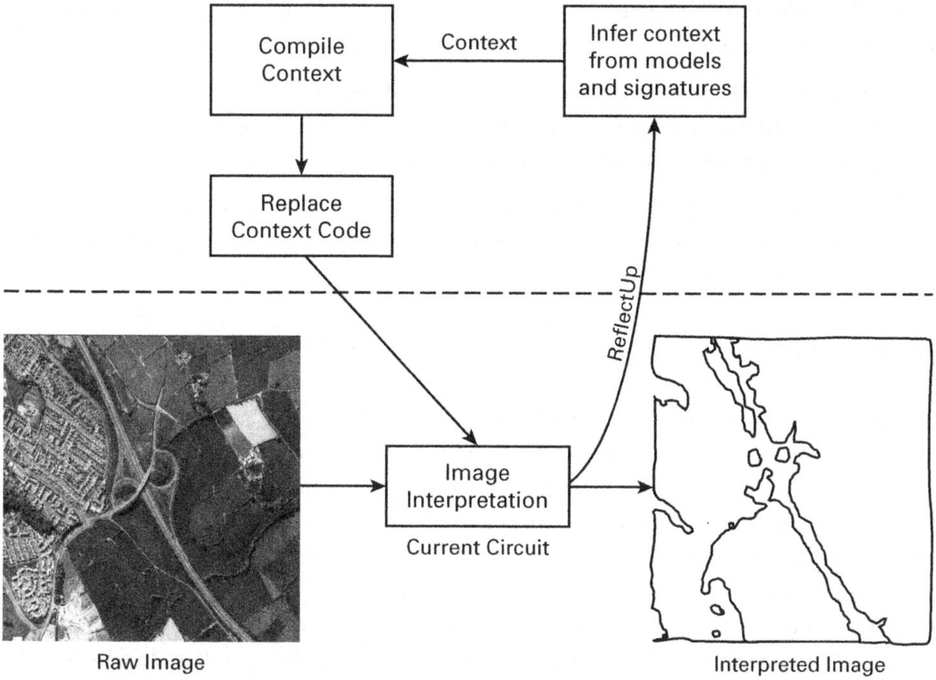

Figure 7.5
Adaptation of context in GRAVA.

We also said earlier that the chief engineering issue for self-adaptive software was evaluation of program performance. It is possible to evaluate without diagnosis, if we simply respond by randomly picking a different algorithm or implementation. Although this fits a broad definition of self-adaptive software, our goals are much higher.

Instead, the kind of evaluation we envision is one that includes and partially depends on a diagnosis of at least the proximate cause, and where possible the root cause, of the failure or performance problem. In this sense, the entire self-adaptive apparatus in the program can be thought of as a model-based diagnosis system in support of the program's main goals. The program, its goals, and the environment that it runs in are all modeled in the running system, and diagnostic reasoning is employed to evaluate program performance. Thus model-based diagnosis realizes the self-aware metaphor for self-adaptive software.

In addition to metareasoning, reasoning about the task decomposition also takes place in order to consider the need to rebuild a new child program. Finally, the goal of the program is also subject to change. If the priorities of the system change during a run, the system can self-adapt to reflect those changes. Adaptation therefore is driven by these three aspects of the system state:

metaknowledge about system performance on the current images;
the abstract representation of the knowledge extracted from the image; and
the changing state of the goals for the system.

We have focused on the first of these mechanisms in this chapter. The three sources of knowledge are managed by a theorem prover that plays a central role in the child program synthesis.

GRAVA and the Manifesto

The principal model of the Manifesto refers to a ground level, an object level and a metalevel. The corresponding levels in GRAVA are the base or image-interpretation level, which incorporates the manifesto's ground level and much of the manifesto's object level, and the metalevels, which include some of the manifesto's object level and all of the manifesto's metareasoning level. In GRAVA, the image-interpretation level applies operations to the image in order to segment, label, and thus interpret the image, but it also invokes evaluation of the fit of the interpretation. In the manifesto the ground level doesn't actually reason, but in GRAVA, the base level not only computes an interpretation of an image, it also evaluates the interpretation and can act by choosing to reflect the problem and results back to the first metalevel. We have considered the possibility of separating GRAVA's base layer into ground and object layers, but have not yet performed experiments to determine both the ease and utility of such a transformation.

In GRAVA, there can be many metalevels, each treating the level below as an object level. This is also a departure from the manifesto model, but in practice, GRAVA doesn't usually use more than one metalevel. We have, however, proposed a second metalevel to deal with stabilizing GRAVA programs (Laddaga, 2006).

The image-interpretation level (qua *object level*) is passed control along with a configured set of operators, and applies the operators (qua *ground level*). It retains control until it fails an evaluation, and then returns control to its metalevel. When control is passed to the metalevel, the metalevel must directly interact with the image-interpretation level (qua *ground level*), in order to estimate a new context, from which it will derive a new configuration for the image-interpretation level. Thus information from the ground level is directly interpreted in the metalevel to estimate a context.

Currently, GRAVA does not interact with other agents, although GRAVA components are all agents that interact with each other via responding to task goal postings at the object (image-interpretation) level. Since GRAVA accepts the notion of multiple metalevels, in principle, GRAVA can support multiple agents by having multiple instantiations of GRAVA controlled by cooperating top metalevels. This approach would probably not support cross-level cooperation to the degree that might be needed depending on the nature of the distributed application.

The manifesto's model is a fairly good abstract description of GRAVA's operation. Differences are GRAVA's support for multiple metalevels, GRAVA's simplified control regime, GRAVA's combination of ground and object levels as a single level, and GRAVA's placement of evaluation of object-level performance in the object level. A more significant difference is the central role we place on reasoning about contexts and having environmental context centered in the metalevel rather than the object level. This difference means that GRAVA never considers the state of its reasoning at the object level, without also referring to its estimate of the object-level context.

Discussion

The GRAVA architecture and image-interpretation programs coded in GRAVA provide a case study in the advantages and issues of systems incorporating metareasoning. A number of important and general lessons have emerged from the effort. Some of these that relate to the advantages of separating reasoning and metareasoning have already been mentioned in the metareasoning section. The first of these is *synchronization*: often a system needs to invoke metareasoning asynchronously with the reasoning system, especially when metareasoning may be computationally expensive. Another of these is *metareasoning reuse*: Even within a single system, metareasoning modules and approaches may apply to several different reasoning elements and contexts, and thus there are *representational efficiencies* to separating metareasoning from reasoning.

Another important lesson we've learned is that making metareasoning less computationally expensive is valuable and leads to significant improvements in overall system performance, as well as more prevalent and advantageous use of the metareasoning modules. In GRAVA, this was achieved by adding learning to the metareasoning module, to reduce the need to invoke the theorem prover.

Perhaps the most important lesson we learned is the importance of the metaproblem-solving methodology of "divide and conquer." For vision systems, and probably all perceptual systems, dividing the perceived world into context and object provides an enormous range of computational and conceptual advantages.

Entanglement It is nice to think of metareasoning and reasoning as separate activities, and it is advantageous to do so in terms of modularity, as we have argued. In practice, however, metareasoning and reasoning are entangled in such a way that it is impossible to separate them clearly by role.

Dimensions of metareasoning Metareasoning is not a one-dimensional activity. For example, we may reason about what are the best modules to apply in a given context in order to obtain the most useful result, but we may also reason about how long we expect a computation to take in order to decide how best to allocate our computational resources—perhaps choose a faster method with some loss of precision or perhaps steal resources from somewhere else. Finally, we may want to reason about whether our recent actions have helped the situation. This latter kind of metareasoning can assist in avoiding a perpetual cycle of unhelpful adaptations.

Conclusions

We have interleaved the description of the GRAVA architecture and of the satellite aerial image understanding program that was implemented using it. Some of the choices made in the implementation, such as the learning and subsequent use of contexts, were arbitrary and driven by the problem domain. Others, such as the relationships between parent and child levels, are general and would be common to other GRAVA applications. The domain discussed in this chapter uses an efficient and simple representation of program structure choices (contexts), but more complex domains could use richer representations with correspondingly richer metareasoning. We have described how self-adaptation draws upon both metaknowledge and abstract knowledge in order to effect adaptation to changes in the environment (i.e., changing makeup of the scene.)

While many image interpretation programs will merrily continue to interpret images that do not reflect the program's domain of competence, the described program, by using meta- and abstract knowledge, catches itself in the act of doing something silly and self-adapts into a program that can do better. In this way metareasoning leads to a program that, through self-knowledge, produces robust performance. In the cases where a good interpretation cannot be arrived at through self-adaptation, it can at least indicate that its best interpretation is unreliable.

Acknowledgments

This work was sponsored in part by the Defense Advanced Research Projects Agency (DARPA) and Air Force Research Laboratory, Air Force Material Command, USAF, under agreement number F30602-98-0056. The U.S. Government is authorized to reproduce and distribute reprints for Governmental purposes notwithstanding any copyright annotation thereon. The views and conclusions contained herein are those of the authors and should not be interpreted as necessarily representing the official policies or endorsements, either expressed or implied, of the Defense Advanced Research Projects Agency (DARPA), the Air Force Research Laboratory, or the U.S. Government.

References

Erman, L. D., Hayes-Roth, F., Lesser, V. R., & Reddy, D. R. (1980). The HEARSAY-II speech-understanding system: Integrating knowledge to resolve uncertainty. *ACM Computing Surveys, 12*(2), 213–253.

Hamscher, W., Console, L., & de Kleer, J. (1992). *Readings in model-based diagnosis*. San Francisco: Morgan Kaufmann.

Laddaga, R. (2001). Active software. In P. Robertson, H. Shobe, & R. Laddaga (Eds.), *Self adaptive software* (pp. 11–26). New York: Springer.

Laddaga, R. (2006). Self adaptive software problems and projects. In *SE '06: Second International IEEE Workshop on Software Evolvability, 2006* (pp. 3–10). http://www.citeulike.org/user/ekoenig/article/2443437.

Robertson, P. (2002). *A self adaptive architecture for image understanding*. DPhil Thesis, Department of Engineering Science, University of Oxford.

Robertson, P., & Laddaga, R. (2002a). Principle component decomposition for automatic context induction. In *Proceedings of the Artificial and Computational Intelligence Conference* (pp. 23–31). Tokyo Japan, ACTA Press.

Robertson, P., & Laddaga, R. (2002b). A self adaptive architecture and its application to robust face identification, In *Proceedings of the Pacific Rim Conference on Artificial Intelligence* (pp. 542–551). Berlin: Springer-Verlag.

Robertson, P., & Laddaga, R. (2003). GRAVA: An architecture supporting automatic context transitions and its application to robust computer vision. In *Proceedings of the 4th International and Interdisciplinary Conference CONTEXT* (pp. 499–506). Berlin: Springer Verlag LNAI 2680.

Shrobe, H. (2002). Computational vulnerability analysis for information survivability. *AI Magazine, 23*(4), 81–94.

References

8 Metareasoning as a Formal Computational Problem

Vincent Conitzer

An agent acting in the world generally needs to spend some time and other resources on *deliberation*, to assess the quality of the various plans of action available to it. To find the absolutely optimal plan, an agent generally needs to perform a very large amount of deliberation: it has to consider all the relevant implications of all the relevant facts that it knows about the world, and, if the agent is able to gather additional information, it also has to take all relevant information-gathering actions (and consider the implications of the resulting information). This is not always feasible: for example, if the agent has a deadline for choosing an action, there may not be enough time for all of this deliberation. Still, the agent may be able to find a plan of action that is close to optimal. To do so, the agent needs to focus on the parts of the deliberation (*deliberation actions*) that have the greatest impact on the quality of its plan. Determining which deliberation actions to perform is the *metareasoning problem*, in which the agent needs to reason about the reasoning it will perform.

Though this sounds natural, doing it well is far from easy. For one, the usefulness of one deliberation action may not be separable from another. For example, if there is a particularly risky plan that the agent is considering, the agent may need to rule out two ways in which this plan could potentially fail. If the agent only manages to rule out one of the two failure possibilities, and does not deliberate on the other, then the plan is still too risky and will not be chosen. Hence, the deliberation on the first failure possibility was a waste of time: the agent does not obtain any benefit from deliberation unless it considers both failure possibilities. To make things more complicated, the agent generally has to consider the outcomes of earlier deliberation actions in choosing the next deliberation action. For instance, in the above example, if the agent considers the first failure possibility and realizes that the plan would in fact fail in this way, then there is no point in considering the other failure possibility: the agent should spend its valuable time considering other options rather than pointlessly figuring out in exactly how many ways the risky plan would have failed. Hence, in general, the agent does not merely need to choose a subset of the deliberation actions; rather, it needs to create a complete *contingency plan* for deliberating.

From the above, it should be clear that the metareasoning problem is nontrivial, and may in fact be computationally hard. This is an issue of concern, since we want to avoid the ironic situation in which the agent spends so much time solving the metareasoning problem that there is no time left to take any actual deliberation actions. However, even if the problem does turn out to be computationally hard, this does not mean that we should abandon the metareasoning approach altogether: we could still find fast heuristics or approximation algorithms that find close-to-optimal solutions to the metareasoning problem, or algorithms that find the optimal solution fast under certain conditions. (See also the discussion on optimal metareasoning by Zilberstein, this vol., chap. 3.)

In the remainder, we first discuss some known results (Conitzer & Sandholm, 2003) that imply that certain variants of the metareasoning problem are in fact computationally hard. While these variants by no means capture all the interesting parts of all metareasoning problems, they are useful for illustrating some computational difficulties that metareasoning systems must face. As such, these results set the stage for the remainder of this chapter, in which we discuss their implications for real metareasoning systems.

Variants of the Metareasoning Problem and Their Complexity

Before we can determine whether the metareasoning problem is computationally hard, we first need to define it as a computational problem. However, there are many different settings in which metareasoning is essential, and each of these settings leads to a different variant of the metareasoning problem. We could try to create a computational definition of the metareasoning problem that is so general that it captures every variant that we might reasonably encounter. It would not be very surprising if such a general problem turned out to be computationally hard; moreover, it is not clear that such a hardness result would tell us anything very interesting, because it could still be the case that most reasonable variants are in fact quite easy to solve.

Instead, we will consider definitions of some very restricted variants of the metareasoning problem that still turn out to be computationally hard. Such results are much more meaningful, because it seems likely that most real-world metareasoning systems need to solve a problem that is at least as hard as at least one of these problems. We discuss mostly the results of Conitzer and Sandholm (2003). Later in the chapter, we discuss the implications of these results for the design of metareasoning systems.

Variant 1: Deliberation That Leads to Predictable Improvements

As we mentioned above, one of the main difficulties in metareasoning is that the outcomes of the deliberation actions are uncertain, and what deliberation action should be taken next in general depends on the outcomes of the current and past deliberation actions. Hence, in general, a solution to the metareasoning problem consists of a full contingency plan (at least if we aim to solve the problem to optimality).

In this subsection, however, we consider a simplified variant of the metareasoning problem in which the outcomes of deliberation actions are completely predictable. Specifically, suppose that the agent has m tasks that it needs to complete. For each of the tasks, it has a default plan that has some cost; however, by deliberating on the plan more, the agent can reduce this cost. (For example, Conitzer and Sandholm consider a setting where the agent needs to solve m unrelated vehicle-routing problem instances, and it can improve the quality of its solution for each routing problem instance by spending more computation on it—that is, it has an anytime algorithm for the vehicle routing problem.) The agent also has a deadline T by which it needs to finalize all of its plans. Finally, we assume that for each task i, there is a function f_i, where $f_i(t_i)$ is the reduction in the cost of the plan for the ith task that results from spending t_i units of deliberation time on that task. Of course, in reality, this improvement is not so perfectly predictable, but these functions are often used as a modeling simplification. They are called *(deterministic) performance profiles* (Boddy & Dean, 1994; Horvitz, 1987; Zilberstein & Russell, 1996). (Performance profiles were discussed earlier by Zilberstein, this vol., chap. 3.)

The goal is to obtain the maximum total savings given the time limit. That is, we want to choose the times $t_1, t_2, \ldots, t_m$ to spend on deliberating on the tasks, with the goal of maximizing $\sum_{i=1}^{m} f_i(t_i)$, under the constraint $\sum_{i=1}^{m} t_i \leq T$. Conitzer and Sandholm (2003) show that (the decision variant of) this problem is NP-complete, even if the f_i are piecewise linear. In contrast, if we require that the f_i are concave, then the problem can be solved in polynomial time (Boddy & Dean, 1994).[1] However, Conitzer and Sandholm argue that the f_i are generally not concave: for example, anytime algorithms generally go through distinct phases, and often the end of one phase does not produce as much improvement as the beginning of the next phase.

It is quite a negative result that even this simple deterministic variant of the metareasoning problem is hard. Still, the implications of this hardness result for metareasoning are limited, because there are variants of the metareasoning problem that do not include the above problem as a subproblem. In a sense, in the above problem, the deliberation actions reveal new plans of action (e.g., vehicle routes). However, there are many metareasoning settings in which the set of available plans is known from the beginning, and the only purpose of deliberation is to discover which plan is best. If the results of deliberation were perfectly predictable in such a setting, then we would know from the beginning which plan is best, and hence there would be no point in doing any deliberation. That is, the metareasoning problem only makes sense in this

1. Similar results based on concavity are common in metareasoning. See, e.g., Horvitz (2001).

context if the outcomes of the deliberation actions are uncertain. This is the topic of the next subsection.

Variant 2: Deliberation to Evaluate a Fixed Set of Plans

In this subsection, we consider a different variant of the metareasoning problem. Suppose there is a fixed set of possible plans of action that the agent can choose from. Each plan gives the agent some expected utility. The agent can take some deliberation actions on each plan; depending on the outcome of the deliberation action, the expected utility of that plan changes. For example, Conitzer and Sandholm (2003) consider a setting in which a robot must choose a site for digging for precious metals, and before starting to dig, the robot can perform tests (deliberation actions) at each site that will change its beliefs about what metals may be there. Each deliberation action requires some time (the amount of time is not necessarily the same for each deliberation action), and there is a deadline.

Also, we assume that the agent has a probability distribution over how its beliefs about a plan will change upon taking a deliberation action for that plan. For instance, in the digging example above, the agent may believe that if it tests at site A, then with probability 0.6, after the test it will believe that there is a probability of 0.1 that there is gold at A, and with probability 0.4, after the test it will believe that there is a probability of 0.2 that there is gold at A. This implies that before the test, it believes that there is a probability of $0.6 \cdot 0.1 + 0.4 \cdot 0.2 = 0.14$ that there is gold at A. At the end of the deliberation, the agent will choose the plan that currently has the highest expected utility.

The goal here is to find a deliberation strategy that maximizes the expected utility of the agent. Conitzer and Sandholm (2003) show that this problem is NP-hard, even if there is at most one deliberation action (with only two outcomes) per plan. They do not even prove that the problem is in NP; it could be that it is, for example, PSPACE-hard.[2]

The problem that we studied in this subsection has the nice property that each deliberation action only affects the agent's beliefs for a single plan, and for each plan there is only a single deliberation action to choose. In the next subsection, we consider a variant of the metareasoning problem without such properties.

Variant 3: Deliberation to Disambiguate State

In the final variant of the metareasoning problem that we consider, the agent knows that the world can be in any one of several states. To obtain nonzero utility, the agent needs to determine (by deliberation) the state of the world with certainty. If the agent

2. A closely related class of problems that has been receiving attention more recently is that of "budgeted learning" problems (Guha & Munagala, 2007; Madani, Lizotte, & Greiner, 2004).

succeeds in determining the state of the world, then the agent's utility depends on which state it is. The agent has a set of available deliberation actions; the outcome of each deliberation action rules out certain states. The outcome of a deliberation action is not deterministic. For example, Conitzer and Sandholm (2003) consider a setting in which a robot is trying to determine the nature of a gap in the floor in front of it. If it cannot determine the nature of the gap with certainty, it should be conservative and turn around, getting utility zero. If it determines the nature of the gap, it may be able to get past the gap and get some utility, depending on what kind of gap it is. The agent can take only a certain number of deliberation actions (there is a deadline).

Again, the goal for the agent is to find a deliberation strategy that maximizes its expected utility. Conitzer and Sandholm (2003) show that this problem is PSPACE-hard, making it the hardest of the metareasoning problems that we have considered (unless the previous problem also turns out to be PSPACE-hard). They also show that the problem remains NP-hard even if, for every state and every deliberation action, there is only a single possible outcome for that deliberation action when the world is in that state (so that the outcomes of deliberation actions are deterministic).

Implications for Metareasoning Systems

What is the relevance of these complexity results to the design of metareasoning systems? Of course, this depends first of all on whether the problems that we considered are indeed (sub)problems that need to be solved in real metareasoning systems. It seems likely that they are, but we will consider this question in more detail later in this section. For now, let us consider metareasoning systems that indeed need to solve one of the above problems.

We first note that in all of the above problems, the deliberation that the agent can perform is limited by a deadline. So, all the time that the agent spends on the metareasoning problem (deciding what deliberation actions to take) is time that can no longer be spent on actual deliberation. If the metareasoning problem were solvable to optimality in polynomial time, then perhaps the amount of time spent on the metareasoning problem would always be negligible. But the hardness results discussed above imply that more than polynomial time will be required on at least some instances of the metareasoning problem (unless P = PSPACE, or P = NP for the easier problems). Now, it is certainly possible that these hard instances do not occur in practice very often. For example, we already noted that the first problem that we studied can be solved in polynomial time if the f_i are concave; and it may well be the case that for a particular application, in practice, these functions are in fact always concave. If so, then the hardness result becomes irrelevant (for this particular application). However, we cannot decide whether this is the case if we do not know what instances occur in practice. Moreover, even if the hard metareasoning instances occur only rarely, we would still like to handle them properly. So, it might be the case that in practice most metareasoning instances lie in a class of "easy" instances, and this would mitigate the problem; but it would not eliminate it.

Once the time spent on the metareasoning problem becomes a significant fraction of the total time until the deadline, the agent faces a moving-target problem: the amount of time left for deliberation changes as the metareasoning problem is being solved—but the time left for deliberation is part of the input of the metareasoning problem. This can be resolved in various ways. The simplest is to budget some fixed amount of time B for metareasoning, so that the time for taking deliberation actions is $T - B$, where T was the original deadline. $T - B$ is thus the deadline that is used in the input of the metareasoning problem. This approach requires us to have a metareasoning algorithm that is guaranteed to give a reasonable solution in B units of time; this could be an approximation algorithm with a running time bound of B, or an anytime algorithm that we can simply interrupt at time B.

Another approach would be to have a metareasoning algorithm that, in the first B_1 units of time, finds a solution that requires $T - B_1$ units of deliberation time; then, in the next B_2 units of time, it finds a solution that requires $T - B_1 - B_2$ units of deliberation time; and so on. At the end of each phase, we can stop this metareasoning algorithm and use the latest solution it provided. One reasonable termination condition for such a metareasoning algorithm is the following: stop when the quality of the solution decreased in the latest phase. One downside to this general approach is that it is not clear that we can reuse any of the computation performed in one phase of the metareasoning algorithm in a later phase, because the phases are effectively solving different problem instances. Still, there seems to be some hope for such reuse, because these instances are closely related. Another key question is how to set the B_i; this may be done dynamically, based on the solutions found in the earlier phases. This type of analysis of the metareasoning algorithm is getting us into meta-metareasoning.

We have implicitly assumed so far that the metareasoning problem is solved first, and then deliberation starts. This makes sense in a setting where the results of deliberation are deterministic, as in the first problem that we studied. However, if the results of deliberation are not deterministic, then it may make sense to interleave metareasoning and deliberation actions. The results of the deliberation actions will allow us to prune the search space for metareasoning. For instance, in the digging example, if we do the metareasoning first, then we have to consider both the case where the test for gold at site A turns out positive and the case where it turns out negative. However, if we have already decided that the first deliberation action should be to test for gold at A, then we should go ahead and perform this test before we return to metareasoning: if the test turns out (say) positive, then we no longer need to consider what we would have done if the test had turned out negative.

Finally, let us briefly return to the question of whether our variants of the metareasoning problem were the right ones to study. One debatable aspect is that each of these variants has a deadline that limits the amount of deliberation that can be performed. Though having such a deadline is realistic in many situations, we could also consider a model in which there is no deadline, but each deliberation action comes at a cost. Indeed, such models are common in metareasoning, for example, in the work on using the expected value of computation to determine when to stop computing (Horvitz, Cooper, & Heckerman, 1989; Horvitz & Breese, 1990). This modification from a deadline-based model to a cost-based model can affect the complexity of metareasoning. For example, after this modification, the first problem that we studied (where the effect of deliberation is deterministic) becomes easy to solve: now, for each task i *separately*, we can determine the optimal amount of deliberation t_i^*, that is, $t_i^* \in \arg\max_{t_i} f_i(t_i) - ct_i$ (where c is the cost of a unit of deliberation time). Effectively, even though the tasks are in and of themselves unrelated, the deadline caused the decisions about how much time to spend on each task to become interrelated; if we switch from the deadline model to the cost model, this effect disappears.

Conclusions

Metareasoning research often lays out high-level principles, which are then applied in the context of larger systems. While this approach has proven quite successful, it sometimes obscures how metareasoning can be seen as a crisp computational problem in its own right. This alternative view allows us to apply tools from the theory of algorithms and computational complexity to metareasoning.

In this chapter, we saw how to formulate variants of the metareasoning problem as computational problems, and that these computational problems are generally hard. This approach to the metareasoning problem has at least the following benefits:

Crisp computational formulations of the metareasoning problem make it easier to consider the key variants of the problem, and to determine what makes the problem hard.

The hardness results force us to confront the fact that optimal metareasoning is not computationally feasible in general, so that we have to consider approximation algorithms, heuristics, and anytime algorithms for the metareasoning problem, as well as more involved meta-metareasoning approaches. (It is interesting to contrast this with the discussion of "hierarchical vs. loopy" in Perlis, this vol., chap. 2.)

The reader may be disappointed that we have not given a single, all-encompassing definition of the general metareasoning problem. Certainly, it seems difficult to create such a definition: it seems likely that one would leave out some aspect of the problem. Nevertheless, it may well be interesting to attempt such a definition, even if it is for no other purpose than to provide a starting point for discussion. However, the difficulty of giving a truly general definition is not the main reason that we focused on more restricted variants in this chapter. Rather, the main reason for this is that these simple variants are already computationally hard. Any fully general definition of the metareasoning problem would presumably include all of these variants as special cases. Because computational problems inherit the hardness of their special cases, this means that we have already shown that the general metareasoning problem is hard (even without giving its precise definition).

The above also casts some doubt on the value of coming up with a single, general definition of the metareasoning problem as a formal computational problem. If one were to write an algorithm to solve such a general problem, it would have to address a tremendous variety of complexities, including all the ones studied here as well as, presumably, numerous others. As long as we are not trying to solve the general AI problem, it is probably more productive to focus on the special cases of the metareasoning problem that are important for the application at hand, thereby avoiding some of the irrelevant complexities. This is absolutely not to say that there is no value in *studying and discussing* metareasoning in general: in fact, doing so is vital to help us understand the relationships among the different variants of the metareasoning problem, and will allow for the smooth transfer of techniques across these variants.

There are still many open questions. For many key variants, the complexity of the metareasoning problem has not yet been established (including many variants where there is no deadline but deliberation is costly). For the variants where optimal metareasoning has been shown to be hard, there is still a need for approximation algorithms or inapproximability results, as well heuristics and anytime algorithms without formal guarantees but with good practical performance. Perhaps more important, it is not yet entirely clear what the best high-level framework is for metareasoning when optimal metareasoning is hard, especially when time is limited and the metareasoning is using up time that could have been used for deliberation actions. As discussed above, we run into the issue that the problem instance becomes a moving target, because the available time for deliberation is changing. Moreover, when the results of deliberation are uncertain, it makes sense to interleave metareasoning and deliberation, because the outcomes of deliberation actions will allow us to prune the possibilities that the metareasoning algorithm no longer needs to consider.

References

Boddy, M., & Dean, T. (1994). Deliberation scheduling for problem solving in time-constrained environments. *Artificial Intelligence, 67*, 245–285.

Conitzer, V., & Sandholm, T. (2003). Definition and complexity of some basic metareasoning problems. In *Proceedings of the Eighteenth International Joint Conference on Artificial Intelligence (IJCAI)* (pp. 1099–1106). San Francisco: Morgan Kaufmann.

Guha, S., & Munagala, K. (2007). Multi-armed bandits with limited exploration. In *Proceedings of the 39th Annual ACM Symposium on Theory of Computing (STOC)* (pp. 104–113). New York: ACM.

Horvitz, E. J., & Breese, J. S. (1990). *Ideal partition of resources for metareasoning*. Technical Report KSL-90–26, Stanford University Computer Science Department.

Horvitz, E. J., Cooper, G. F., & Heckerman, D. E. (1989). Reflection and action under scarce resources: Theoretical principles and empirical study. In *Proceedings of the Eleventh International Joint Conference on Artificial Intelligence (IJCAI)* (pp. 1121–1127). Los Altos, CA: Morgan Kaufmann.

Horvitz, E. J. (1987). Reasoning about beliefs and actions under computational resource constraints. In *Proceedings of Third Workshop on Uncertainty in Artificial Intelligence* (pp. 429–444). Amsterdam: North Holland.

Horvitz, E. (2001). Principles and applications of continual computation. *Artificial Intelligence, 126*, 159–196.

Madani, O., Lizotte, D. J., & Greiner, R. (2004). Active model selection. In M. Chickering & J. Halpern (Eds.), *Proceedings of the 20th Annual Conference on Uncertainty in Artificial Intelligence (UAI)* (pp. 357–365). Arlington, VA: AUAI Press.

Zilberstein, S., & Russell, S. (1996). Optimal composition of real-time systems. *Artificial Intelligence, 82*(1–2), 181–213.

III Introspective Monitoring

9 Metareasoning, Monitoring, and Self-Explanation

Michael T. Cox

A significant research history exists with respect to metareasoning in artificial intelligence (Anderson & Oates, 2007; Cox, 2005), and much of it is driven by the problems of bounded rationality (see Zilberstein, this vol., chap. 3). That is because of the size of the problem space, the limitations on resources, and the amount of uncertainty in the environment; as a result, only approximate solutions can be obtained for finite agents. So, for example, with an anytime algorithm that incrementally refines plans, an agent must choose between executing the current plan or further deliberation with the hope of improving the plan. To make this choice, the agent is reasoning about its own reasoning (i.e., planning) as well as its potential actions in the world (i.e., the plan). As such this represents the problem of explicit control of reasoning.

Figure 1.2 in the manifesto illustrates the control side of reasoning along its upper portion. Reasoning controls action at the ground level in the environment, whereas metareasoning controls the reasoning at the object level. For the anytime controller, metareasoning decides when reasoning is sufficient and thus action can proceed. Although other themes exist within the metareasoning tradition, this characterization is a common one (e.g., Conitzer, this vol., chap. 8; Horvitz, 1987; Raja, Alexander, Lesser & Krainin, this vol., chap. 13; Russell & Wefald, 1991).

The complementary side of metareasoning, however, is less well studied. The introspective monitoring of reasoning performance requires an agent to maintain some kind of internal feedback in addition to perception, so that it can perform effectively and can evaluate the results of metareasoning. For instance, Zilberstein (1993; Zilberstein & Russell, 1996) maintains statistical profiles of past metareasoning choices and the associated performance and uses them to mediate the subsequent control and dynamic composition of reasoning processes.

But introspective monitoring can be even more explicit. If the reasoning that is performed at the object level, and not just its results, is represented in a declarative knowledge structure that captures the mental states and decision-making sequence, then these knowledge structures can themselves be passed to the metalevel for monitoring. For example, the Meta-AQUA system (Cox & Ram, 1999) keeps a trace of its story understanding decisions in structures called a trace meta-explanation pattern

(TMXP). Here the object-level story understanding task is to explain anomalous or unusual events in a ground-level story perceived by the system.[1] Then, if this explanation process fails, Meta-AQUA passes the TMXP and the current story representation to a learning subsystem. The learner performs an introspection of the trace to obtain an explanation of the explanation failure called an introspective meta-explanation pattern (IMXP). The IMXPs are used to generate a set of learning goals that are passed back to control the object-level learning and hence improve subsequent understanding. TMXPs explain *how* reasoning occurs; IMXPs explain *why* reasoning fails.

Unfortunately these meta-explanation structures are so complicated that, although they have been shown empirically to support complex learning, they cannot be understood easily by humans. Indeed before I demonstrate the Meta-AQUA system to others, I often spend twenty minutes reviewing the TMXP and IMXP schemas, so that I can answer questions effectively. However, I claim that all metareasoning systems share this characteristic. The kinds of recursive processing an agent must do to perform metareasoning (e.g., within the metacognitive loop of this vol., chap. 12) and the types of knowledge structures used to support metareasoning (e.g., the introspective explanations in this vol., chap. 11, or the workflow trace representations in this vol., chap. 6) produce a severe cognitive demand on even the most sophisticated observer. What is required is the implementation of an infrastructure to support interactive explanation of an agent's own reasoning.[2] By so building such an infrastructure, we not only improve our understanding of the design of intelligent agents, but we also move toward agents that truly understand what they are doing and why. A solution lies along the monitoring side of metareasoning.

This chapter will examine further the potential that the monitoring of reasoning provides and will consider what implications exist. For metareasoning in agent-based systems, the self is the object of the processing, yet for many researchers the centrality of this statement is left wholly implicit. Here we will briefly discuss four characteristics or aspects of self from a computational stance. We consider in turn self-modifying code, self-knowledge, self-understanding, and finally self-explanation. After discussing the issue of evaluation, we will conclude by enumerating some outstanding problems related to metareasoning.

Self-Modifying Code

Like many novice programmers, I was fascinated by the idea of self-modifying code as an undergraduate. It seemed to capture in a direct and elegant way the idea of

1. Note that no action-selection occurs with the story understanding task.

2. McGuinness and associates (McGuinness, Ding, Glass, Chang, Zeng, & Furtado, 2006; McGuinness & Patel-Schneider, 2003) have made a similar claim with respect to explanation for the semantic web.

learning and intelligence. Of course my instructor quickly pointed out that this was a bad idea from a software engineering perspective and constituted a poor design. It generates hard-to-understand code that is very difficult to debug, because the flow of control lacks transparency. Instead, the goal of top-down design is to abstract the environment using relevant data structures and to model the dynamics and interactions with these data structures. To effect a change in the behavior of the program, it was preferable to modify the data, not the code. Yet for some of us, it is easy to confuse techniques of self-modification with the principles of metareasoning.

For example, in the concluding paragraph of a chapter from an expert-systems textbook, Lenat et al. (1983) proclaim the following:

> Once self-description is a reality, the next logical step is self-modification. Small, self-modifying, automatic programming systems have existed for a decade; some large programs that modify themselves in very small ways also exist; and the first large fully self-describing and self-modifying programs are being built just now. The capability of machines has finally exceeded human cogni-

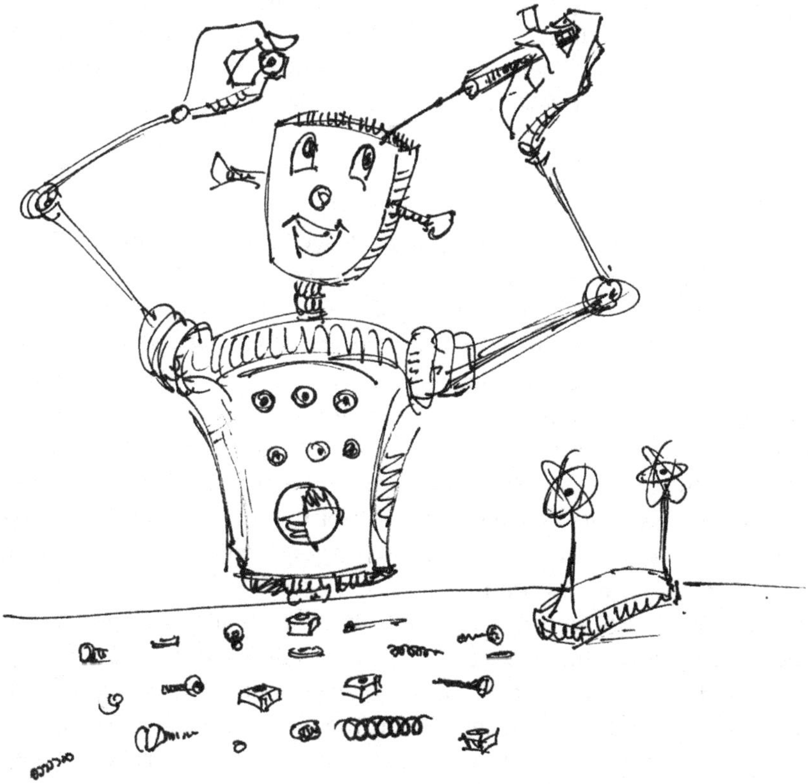

Figure 9.1
Self-modifying code.

tive capabilities in this dimension; it is now worth supplying and using meta-knowledge in large expert systems. (p. 238)

Given that this quote is more than a quarter of a century old, we can attribute the over-enthusiastic response to some amount of naïveté, but this assertion remains astonishing nonetheless. To what dimension are they referring when they claim that human capabilities have been supplanted by machines, and in what manner are self-modification and metaknowledge the prime factors? Surely, by most accounts, this exaggerates. The primary issue should be the relationship between learning and metareasoning.

To improve performance an agent must be able to adapt and change so that over time better decisions accrue. Changes can occur in essentially two ways. Agents are commonly construed as functions from a current state to some action that will change the state. Self-modification can be cast as adaptive changes to this function given a suitable representation for the function in a particular data structure and rigorous algorithms that transform the function. Alternatively, learning can be cast as an accumulation of knowledge. As an agent acquires more knowledge and as its knowledge base is refined and reorganized, its performance and action selections should improve as a result. Yet it is unclear how metaknowledge is related to successful change and whether the two alternatives just described can be related.

Self-Knowledge

Many researchers stress the importance of metaknowledge in the design of intelligent agents, and certainly many papers on metareasoning discuss metaknowledge (e.g., Arkoudas & Bringsjord, 2005; Barklund, Dell'Acqua, Constantini, & Lanzarone, 2000; Cox, 2005; Davis, 1980; Hahn, Klenner, & Schnattinger, 1996; Raja & Goel, 2007). Metaknowledge being knowledge about knowledge seems at first blush to be crucial to learning if not action. That is, how can an agent improve its knowledge without understanding the knowledge? Indeed, the area of knowledge refinement appears to need much in addition to lone assertions in order to evaluate a knowledge base and to be able to make the necessary changes. Yet much of the recent trend in learning research demonstrates just how much an agent can learn using data-driven statistical approaches such as reinforcement learning.

Much ambiguity also exists with respect to metaknowledge and planning agents. Confusion results when a cognitive process such as planning and when knowledge concerning the world such as plans are mistaken for metacognitive processes and self-knowledge at the metalevel. Part of this problem is the fact that metaknowledge can exist at both the object and metalevels and that interactions occur between levels. Consider the statement "The robosoccer agent followed its plan and won the championship because the plan was a good one." I claim that, although this statement

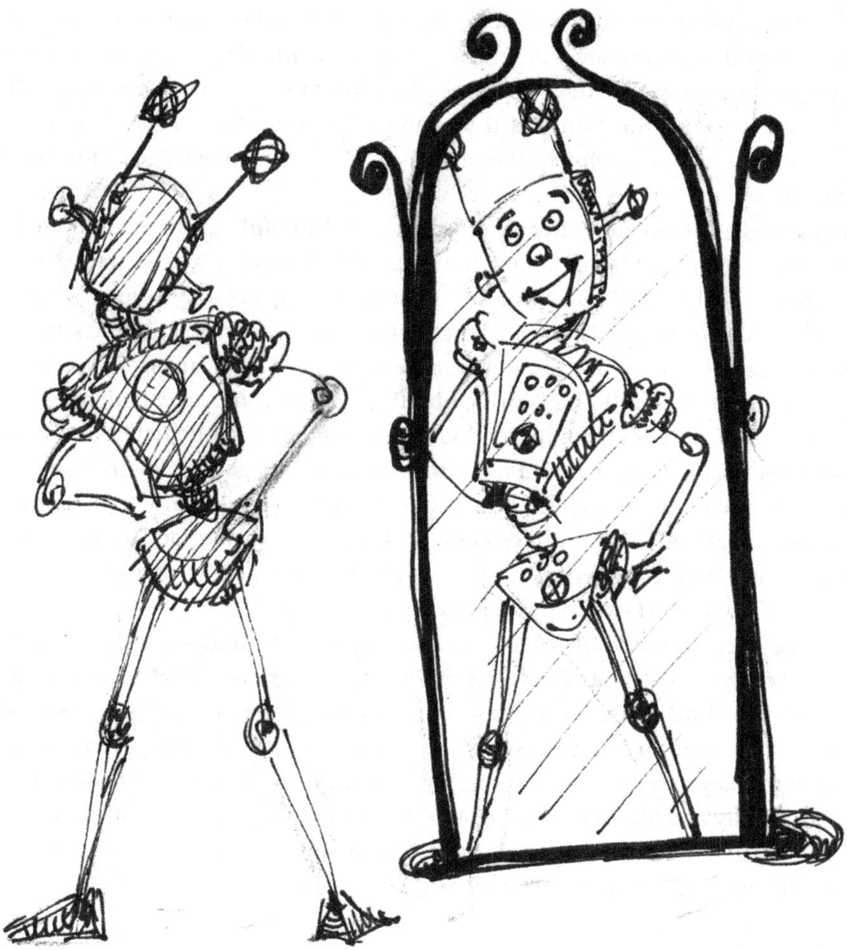

Figure 9.2
Self-knowledge.

contains metaknowledge, it does not necessarily involve metareasoning. Instead, it refers to action at the ground level (i.e., soccer actions) controlled by an object-level constructed piece of knowledge (i.e., the game plan). To state that the plan was a good one is an assertion about the plan and thus knowledge about knowledge, but at no point must we infer metareasoning or the metalevel. Thus metaknowledge is independent of metareasoning.[3]

Furthermore, the statement concerns another agent and does not involve the self. Self-knowledge arises in part from the psychological distinction between semantic and episodic memory (Tulving, 1972). Semantic knowledge is general knowledge about objects such as "All psychologists know a lot about human thinking." Episodic knowledge concerns actual events or episodes in a person's life or in an agent's action history. Much of human reasoning is driven by this type of concrete experience. For example, I might know that all computer scientists are good at mathematics and that I am a computer scientist. But I would not conclude that I am good at math through logical deduction with this semantic knowledge. Instead, I have many experiences with performing mathematics and have come to trust my ability to do similar problems in the future. Such confidence in my own ability is metaknowledge derived by reasoning about my own reasoning experiences.

Such an approach to self-knowledge uses a case-based reasoning (Kolodner, 1993; Leake, 1996; Lopez de Mántaras et al., 2006; Riesbeck & Schank, 1989) perspective. That is, a case-based agent performs reasoning by being reminded of past cases of experience and by adapting these cases to the current situation when interpreting perceptions (case-based understanding) or choosing an action to perform (case-based planning). Ironically and like most AI programs, few case-based implementations focus on an explicit representation of the self or otherwise operationalize the self despite specific case libraries that represent experience.[4]

Self-Understanding

Early research in the case-based reasoning community concentrated on cognitive modeling of the human comprehension process, especially in terms of how humans acquire a conceptual understanding of stories or textual representations (e.g., Schank & Abelson, 1977; Schank & Riesbeck, 1981). As is the case with Meta-AQUA, the story

3. Note that this statement is an assertion about metaknowledge and therefore meta-metaknowledge. However, this distinction is not necessarily very important or useful. What is important is simply that we as researchers be clear with our categories for purposes of *communication* of agent design and implementation.

4. An interesting exception exists with the research of Forbus and Hinrichs (2004) that tracks agent activity logs to ascertain episodic information with respect to self-knowledge.

understanding task is to take as input a representation (either conceptual or textual) of the story and to produce as output an interpretation of the input. Although interpretation can take many forms, the CBR stance is to retrieve a piece of experience (i.e., a script or case) that matches the content of the current sentence and to adapt it to produce the interpretive understanding. So the story is understood, if the program can successfully answer questions about the story, paraphrase it, or connect the representations into a coherent whole that predicts further events in the story. More generally, this same process can be applied to monitor one's own plans or exogenous events executed in the world or to monitor reasoning performed in the head. The key is that monitoring, like control, is a "first-class citizen" in both the reasoning and metareasoning processes (Cox, 1996b; So & Sonenberg, 2007).

An initial introspective cognitive agent called INTRO (Cox, 2007) combines planning and understanding within a Wumpus World environment (Russell & Norvig, 2003) by integrating the PRODIGY planning and learning architecture (Carbonell, Knoblock, & Minton, 1991; Veloso et al., 1995) with the Meta-AQUA story understanding and learning system. Rather than input all goals for the agent to achieve, the understanding component compares expected states and events in the world with those actually perceived to create an interpretation. When the interpretation discloses divergence from those expectations, INTRO generates its own goals to resolve the conflict. These new goals are then passed back to the PRODIGY component so that a plan can be generated and then executed. As such, introspective monitoring controls action through the creation of new goals.

This understanding process depends on declaratively represented percepts of ground-level states and actions. If the reasoning processes at the object level (i.e., the mental states and inferences) are likewise represented declaratively, metareasoning can monitor such activity to obtain some measure of self-understanding. As mentioned in the introduction, the Meta-AQUA system implements a theory of introspective multistrategy learning whereby the system builds and executes a learning plan to achieve a set of learning goals. These goals are spawned in response to explanations of explanation failures, which allow the system to decide what to learn. However, much remains to be implemented in the INTRO system to achieve a full integration of reasoning and metareasoning and of world knowledge and self-knowledge.

For example, other than control over goal generation, monitoring has no control over INTRO's reasoning. Consider the possible responses to a failed robosoccer plan. If an agent was to reason about why its game plan did not succeed by considering its prior planning (e.g., "I focused on our ball-handling when creating the plan rather than the defender's capabilities") as opposed to simply analyzing the plan or the plan execution, then metareasoning and monitoring would be involved. But INTRO cannot use such inferences to improve its future planning performance. Furthermore, planning itself is not influenced by cases of prior planning, although an introspective

Figure 9.3
Self-understanding.

version of PRODIGY called Prodigy/Analogy (Veloso, 1994) has that capability. Certainly INTRO has never felt a familiarity at planning time so that it might say to itself, "This partial plan must be close to a correct one, because I have performed similar planning before."[5] Also, INTRO cannot decide whether it is competent enough for a task (at either the ground or object level) or whether it should ask another agent to perform the task instead. Finally, despite the fact that INTRO might invoke the Meta-AQUA component to explain some failed reasoning, it cannot actually explain the failure to you. Here I claim that not only INTRO but all metareasoning agents would benefit from similar capabilities.

Self-Explanation

Explanation-aware computing is seeing a recent resurgence in the AI and cognitive science communities as indicated by the existence of mainstream workshops (Roth-Berghofer & Schultz, 2005; Roth-Berghofer, Schultz, Bahls & Leake, 2007) and compilations (e.g., Roth-Berghofer & Richter, 2008; Keil & Wilson, 2000). Explanations provide numerous functions including event prediction, assignment of personal (e.g., legal) blame, and diagnosis for repair (Keil, 2006), but their most central purpose is to determine causal connectedness in service of learning (Keil, 2006; Ram & Leake, 1991; Schank, 1986). Explanation provides a key capability for elaborating the understanding that agents produce when processing the environment, especially when agents' perceptions diverge from their expectations. An explanation likewise provides a causal accounting of mental anomalies discovered during monitoring.

Explanation is ubiquitous. While discussing self-knowledge, I provided an explanatory sentence as an example. To assert that a robosoccer agent won a championship because the plan was a good one is to causally link the characteristics of the plan to successful performance (i.e., following the plan). A story-understanding agent comprehends an input, if it can explain why the characters in the story do surprising things by inferring what their goals and motivations are and by enumerating those events that follow from earlier ones in a causally determined manner (e.g., event e_1 results in a state that is the precondition or determinant for another event e_2). Such explanations link the causally relevant past events with the desired future states to account for current observations.[6] Yet explanation is all too absent in many agent-based implementations.

5. But see the DIAL case-based planner (Leake, Kinley, & Wilson, 1996) that considers familiarity with past reasoning.

6. Such *self-projection* into the future and past has been linked to central human cognitive abilities (Buckner & Carroll, 2007).

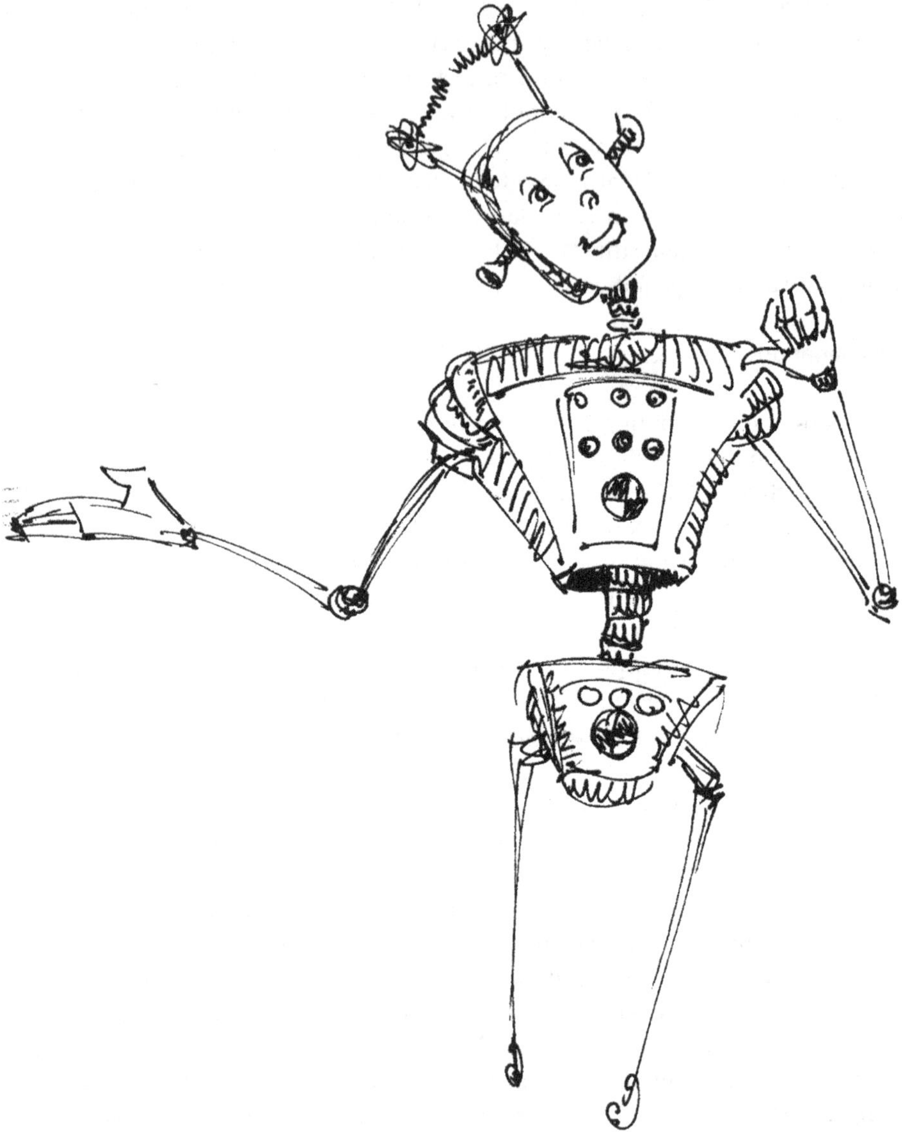

Figure 9.4
Self-explanation.

Like Rats in a Maze

As commented upon in the above section on self-knowledge, statistical techniques have proven to be a powerful means of enabling agent-based systems to learn complex behaviors from interactions with regularities in the environment. Indeed, given the Markov assumption of independent decisions, we can model an agent with the policy $\pi^*(s)$ that returns an optimal action, a, from any given state, s. Even though an agent may not know the environmental probability distribution between states and actions, an agent that explores states through its actions can converge on the optimal policy by experiencing rewards and using Q-learning.

The technique has been used in many complex situations and under various conditions of uncertainty to model behavior in the natural world. For example, both Konidaris and Hayes (2005) and Sharma (2003) have shown reinforcement learning to be capable of simulating the maze learning behavior of rats. In the simplest of trials, one can place a rat at the base of a T-maze with cheese in one of the two arms. The task is for the rat to find the food. Given a sufficient number of trials, the algorithms will learn the correct set of actions to find the reward. More complex mazes can be assembled by connecting multiple Ts, each representing a binary decision. But consider the following. The artificial rats may learn to find the reward, but do they know where the cheese is?

Many years ago, Tolman (1948) ran a very interesting experiment at Berkeley with actual rats. They had two groups that experienced very different conditions. The first group of rats represented the standard condition. These rats were deprived of food for a length of time so that they were hungry, and they were trained over an eleven-day period through a complex maze system. By the end of the period, they had reached a high level of performance so that they made few errors when running the maze. The second group of rats were fed until satiation and then were strapped into small wheelbarrows. The experimenters then pushed the wheelbarrows through the maze to the location of the cheese. After eleven days the second group was tested using a standard test (hungry and on foot). The surprising discovery was that the group very quickly gained performance equal to that of the standard learning condition. The experiment demonstrated latent learning in the absence of reward. That is, the reward was necessary for performance but not for learning.

This is relevant to metareasoning, because many forms of metareasoning use data-driven statistical methods and reinforcement-learning driven only by performance as determined by a reward schedule (e.g., Hansen & Zilberstein, 2001; Raja & Lesser, 2007). Moreover, it is difficult to claim that these systems can understand themselves in an explicit way, although they have a statistical model of their own reasoning and reason recursively about the model. This is true at both the object and the ground levels. The reinforcement-learning agent reported by Perlis and colleagues (Anderson & Perlis, 2005; Schmill et al., this vol., chap. 12) contains an internal metacognitive loop that detects when the rewards in the environment diverge from its expectations. Analysis of such perturbations leads to improved performance with respect to standard reinforcement learners. But can this type of agent explain how and why it learns? Because the statistical models have no symbolic content, explanation is handicapped. Instead, we should consider how an agent might learn an explainable policy $\pi^e(s)$ that decides to take action, *a*, when in state, *s*, because of justification, *j*. For example, such a policy would suggest that the rat turns left at the T junction *because the cheese is at the end of the left arm*. When the cheese is no longer to be found to the left and is instead at the end of the right arm, a straightforward explanation of failure should result in more effective learning. Granted, Raja and Goel (2007) are making progress toward enabling introspective explanations, but as mentioned previously, the kinds of explanations structures used in metareasoning (i.e., meta-explanations and introspective explanations) are of less use to humans trying to understand the metareasoning.

From Rats to Cognitive Agents

Two characteristics separate humans from all other species including rats. First is our creative use of natural language and our ability to communicate to others (and to ourselves). Second is the (albeit limited) ability to introspect and to explain our identity as individuals. This chapter challenges the metareasoning community to develop computational frameworks within which these two characteristics synthesize. The goal is to create cognitive agents that can explain themselves to others in plain English. Evidence exists that such self-explanation behavior can help agents learn better (Cox, 2007; Cox & Ram, 1999), and lucid English translations will clearly help humans gain trust in their cognitive assistants.

The general problem faced by users of cognitive systems is that of trust calibration. Some users overestimate the ability of systems, whereas others underestimate or mistrust them. The root cause in both cases is that users do not understand how or why computers do what they do. If a system could explain itself in English and tell a user why it makes a particular decision, the user will more likely know the correct uses and limits of that system. But most important, it is the very act of explaining itself that allows a system to improve its performance in ways that ordinary machine learning programs never will.

The problem faced by designers of cognitive systems is that the intelligent agents they wish to develop are so complicated that existing and foreseeable design techniques are unable to effectively engineer them with existing technology alone. Yet if a learning agent could participate in its own testing and debugging, the agent might explain those components of its software that have implementation failures so that engineering bottlenecks can be overcome. One direction toward this ideal is to formulate systems that generate detailed explanation graph structures of their internal

Table 9.1
Ten simple mental explanations

1	I forgot that X.
2	I am good at Y.
3	I did not see (or notice) Z.
4	I mistook an M for an N.
5	I assumed that I is the case because B.
6	I thought that all J could K.
7	I learned that Q today.
8	I did not have enough time to think about R. I wasted time worrying (thinking) about R.
9	S surprised me because B.
10	I chose to do A1 instead of A2 because B. I wanted to achieve G1 rather than G2 because B.

behavior and provide interactive graph-navigation aids with English-generation abilities.

Many reasons exist for self-explanation, but it is not an easy task. Table 9.1 lists my top ten favorite explanations I would like to hear a cognitive agent communicate. Consider the first. Many humans have explained to their friends that they were late for an appointment because they forgot to fill up their car with gas. Cox (1994) notes that, if a case-based planner uses an indexed memory for retrieval of past cases in lieu of exhaustive search, then forgetting is a potential causal factor in planning failures.

Figure 9.5 illustrates the IMXP explanation structure for such a reasoning failure. The language task then is to take this graph as input and to output either a paraphrase or elaboration in English text. A suitable paraphrase might be "I forgot to fill up the car with gas when I was at the store." An elaboration might be something similar to the following text. "The context, *C*, of being at the store did not sufficiently match the index, *I*, with which the goal, *G*, to fill up with gas was stored in memory, so I failed to retrieve the goal at the right time and thus did not put gas in the tank. Because the tank was low, I did not have enough fuel and then ran out of gas." Being able to generate such text might be possible using existing language-generation algorithms (Lester & Porter, 1996; McDonald, 2010), although many problems of generative focus exist.

Another open research question remains as to the best method of quantitatively evaluating subjective explanation. An explanation can be true but totally miss the point. For example, it does not help us understand why firemen wear red suspenders if we are told that the suspenders hold their pants up (Ram, 1989). What is most important in evaluating an explanation is not its veracity per se, but whether it serves

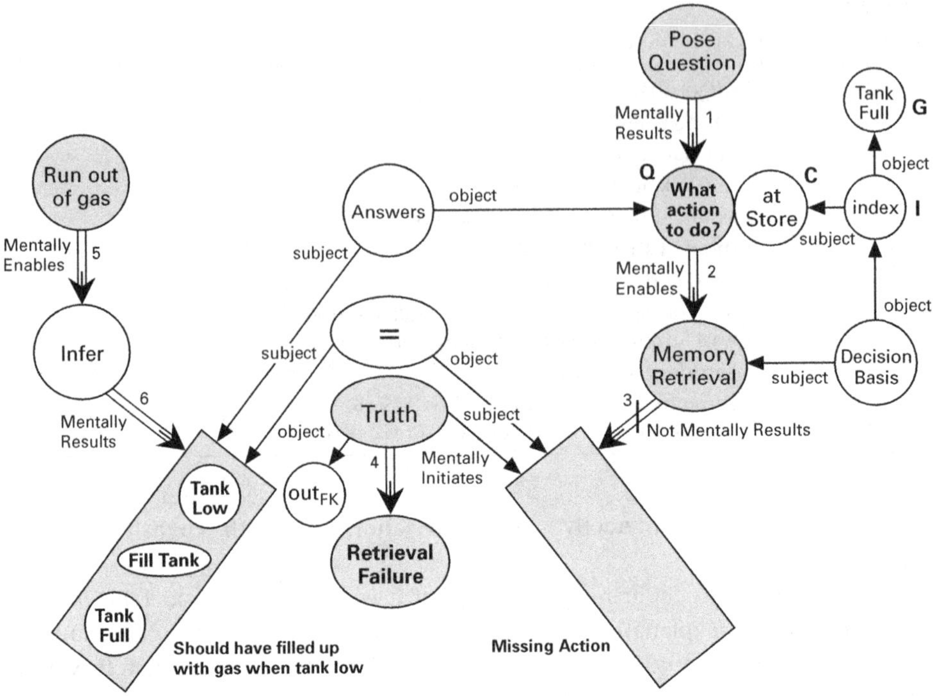

Figure 9.5
"Forgetting to fill up with Gas" Meta-XP structure.

the need of the agent (either self or other) targeted by the explanation. The need is in terms of the current knowledge of the agent and gaps in the knowledge that the explanation fills (Leake, 1994; Ram & Leake, 1991). So when knowledge is missing, incorrect, or disconnected from related knowledge, the best explanation fills the gap, corrects the misconception, or causally links assertions that provide further coherence and relational structure.

The challenge is to take these long-standing, subjective principles and to operationalize them constructively. A numeric criterion may be a poor substitute for evaluating the extent to which a large graph structure fulfills conceptual needs as opposed to strictly syntactic ones (e.g., the number of connected components in an explanation), but the loss due to abstraction and approximation is compensated by the ability to compare and contrast explanatory solutions. In a very simple way, the dissertation research of Cox (1996a,b) provides a start toward this goal. Each anomaly in a story represents a source of knowledge discrepancy for Meta-AQUA and a potential explanation target. For each anomaly, up to three points are awarded: one point for identifying that a question needs to be posed, a second for providing any explanation, and a third for matching the "correct" explanation as enumerated by an oracle. With this or any like function, the evaluator should generate a real number between 1 and 0. Then, to normalize the explanation criterion with performance (given a performance measure also between 1 and 0), it is sufficient to calculate *performance/(2-explanation)*. When explanation is 1, the measure reflects performance alone; otherwise, the measure can be reduced by as much as half the normal performance. Without the incorporation of self-explanation into the overall performance measure, many metareasoning implementations can simply optimize performance first and then sprinkle on a bit of metasugar after the fact.

Conclusion

I am not the first to call for agents that truly know what they are doing and why. Raja and Goel (2007) make many of the same arguments, and Brachman (2002) issued the challenge beforehand. Indeed, Brachman initiated DARPA's cognitive computing vision that seeks to solve basic research and development problems related to those described here (Defense Advanced Research Projects Agency [DARPA], 2009). One difference is that I claim that, if an agent really understands what it is doing and why, then it should be able to explain this self-understanding to others as well.

I will simply close with a list of hard problems that, in addition to the problems of text generation and evaluation, seriously impede progress toward agents that can meaningfully claim to know themselves.

The problem of appropriateness Given that metareasoning creates an additional computational burden, how can an agent decide when the potential benefit of metareasoning will outweigh the cost of its overhead?

The homunculus problem How can we effectively control metareasoning without substituting yet another computational layer above the metalevel?

The problem of consciousness How can the many heterogeneous reasoning functions such as problem solving, understanding, and learning be multiplexed with metareasoning into a whole that represents the unity of experience?[7]

The existential problem What are the computational properties that lie beneath the illusion of separate, independent existence and free will?[8]

The problem of identity What knowledge structure best represents the abstract notion of self?

7. See Sloman (this vol., chap. 20) for a discussion.

8. For some prominent comments on this issue, see Minsky (1968) and Sloman (1992).

Acknowledgments

The views, opinions, and findings contained in this chapter are those of the author and should not be interpreted as representing the official views or policies, either expressed or implied, of the Defense Advanced Research Projects Agency or the Department of Defense. This document has been approved for public release by DARPA for unlimited distribution. I thank Deborah Dixon for the illustrations used in the first four figures.

References

Anderson, M., & Oates, T. (2007). A review of recent research in metareasoning and metalearning. *AI Magazine, 28*(1), 7–16.

Anderson, M., & Perlis, D. (2005). Logic, self-awareness and self-improvement: The metacognitive loop and the problem of brittleness. *Journal of Logic and Computation, 15*(1), 21–40.

Arkoudas, K., & Bringsjord, S. (2005). Metareasoning for multi-agent epistemic logics. In J. Leite & P. Torroni (Eds.), *Computational Logic in Multi-Agent Systems: 5th International Workshop, CLIMA V, Lisbon, Portugal, September 29–30, 2004* (pp. 111–125). Berlin: Springer.

Barklund, J., Dell'Acqua, P., Constantini, S., & Lanzarone, G. A. (2000). Reflection principles in computational logic. *Journal of Logic and Computation, 10*(6), 743–786.

Brachman, R. J. (2002). Systems that know what they are doing. *IEEE Intelligent Systems, 17*(6), 67–71.

Buckner, R. L., & Carroll, D. C. (2007). Self-projection and the brain. *Trends in Cognitive Sciences, 11*(2), 49–57.

Carbonell, J. G., Knoblock, C. A., & Minton, S. (1991). PRODIGY: An integrated architecture for planning and learning. In K. VanLehn (Ed.), *Architectures for intelligence: The 22nd Carnegie Mellon Symposium on Cognition* (pp. 241–278). Hillsdale, NJ: Lawrence Erlbaum.

Cox, M. T. (1994). Machines that forget: Learning from retrieval failure of mis-indexed explanations. In A. Ram and K. Eiselt (Eds.), *Proceedings of the Sixteenth Annual Conference of the Cognitive Science Society* (pp. 225–230). Hillsdale, NJ: LEA.

Cox, M. T. (1996a). An empirical study of computational introspection: Evaluating introspective multistrategy learning in the Meta-AQUA system. In R. S. Michalski & J. Wnek (Eds.), *Proceedings of the Third International Workshop on Multistrategy Learning* (pp. 135–146). Menlo Park, CA: AAAI Press.

Cox, M. T. (1996b). *Introspective multistrategy learning: Constructing a learning strategy under reasoning failure* (Tech. Rep. No. GIT-CC-96-06). Unpublished doctoral dissertation, Georgia Institute of Technology, College of Computing, Atlanta.

Cox, M. T. (2005). Metacognition in computation: A selected research review. *Artificial Intelligence, 169*(2), 104–141.

Cox, M. T. (2007). Perpetual self-aware cognitive agents. *AI Magazine, 28*(1), 32–45.

Cox, M. T., & Ram, A. (1999). Introspective multistrategy learning: On the construction of learning strategies. *Artificial Intelligence, 112*, 1–55.

Davis, R. (1980). Meta-rules: Reasoning about control. *Artificial Intelligence, 15*, 179–222.

Defense Advanced Research Projects Agency (DARPA). (2009). *Strategic plan*. Washington, D.C.: U.S. Government.

Forbus, K., & Hinrichs, T. (2004). Companion cognitive systems: A step towards human-level AI (pp. 30–34). In *AAAI Fall Symposium on Achieving Human-level Intelligence through Integrated Systems and Research*. Menlo Park, CA: AAAI Press.

Hahn, U., Klenner, M., & Schnattinger, K. (1996) Automated knowledge acquisition meets metareasoning: Incremental quality assessment of concept hypotheses during text understanding (pp. 9–14). In *Proceedings of the 10th Banff Knowledge Acquisition for Knowledge-Based Systems Workshop*. Calgary: Knowledge Science Institute.

Hansen, E. A., & Zilberstein, S. (2001). Monitoring and control of anytime algorithms: A dynamic programming approach. *Artificial Intelligence, 126*(1–2), 139–157.

Horvitz, E. (1987). Reasoning about beliefs and actions under computational resource constraints. In *Proceedings of the Third Workshop on Uncertainty in Artificial Intelligence* (pp. 429–444). Amsterdam: North-Holland.

Keil, F. C. (2006). Explanation and understanding. *Annual Review of Psychology, 57*, 227–254.

Keil, F. C., & Wilson, R. A. (Eds.) (2000). *Explanation and cognition*. Cambridge, MA: MIT Press.

Kolodner, J. L. (1993). *Case-based reasoning*. San Mateo, CA: Morgan Kaufmann.

Konidaris, G. D., & Hayes, G. M. (2005). An architecture for behavior-based reinforcement learning. *Adaptive Behavior, 13*(1), 5–32.

Leake, D. (1994). Accepter: Evaluating explanations. In R. C. Schank, A. Kass, & C. K. Riesbeck (Eds.), *Inside case-based explanation* (pp. 168–206). Hillsdale, NJ: Lawrence Erlbaum Associates.

Leake, D. (Ed.) (1996). *Case-based reasoning: Experiences, lessons, and future directions*. Menlo Park: AAAI Press/MIT Press.

Leake, D., Kinley, A., & Wilson, D. (1996). Linking adaptation and similarity learning (pp. 591–596). In *Proceedings of the Eighteenth Annual Conference of the Cognitive Science Society*. Hillsdale, NJ: LEA.

Lenat, D. B., Davis, R., Doyle, J., Genesereth, M., Goldstein, I., & Schrobe, H. (1983). Reasoning about reasoning. In F. Hayes-Roth, D. A. Waterman, & D. B. Lenat (Eds.), *Building expert systems* (pp. 219–239). London: Addison-Wesley Publishing.

Lester, J., & Porter, B. (1996). Scaling up explanation generation: Large-scale knowledge bases and empirical studies (pp. 416–423). In *Proceedings of the Thirteenth National Conference on Artificial Intelligence*. Menlo Park: AAAI Press/MIT Press.

Lopez de Mántaras, R., McSherry, D., Bridge, D., Leake, D., Smyth, B., Craw, S., et al. (2006). Retrieval, reuse and retention in case-based reasoning. *Knowledge Engineering Review, 20*(3), 215–240.

McDonald, D. (2010). Natural language generation (pp. 121–144). In N. Indurkhya & F. J. Damerau (Eds.), *Handbook of natural language processing* (2nd ed.). Boca Raton, FL: CRC Press.

McGuinness, D. L., Ding, L., Glass, A., Chang, C., Zeng, H., & Furtado, V. (2006). Explanation interfaces for the semantic web: Issues and models. In *Proceedings of the 3rd International Semantic Web User Interaction Workshop* (collocated with ISWC 2006). Berlin: Springer.

McGuinness, D., & Pinheiro da Silva, P. (2003). Infrastructure for web explanations (pp. 113–129). In *Proceedings of 2nd International Semantic Web Conference (ISWC2003)*. Berlin: Springer.

Minsky, M. L. (1968). Matter, mind, and models. In M. Minsky (Ed.), *Semantic information processing* (pp. 425–432). Cambridge, MA: MIT Press.

Raja, A., & Goel, A. (2007). Introspective self-explanation in analytical agents. In A. Raja & M. T. Cox (Eds.), *Proceedings of the First International Workshop on Metareasoning in Agent-based Systems* (pp. 76–91). Collocated with AAMAS-07. Columbia, SC: IFAAMAS.

Raja, A., & Lesser, V. (2007). A framework for meta-level control in multi-agent systems. *Autonomous Agents and Multi-Agent Systems, 15*(2), 147–196.

Ram, A. (1989). *Question-driven understanding: An integrated theory of story understanding, memory and learning* (Tech. Rep. No. 710). Doctoral dissertation, Yale University, Department of Computer Science, New Haven, CT.

Ram, A., & Leake, D. (1991). Evaluation of explanatory hypotheses. In *Proceedings of the Thirteenth Annual Conference of the Cognitive Science Society* (pp. 867–871). Hillsdale, NJ: Lawrence Erlbaum.

Riesbeck, C. K., & Schank, R. C. (Eds.) (1989). *Inside case-based reasoning*. Hillsdale, NJ: Lawrence Erlbaum.

Roth-Berghofer, T., & Richter, M. M. (Eds.) (2008). Special issue on explanation. *Künstliche Intelligenz (Artificial Intelligence), 22* (2).

Roth-Berghofer, T., & Schultz, S. (Eds.) (2005). *Explanation-aware computing: Papers from the AAAI Fall Symposium* (Technical Report No. FS-05-04). Menlo Park, CA: AAAI Press.

Roth-Berghofer, T., Schultz, S., Bahls, D., & Leake, D. B. (Eds.) (2007). *Explanation-aware computing: Papers from the 2007 AAAI Workshop* (Technical Report No. WS-07–06). Menlo Park, CA: AAAI Press.

Russell, S. J., & Norvig, P. (2003). *Artificial intelligence: A modern approach* (2nd ed.). Upper Saddle River, NJ: Prentice Hall.

Russell, S. J., & Wefald, E. (1991). Principles of metareasoning. *Artificial Intelligence, 49,* 361–395.

Schank, R. C. (1986). *Explanation patterns: Understanding mechanically and creatively.* Hillsdale, NJ: Lawrence Erlbaum.

Schank, R. C., & Abelson, R. P. (1977). *Scripts, plans, goals and understanding: An inquiry into human knowledge structures.* Hillsdale, NJ: Lawrence Erlbaum.

Schank, R. C., & Riesbeck, C. (Eds.) (1981). *Inside computer understanding: Five programs plus miniatures.* Hillsdale, NJ: Lawrence Erlbaum.

Sharma, R. (2003). *Latent learning in agents.* Unpublished. (Available at http://paul.rutgers.edu/~ratis/LatentLearningiCML.pdf.)

Sloman, A. (1992). How to dispose of the free-will issue. *AISB Quarterly, 82,* 31–32.

So, R., & Sonenberg, L. (2007). Situation awareness as a form of meta-level control. In A. Raja & M. T. Cox (Eds.), *Proceedings of the First International Workshop on Metareasoning in Agent-based Systems* (pp. 61–75). Colocated with AAMAS-07. Columbia, SC: IFAAMAS.

Tolman, E. C. (1948). Cognitive maps in rats and man. *Psychological Review, 55,* 189–208.

Tulving, E. (1972). Episodic and semantic memory. In E. Tulving & W. Donaldson (Eds.), *Organization of memory* (pp. 381–403). New York: Academic Press.

Veloso, M. M. (1994). *Planning and learning by analogical reasoning.* Berlin: Springer.

Veloso, M., Carbonell, J. G., Perez, A., Borrajo, D., Fink, E., & Blythe, J. (1995). Integrating planning and learning: The PRODIGY architecture. *Journal of Theoretical and Experimental Artificial Intelligence, 7*(1), 81–120.

Zilberstein, S. (1993). *Operational rationality through compilation of anytime algorithms.* Unpublished doctoral dissertation, University of California at Berkeley.

Zilberstein, S., & Russell, S. J. (1996). Optimal composition of real-time systems. *Artificial Intelligence, 82*(1–2), 181–213.

10 Metareasoning for Self-Adaptation in Intelligent Agents

Ashok K. Goel and Joshua Jones

It is generally agreed in artificial intelligence (AI) that the capability of metareasoning is essential for achieving human-level intelligence (e.g., Brachman, 2002; Minsky, Singh, & Sloman, 2004). Past AI research has shown that metareasoning is useful for many tasks, including planning about reasoning (Cox & Ram, 1999; Wilensky, 1981), control of reasoning (Davis, 1980; Hansen & Zilberstein, 2001; Hayes-Roth & Larsson 1996; Punch, Goel, & Brown, 1995; Raja & Lesser, 2007; Stefik, 1981), bounding reasoning (Horvitz, 2001; Horvitz, Cooper, & Heckerman, 1989; Russell, 1991), revision of beliefs (Doyle, 1979), revision of reasoning processes (Leake, 1996; Murdock & Goel, 2008; Stroulia & Goel, 1995), refinement of knowledge indices (Fox & Leake, 2001), self-explanation (Cox & Ram, 1999; Goel & Murdock, 1996), and guidance of situated learning (Anderson et al., 2006; Ulam, Jones, & Goel, 2008). Cox (2005) provides a useful review of some AI research on metareasoning.

Our work on metareasoning since the early 1990s has focused on self-adaptation in intelligent agents (e.g., Murdock & Goel, 2001a,b, 2003; Stroulia & Goel, 1996, 1997). We adopt a design stance toward self-adaptation in intelligent agents. In particular, we view an intelligent agent as an abstract information-processing device with a design that is intended to achieve specific functions. Self-adaptation in an intelligent agent then means that the intelligent agent autonomously modifies elements in its design to either better achieve a function or achieve a new function. This characterization covers a large range of self-adaptation situations. First, self-adaptations to an agent's design may be retrospective (i.e., when the agent fails to achieve the desired function; Birnbaum et al., 1990; Leake, 1996; Stroulia & Goel, 1995, 1999), or proactive (i.e., when the agent is asked to deliver a new behavior; Murdock & Goel, 2008). Second, adaptations may be to the deliberative element in the agent design (Birnbaum et al., 1990; Leake, 1996; Murdock & Goel, 2008; Stroulia & Goel, 1995), to the reactive element (Stroulia & Goel, 1999), or both. Third, adaptations to the deliberative element may be modifications to its reasoning process (i.e., to its task structure, selection of methods, or control of reasoning; e.g., Birnbaum et al., 1990; Murdock & Goel, 2008; Stroulia & Goel, 1995), to its domain knowledge (i.e., the content, representation, and organization of its knowledge [e.g., Jones & Goel, 2007; Leake, 1996]), or both.

A core and long-standing problem in self-adaptation is that of credit (or blame) assignment (Minsky, 1961; Samuel, 1959). It is useful to distinguish between two kinds of credit assignment problems: temporal and structural. In temporal credit assignment, given a sequence of many actions by an agent that leads to a failure, the task is to identify the action(s) responsible for the failure. Reinforcement learning is one method for addressing the temporal credit assignment problem (Sutton & Barto, 1998). In structural credit assignment, given an agent composed of many knowledge and reasoning elements that fails to achieve a goal, the task is to identify the element(s) responsible for the failure. Metareasoning for self-adaptation typically addresses the problem of structural credit assignment, though it can also be used to guide reinforcement learning (Anderson et al., 2006; Ulam, Jones, & Goel, 2008). It is also useful to note the close relationship between agent self-adaptation and agent learning: the use of metareasoning for self-adaptation views learning as a deliberative, knowledge-based process of self-diagnosis and self-repair. In this sense, research on self-adaptation through metareasoning can be viewed as a bridge between knowledge-based AI and machine learning.

Our past work on structural credit assignment over reasoning processes has investigated the hypothesis that a declarative self-model that captures the teleology of the agent's design (i.e., the agent's functions in the external world and the internal causal mechanisms that result in the achievement of the functions) may enable localization, if not also identification, of the elements in the reasoning process responsible for a given behavior. Thus, the core theme of our previous work on metareasoning for self-adaptation in intelligent agents has been that teleology is a central organizing principle of self-adaptation of reasoning processes. In recent work, we have explored the use of metareasoning for self-adaptation of domain knowledge. Since classification is a ubiquitous task in AI, we have focused on the problem of using metaknowledge for repairing classification knowledge when the classifier supplies an incorrect class label. In this chapter, we first briefly summarize our previous work on self-adaptation of reasoning processes and then describe our recent work on self-adaptation of domain knowledge.

An Example from Game-Playing Software Agents

To make the problem concrete, consider an example from the turn-based strategy game called FreeCiv (www.freeciv.org), an open-source variant of a class of Civilization games with similar properties. A human player typically plays the game against multiple software agents. FreeCiv offers a challenging domain for studying the use of metareasoning for self-adaptation in a software agent. The game is only partially observable and nondeterministic. Also, the game has a huge state space, making it computationally infeasible to learn to play well without substantial decomposition of the game-playing task. However, a neat decomposition of the game-playing task into a hierarchical task structure is impossible too, because of complex interactions among multiple subtasks. In one single turn, for example, a software agent designed to play FreeCiv may need to address several interacting tasks such as managing existing cities, managing offensive and defensive units, exploring the world, and building new cities. Building new cities on the game map is a critical action because each city produces resources on subsequent turns that can then be used by the agent to further advance its civilization. The quantity of resources produced by a city on each turn is based on various factors including the terrain and special resources surrounding the city's location on the map and the skill with which the city's operations are managed. So the question becomes: How might a game-playing software agent use metareasoning to adapt its reasoning processes based on failures in its game-playing experiences? A closely related question is: How may the agent use metareasoning to adapt its domain knowledge when its predictions about the game turn out to be incorrect?

Self-Adaptation of Reasoning Processes

When our game-playing software agent fails in some task in playing FreeCiv, then the agent may want to reason about its own design that led to the failure. This metareasoning requires that the agent have a representation of the teleology of its design. We have developed a computational architecture called the Task-Method-Knowledge model that captures the teleology of the agent design at multiple levels of aggregation and abstraction (Murdock & Goel, 2001a,b, 2003) and a corresponding Task-Method-Knowledge Language (TMKL) for specifying the TMK model in a declarative form (Murdock & Goel, 2008). Figure 10.1 illustrates the tasks (rectangles) and methods (rounded rectangles) in a small portion of the TMK model for a software agent that plays the FreeCiv game.

Briefly, TMK models of designs of intelligent agents are expressed in terms of tasks, methods, and knowledge. A *task* describes the designer's intent in terms of a computational goal of producing a specific result. A *method* is a unit of computation that produces a result in a specified manner. A method decomposes a task into subtasks, specifies the ordering among the subtasks, and is represented as a finite state machine. This decomposition may go on up to a primitive level of abstraction at which either the task corresponds to an action in the game, or domain knowledge about the game directly accomplishes the task. The *knowledge* portion of the TMK model describes the concepts and relations that tasks and methods in the model can use and affect as well as logical axioms and other inferencing information involving those concepts and relations. Hoang, Lee-Urban, and Muñoz-Avila (2005) have compared TMKL

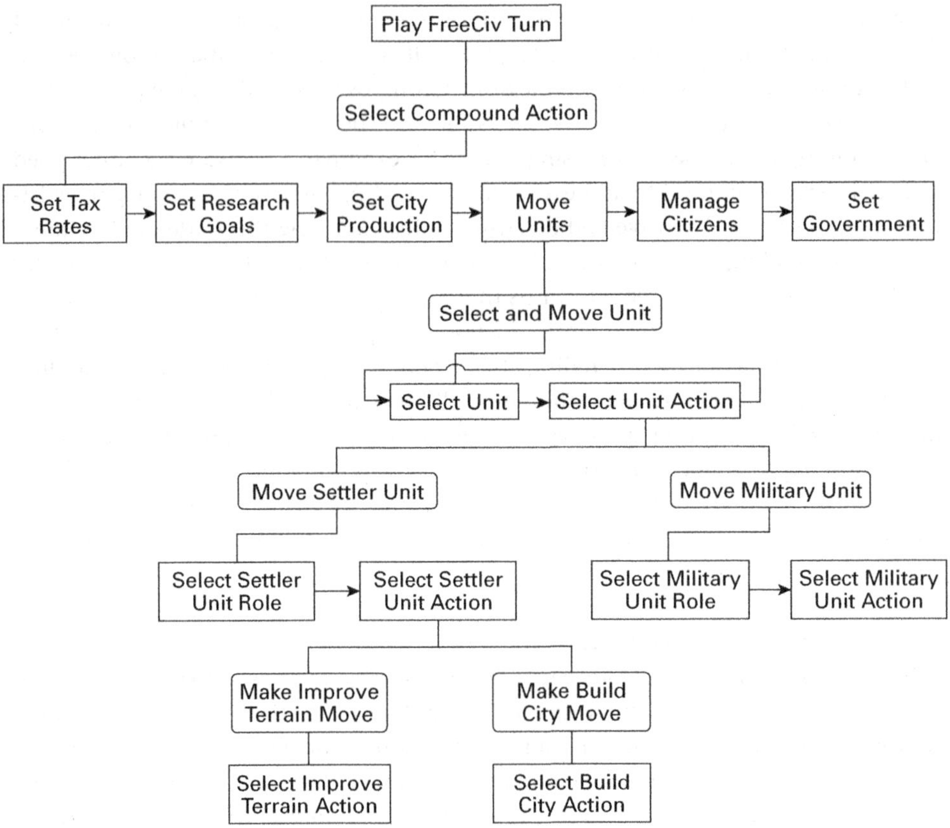

Figure 10.1
A Task-Method-Knowledge model of a small portion of a software agent that plays the FreeCiv game. Rectangles indicate tasks; rounded rectangles indicate methods.

with hierarchical task networks (HTNs; Erol, Hendler, & Nau, 1994) for designing game-playing agents. They found that since TMKL enables explicit representation of subgoals, multiple plans for achieving a goal, and other control structures, TMKL is more expressive than HTN, but that a translation from one to the other is always possible.

Given a TMK model of a portion of the game-playing agent, consider what may happen when introspective monitoring in the REM metareasoning system (Murdock & Goel, 2008) detects that the agent has met some failure due to an error in managing its cities and units in a given turn. At this point, REM would use the TMK model of the agent, together with the trace of processing that led to the failure, to diagnose the causes of the error. While the trace of processing provides REM with an account of the actual processing that led to the failure, the TMK model provides an account of the desired processing. REM uses these two accounts and information about the specific error to identify the causes for the error. If REM succeeds in generating a hypothesis about the cause for the error at the level of some nonprimitive task or method, then it uses information about the specific error and its cause to access an abstract adaptation plan and instantiates this plan in the context of the cause of the error. Murdock and Goel (2001a,b, 2003, 2008) provide details of this process, including results of experimental studies with it.

Adaptation of Domain Knowledge

In some situations, the above process of diagnosis may lead to the identification of some primitive task in the TMK model as a cause of the agent's failure. For example, given the TMK model illustrated in figure 10.1, the metareasoner may identify the *Select Build City Action* primitive task as the cause of failure, based on an analysis of the goals encoded in the model in conjunction with a trace of processing that led to the failure. We address this problem by providing the agent not only with a model of its own reasoning but also of the domain knowledge used in that reasoning. Then, when a primitive task is identified as responsible for some failure in the reasoning, self-diagnosis can operate over the model of the knowledge used by that primitive task and enable the repair of that knowledge. In the work described here, we have not yet actually implemented the integration of the self-diagnosis and repair of knowledge with the self-diagnosis of reasoning provided by REM. Instead, we have experimented with the *Select Build City Action* classifier operating independently and interacting directly with the environment. However, our intent is that this procedure could be integrated with a system such as REM to form a unified metareasoning system implementing self-diagnosis and repair over both object-level process and knowledge.

The domain knowledge used in *Select Build City Action* is classification knowledge: The agent determines if the tile that a settler unit currently occupies is a good location in which to build a city (classifies the location), and if so instructs the unit to build a city. If not, the unit will instead be moved. Figure 10.2 illustrates a knowledge hierarchy for the *Select Build City Action* task used by our FreeCiv game-playing agent. This classification task is an instance of classification problems that can be decomposed into a hierarchical set of smaller classification problems; alternatively, problems in which features describing the world are progressively aggregated and abstracted into higher-level abstractions until a class label is produced at the root node. This subclass of classification problems are recognized as capturing a common pattern of classification (Bylander, Johnson, & Goel, 1991; Goel & Bylander, 1989; Russell, 1988). We will call this classification task *compositional classification*, and the hierarchy of abstractions an *abstraction network*.

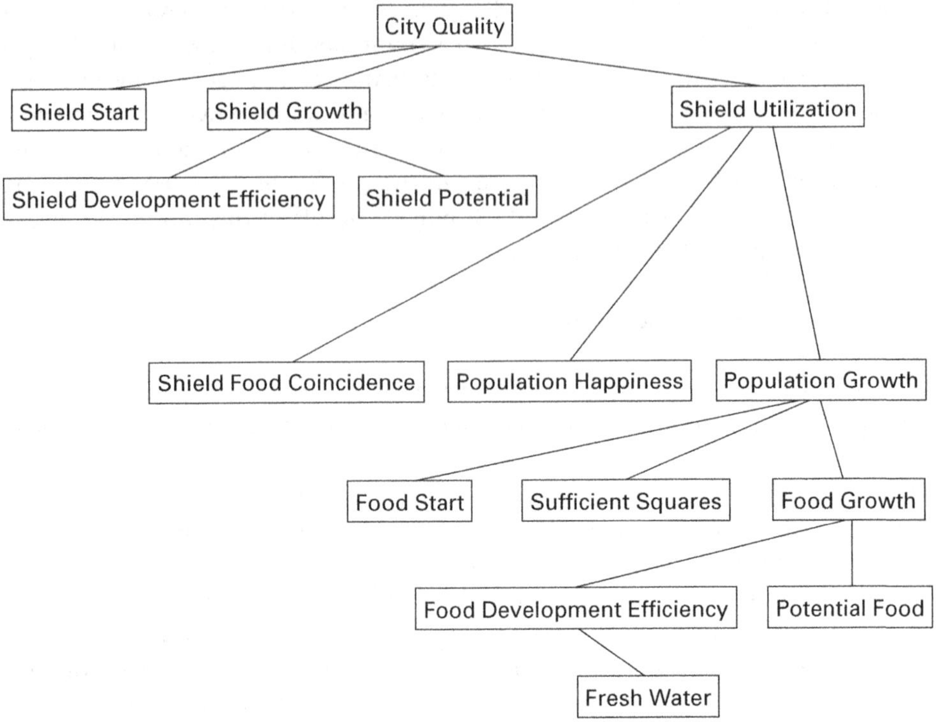

Figure 10.2
A game-playing agent's abstraction network for the classification of city quality in FreeCiv.

We consider the problem of retrospective adaptation of the content of the intermediate abstractions in the abstraction network (and *not* its structure) when the classifier makes an incorrect classification. Note that once again structural credit assignment becomes a core problem: given the error at the root node, the structural credit assignment problem now is to identify the intermediate abstractions in the abstraction network responsible for the error. Note also that the hypothesis about using teleological knowledge that works so well for adapting reasoning processes is not useful in this setting because there is no complex reasoning process to model here. Instead, we explore an alternative hypothesis for using metareasoning for self-adaptation of domain knowledge: If the semantics of the domain concepts that form the intermediate abstractions in the hierarchy can be grounded in predictions about percepts in the world, then metaknowledge in the form of verification procedures associated with those domain concepts is useful for addressing the structural credit assignment problem. Metareasoning can then use verification procedures associated with domain concepts to verify the predictions made by those concepts. In the case of compositional classification, this means that intermediate abstractions in the abstraction network are chosen such that each abstraction corresponds to a prediction about percepts in the world, metaknowledge comes in the form of verification procedures associated with the abstractions, and metareasoning invokes the appropriate verification procedures to perform structural credit assignment and then adapt the abstractions. The verification procedures explicitly encode the grounding of intermediate abstractions in percepts from the environment. Below we illustrate, formalize, and evaluate these ideas, and briefly discuss the implications of this scheme for a metareasoning architecture.

Compositional Classification

To more formally describe compositional classification, let T be a discrete random variable representing the class label. Let $S = \{s{:}s$ is empirically determinable and $h[T] > h[T|s]\}$, where $h[x]$ denotes the entropy of x. S is a set of discrete random variables that have nonzero mutual information with the class label and are *empirically determinable*, meaning that there is some way to interact with the environment to determine which value has been taken by each member of S. Each member s of S represents a related set of equivalence classes, where each value taken by s is a unique equivalence class. In the case of our running FreeCiv example, things like the future population growth of the potential city and the amount of food provided by terrain squares around the city location constitute S. A task instance is generated by jointly sampling the variables in $S \cup T$. In FreeCiv, the game engine handles this for us by randomly generating a game map and managing game dynamics that govern the relationships among the variables in S.

Empirical determinability captures the notion of perceptual grounding of concepts, indicating that each equivalence class represents some verifiable statement about the world. In the simplest case, empirical determinability means that the value taken by the variable in a given task instance is directly observable at some later time after classification has occurred. In general, some experiment may need to be performed in order to observe the value of some $s \in S$. In FreeCiv, all of the values can be directly observed, though some only after classification has occurred. This is because in order to be useful, the prediction of city resource production must be made before the city is actually constructed and its resource production rate and the values of the intermediate nodes in the hierarchy can be observed. However, we can obtain the true values later in order to perform self-diagnosis over the knowledge structure used for the classification. We call the problem of predicting T in such a setting *compositional classification*. In order to make such predictions, our agent will make use of a structured knowledge representation called an *abstraction network*, defined in the next section. This representation will capture knowledge about the relationships between variables in S. Knowledge repair will be required if the distributions $P(s|K)$, $s \in S \cup T$, $K \subseteq S$ are not always accurately known by the agent, but must instead be inferred from experience.

Knowledge Representation

Here we formally define the knowledge representation used at the object level for the compositional classification task. This representation is annotated with metaknowledge used by metalevel reasoning process for self-diagnosis. We call this diagnostic self-knowledge *empirical verification procedures*, described in more detail below.

The knowledge structure contains a node for each $s \in S \cup T$. These nodes are connected in a hierarchy reflecting direct dependence relationships organized according to background knowledge. Each node will handle the subproblem of predicting the value of the variable with which it is associated given the values of its children.

Definition 10.1 *A* supervised classification learner *(SCL) is a tuple <I,O,F,U>, where I is a set of input strings (input space), O is a set of output symbols (output space), F is a function from I to O, and U is a function from (i,o): $i \in I, o \in O$ to the set of SCLs that share the same input and output spaces I and O.*

Definition 10.2 *An* empirical verification procedure *(EVP) is a tuple <E,O> where O is a set of output symbols (output space) and E is an arbitrary, possibly branching sequence of actions in the environment and observations from the environment concluding with the selection of an $o \in O$.*

Any output space *O* of an empirical verification procedure is an empirically determinable set of equivalence classes. So, a set of equivalence classes is empirically determinable if an empirical verification procedure can be defined with an output space equal to that set of classes.

Definition 10.3 *An* abstraction network *(AN) is a tuple <N,O,L,P>, where N is a (possibly empty) set of ANs, O is a set of output symbols, L is an SCL, and P is an empirical verification procedure. Let I be the set of strings that can be formed by imposing a fixed order on the members of N and choosing exactly one output symbol from each $n \in N$ according to this order. The SCL L has input space I and output space O, and the empirical verification procedure P has output space O.*

When *N* is empty, *L* is trivial and has no use because the input space is empty. In these cases (the leaves of the AN), a value determination must always be made by invoking *P*. Thus, EVP execution must be possible before classification in the case of AN leaves, although it is never possible until some time after classification for nonleaf nodes.

Object-Level Reasoning

In a given task instance, the values of the leaf nodes are fixed by observation. Each node with fixed inputs then produces its prediction. This is repeated until the value of the class label is predicted by the root of the hierarchy (see table 10.1).

Table 10.1
Abstraction network object-level reasoning procedure

begin AN-reasoning(a)

1. If $a.N = \varnothing$, execute $a.P$ and return the result.
2. Else, recursively execute this procedure for each $n \in N$ to generate an input string i for $a.L$, then return $a.L.F(i)$ and store this value and i for the purpose of the self-diagnosis procedure (called *a.last_value* and *a.last_input* below).

end

Table 10.2
Abstraction network metalevel reasoning procedure

begin AN-diagnose-and-repair(a)

1. If $a.P$ = *a.last_value* then return *true*.
2. $\forall n \in a.N$, call AN-diagnose-and-repair(n). If $\exists n \in a.N$ s.t. AN-diagnose-and-repair(n) = *false* then return *false*.
3. *a.L ← a.L.U(a.last_input, a.P)*, return *false*.

end

Metalevel Reasoning

At some time after classification, the true value of the class label is obtained by the monitoring process. If the value produced by object-level reasoning was correct, no further action is taken. If the value is found to be incorrect, the self-diagnosis and repair procedure shown in table 10.2 is followed, operating over knowledge used at the object level.

It should be noted that not all supervised classification learners can operate properly under this diagnosis and repair procedure—specifically, learners that require problem instances to be drawn from a stationary distribution require an alternative procedure that inspects each AN node for each repair episode. However, in situations where this more selective diagnosis procedure *can* be used, it is parsimonious in terms of requiring the fewest EVP executions to diagnose a failure. This procedure has a base case when the leaves are reached, as their true values were obtained before classification and thus cannot be found to be incorrect.

Notice that an AN abstracts in two ways. One is apparent in the object-level reasoning procedure; information is progressively lost at each node in the hierarchy during reasoning as information is aggregated into equivalence classes, so abstraction takes place during inference. The second source of abstraction becomes clear in the self-diagnosis and repair procedure. The EVPs explicitly encode a process of abstraction from raw state to the equivalence classes produced at nodes in the AN.

FreeCiv Experiments

We have implemented the AN theory of adaptation of classification knowledge in a computer program called Augur. Augur runs in the FreeCiv domain using the AN depicted in figure 10.2. This AN was used to produce outputs from a set containing three values, corresponding to poor, moderate, and good city resource production. These values indicate predictions about the resource production expected from a city built on a considered map location. Specifically, the values correspond to an expected degree and direction of deviation from a logarithmic baseline resource production function that was manually tuned to reflect roughly average city resource production. Each of the intermediate nodes in the AN has an output set consisting of five values in this experiment. The empirical verification procedures simply discretize observed game features. We placed a very simple rote learner within each node in the AN. These simple learners offer no generalization power of their own, so this experiment relies on the power of the AN representation itself rather than on powerful learners within nodes. The content of each rote learner was initialized arbitrarily in a way that was known to be incorrect in some cases for each of the learners. Because we expect resource production from cities built on various kinds of map locations to potentially differ qualitatively as games progress, we trained three separate AN-based learners with one of each learning to make predictions about resource production in the early, middle, or late stages of the game. Results reported are cumulative across all three learners of the appropriate type.

To test our self-diagnosis and self-repair procedure, we ran 60 independent trials, each consisting of a sequence of 49 games played by Augur using the AN of figure 10.2. Results reported in this section are an average across these trials. Each game played used a separate randomly generated map, with no opponents. Augur always builds a city on the first occupied square, after making an estimate of the square's quality. Building in the first randomly generated occupied square ensures that Augur will have opportunities to test its knowledge in a variety of states. We evaluated the result of Augur's self-diagnosis and self-repair procedure by comparing Augur's average performance during the first seven games to the average performance during the last seven games. Making this comparison, we observed an average 52 percent decrease in the error rate of the agent. This improvement in performance is evidence that the metalevel process has been successful in repairing faulty knowledge at the object level. We have also experimented with the AN self-diagnosis and self-repair procedure in other domains such as prediction of the direction of the Dow Jones Index (Jones & Goel, 2007) and in synthetic settings with similarly positive results.

Related Research

As we mentioned in the introduction, the use of metareasoning for self-adaptation in intelligent agents is related to agent learning: Our work on metareasoning for self-adaptation views learning as a deliberative problem-solving activity. In particular, our work on the use of metareasoning for structural credit assignment in compositional classification is related to past work on tree-structured bias (TSB) (Russell, 1988; Tadepalli & Russell, 1998). However, while TSB research relies on carefully constructed queries to the environment to learn the functions at internal nodes in a classification hierarchy, in our work, EVPs encode the metaknowledge used in the self-diagnostic procedure. That is, rather than using explicitly represented metaknowledge to perform self-diagnosis, TSB has a fixed training procedure that implicitly relies on a given type of query. This procedure can be seen as requiring a very specific kind of empirical verifiability for internal nodes—thus forcing a particular (and rather complex) form on the EVPs that a designer would write if applying TSB procedures within the AN framework. In the work described here, we take the stance that, in general, a broader set of queries to the environment may be possible. If this is the case, it will be more efficient to make use of the observations that most directly allow us to determine the value of an internal node when learning. In fact, the motivating example given by Tadepalli and Russell (1988), concerning a credit-card domain, appears clearly to have a strong kind of direct empirical verifiability at internal nodes that could be exploited by ANs using very simple EVPs. The explicit representation of EVPs is another major difference between our work on ANs and past research on TSB. EVPs represent an abstraction from observable quantities to concepts used in an AN. Since the grounding of concepts in observable quantities is explicitly represented, it becomes fair game to be operated on during adaptation. It also means that we are able to adapt intermediate concepts themselves according to their functional roles—recognizing that intermediate concepts are not fixed by the environment, but that they are constructs that exist in order to allow for correct overall classification.

It is also interesting to note the relationship of our work with two other techniques described in this volume. At a high level, REM, the metacognitive loop (MCL) (chap. 12), GRAVA (chap. 7), and Augur all use an agent's understanding of itself, and an agent's expectations of its own performance, to detect failures and diagnose faults. REM and MCL provide overarching frameworks for metareasoning that include not only diagnosis and repair of deliberative reasoning, but also guidance of situated learning (Anderson et al., 2006; Ulam, Jones, & Goel, 2008). GRAVA and Augur, on the other hand, focus on adaptation of domain knowledge. Whereas GRAVA is more concerned with selection and configuration of domain models, Augur focuses on diagnosis and repair of domain knowledge.

Relationship to the Canonical Metareasoning Architecture

Figure 1.2 (Cox & Raja, this vol., chap. 1) illustrates a canonical architecture for metareasoning. On one hand, our past and current work on self-adaptation of an agent's *reasoning processes* fits well with this architecture; we can imagine the teleological model of the agent's deliberative reasoning element and the metareasoner using that teleological knowledge for structural credit assignment over the deliberative reasoning processes as residing in the metareasoning element in the canonical architecture.

Of course, the architecture in figure 1.2 is an idealized abstraction. Our work suggests several elaborations. First, the canonical architecture implies that an "object-level" reasoning element mediates between the "ground-level" and the "metalevel" elements. However, our work on structural credit assignment and self-adaptation in reactive control agents (Stroulia & Goel, 1999) directly applies metareasoning over reactive control without any intermediate object-level element for deliberative reasoning. In principle, we see no particular reason why deliberative reasoning must necessarily mediate between "doing" and metareasoning. Second, the canonical architecture implies that the ground, object, and metalevels are distinct and separate. However, our work on using metareasoning for guiding reinforcement learning (Ulam, Jones, & Goel, 2008) views the three levels as substantially overlapping. Again, in principle, we see no particular reason for a complete separation between the ground, object, and metalevels. Third, our current work described in this chapter suggests that some of the actions at the ground level may be in service of verifying predictions made by semantics of the domain knowledge at the object level. Thus, in this work, metareasoning uses metaknowledge of the relation between knowledge used at the object level and predictions about percepts accessible from the ground level. Finally, this work suggests that metaknowledge useful for adapting domain knowledge may be distributed over the domain concepts in the object level, and not necessarily confined to the metalevel as in the canonical architecture.

Conclusions

In this chapter, we described a scheme for using metareasoning in intelligent agents for self-adaptation of domain knowledge. In particular, we considered retrospective adaptation of the content of intermediate abstractions in an abstraction network used for compositional classification when the classifier makes an incorrect classification. We showed that if the intermediate abstractions in the abstraction network are organized such that each abstraction corresponds to a prediction about a percept in the world, then metaknowledge comes in the form of verification procedures associated with the abstractions, and metareasoning invokes the appropriate verification procedures in order to first perform structural credit assignment and then adapt the abstractions. This lends credence to our hypothesis about the use of metareasoning for self-adaptation of domain knowledge; if the semantics of domain concepts can be grounded in predictions about percepts in the world, then metaknowledge in the form of verification procedures associated with the domain concepts is useful for addressing the structural credit assignment problem.

This result can be taken as prescriptive by designers of AI agents, suggesting that whenever possible, the domain concepts used by agent should be grounded in the agent's perceptions. While the computational advantages of the grounding of domain knowledge in the agent's perceptions for deliberative reasoning have been long understood, our work indicates that this grounding also offers computational benefits for metareasoning-based adaptation of the domain knowledge used by deliberative reasoning.

Acknowledgments

This research is supported by an NSF (SoD) Grant (0613744) on "Teleological Reasoning in Adaptive Software Design."

References

Anderson, M. L., Oates, T., Chong, W., & Perlis, D. (2006). The metacognitive loop I: Enhancing reinforcement learning with metacognitive monitoring and control for improved perturbation tolerance. *Journal of Experimental & Theoretical Artificial Intelligence, 18*(3), 387–411.

Birnbaum, L., Collins, G., Freed, M., & Krulwich, B. (1990). Model-based diagnosis of planning failures. In *Proceedings of the 8th National Conference on Artificial Intelligence* (pp. 318–323). Menlo Park, California: AAAI Press.

Brachman, R. J. (2002). Systems that know what they're doing. *IEEE Intelligent Systems, 17*(6), 67–71.

Bylander, T., Johnson, T. R., & Goel, A. K. (1991). Structured matching: a task-specific technique for making decisions. *Knowledge Acquisition, 3*(1), 1–20.

Cox, M. T., & Ram, A. (1999). Introspective multistrategy learning: On the construction of learning strategies. *Artificial Intelligence, 112*(1–2), 1–55.

Cox, M. T. (2005). Metacognition in computation: A selected research review. *Artificial Intelligence, 169*(2), 104–141.

Davis, R. (1980). Meta-rules: Reasoning about control. *Artificial Intelligence, 15*(3), 179–222.

Doyle, J. (1979). A truth maintenance system. *Artificial Intelligence, 12*(3), 231–272.

Erol, K., Hendler, J., & Nau, D. S. (1994). HTN planning: Complexity and expressivity. *Proceedings of the Twelfth National Conference on Artificial Intelligence (AAAI-94)*, vol. 2 (pp. 1123–1128). Menlo Park, CA: AAAI Press/MIT Press.

Fox, S., & Leake, D. (2001). Introspective reasoning for index refinement in case-based reasoning. *Journal of Experimental & Theoretical Artificial Intelligence, 13*(1), 63–88.

Goel, A. K., & Bylander, T. (1989). Computational feasibility of structured matching. *IEEE Transactions of Pattern Matching and Machine Intelligence, 11*(2), 1312–1361.

Goel, A. K., & Murdock, J. W. (1996). Meta-cases: Explaining case-based reasoning. *Proceedings of the Third European Workshop on Case-Based Reasoning* (pp. 150–163). Berlin: Springer.

Hansen, E. A., & Zilberstein, S. (2001). Monitoring and control of anytime algorithms: A dynamic programming approach. *Artificial Intelligence, 126*(1–2), 139–157.

Hayes-Roth, B., & Larsson, J. E. (1996). A domain-specific software architecture for a class of intelligent patient monitoring systems. *Journal of Experimental & Theoretical Artificial Intelligence, 8*(2), 149–171.

Hoang, H., Lee-Urban, S., & Muñoz-Avila, H. (2005). Hierarchical plan representations for encoding strategic game AI. In R. M. Young & J. E. Laird (Eds.), *Artificial Intelligence and Interactive Digital Entertainment* (pp. 63–68). Menlo Park, CA: AAAI Press.

Horvitz, E. J., Cooper, G. F., & Heckerman, D. E. (1989). Reflection and action under scarce resources: Theoretical principles and empirical study. In *Proceedings of the Eleventh International Joint Conference on Artificial Intelligence (IJCAI-89)* (pp. 1121–1127). San Francisco: Morgan Kaufmann.

Horvitz, E. (2001). Principles and applications of continual computation. *Artificial Intelligence, 126*(1–2), 159–196.

Jones, J., & Goel, A. K. (2007). Structural credit assignment in hierarchical classification. In *Proceedings of the International Conference on AI* (pp. 378–384). Athens, GA: Computer Science Research, Education and Applications (CSREA) Press.

Leake, D. B. (1996). Experience, introspection and expertise: Learning to refine the case-based reasoning process. *Journal of Experimental & Theoretical Artificial Intelligence, 8*(3–4), 319–339.

Minsky, M. (1961). Steps Toward Artificial Intelligence. In E. A. Feigenbaum & J. Feldman (Eds.), *Computers and thought* (pp. 406–450). New York: McGraw Hill.

Minsky, M., Singh, P., & Sloman, A. (2004). The St. Thomas common sense symposium: Designing architectures for human-level intelligence. *AI Magazine, 25*(2), 113–124.

Murdock, J. W., & Goel, A. K. (2001a). Meta-case-based reasoning: Use of functional models to adapt case-based agents. In *Proceedings of the 4th International Conference on Case-Based Reasoning (pp. 407–421),* Berlin: Springer-Verlag.

Murdock, J. W., & Goel, A. K. (2001b). Learning about constraints by reflection. In *Proceedings of the 14th Biennial Conference of Canadian AI Society* (pp. 131–140). Berlin: Springer-Verlag.

Murdock, J. W., & Goel, A. K. (2003). Localizing planning with functional process models. In E. Giunchiglia, N. Muscettola, & D. S. Nau (Eds.), *Proceedings of the Thirteenth International Conference on Automated Planning and Scheduling* (pp. 73–81). Menlo Park, CA: AAAI Press.

Murdock, J. W., & Goel, A. K. (2008). Meta-case-based reasoning: Self-improvement through self-understanding. *Journal of Experimental & Theoretical Artificial Intelligence, 20*(1), 1–36.

Punch, W., Goel, A. K., & Brown, D. (1995). A knowledge-based selection mechanism for strategic control with application in design, assembly, and planning. *International Journal of Artificial Intelligence Tools, 4*(3), 323–348.

Raja, A., & Lesser, V. (2007). A framework for meta-level control in multi-agent systems. *Autonomous Agents and Multi-Agent Systems, 15*(2), 147–196.

Russell, S. (1988). Tree-structured bias. In *Proceedings of the Seventh National Conference on Artificial Intelligence (AAAI-88)* (pp. 641–645). Menlo Park, CA: AAAI Press.

Russell, S. (1991). Principles of metareasoning. *Artificial Intelligence, 49*(1–3), 361–395.

Samuel, A. (1959). Some studies in machine learning using the game of checkers. *IBM Journal, 3*(3), 210–229.

Stefik, M. (1981). Planning and meta-planning (Molgen: Part 2). *Artificial Intelligence, 16*(2), 141–170.

Stroulia, E., & Goel, A. K. (1995). Functional representation and reasoning in reflective systems. *Journal of Applied Intelligence, Special Issue on Functional Reasoning, 9*(1), 101–124.

Stroulia, E., & Goel, A. K. (1996). A model-based approach to blame assignment: Revising the reasoning steps of problem solvers. In *Proceedings of the Thirteenth National Conference on Artificial Intelligence (AAAI-96)* (pp. 959–964). Menlo Park, CA: AAAI Press.

Stroulia, E., & Goel, A. K. (1997). Redesigning a problem-solver's operations to improve solution quality. In *Proceedings of the Fifth International Conference on Artificial Intelligence (IJCAI-97)* (pp. 562–567). San Francisco: Morgan Kaufmann.

Stroulia, E., & Goel, A. K. (1999). Evaluating PSMs in evolutionary design: The autognostic experiments. *International Journal of Human-Computer Studies, 51*(4), 825–847.

Sutton, R., & Barto, A. (1998). *Reinforcement learning: An introduction.* Cambridge, MA: MIT Press.

Tadepalli, P., & Russell, S. (1998). Learning from examples and membership queries with structured determinations. *Machine Learning, 32*(3), 245–295.

Ulam, P., Jones, J., & Goel, A. K. (2008). Combining model-based metareasoning and reinforcement learning for adapting game-playing agents. In *Proceedings of the Fourth AAAI Conference on AI in Interactive Digital Entertainment* (pp. 132–137). Menlo Park, CA: AAAI Press.

Wilensky, R. (1981). Meta-planning: Representing and using knowledge about planning in problem solving and natural language understanding. *Cognitive Science, 5*(3), 197–234.

11 Using Introspective Reasoning to Improve CBR System Performance

Josep Lluís Arcos, Oğuz Mülâyim, David B. Leake

When AI technologies are applied to real-world problems, it is often difficult for developers to anticipate all possible eventualities. Especially in long-lived systems, changing circumstances may require changes not only to domain knowledge but also to the reasoning process that brings it to bear. This requires *introspective reasoning*, metareasoning by a system about its own internal reasoning processes. This chapter investigates applying introspective reasoning to improve the performance of a case-based reasoning system, by guiding learning to improve how a case-based reasoning system applies its cases.

Case-based reasoning (CBR) is a problem-solving methodology that exploits prior experiences when solving new problems, retrieving relevantly similar cases and adapting them to fit new needs (for an overview and survey, see Mantaras et al., 2005). Many CBR systems store each newly solved problem and its solution as a new case for future use, enabling them to continuously improve their case knowledge. Nevertheless, the success of a CBR system depends not only on its cases, but also on its ability to use those cases appropriately in new situations, which depends on factors such as the system's similarity measure and the case adaptation mechanism. Consequently, it is desirable to enable CBR systems to improve the knowledge and processes by which they bring their cases to bear.

Metareasoning techniques provide a promising basis for self-improving systems (see Anderson & Oates, 2007, or Cox, 2005, for recent reviews). As described by Cox and Raja (this vol., chap. 1), the metareasoning approach incorporates a metareasoning layer, with monitoring and control capabilities over the reasoning process, to adjust that reasoning process as needed. Introspective learning techniques have used *self-models* as a way to determine when, what, and how to improve the reasoning of systems. Here we focus on how a self-model may be exploited; an open challenge is how to provide capabilities for extending and refining self-models that are themselves imperfect or incomplete (Leake & Wilson, 2008).

Previous research on introspective CBR has shown that metareasoning can enable a CBR system to learn by refining its own reasoning process. That work has tended to apply the introspective approach only to a single aspect of the CBR system, for example, to adjust the indices used for retrieval. This chapter presents research on developing an introspective reasoning model enabling CBR systems to autonomously learn to improve multiple facets of their reasoning processes.

The remainder of this chapter describes an approach in which an introspective reasoner monitors the CBR process with the goal of adjusting the retrieval and reuse strategies of the system to improve solution quality. Novel aspects of this approach, compared to previous work on introspective reasoning for CBR, include that it applies a unified model for improving the two main stages of the CBR process, that a single failure may prompt multiple forms of learning, and that it performs internal tests to empirically assess the value of changes proposed by the introspective reasoner, to determine which ones should be retained.

The next section discusses previous work on introspective learning for case-based reasoning. The following section presents a detailed description of our approach and its implementation. The approach has been evaluated on problems from a fielded industrial application for design of pollution control equipment, for which we provide results in the next section. Before concluding the chapter, we put our model into context with respect to the metareasoning models discussed in chapter 1 of this volume. In the last section we present our conclusions and directions for future research.

Related Work

Birnbaum et al. (1991) first proposed the use of self-models within case-based reasoning. Work by Cox and Ram (1999) develops a set of general approaches to introspective reasoning and learning that automatically select the appropriate learning algorithms when reasoning failures arise. Their work defines a taxonomy of causes of reasoning failures and proposes a taxonomy of learning goals, used for analyzing the traces of reasoning failures and responding to them. Here case-based reasoning is a vehicle for supporting introspective reasoning: CBR is used to explain reasoning failures and generate learning goals.

A number of studies apply introspective approaches to improve the performance of CBR systems. Leake (1996) identifies the knowledge sources a CBR system uses in its reasoning process and the required self-knowledge about these sources, and provides examples of refinement of retrieval knowledge using model-based reasoning and of acquisition of adaptation knowledge by search plans. Fox and Leake (2001) developed a system inspired by the Birnbaum et al. proposal to refine index selection for case-based reasoners. Fox and Leake's work develops a declarative model for describing the expectations for correct reasoning behavior, and applies that model to detect and diagnose reasoning failures. When the introspective reasoner is able to identify the feature that caused the failure, the system's memory is reindexed, resulting in significant performance improvement. The DIAL system (Leake et al., 1995) improves case adaptation using introspection. This research focuses on improving the performance of the system by storing the traces of successful adaptation transformations and memory search paths for future reuse. Likewise, Craw (2006) proposes an introspective learning approach for acquiring adaptation knowledge, making it closely related to our work. However, a key difference is that their learning step uses the accumulated case base as training data for adaptation learning, in contrast to our approach of incrementally refining adaptation knowledge in response to failures for individual problems.

Arcos (2004) presents a CBR approach for improving solution quality in evolving environments. His work focuses on improving the quality of solutions for problems that arise only occasionally, by analyzing how the solutions of more typical problems change over time. Arcos's algorithm improves the performance of the system by exploiting the neighborhoods in the solution space but, unlike the model presented in this chapter, learns only from success.

The REM reasoning shell (Murdock & Goel, 2008) presents a meta-case-based reasoning technique for self-adaptation. The goal of REM is the design of agents able to solve new tasks by adapting their own reasoning processes. Meta-case-based reasoning is used for generating new task-method decomposition plans. Because the goal in REM is the assembly of CBR reasoning components, the metamodel is focused on describing the components in terms of their requirements and their effects. In contrast, our model is focused on describing the expected correct properties of the components and their possible reasoning failures.

Introspective reasoning to repair problems may also be seen as related to the use of confidence measures for assessing the quality of the solutions proposed by a CBR system (Cheetham & Price, 2004; Delany et al., 2005). Confidence measures provide expectations about the appropriateness of proposed solutions. A high confidence solution that is determined to be erroneous reveals a failure of the reasoning process used to form the prediction, which points to the need to refine the self-model. The unexpected success of a low-confidence solution may do so as well. Nevertheless, because confidence measures provide no explanations for their assessments, they are not helpful for revealing the origin of the reasoning failure, making their failures hard to use to guide repairs.

Introspective Reasoning Approach

The goal of our introspective reasoning system is to detect reasoning failures and to refine the function of reasoning mechanisms, to improve system performance on future problems. To achieve this goal, the introspective reasoner monitors the reasoning process, determines the possible causes of its failures, and performs actions that will affect future reasoning processes.

To give our system criteria for evaluating its case-based reasoning performance, we have created a model of the correctly-functioning CBR process itself, together with a taxonomy of reasoning failures. Failures of a CBR system's reasoning process are modeled as conflicts between observed system performance and predictions from the model. These failures, in turn, are related to possible learning goals. Achieving these goals repairs the underlying cause of the failure.

As illustrated in the bottom portion of figure 11.1, the case-based reasoning process consists of four steps: (1) *case retrieval/similarity assessment*, which determines which cases address problems most similar to the current problem, to identify them as starting points for solving the new problem; (2) *case adaptation*, which forms a new solution by adapting/combining solutions of the retrieved problems; (3) *case revision*, which evaluates and adjusts the adapted solution; and (4) *case retention*, in which the system learns from the situation by storing the result as a new case for future use.

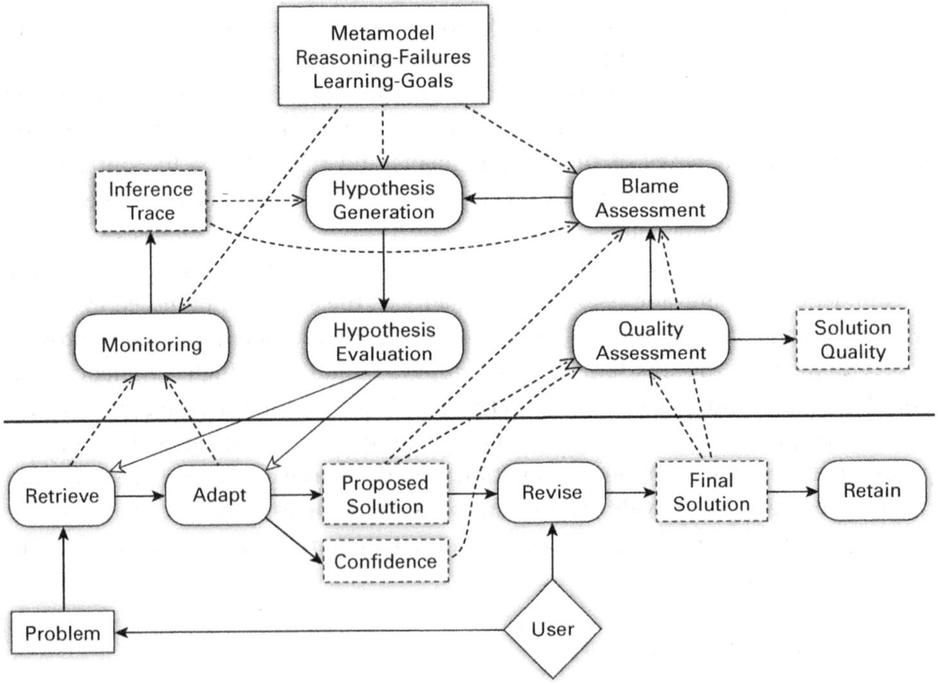

Figure 11.1
Introspective reasoner components. The horizontal line divides the CBR process (bottom) and the introspective reasoner (top).

Reasoning failures may be revealed by either of two types of situation: (i) when the retrieval or adaptation step is unable to propose a solution, or (ii) when the solution proposed by the system differs from the desired final solution. Failures of the retrieval or adaptation steps are identified directly by contrasting their performance with model predictions. The second type of failure can be detected by monitoring the revision step. In CBR systems, the revision step often involves interaction with the user to determine the final solution. This interaction provides a feedback mechanism for assessing the real quality of the solution initially proposed.

For each of the four CBR steps, the model encodes expectations, and the expectations are associated with learning goals that are triggered if the expectations are violated. For example, the expected behavior of the similarity assessment step is to rank the retrieved cases correctly. If they are ranked incorrectly, the failure may be due to using an inappropriate weighting when similarity assessments along different dimensions are aggregated. Consequently, a possible strategy for solving the failure is to refine the weight model, and a corresponding learning goal is to learn new weightings.

Our model is domain independent, that is, it is focused on the general case-based reasoning process for retrieval and adaptation, rather than on specific details of those processes for any particular domain. The model deals with three types of knowledge: indexing knowledge, ranking knowledge, and adaptation knowledge. To apply the model to any concrete application, domain-specific retrieval and adaptation mechanisms must be linked to the model.

Indexing knowledge determines the subspace of the case base considered relevant to a given problem. Ranking knowledge identifies the features considered most relevant to determining similarity, given a collection of retrieved cases. Adaptation knowledge defines transformative and/or generative operations for fitting previous solutions to a current problem.

Our approach is shaped by two assumptions about the underlying CBR system. The first is that the system is initially provided with general retrieval and adaptation mechanisms, which apply uniform criteria to problems throughout the problem space. This is a common property of many case-based reasoning systems, but experience developing CBR systems has shown that this uniform processing may result in sub-optimal processing, in turn resulting in the generation of low-quality solutions. Consequently, one of the focuses of our approach is to address this problem: One of the learning goals of the introspective reasoner is to determine the real scope of cases, to weight the different ranking criteria, and to refine the adaptation model for different problem space regions.

The taxonomy defined for the learning goals borrows partially from the taxonomy of learning goals proposed by Cox and Ram (1999). Nevertheless, in our approach the learning goals are oriented specifically toward refining the CBR process. For example, determining the scope of cases is modeled in terms of differentiation/reconciliation goals, whereas improving the ranking criteria is modeled in terms of refinement/organization goals.

The second working assumption is that the CBR system is able to determine internal confidence estimates for its solutions to new problems. Because confidence assessment will be domain specific, it is not part of our general model. In the application we consider, the system always serves in an advisory role to an engineer, who assesses the system-generated solution before applying it. The engineer's assessment provides a natural source of feedback for judging whether the system's confidence value was appropriate.

Rather than reasoning about numeric confidence values, we deal with confidence using three qualitative values: *low confidence*, *medium confidence*, and *high confidence*. The mapping to the numeric intervals that represent the qualitative values must be defined in each application. For instance, in our chemical application, due to the importance of safety constraints in the chemical processes, high confidence is ascribed to values greater than 0.8 on a 0–1 scale, and the threshold for low confidence is 0.6.

The system's introspective reasoning is organized into five tasks: (1) the *monitoring* task, in charge of maintaining a trace of the CBR process; (2) the *quality assessment* task, which analyzes the quality of the solutions proposed by the system; (3) the *blame assessment* task, responsible for identifying the reasoning failures; (4) the *hypothesis generation* task, in charge of proposing learning goals; and (5) the *hypothesis evaluation* task, which assesses the impact of proposed improvements on solution generation.

Figure 11.1 depicts the introspective reasoning components. The horizontal line divides the CBR process (bottom) from the Introspective Reasoner (top). Rounded boxes represent inference processes; dashed boxes represent knowledge generated by inference; dashed lines show knowledge dependencies; black-tipped arrows show inference flows; and hollow-tipped arrows denote control relationships.

Monitoring

The monitoring task tracks the case-based reasoning process. For each problem solved by the CBR system, the monitor generates a trace containing: (1) the cases retrieved, with a link to the indexing knowledge responsible for the retrieval; (2) the ranking criteria applied to the cases, together with the values that each criterion produced and the final ranking; and (3) the adaptation operators that were applied, with the sources to which they were applied (the cases used) and the target changes produced (the solution features).

Note that our model does not require that the adaptation step use only a single case, nor that all the retrieved cases be involved in all adaptations; any such constraints depend on specific applications, independent of the general model. Similarly, our model distinguishes application of indexing criteria and ranking criteria as two subprocesses involved in the retrieval step, but it does not require that they be decoupled in the implementation being monitored. For instance, a K-nearest neighbor approach (Cover & Hart, 1967) uses the value of K to determine the number of cases considered and uses the distance measure as a ranking criterion. Other approaches might separate indexing and ranking by, for example, using crude criteria for indexing and finer-grained criteria for case ranking.

Quality Assessment

When the user's final solution is provided to the system, quality assessment is triggered to determine the "real" quality of the system-generated solution, by analyzing the differences between the system's proposed solution and the final solution. Quality assessment provides a result in qualitative terms: *low quality*, *medium quality*, or *high quality*.

Given the system's initial confidence assessment and the final quality assessment, the introspective reasoner fires learning mechanisms when there is a mismatch between the two. There are two main types of possible mismatches. When the confidence was high but the actual quality is low, the conflict points to a failure at the retrieval stage, because the confidence of a solution has a strong relationship with the coverage of the retrieved cases (Cheetham, 2000).

On the other hand, when the confidence was low but the quality is demonstrated to be high, the unexpected success may be due either to low coverage from cases (none of the system's cases appeared highly relevant) or to bad ranking of the retrieved cases (the most relevant cases were not considered, due to a failure of the ranking polices to identify them). When the mismatch between the confidence and the quality assessments is small (i.e., high versus medium, medium versus high, medium versus low, and low versus medium) it may suggest a failure in the adaptation stage.

Blame Assessment

Blame assessment starts by identifying the source of the failure. It takes as input the differences between the solution and expected result, and tries to relate the solution differences to the retrieval or the adaptation mechanisms. The system searches the taxonomy of reasoning failures and selects those that apply to the observed solution differences. For instance, when a final solution is radically different from the solution proposed by the system, the failure may be caused by the indexing knowledge, that is, either the relevant precedents have not been retrieved or too many cases have been retrieved.

Search for applicable failures in the failure taxonomy uses the trace generated by the monitoring module. It starts by analyzing the index failures. There are three types of index failures: *wrong index, broad index,* and *narrow index.* When none of the retrieved cases has a solution close to the current solution, the wrong index failure is selected. A broad index failure is selected when many cases are retrieved and their solutions are diverse. On the other hand, when a small set of cases is retrieved, the narrow index failure is selected.

Ranking failures are identified by comparing the retrieval rankings with the solution differences they generate. Examples of ranking failures are *inappropriate ranking scheme, overestimated weights,* and *underestimated weights.*

Adaptation failures are identified by linking the solution differences to the adaptation operators stored in the monitoring trace. When adaptation uses interpolation, adaptation failures originate in inappropriate interpolation policies.

Because the introspective reasoner will often not be able to determine a unique source for a failure, all the possible causally supported failures are chosen, resulting in multiple types of learning goals from a single failure.

Hypothesis Generation

The fourth reasoning stage, hypothesis generation, identifies the learning goals related to the reasoning failures selected in the blame assignment stage. Each failure may be associated with more than one learning goal. For instance, there are multiple ways of solving overestimated weights. For each learning goal, a set of plausible local retrieval/adaptation changes in the active policies is generated, using a predefined taxonomy.

Table 11.1 shows some of the types of hypotheses generated to explain failures in the retrieval and adaptation stages. The changes must be local because their applicability is constrained to the neighborhood of the current problem. For instance, when a refinement goal is selected for the adaptation knowledge, an adaptation adjustment is selected from a predefined collection of tuning actions depending on the nature of the original adaptation. Specifically, when adaptations are related to numerical features the tuning actions determine different types of numerical interpolations. The two main types of changes in numeric features affect the *shape* and *slope* of the interpolation curve.

Table 11.1
Examples of types of hypotheses used by the introspective reasoner

Failure	Learning Goal
Missing index	Create index
Broad index	Refine index
Underestimated weight	Adjust weighting
Inappropriate interpolation	Change shape Increase slope

Hypothesis Evaluation

The fifth reasoning stage, hypothesis evaluation, evaluates the impact of introducing retrieval/adaptation changes. Because the introspective reasoner does not have a complete model of the inference process, it is not possible for it to definitively predict the effects of changes. Consequently, before altering the CBR system, some empirical evidence about the impact of the change must be obtained. In our current design this evidence is obtained by re-solving the problem, applying each proposed change and evaluating its impact. Retrieval/adaptation changes that improve the quality of the solution are incorporated into the CBR inference mechanisms. Note that when the introspective reasoner provides a problem to the CBR system for testing purposes, the case retention step is deactivated.

Experiments

We have tested the introspective reasoner as an extension to a fielded industrial design application. We have developed a case-based reasoning system for aiding engineers in the design of gas treatment plants for the control of atmospheric pollution due to corrosive residual gases that contain vapors, mists, and dusts of industrial origin (Arcos, 2001). A central difficulty for designing gas treatment plants is the lack of a complete model of the chemical reactions involved in the treatment processes. Consequently, the expertise acquired by engineers from their practical experience is essential for solving new problems. Engineers have many preferences and deep chemical knowledge, but our interactions have shown that it is hard for them to determine in advance (i.e., without a new specific problem at hand) the scope and applicability of previous cases. They apply some general criteria concerning factors such as cost and safety conditions, but other criteria depend on specific working conditions of the treatment process.

On the other hand, because engineers make daily use of the application system to provide the final solutions to customers, the system has the opportunity to compare its proposed solutions with the solutions finally delivered. Thus, we have the opportunity to assess the impact of the introspective reasoner on the quality of the solutions proposed by the CBR system.

Applying the CBR Process

The inference process in this design application is decomposed into three main stages: (1) selecting the class of chemical process to be realized; (2) selecting the major equipment to be used; and (3) determining the values for the parameters for each piece of equipment.

The quality of proposed solutions is computed automatically, by comparing the proposed solution to the solution applied by the experts at these three different stages.

Mismatches at earlier steps are more serious than at later ones. For example, except in the case of underspecified problems, a mismatch with the class of the chemical process would indicate a very low-quality solution.

The retrieval and adaptation steps were designed taking into account the three knowledge sources described in the previous section: indexing criteria, ranking criteria, and adaptation operators. Here the problem features are related to the detected pollutants, the industrial origin of the pollutants, and working conditions for the pollution-control equipment (flow, concentrations, temperature). Indexing criteria determine the conditions for retrieving cases. The main indexing criteria are related to the initially defined chemical relations among pollutants. Ranking criteria determine a preference model defined as a partial order. Initially, the preferences are homogeneous for the whole problem space. Throughout the experiments, the introspective reasoner automatically refines the initial model.

Reasoning failures originate from situations in which the criteria do not properly identify the main pollutants or critical working conditions. The consequences are manifested in solutions for which the proposed chemical process is not correct or there are inappropriate washing liquids, or by mismatches on equipment parameters.

Testing Scenario

The design application can solve a broad range of problems. However, to test the effects of introspective reasoning for learning to handle novel situations, it is desirable to focus the evaluation on sets of frequently occurring problems which share at least a pollutant (the minimal indexing criterion), in order to have reuse. On the other hand, it is necessary to have sufficient diversity: Good performance on quasi-identical problems can be obtained by case learning alone, so such problems do not generate opportunities for the introspective reasoner.

We decided to focus the evaluation of the system on problems with the presence of hydrogen sulfide, a toxic gas produced by industrial processes such as wastewater treatment. From the existing application, we had access to the 510 such solved problems, ordered chronologically. We divided the problems into two sets: 300 initial system cases and 210 testing problems.

To evaluate the contribution of the introspective reasoner we performed an ablation study, comparing the performance of the system when presenting the problems sequentially for five different reasoning strategies. In addition to testing inputs in chronological order, we repeated the experiments ten times with random orders for the testing problems, to assess the sensitivity of learning to problem ordering. The tested reasoning strategies are the following:

No-Retain, a strategy that solved the problems without introspective reasoning and without incorporating the solved cases into the case memory;

Retain, which solved the problems without introspective reasoning but incorporated solved cases into the system (the only learning normally done by CBR systems);
Int-Retr, which combined *Retain* with introspective reasoning only for retrieval refinement;
Int-Adapt, which combined *Retain* with introspective reasoning only for adaptation refinement; and
Int-Compl, which combined Retain with introspective reasoning for both retrieval refinement and adaptation refinement.

Results

Table 11.2 shows the results of the evaluation for chronological problem presentation (results for random ordering were similar). Results support that the storage of solved problems—case learning alone—improves the performance of the system, but also show that this policy is not sufficient. Although the number of high-confidence solutions increased significantly, the decrease of low-quality solutions is not statistically significant (see second column in table 11.2).

A second conclusion from the results is that the main contribution of using introspection to refine retrieval knowledge is to reduce the number of low-quality solutions (a 36.67 percent reduction compared with case learning alone). In our design application this improvement is achieved by providing more accurate ranking policies for determining the chemical process to be realized.

The main contribution of using introspection for refining adaptation knowledge (see fourth column in table 11.2) is an increase in the number of high-quality solutions (a 12.5 percent increment from *Retain*). In our task, learning more appropriate adaptation policies enables better determination of the different equipment parameters.

Interestingly, when introspection adjusts both retrieval and adaptation (last column in table 11.2), the improvement in the retrieval step has an indirect effect on the adaptation step, increasing the number of high-quality solutions. An intuitive explanation is that better retrieval also facilitates the adaptation process. Thus, using both introspection strategies, the increase in the number of high-quality solutions, with respect to case learning alone, reaches 15.63 percent.

Table 11.2
Average solution quality for all the strategies

	No-Retain	Retain	Intr-Retr	Int-Adap	Int-Compl
High-Quality	23.81%	30.92%	30.95%	34.29%	35.75%
Medium-Quality	59.52%	54.59%	60.00%	52.86%	56.04%
Low-Quality	16.67%	14.49%	9.05%	12.85%	8.21%

Comparing the number of problems that changed their quality of solution, 12 percent of the total solved problems qualitatively increased their solution quality when introspection was used. Solution qualities varied, but the use of introspection did not decrease the solution quality for any problem. Moreover, the reduction in low-quality solutions is statistically significant ($\rho < 0.05$), even though the increase in high-quality solutions is not statistically significant. Consequently, we conclude that the number of problems whose solution quality was improved by the use of introspection is statistically significant.

Table 11.3 summarizes the introspective reasoner's processing. Results summarize the experiments using both introspection strategies, reflecting learning goals triggered from the detection of 135 non-high-confidence solutions. Most activity was focused on ranking and adaptation failures, because these are the most difficult tasks. Note that not all the generated hypotheses were considered useful by the system (see third and fourth columns): revisions to the reasoning process were performed for 17 percent of the instances for which learning goals were triggered. This result illustrates that the introspective reasoner is dealing with partial understanding of the CBR process and that the introspective learner's hypotheses should be tested before being applied.

It is clear that the incorporation of the introspective reasoner entails some computational overhead. However, it does not interfere with normal system performance: The introspective reasoner is triggered only *after* a problem is solved and is a background process without user intervention. Most of the cost of introspective reasoning arises from hypothesis generation. Table 11.3 shows that the ratio between failures and hypotheses generated is 0.6, because only failures highly explained by the model become hypotheses. Consequently, the number of hypotheses to verify is limited.

A risk of triggering metareasoning in response to individual reasoning failures is the possibility of treating exceptions as regular problems. In the current experiments, such situations did not arise, but in general we assume that the user is responsible for recognizing the exceptions. In addition, only taking action in response to clearly identified failures helps the system to avoid reasoning about exceptions.

Table 11.3

Summary of the number of times learning goals are triggered. Occ stands for failure occurrences, Prop stands for hypotheses generated, and Inc stands for changes incorporated into the CBR process

Failures	Occ.	Prop.	Inc.
Indexing Knowledge	12	5	3
Ranking Knowledge	83	41	8
Adaptation Knowledge	74	56	12

Research on humans has shown that introspection may sometimes have negative consequences. Experiments reported by Wilson and Schooler (1991) showed that, when people are asked to think about the reasons for a given decision, their attempt to form plausible explanations for the specific context of the current decision may result in nonoptimal explanations, negatively affecting future decisions. However, such risks do not apply directly to our approach. First, only the changes incorporated into the CBR process affect future decisions, that is, not the exploration of plausible hypotheses. Second, the goal of the hypothesis evaluation process is to verify the effect of candidate changes on the system. Third, the changes incorporated only have local effects.

Relationship to the Metareasoning Manifesto

Compared to the metareasoning models described in chapter 1 of this volume, our approach is closely related to the use of metalevel control to improve the quality of decisions. Taking the "Duality in reasoning and acting" diagram (fig. 1.2) of chapter 1 as a starting point, our approach incorporates some revisions, as illustrated in figure 11.2 and described in the following points.

First of all, at the ground level, our approach adds the user of the system. The role of the user is twofold: the user (1) presents new problems to the system and (2) provides feedback by revising the solution proposed by the object level. This second role is crucial because it allows the metalevel to estimate the performance of the object level.

In our system, the metalevel continuously monitors the object level (the case-based reasoning process) and assesses the quality of the solutions proposed by the reasoner (using the quality assessment module). The feedback of the user's final solution is exploited to assess the mismatch between system's expectations for its solution (the solution proposed at the object level) and the correct solution (the solution obtained from the ground level).

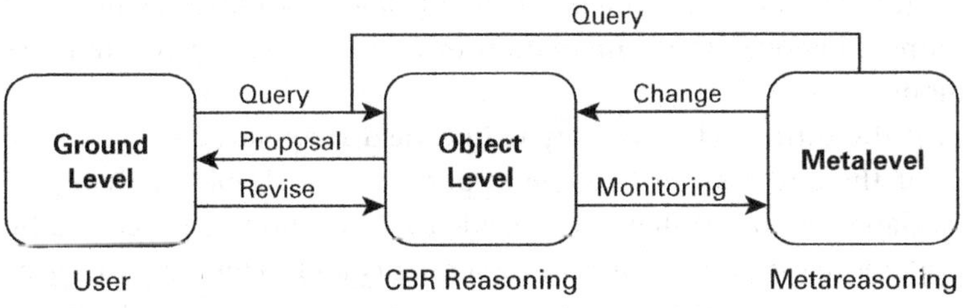

Figure 11.2
Relating our model with existing metareasoning models.

We note the importance of the hypothesis evaluation step. Because the introspective reasoner cannot completely predict the effects of changing the reasoning level, the hypothesis evaluation phase acts as an online trainer. Thus, the metalevel, analogously to the ground level, has the ability to require that the object level solve new problems (top-most query arrow in figure 11.2). Moreover, when the metalevel is testing the performance of the object level, it can temporally deactivate the retention step (in our experiments this is achieved by activating the No-Retain policy).

The control of the object level is achieved by acting over three types of knowledge components used in the reasoning process at the object level: indexing knowledge, ranking knowledge, and adaptation knowledge.

Conclusions

This chapter presented a new introspective model for autonomously improving the performance of a CBR system by reasoning about system problem-solving failures. To achieve this goal, the introspective reasoner monitors the reasoning process, determines the causes of the failures, and performs actions that will affect future reasoning processes.

The introspective level reasons about the reasoning at the object level and about alternative choices to improve the object-level reasoning. Specifically, it relies on a causal model of the correctly functioning retrieval and adaptation stages of CBR. Failures of a CBR system's reasoning process are modeled as conflicts between observed system performance and predictions from the causal model. The sources of these conflicts are identified and associated learning goals are introduced, sometimes triggering multiple types of learning. As a result the case-based reasoning process is improved for future problem solving.

We have tested the introspective reasoner in a fielded industrial design application. Experiments show that the use of the introspective reasoner improved the performance of the system. Introspection-based refinements of retrieval knowledge reduced the number of low-quality solutions; refinements to adaptation knowledge increased high-quality solutions. Moreover, the combination of both is able to generate more high-quality solutions.

Because we tested the introspective prototype in a fielded application previously developed by one of the authors, we had the opportunity to deeply analyze and compare the performance of both systems. The fielded application was developed by introducing many ad hoc mechanisms (concerning similarity and adaptation), whereas the introspective prototype was initially provided with only some broad mechanisms. Over the course of the experiments, the introspective prototype was able to refine its initial reasoning and reach a performance comparable to that of the fielded application. Thus, one lesson of this research is that a domain-independent introspective reasoner is a powerful tool that facilitates the design of a CBR system by providing a mechanism that can autonomously improve the system's reasoning when required.

Because our model of the CBR reasoning process is domain independent, it can be applied in other domains. The engineering effort for incorporating the metareasoning component to other domains would be concentrated on linking domain-specific aspects of the CBR reasoning process to the appropriate parts in the model (retrieval, adaptation, and revision models). The application of the metareasoning component to other design domains would provide an opportunity to validate the completeness of the taxonomies of reasoning failures and learning goals. Our current work aims at exploring the generality of our approach.

Acknowledgments

This research has been partially supported by the Spanish Ministry of Education and Science project MID-CBR (TIN2006-15140-C03-01), EU-FEDER funds, and by the Generalitat de Catalunya under the grant 2005-SGR-00093. This work has been conducted in the framework of the Doctoral Program in Computer Science of the Universitat Autònoma de Barcelona. This material is also based upon work supported by the National Science Foundation under grant No. OCI-0721674.

References

Anderson, M. L., & Oates, T. (2007). A review of recent research in metareasoning and metalearning. *AI Magazine, 28*(1), 7–16.

Arcos, J. L. (2001). T-air: A case-based reasoning system for designing chemical absorption plants. In D.W. Aha & I. Watson (Eds.), *Case-based reasoning research and development.* No. 2080 in Lecture Notes in Artificial Intelligence (pp. 576–588). Berlin: Springer-Verlag.

Arcos, J. L. (2004). Improving the quality of solutions in domain evolving environments. In P. Funk & P. A. Conzález-Calero (Eds.), *Proceedings of the 7th European Conference on Case-Based Reasoning.* No. 3155 in Lecture Notes in Artificial Intelligence (pp. 464–475). Berlin: Springer-Verlag.

Birnbaum, L., Collins, G., Brand, M., Freed, M., Krulwich, B., & Pryor, L. (1991). A model-based approach to the construction of adaptive case-based planning systems. In R. Bareiss (Ed.), *Proceedings of the DARPA Case-Based Reasoning Workshop* (pp. 215–224). San Mateo, CA: Morgan Kaufmann.

Cheetham, W., & Price, J. (2004). Measures of solution accuracy in case-based reasoning systems. In P. Funk & P. A. Conzález-Calero (Eds.), *Proceedings of the 7th European Conference on Case-Based Reasoning.* No. 3155 in Lecture Notes in Artificial Intelligence (pp. 106–118). Berlin: Springer-Verlag.

Cheetham, W. (2000). Case-based reasoning with confidence. In E. Blanzieri & L. Portinale (Eds.), *Proceedings of the 5th European Workshop on Case-Based Reasoning.* No. 1898 in Lecture Notes in Artificial Intelligence, (pp.15–25). Berlin: Springer-Verlag.

Cover, T. M., & Hart, P. E. (1967). Nearest neighbor pattern classification. *IEEE Transactions on Information Theory, 13,* 21–27.

Cox, M. T., & Ram, A. (1999). Introspective multistrategy learning: On the construction of learning strategies. *Artificial Intelligence, 112,* 1–55.

Cox, M. T. (2005). Metacognition in computation: A selected research review. *Artificial Intelligence, 169*(2), 104–141.

Craw, S., Wiratunga, N., & Rowe, R. C. (2006). Learning adaptation knowledge to improve case-based reasoning. *Artificial Intelligence, 170,* 1175–1192.

Delany, S. J., Cunningham, P., Doyle, D., & Zamolotskikh, A. (2005). Generating estimates of classification confidence for a case-based spam filter. In H. Muñoz-Avila & F. Ricci (Eds.), *Proceedings of the 6th International Conference, on Case-Based Reasoning.* No. 3620 in Lecture Notes in Artificial Intelligence (pp. 177–190). Berlin: Springer-Verlag.

Fox, S., & Leake, D. B. (2001). Introspective reasoning for index refinement in case-based reasoning. *Journal of Experimental & Theoretical Artificial Intelligence, 13,* 63–88.

Leake, D. B., Kinley, A., & Wilson, D. C. (1995). Learning to improve case adaption by introspective reasoning and CBR. In M. Veloso & A. Aamodt (Eds.), *Proceedings of the First International Conference on Case-Based Reasoning.* No. 1010 in Lecture Notes in Artificial Intelligence (pp. 229–240). Berlin: Springer-Verlag.

Leake, D. B., & Wilson, M. (2008). Extending introspective learning from self-models. In M. T. Cox & A. Raja (Eds.), *Metareasoning: Thinking about thinking, Papers from the AAAI Workshop* (pp. 143–146). Technical Report WS-08-07. Menlo Park, CA: AAAI Press.

Leake, D. B. (1996). Experience, introspection, and expertise: Learning to refine the case-based reasoning process. *Journal of Experimental & Theoretical Artificial Intelligence, 8*(3), 319–339.

Mantaras, R., McSherry, D., Bridge, D., Leake, D., Smyth, B., Craw, S., et al. (2005). Retrieval, reuse, revision, and retention in CBR. *Knowledge Engineering Review, 20*(3), 215–240.

Murdock, J. W., & Goel, A. K. (2008). Meta-case-based reasoning: Self-improvement through self-understanding. *Journal of Experimental & Theoretical Artificial Intelligence, 20*(1), 1–36.

Wilson, T. D., & Schooler, J. W. (1991). Thinking too much: Introspection can reduce the quality of preferences and decisions. *Journal of Personality and Social Psychology, 60*(2), 181–192.

12 The Metacognitive Loop and Reasoning about Anomalies

Matthew D. Schmill, Michael L. Anderson, Scott Fults, Darsana Josyula, Tim Oates, Don Perlis, Hamid Shahri, Shomir Wilson, and Dean Wright

Murphy's Law states, "if anything can go wrong, it will." Though it is more of an adage than a law, it is surprisingly predictive. For each of the fifteen participants in the 2004 DARPA Grand Challenge driverless car competition, Murphy's Law held true. Each of the entries was an impressive engineering feat; to receive an invitation each team's vehicle had to navigate a mile-long preliminary obstacle course. Yet in the longer course, every one of the driverless vehicles encountered a situation for which it was unprepared: some experienced mechanical failures, while others wandered off course and into an obstacle their programming could not surmount (Hooper, 2004).

The DARPA Grand Challenge highlights the enormity of the defensive design task, in which the engineer must attempt to enumerate the ways in which a system might fail so that they can be appropriately managed. For sophisticated computer systems, particularly autonomous systems operating in the real world, this is a great challenge. In general, no system designer, whether we are talking about a learning system, a planning system, or any other artificial intelligence (AI) technology, can enumerate all the possible contingencies his or her system will encounter. This is not a unique observation. Such a view has been pointed out before (Brachman, 2006). Systems that learn and adapt attempt to address this, but learning processes themselves are also constrained to work in the space for which they were designed. Learning systems can improve robustness, but only in the situations for which they are designed.

Consider, though, a driverless vehicle that has become stuck on an embankment (a fate of several of the participants in the grand challenge). If that vehicle had a self-model that allowed it to reason about its own control and sensing capabilities, it may have been in a position to notice and diagnose its own failure. Such a system would also have the ability to reason about which of its cognitive components, whether they be controllers, learning algorithms, or planners, might allow the system to recover from the current failure, or at least prevent it from happening the next time. How can an AI system create such a self-model so that it can diagnose its own failures?

We propose that at some level of abstraction, the ways in which a system can fail are finite. Thus, a domain-general metareasoning component can be developed and equipped with knowledge of how systems fail (and how to recover from these failures). This component, when integrated with an existing AI system (which we will call the *host*), will allow that system to diagnose failures and thus become more robust.

In this chapter we present our architecture for generalized metacognition aimed at making AI systems more robust. The key to this enhancement is to characterize a system by its expectations each time it engages in activity, to watch for violations of system expectations, and to attempt to reason in an application-general way about the violation to arrive at a diagnosis and plan for recovery. Our architecture is called the *metacognitive loop* (MCL), and we present it here along with details of its implementation.

The Metacognitive Loop

Human intelligence manages to work not just in everyday situations, but also in novel situations, and even in significantly perturbed situations. For our purposes, we define a perturbation as a change in conditions under which an agent (human or artificial) has obtained competency.

Suppose someone who has spent his entire life in the desert is suddenly dropped in the middle of a skating rink. This person has learned to walk, but never on ice. His usual gait will not produce the desired result. In coping with this new situation, he starts by noticing that the proprioceptive feedback he is receiving is unusual in the context of walking. He must become more aware of what he is doing and reason sensibly about the situation. This allows him to assess what has changed or gone awry. Once he has made an assessment, he must respond to the perturbation by modifying his usual behavior: become more cautious and deliberate, or attempt to learn the dynamics of walking on ice.

Dealing with perturbations invariably involves reasoning about one's own self: about one's abilities, expectations, and adaptivity. We recognize when we possess a necessary capacity or whether we need to acquire it. What would be required of a computer system that endeavored to have that same level of robustness?

An AI system capable of reasoning about its own (reasoning) capabilities is said to possess the ability of metareasoning. A typical metareasoner can be laid out as in figure 12.1, consisting of a sensorimotor subsystem, shown in the figure as the ground level and responsible for sensing and effecting changes in an environment; a reasoning subsystem, shown as the object level and responsible for processing sensory information and organizing actions at the ground level; and a metareasoning component, shown as the metalevel and responsible for monitoring and controlling the application of components at the object level (see Cox and Raja, this vol., chap. 1).

We are developing an embedded, general-purpose metareasoner based on this basic architecture. The metacognitive loop (MCL) is a metalevel component that endows

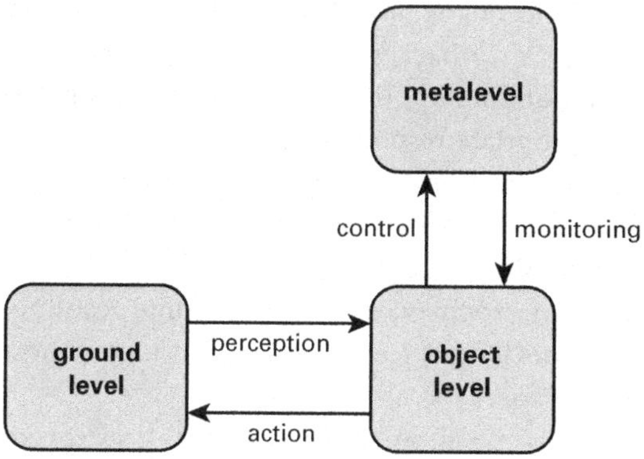

Figure 12.1
An overview of a typical metareasoning system.

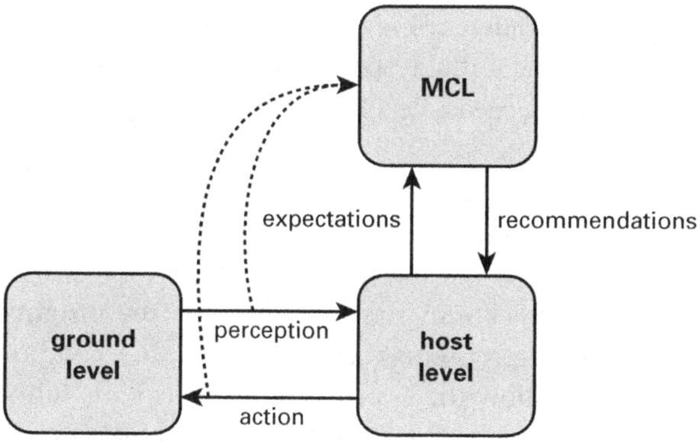

Figure 12.2
An overview of an MCL-enhanced AI system.

AI systems with self-modeling, monitoring, and repair capabilities. An overview of an MCL-enhanced system can be seen in figure 12.2. A reasoning system that employs MCL (called the *host system*) makes explicit its components, capabilities, actions, percepts, and internal state information to compile the infrastructure necessary for a self-model. Additionally, the host declares expectations about how its activities will affect the perceptual and state information. MCL monitors the operation of the host (including its actions and sensory feedback) against its expectations, waiting for violations to occur. When a violation of expectations is detected, it employs a combination of a domain-general problem solver and the host's self-model to make recommendations on how to devote computational resources to anomalous host behavior.

The operation of MCL is analogous to the thought process of the human walking on ice presented above. It can be thought of as a background process consisting of three steps: (i) monitoring for and noticing anomalies; (ii) assessing them (probable causes, or severity); and (iii) guiding an appropriate response into place.

The monitoring phase corresponds to an agent's "self-awareness." As an agent accumulates experience with its own actions, it develops expectations about how they will unfold. An agent might expect an internal state to change to a new value, for a sensor to increase at some rate, or for an action to achieve a goal before some deadline. As the agent engages in a familiar behavior, deviations from expectations (anomalies) cause surprise, and initiate the assessment phase.

In the assessment stage of MCL, a profile of the anomaly is generated. How severe is the anomaly? Must it be dealt with immediately? What is its likely cause? This anomaly profile enables MCL to move on to the guide state, where a response will be selected to either help the agent recover from the failure, prevent it from happening in the future, or both. Once this response is guided into place by the host system, MCL can continue to monitor the situation to determine whether or not the response has succeeded. Should MCL determine that its initial response has failed, it can move down its list of possible responses until it succeeds, decides to ask for help, or move on to work on something else.

Domain-General MCL

Implementing our MCL-enhanced pilot applications has provided two key insights into building robust AI systems. First, building systems that employ an MCL component requires a structured understanding of how the system and all of its parts function. Object-level capabilities and expected behaviors must be known or learnable such that the metareasoner can detect any perturbations to the system. Indeed, in similar work great attention is paid to the methodologies that enable self-modeling and robust behavior in AI (Stroulia, 1994; Ulam, Goel, Jones, & Murdoch, 2005; Williams & Nayak, 1996), and in the literature of fault detection, isolation, and recovery (FDIR) (Frank, 1990; Isermann, 1997).

The second insight is that although there may be many different perturbations possible in a given domain, there are a limited number of distinct ways in which they may create system failures, and generally an even smaller number of coping strategies. Can we produce a taxonomy of the ways in which AI systems fail, and reason about failures using the general concepts present in that taxonomy, such that one general-purpose reasoner can be useful to a wide variety of host systems and domains? Indeed, our primary scientific hypothesis is that the answer to this question is "yes," and our current research seeks to determine to what extent this hypothesis is correct.

It is useful to consider two different forms of generalized utility here. A system/domain-general MCL would be coupled "out-of-the-box" with any of a wide variety of host systems and in a wide variety of domains; the host would at a minimum need only provide MCL with expectations and monitoring information and specify any tunable actions it might have. An anomaly-general MCL would have a sufficiently high-level typology of anomalies such that virtually all specific anomalies would fall into one type or another. Since actual instances of anomalies tend to be system or domain specific, the two dimensions are not totally independent. However, a system/domain-general MCL would have a protocol design facilitating a kind of "plug and play" symbiotic hook-up, where the system/host need only provide and receive data from MCL in a specified format, even if MCL might not be equipped to handle anomalies in some domains. An anomaly-general MCL, by contrast, would be equipped to process virtually any anomaly for any system or domain, even if it might be tedious to provide the add-on interface between them. Combining the two gives the best of both worlds: easy hook-up to any host (as long as the designer follows the communication protocol) and an ability to deal flexibly with whatever comes its way. Indeed, the primary difference between MCL and much of the related work, perhaps best exemplified by that of Goel, is that rather than requiring a complete self-model, MCL can operate with more modest knowledge about expectations, the failures (probabilistically) indicated by violations thereof, and potentially effective repairs.

The current generation of MCL implements such a generalized taxonomy and uses it to reason through anomalies that a host system experiences. MCL breaks the universe of failures down into three ontologies that describe different aspects of anomalies, how they manifest in AI agents, and their prescribed coping mechanisms. The core of these ontologies contains abstract and domain-general concepts. When an actual perturbation is detected in the host, MCL attempts to map it into the MCL core so that it may reason about it abstractly. Nodes in the ontologies are linked, expressing relationships between the concepts they represent. The linkage both within the ontologies and between them provides the basis that MCL uses to reason about failures.

Although the hierarchical network structure of the ontologies lends itself to any of a number of graph-based algorithms, our implementation represents the ontologies as a Bayesian network. This allows us to express beliefs about individual concepts within the ontologies by probability values, to model the influence that the belief in one concept has on the others, and to use any of the many Bayesian inference algorithms to update beliefs across the ontologies as new observations are made by MCL. The core of our implementation is based on the SMILE reasoning engine.[1]

1. The SMILE engine for graphical probabilistic modeling, contributed to the community by the Decision Systems Laboratory, University of Pittsburgh (http://dsl.sis.pitt.edu).

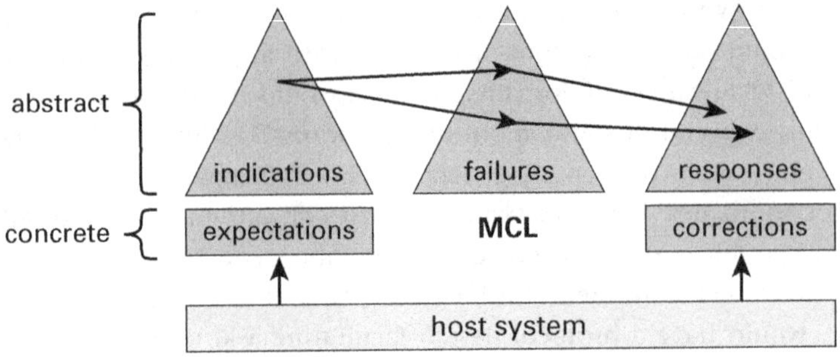

Figure 12.3
An overview of the MCL ontologies.

Each of the three phases of MCL (note, assess, guide) employs one of the ontologies to do its work (Schmill, Josyula, Anderson, Wilson, Oates, Perlis, Wright, & Fults, 2007). A flow diagram is shown in figure 12.3. The note phase uses an ontology of indications. An indication is a sensory or contextual cue that the system has been perturbed. Processing in the indication ontology allows the assess phase to hypothesize underlying causes by reasoning over its failure ontology. This ontology contains nodes that describe the general ways in which a system might fail. Finally, when failure types for an indication have been hypothesized, the guide phase maps that information to its own response ontology. This ontology encodes the means available to a host for dealing with failures at various levels of abstraction. Through these three phases, reasoning starts at the concrete, domain-specific level of expectations, becomes more abstract as MCL moves to the concept of a system failure, and then becomes more concrete again as it must realize an actionable response based on the hypothesized failure.

In the following sections, we will describe in greater detail how the three ontologies are organized and how MCL gets from expectation violations to responses that can be executed by the host system, using the MCL-enhanced reinforcement learning system as an example. To help illustrate the functions of the ontologies, we will use a previous study of ours as an example (Anderson, Oates, Chong, & Perlis, 2006). In this study we deployed MCL in a standard reinforcement learner. There, learned reward functions in a simple 8×8 grid world formed the basis for expectations.[2] When reward conditions in the grid world were changed, MCL noted the violation and would respond in a number of ways appropriate to relearning or adapting policies in RL systems. In a variety of settings, the MCL-enhanced learner outperformed standard

2. Q-learning (Watkins & Dayan, 1992), SARSA (Sutton & Barto, 1995), and prioritized sweeping (Moore & Atkeson, 1993) were used.

reinforcement learners when perturbations were made to the world's reward structure.

Indications

A fragment of the MCL indication ontology is pictured in figure 12.4. The indication ontology consists of two types of nodes separated by a horizontal line in the figure: domain-independent indication nodes above the line, and domain-specific expectation nodes below it. Indication nodes belong to the MCL core and represent general classes of sensory events and expectation types that may help MCL disambiguate anomalies when they occur. Furthermore, there are two types of indication nodes: fringe nodes and event nodes. Fringe nodes zero in on specific properties of expectations and sensors. For example, a fringe node might denote what type of sensor is being monitored: internal state, time, or reward. Event nodes synthesize information in the fringe nodes to represent specific instances of an indicator (for example, reward not received). Expectation nodes (shown below the dashed line) represent host-level expectations of how sensor, state, and other values are known to behave. Expectations are created and destroyed based on what the host system is doing and what it believes the context is. Expectations may be specified by the system designer or learned by MCL, and are linked dynamically into indication fringe nodes when they are created.

Consider the ontology fragment pictured in figure 12.4. This fragment shows three example expectations that the enhanced reinforcement learner might produce when it attempts to move into a grid cell containing a reward. First, a reward *x* should be

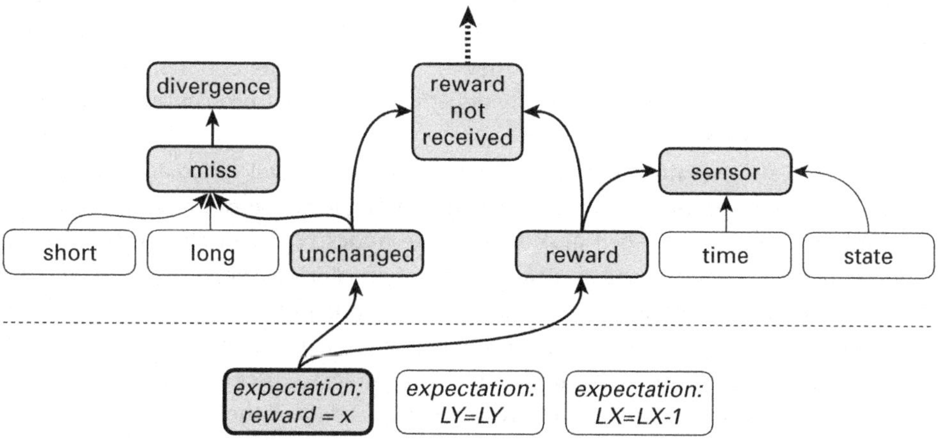

Figure 12.4

A fragment of the MCL indication ontology.

experienced at the end of the movement. Second, the sensor LY should not change. Lastly, the sensor LX should decrease by one unit.

Suppose that someone has moved the location of the reward, but LY and LX behave as if the reward were still in the original position. MCL will notice an expectation violation for the reward sensor and create a fresh copy of the three ontologies to be used as a basis for reasoning through a repair. Based on the specifics of the violation, appropriate evidence will be entered into the indication fringe to reflect the fact that a violation occurred: a change in a reward sensor was expected, but the change never occurred. The relevant expectation node in the fragment in figure 12.4 is denoted by boldface, and its influence on associated nodes in the indication ontology is denoted by heavy arrows. Through the conditional probability tables maintained by the Bayesian implementation of the ontology, MCL's belief in fringe nodes "reward" and "unchanged" will be boosted. From there, influence is propagated along abstraction links within the indication core (activating the sensor node and others). Finally, fringe-event links combine the individual beliefs of the separate fringe nodes into specifically indicated events. In figure 12.4, the "reward not received" node is believed to be more probable due to the evidence for upstream nodes. Once all violated expectations have been noted, and inference is finished, the note phase of MCL is complete.

Failures

The note stage having been completed, MCL can move to the assessment stage, in which indication events are used to hypothesize a cause of the anomaly experienced. The failure ontology serves as the basis for processing at the assessment stage.

Belief values for nodes in the failure ontology are updated based on activation in the indication ontology. Indication event nodes are linked to failure nodes via interontological links called diagnostic links. They express which classes of failures are plausible given the active indication events and the conditional probabilities associated with those relationships.

Figure 12.5 shows a fragment of the MCL failure ontology. Dashed arrows indicate diagnostic links from the indications ontology leading to the sensor failure and model error nodes, which are shaded and bold. These nodes represent the nodes directly influenced by updates in the indications ontology during the note phase in our enhanced reinforcement learning example; a "reward not received" event can be associated with either of these types of failure. The remaining links in the figure are intraontological and express specialization. For example, a sensor may fail in two ways: it may fail to report anything, or it may report faulty data. Either of these is a refinement of the sensor failure node. As such, sensor not reporting and sensor malfunction are connected to sensor failure with specialization links in the ontology to express this relationship.

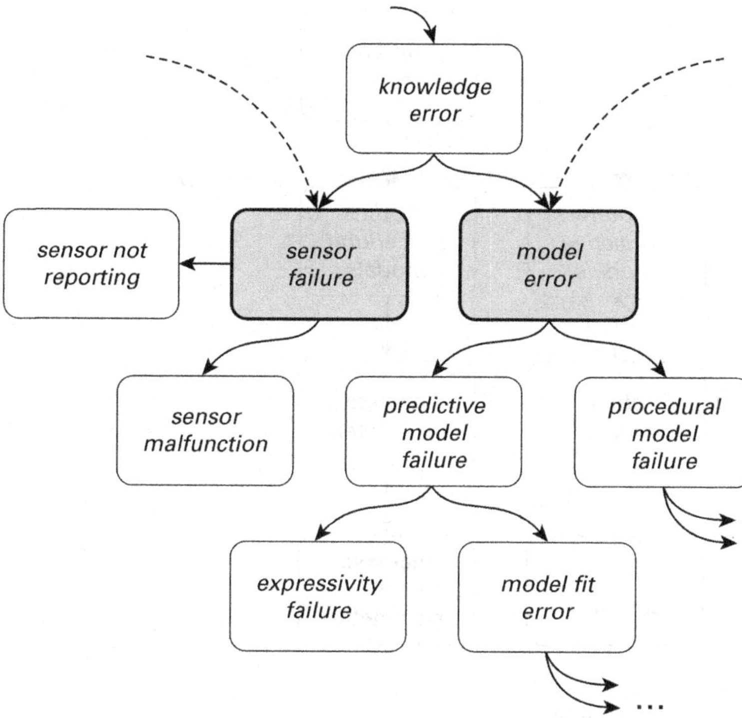

Figure 12.5
A fragment of the MCL failure ontology.

As in the note phase, influence is passed along specialization links to activate more specific nodes based on the probabilities of related abstract nodes and priors. Of particular interest in our RL example is the predictive model failure node, which follows from the model error hypothesis. The basis for action in Q-learning is the predictive model (the Q function), and failure to achieve a reward often indicates that the model is no longer a match for the domain.

Responses

Outgoing interontological links from probable failure nodes allow MCL to move into the guide phase. In the guide phase, potential responses to hypothesized failures are activated, evaluated, and implemented in reverse order of their expected cost. The expected cost for a concrete response is computed as the cost of the response multiplied by one minus the estimated probability that the response will correct the anomaly, where the cost is quantified by the host. Interontological links connecting failures to responses are called prescriptive links.

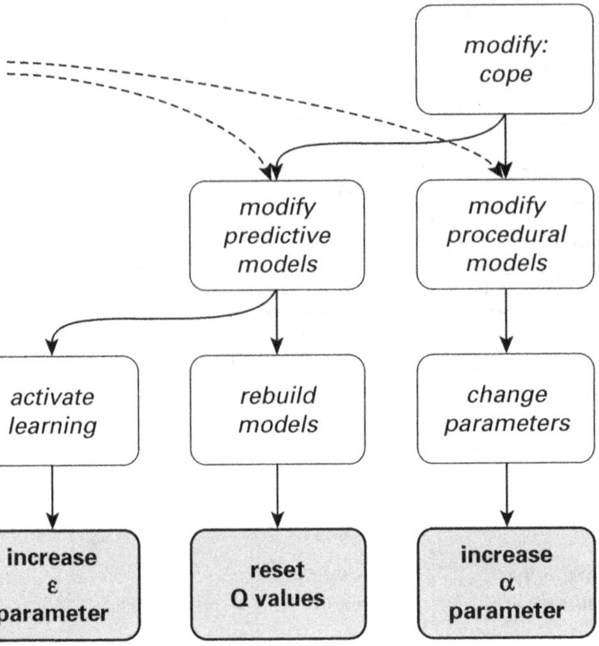

Figure 12.6
A fragment of the MCL response ontology.

Figure 12.6 shows a fragment of the MCL response ontology. Pictured are both MCL core responses (which are abstract, and shown in italics) and host-level responses (pictured in bold), which are concrete actions that can be implemented by a host system. Host system designers specify the appropriate ways in which MCL can effect changes by declaring properties (such as "employs reinforcement learning") that are incorporated into the conditional probability tables for the response nodes. Declaring "employs reinforcement learning," for example, will make nonzero the prior belief that responses, such as "reset Q values" as seen in figure 12.6, will be useful.

In the portion of the response ontology pictured, prescriptive links from the failure ontology are pictured as dashed arrows. These links allow influence to be propagated to the nodes "modify predictive models" and "modify procedural models." Like the failure ontology, internal links in the response ontology are primarily specialization links. They allow MCL to move from general response classes to more specific ones, eventually arriving at responses that are appropriate to the host. In our example, concrete nodes correspond to either parameter tweaks in Q-learning or resetting the Q function altogether.

Iterative and Interactive Repairs

Once MCL has arrived at a concrete response in the guide phase, the host system can implement that response. In our enhanced RL example, this may mean clearing the Q values and starting over, or boosting the ε parameter to increase exploration or the α parameter to accelerate learning. A hybrid system, with many components, may have several probable responses to any given indication. This is why all the activated ontology nodes are considered hypotheses with associated conditional probabilities. MCL will not always have enough information to arrive at an unambiguously correct response. MCL must verify that a response is working before it considers the case of an anomaly closed.

When a response is found to have failed, either by explicit feedback from the host, or implicitly by recurrence of expectation violations, MCL must recover its record of the original violation and reinitiate the reasoning process. The decision of when to recover a reasoning process is actually quite complex: repairs may be durative (requiring time to work), interactive (requiring feedback from the host), or stochastic. Each time an anomaly is experienced, it may be a manifestation of an all-new failure, the recurrence of a known failure, or even a failure introduced by an attempted repair. The heuristics required to make the decision of whether to initiate a new reasoning process or resume an existing one remain a topic of our ongoing research.

Once the decision has been made that a response has failed and a reasoning process should be resumed, MCL reenters and updates the ontologies in two ways. First, it revises down the belief that the "failed response" node will solve the problem, possibly driving it to zero. The inference algorithm is run and the influence of having discounted the failed response is propagated throughout the ontologies. Next, it feeds any new indications that may have occurred during the execution of the original response into the indications ontology and again executes the inference algorithm. Then utility values for concrete responses are recomputed and the next most highly rated response is chosen and recommended for implementation by the host. Once a successful response is implemented and no new expectation violations are received, the changes effected during the repair can be made permanent, and the violation is considered addressed.

Evaluation and Future Work

In this section, we describe a new system architecture we are developing that has the requisite complexity to highlight how a metareasoner can contribute to a more robust system. Through this system we also hope to demonstrate the generality of the reasoner, as MCL will have to cope with a variety of problems encountered as the various system components at the object level interact. We also include a short discussion of our planned evaluation methods.

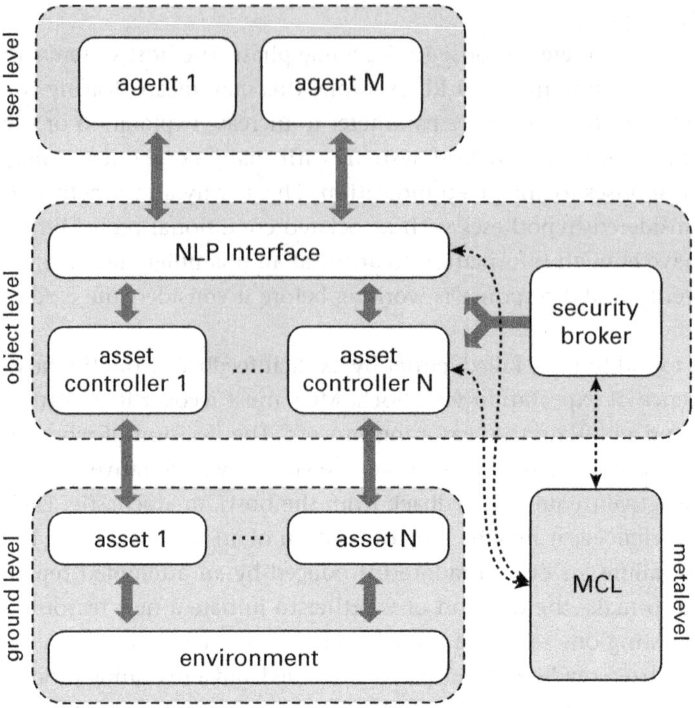

Figure 12.7
An overview of an end-to-end MCL-enhanced AI system.

An overview of our system architecture is pictured in figure 12.7. At the ground level are "assets"—simulated agents with sensing and possibly effecting capabilities that operate in a simulated environment. The architecture is designed to be configurable; the assets might be rover units operating in a simulated Mars environment, or unmanned aerial vehicles operating in a virtual battlefield. The core of the simulation was built based on the Mars rover simulation introduced by Coddington (2007), and is currently discrete, although an obvious development path would be to transition to a two- or three-dimensional, continuous world, and eventually to actual robots acting in the real world. For the purpose of this discussion, we will use the simulated Mars rover as an example.

At the object level of the testbed system are three major cognitive components. First is the monitor and control system of each asset. It is responsible for sequencing execution of effecting and sensing actions on the actual assets. Our Mars rover controller contains a simple planner that performs route planning to navigate between waypoints on a map, while taking reasonable measures to attend to the rover's resource constraints. The rover controller can also learn operator models for the Mars environment, in a form similar to those found in STRIPS (Fikes & Nilsson, 1971).

The second object-level component is a human–computer interface that accepts natural language commands from human users. Users specify their goals to the language processor, which converts them to a goal language usable by the rover controller. The rover controller in turn generates ground-level plans to achieve the user's goals, and also manages the inevitable competition for limited asset resources.

Finally, the system contains a security broker. The security broker places constraints on both the assets and users' access to them. For example, the security broker may state that two rovers may not perform science in the same zone, or the security broker may state that user *U* may access panoramic images taken by the rover, but not specific scientific measurements in a particular zone.

The three object-level components address three distinct classes of AI problems. The rover controller is, obviously, a classic AI control problem. It requires the use of planning, scheduling, and learning, and the coordination of those capabilities to maximize the utility of the system assets. The user–asset interface is a classic AI natural language understanding, learning, and dialogue management problem. Finally, the security broker introduces security policies as a constraint, as well as information fusion.

The domain presents many possibilities for perturbations and associated system failures. Each path between the ground and object level represents a conceptual boundary, whereby one component asserts control and has expectations about the result. Consider a few possible perturbations: the human user may use unknown lexical or syntactic constructs, the user may be denied access to imagery due to conflicting security policies, or the rover may generate useless observations due to unforeseen changes in the Mars environment. Each interaction and its associated expectations will be monitored by MCL, and any violation will be mapped to the core ontologies. Possible explanations and repairs will be considered in an order consistent with prior and learned probabilities in an attempt to prevent further violations.

After building the various components outlined above, our main experimental task will be to build and test the MCL ontologies. We want to show that the MCL approach is effective and results in more perturbation-tolerant systems, and we want to show that the MCL approach is general, that the same MCL core can handle many different kinds of perturbations in many different systems.

For measuring the effectiveness of MCL, the main strategy will involve ablation studies. Performance metrics will include time to task completion and cost of task completion (e.g., fuel burned, number of messages sent), and more particularly the degree of increase in these measures as the scenario difficulty increases (Anderson, 2004). We will compare performance for three versions of the system: (1) full adaptive response: all the components/agents of the system with all parts of MCL enabled.

(2) Fixed maintenance: the components/agents of the system with no MCL, but rather a fixed maintenance policy in which available repair actions are executed in a preventative manner. For instance, the rover rebuilds models every n timesteps, recalibrates sensors every m timesteps, and so on. (3) Fixed response: The components/agents of the system with the MCL note phase working, but with the failure and response ontologies replaced by a single response, which is to run down a list of all available repairs until one succeeds. Insofar as MCL is an effective strategy for ensuring perturbation-tolerance, the performance of system version (1) should be far better than the others.

For measuring the generality of MCL, a different approach must be employed. Recall that we intend for all the MCL instantiations (e.g., for the natural language interpreter and the rover) to have identical core algorithms and core nodes (at least initially), but different fringe nodes (e.g., the type and number of expectations). In the course of development, we expect that the differences between the host systems will suggest changes to the core nodes and their connections, in order to enhance performance. The open research questions are: how much will they end up differing, and can they be reunified after optimization to generate a more truly universal MCL system? We will answer those questions in the following four steps.

First, we will allow each MCL core to be changed and trained however much is required to achieve the best enhancement over base-level performance (as noted above). After this initial training and testing, we will measure the following traits of the MCL systems: (1) which specific nodes get used in each system, and (2) what are the most frequent subtrees used in the ontologies. What we hope to see within each MCL core is that a majority of the nodes and subtrees are being activated in the course of processing the various anomalies.

What we hope to see between any two MCL cores is significant overlap between the subsets of nodes and subtrees being used in each case. Dice's coefficient is a convenient measure for this, as it allows quantification of the overlap between sets, in this case the subset of activated nodes or subtrees, as compared with the full set of available nodes or subtrees (within the MCL core) or as compared with other subsets of activated nodes of subtrees (between MCL cores). Low scores (below 0.5) would indicate poor coverage (extraneous nodes that aren't being used) or insufficient abstraction (different specialized paths being used for each different system), and would trigger a redesign of the MCL core.

Second, once we have generated MCL cores that both serve their host systems and indicate good coverage and abstraction, we will compare the whole cores to one another using a tree-edit distance measure. We hope to see that the MCL cores remain fundamentally similar (requiring few edits to turn one into the other).

Third, we will merge the two MCL cores into one, containing all the nodes and connections of the two. If the unified MCL is domain general, it should work equally well when reattached to the initial host systems. We will test this claim by rerunning the initial performance tests, and seeing if the enhanced, unified MCL works as well as the preunification specialized MCLs.

Fourth and finally, once we have a single, unified MCL core with good coverage and abstraction that works well on both host systems, we will install MCL on a system not designed by us (and with minimum modifications) that we can use as a test-host. We do this to ensure that we have not inadvertently built our original test systems so that they would automatically work with MCL.

Conclusion

We have described a generalized metacognitive layer aimed at providing robustness to autonomous systems in the face of unforeseen perturbations. The metacognitive loop encodes commonsense knowledge about how AI systems fail in the form of a Bayesian network and uses that network to reason abstractly about what to do when a system's expectations about its own actions are violated. Our aim is to provide an engineering methodology for developing metalevel interoperable AI systems and in so doing provide the benefit of adding reactive anomaly-handling using the MCL library. We have also introduced a system architecture with a number of interacting cognitive components at the object level that we believe is a useful testbed for metacognitive research.

Acknowledgments

Supported by NSF (IIS0803739), AFOSR (FA95500910144), and ONR (N000140910328).

References

Anderson, M. L. (2004). Specification of a test environment and performance measures for perturbation-tolerant cognitive agents. In R. M. Jones (Ed.), *Proceedings of the AAAI Workshop on Intelligent Agent Architectures* (pp. 11–18). Technical Report WS-04-07. Menlo Park, CA: AAAI Press.

Anderson, M. L., Oates, T., Chong, W., & Perlis, D. (2006). The metacognitive loop I: Enhancing reinforcement learning with metacognitive monitoring and control for improved perturbation tolerance. *Journal of Experimental & Theoretical Artificial Intelligence, 18*(3), 387–411.

Brachman, R. J. (2006). (AA)AI: More than the sum of its parts. *AI Magazine, 27*(4), 19–34.

Coddington, A. (2007). Motivations as a meta-level component for constraining goal generation. In A. Raja & M. T. Cox (Eds.), *Proceedings of the First International Workshop on Metareasoning in Agent-Based Systems* (pp. 16–30). Collocated with AAMAS-07. Columbia, SC: IFAAMAS.

Fikes, R. E., & Nilsson, N. J. (1971). STRIPS: A new approach to the application of theorem proving. *Artificial Intelligence, 2*(3–4), 189–208.

Frank, P. M. (1990). Fault diagnosis in dynamic systems using analytical and knowledge-based redundancy—A survey and some new results. *Automatica, 26*(3), 459–474.

Hooper, J. (June, 2004). DARPA's debacle in the desert: Behind the scenes at the DARPA grand challenge, the 142-mile robot race that died at mile 7. *Popular Science*, 64–67.

Isermann, R. (1997). Supervision, fault-detection and fault-diagnosis methods—An introduction. *Control Engineering Practice, 5*(5), 639–652.

Moore, A. W., & Atkeson, C. G. (1993). Prioritized sweeping: Reinforcement learning with less data and less time. *Machine Learning, 13*(1), 103–130.

Schmill, M., Josyula, D., Anderson, M. L., Wilson, S., Oates, T., Perlis, D., Wright, D., & Fults, S. (2007). Ontologies for reasoning about failures in AI systems. In A. Raja & M. T. Cox (Eds.), *Proceedings of the First International Workshop on Metareasoning in Agent-Based Systems* (pp. 1–15). Collocated with AAMAS-07. Columbia, SC: IFAAMAS.

Stroulia, E. (1994). *Failure-driven learning as model-based self redesign.* Doctoral dissertation, Georgia Institute of Technology, College of Computing, Atlanta.

Sutton, R. S., & Barto, A. G. (1995). *Reinforcement learning: An introduction.* Cambridge, MA: MIT Press.

Ulam, P., Goel, A., Jones, J., & Murdoch, W. (2005). Using model-based reflection to guide reinforcement learning. In D.W. Aha, H. Muñoz-Avila, & M. van Lent (Eds.), *Proceedings of the IJCAI Workshop on Reasoning, Representation and Learning in Computer Games.* (pp. 107–112). Washington, D.C.: Naval Research Laboratory, Navy Center for Applied Research in Artificial Intelligence.

Watkins, C. J., & Dayan, P. (1992). Q-learning. *Machine Learning, 8*(3–4), 279–292.

Williams, B. C., & Nayak, P. P. (1996). A model-based approach to reactive selfconfiguring systems. In *Proceedings of the National Conference on Artificial Intelligence* (pp. 971–978). Menlo Park, CA: AAAI Press.

IV Distributed Metareasoning

13 Coordinating Agents' Metalevel Control

Anita Raja, George Alexander, Victor R. Lesser, and Michael Krainin

Embedded systems consisting of collaborating agents capable of interacting with their environment are becoming ubiquitous. It is crucial for these systems to be able to adapt to the dynamic and uncertain characteristics of an open environment. The adaptation needs to be based on the priority of tasks, availability of resources, and availability of alternative ways of satisfying these tasks as well as tasks expected in the future. Important issues include the timing of this adaptation process, the level of effort to be invested in the adaptation as opposed to just continuing with the current action plan, and the ramifications of making these decisions in a multiagent context.

The basic idea of bounded rationality arises in the work of Simon with his definition of procedural rationality (Simon, 1976). Simon's work has addressed the implications of bounded rationality in the areas of psychology, economics, and artificial intelligence (AI) (Simon, 1982). He argues that people find satisfactory solutions to problems rather than optimal solutions because people do not have unlimited processing power. In the area of agent design, he has considered how the nature of the environment can determine how simple an agent's control algorithm can be and still produce rational behavior. Bounded rationality, discussed in chapters 3 and 4 of this volume, has been used in the context of beliefs, intentions, and learning (Doyle, 1983); intelligent system design (Horvitz, 1988); problem solving and search (Simon & Kadane, 1974); and planning (Stefik, 1981). Russell, Subramanian, and Parr (1993) cast the problem of creating resource-bounded rational agents as a search for the best program that an agent can execute. In searching the space of programs, the agents, called bounded-optimal agents, can be optimal for a given class of programs or they can approach optimal performance with learning, given a limited class of possible programs. Zilberstein (this vol., chap. 3) discusses the implementation characteristics and formal guarantees of optimal metareasoning that make it a preferred solution approach for bounded rationality.

Cox (2005) provides a review of metacognition research in the fields of AI and cognitive science. In our previous work (Raja & Lesser, 2007), we developed a sophisticated architecture that could reason about alternative methods for computation, including computations that handled simple negotiation between two agents. This chapter builds on results from this earlier work and opens a new vein of inquiry by addressing issues of scalability, partial information, and complex interactions across agent boundaries in real domains. It includes defining a generalized multiagent framework for metalevel control based on a decentralized Markov decision process (DEC-MDP) model.

This chapter is structured as follows: We first describe the taxonomy of agent decisions and their interdependencies from a single-agent perspective and then from a multiagent perspective. The relevance of these research issues within the context of Netrads, a real-world tornado-tracking application, is presented, followed by a description of a generalized framework for metalevel control. We then present the conclusions and future work directions.

Taxonomy of Agent Decisions

Agents in embedded systems operate in an iterative three-step closed loop: receiving sensory data from the environment, performing internal computations on the data, and responding by performing actions that affect the environment either using effectors or via communication with other agents. Two levels of control are associated with this sense, interpretation, and response loop: deliberative and metalevel control (figure 1.2, this vol., ch. 1). The lower control level is deliberative control (also called the object level), which involves the agent making decisions about what domain-level problem solving to perform in the current context and how to coordinate with other agents to complete tasks requiring joint effort. These deliberations may have to be done in the face of limited resources, uncertainty about action outcomes, and real-time constraints. Tasks in these environments can be generated at any time by the environment or other agents and generally have deadlines where completion after the deadline could lead to lower or no utility.

Single-Agent Metalevel Control

At the higher control level is metalevel control, which involves the agent making decisions about whether to deliberate, how many resources to dedicate to this deliberation, and what specific deliberative control to perform in the current context. In practice, metalevel control can be viewed as the process of deciding how to interleave domain and deliberative control actions such that tasks are achieved within their deadlines, and also allocating the required amount of processor and other resources to these actions at the appropriate times. For example, suppose the current time is 10 and an agent is in the midst of executing a set of high-quality tasks with a deadline to complete the task at time 25. At time 15 the agent receives a new medium-quality task T_{new} with expected duration of 10 and a deadline of 40. The sensible metalevel control decision would be for the agent to delay deliberating about how to accomplish task T_{new} in the context of ongoing activities until the existing task set has completed execution (time 25). This would guarantee that the existing task set completes within its deadline and quality can still be gained by processing T_{new} by time 40. The metalevel control decision process should be designed to be computationally inexpensive, obviating the need for meta-metalevel control.

Metalevel control also involves choosing among alternative deliberative action sequences, including choosing among various alternatives for scheduling/planning; choosing between scheduling/planning and coordination; and allocating extra time for learning activities. Consider the following example: suppose the current time is 6 and an agent has two tasks: T_x, a high-quality task with expected duration of 10 and deadline 30; and T_y, a low-quality task with expected duration of 6 and deadline 30. Quality, in this work, is a deliberately abstract domain-independent concept that describes the contribution of a particular action to the overall problem solving. The metacontrol decision could be to spend 5 time units doing a detailed high-quality deliberation about T_x to find a good plan for the high-quality task, and to spend 2 time units doing a quick and dirty deliberation to generate a plan for T_y (the lower-quality task). The remaining time not used by deliberative activities will be allocated to successfully execute both tasks.

Multiagent Metalevel Control

In the multiagent context, metalevel control decisions by different agents that are part of a agent network need to be coordinated. These agents may have multiple high-level goals from which to choose, but if two or more agents need to coordinate their actions, the agents' metacontrol components must be on the same page. That is, the agents must reason about the same problem and may need to be on the same stage of the problem-solving process (e.g., if one agent decides to devote little time to communication/negotiation before moving to other deliberative decisions while another agent sets aside a large portion of deliberation time for negotiation, the latter agent would waste time trying to negotiate with an unwilling partner). Thus, if an agent changes its problem-solving context, it must notify other agents with which it may interact. This suggests that the metacontrol component of each agent should have a multiagent policy in which the progression of what deliberations agents do and when they do them is choreographed carefully and includes branches to account for what could happen as deliberation (and execution) plays out.

Determining the multiagent policy is a complicated problem, as the multiagent policy is not expected to be simply the union of all single-agent metacontrol policies. Consider for instance, two agents: A1 and A2 are negotiating about when A1 can complete method M_1 that enables A2's method M2. This negotiation involves an iterative process of proposals and counterproposals where at each stage A2 generates a commitment request to A1, and A1 performs local optimization computations (scheduling) to evaluate commitment requests; this process repeats until A1 and A2 arrive at a mutually acceptable commitment. The metalevel control decision would be to ensure that A1 completes its local optimization in an acceptable amount of time so that A2 can choose alternate methods in case the commitment is not possible. In setting up a negotiation, the metalevel control should establish when negotiation results will be available. This involves defining important parameters of the negotiation, including the earliest time the target method will be enabled. Two agents with different views of metacontrol policy for negotiation need to be reconciled in order to set up the earliest starting time parameter used in the negotiation process. Rubinstein, Smith, and Zimmerman (this vol., chap. 14) discuss a number of local agent parameters, including coordination-period, quiescence-period, and non-local-freeze period to handle explicit coordination between agents. Kennedy (this vol., chap. 15) introduces distributed metamanagement, where a single agent has multiple metalevels (metareasoning methods) that monitor each other and the same object level. This also requires choreographing the metalevels, albeit within the same agent.

A second multiagent metalevel control issue involves exploring how to dynamically split a network of agents into neighborhoods that are coordinated where each agent in a neighborhood has similar metalevel control parameter settings; different neighborhoods may have different metalevel control settings. Coordinated metalevel control decisions do not mean that metalevel control has to be the same in all parts of the network; instead, it involves finding consistent sets for different parts of the network.

Multiagent metacontrol suggests the need for some kind of metalevel message passing. There are important trade-offs between the amount of communication (both size and number of messages) and resulting overhead, and the usefulness of such communication. Agents must determine what kind of information is contained in a metalevel message. In some situations, it may be enough for the agent to simply let others know that it is thinking about context *X*; in other cases, such as when agents are more tightly coupled, an agent may need to communicate some partial results of its current thinking as well. Agents must also reason about how to handle metacontrol messages from others and coordinate when these messages should be received and handled.

A Real-World Application

The following is a description of a real-world application that will need this type of metalevel control. Netrads (Krainin, An, & Lesser, 2007; Zink et al., 2005) is a network of adaptive radars controlled by a collection of meteorological command and control (MCC) agents that determine for the local radars where to scan based on emerging weather conditions. The Netrads radar is designed to quickly detect low-lying meteorological phenomena such as tornadoes, and each radar belongs to exactly one MCC.

The MCC agent can manage multiple radars simultaneously. It gathers raw data from the radars and runs detection algorithms on weather data to recognize significant meteorological phenomena. The time allotted to the radar and its control systems for data gathering and analysis is known as a heartbeat. Results are used to determine potential weather scanning tasks for the next scanning cycle. Tasks are classified as internal tasks (are squarely under the purview of one agent only) and boundary tasks (shared by multiple MCCs). It is important for MCCs to coordinate both to avoid wasteful redundant scanning as well as to ensure multiple radar scans when required.

Each MCC communicates with its neighbors to agree on what weather scanning tasks it should do and how these tasks should be done in concert with tasks of its neighbors. The MCC then uses a three-step decentralized process to determine the best set of scans for the available radars that will maximize the sum of the utilities of the chosen tasks. It executes a local combinatorial optimization algorithm to determine the best configuration from a local point of view, then exchanges these configurations with neighborhood agents as part of a hill-climbing negotiation protocol to determine which radars to schedule and how much radar time to allocate to each task. This process of local optimization and negotiation is time constrained since radars need to be constantly repositioned to track weather phenomena and recognize the arrival of new phenomena.

For each heartbeat in the Netrads domain, a ground-level action as defined in figure 1.2 would be a radar scan of a weather task. The object level/deliberative action would be the MCC spending some initial time in processing the radar data obtained during the last heartbeat, then performing a local optimization to determine the schedule of the radars under its control, followed by negotiation rounds of alternating communication and recomputation of the local schedule. The metalevel decision involves guiding the schedule optimization and negotiation actions of the MCC to maximize global utility.

Solution Approach

The generalized metalevel control (GeMEC) architecture (figure 13.1) consists of a problem abstraction component, a performance profile learner, a decision process component, and a current state evaluator. A trigger is an event requiring the attention of the metalevel layer. It could be the arrival of a new task or a change in the environment. In Netrads, a triggering event occurs at every heartbeat since emerging weather events need to be scanned and analyzed at each heartbeat.

When the metalevel layer is triggered, the problem abstraction component (PAC) extracts the associated task and identifies high-level alternative ways by which the task can be completed successfully. These alternatives are captured in a task structure called meta-alt task structure. The PAC uses performance profile (Dean & Boddy, 1988

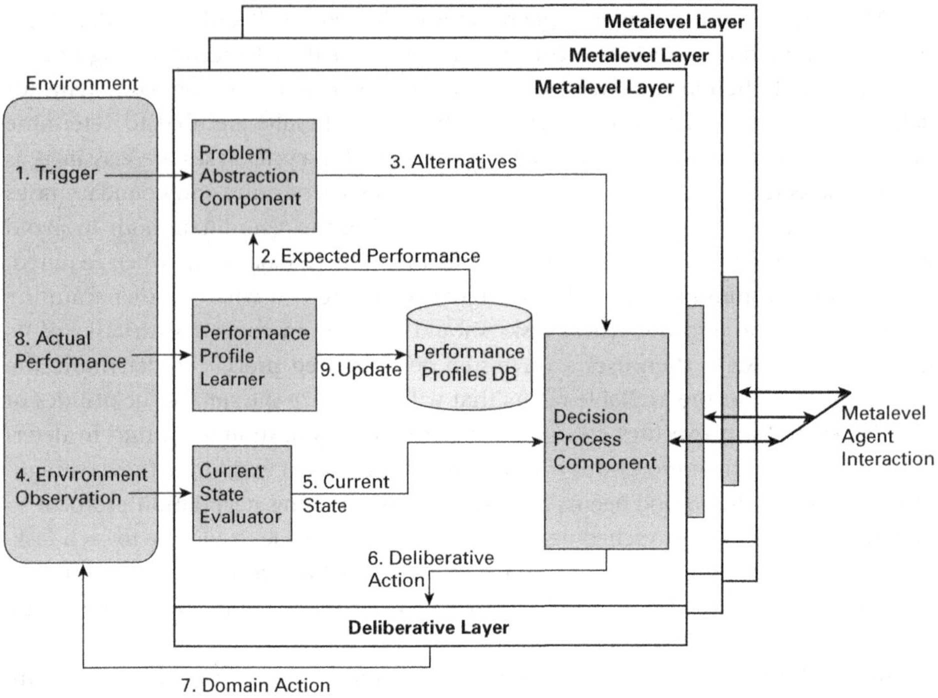

Figure 13.1
Control flow in the generalized metalevel control (GeMEC) architecture.

chap. 3) information about the deliberative action modes from a performance profile database to determine these alternatives. Generally, the performance profile will be a mapping from run time to expected output quality (Zilberstein, this vol., chap. 3). The PAC will help control the complexity of the metalevel decision process by weeding out all superfluous information. This is especially relevant in applications where each deliberation action can be performed in different modes resulting in different performance characteristics. For instance, scheduling, as a deliberation action, can have multiple modes: heuristic scheduler (Wagner, Garvey, & Lesser, 1997), MDP-based scheduler (Musliner et al., 2007), or constraint-based scheduler (Smith, Gallagher, Zimmerman, & Barbulescu, 2006). This framework will be useful to study concavity and close-approximations of the profile function to control complexity of the metareasoning process (Conitzer, this vol., chap. 8).

The GeMEC framework is an extension of figure 1.5 (this vol., ch. 1) that describes metalevel reasoning among multiple agents. Using GeMEC, we elaborate the functionality of the metalevel reasoning module and propose a method for communication as well as for distributed decision making among the agents. In the Netrads application,

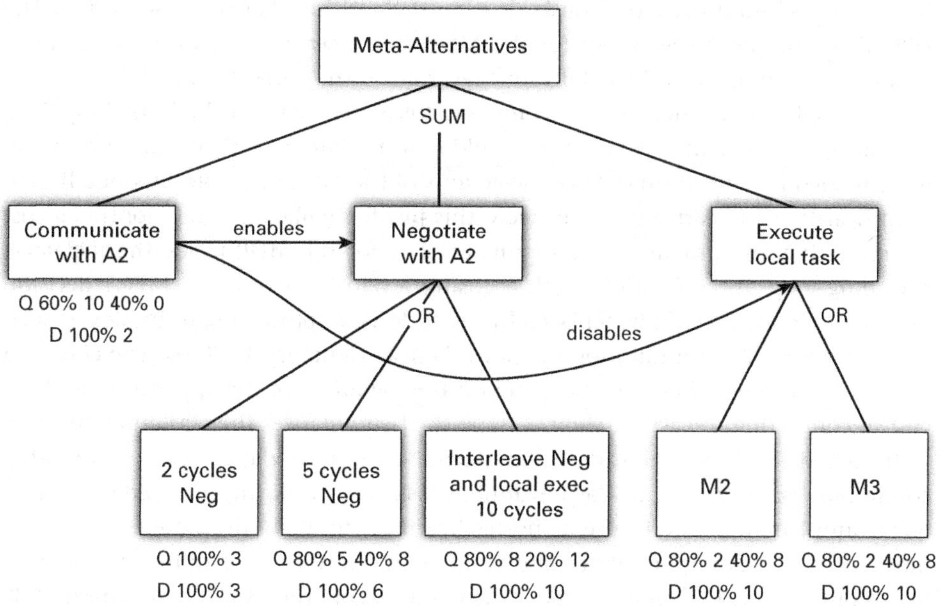

Figure 13.2
Task structure describing metalevel alternatives for a specific Netrads scenario.

an MCC has multiple deliberation modes. Varying amounts of time and resources can be allocated to a single heartbeat, and within a heartbeat, different allocations to optimization and negotiation cycles can be made. Consider a scenario where two agents A1 and A2 share an interdependency requiring negotiation. Figure 13.2 is the task structure representing a set of metalevel alternatives for agent A1 and their associated quality distributions. Agent A1 can choose to communicate (one-shot negotiation in this case) with A2 to determine whether A2 is willing to negotiate about the shared task. If A2 agrees to negotiate then the Negotiate-with-A2 task is enabled and the corresponding alternatives will be chosen based on the resources. If A2 refuses to negotiate, A1 will choose to execute one of its local tasks M2 or M3. The leaf nodes are the domain-level primitive actions and have a quality and duration distribution associated with them. For example, choosing the Communicate-with-A2 has a duration of 2 units and will result in a quality value of 10 (meaning Agent A2 agrees to negotiate) 60 percent of the time, and 0 (Agent A2 refuses to negotiate) 40 percent of the time. Here, agent communication is assumed to be reliable.

Once constructed, the meta-alt task structure is then sent to the decision process component (DPC). In the context of the Netrads application, the DPC converts the metalevel alternative task structure into a Markov decision process (MDP) (Bertsekas

& Tsitsiklis, 1996) using a previously developed algorithm (Raja & Lesser, 2007). The DPC then computes the policy for the MDP and determines the best deliberative action to recommend to the deliberative layer given the current context.

An MDP-based decision process component is appropriate for the Netrads application since the meta-alt task structure would tend to remain static in this application for extended periods of time. Also, the actions of the MCC are typically not adjusted from heartbeat to heartbeat. In our view, this justifies embedding the nontrivial cost of computing an optimal or near-optimal policy for the MDP inside the metalevel reasoning loop. In applications with a greater level of dynamics, GeMEC's decision process component could be replaced by other decision-processing technologies such as stochastic online optimization methods (Bent & Hentenryck, 2004). The choice of the DPC mechanism hence will depend on the dynamics of the application and the cost of computing the action choices. Table 13.1 summarizes the reasoning process.

In Netrads, the DPC could adjust the system heartbeat to adapt to changing weather conditions. For example, if many scanning tasks are occurring in a certain region, metacontrol may decide to use a shorter heartbeat to allow the system to respond more rapidly. It is important to handle different heartbeats for different neighborhoods of MCCs. For example, suppose there is a neighborhood with a heartbeat of 30 seconds and another one with a heartbeat of 60 seconds, with one MCC belonging to both neighborhoods. Also suppose that this MCC is using a 30-second heartbeat. We can choose between one of two protocols. After the end of its first heartbeat, new information is sent to its neighbors in the 60-second neighborhood, or the agent negotiates only with its 30-second neighbors until its slower neighbors have entered their next heartbeat.

The DPC can also adjust the parameters involved in the calculation of an MCC's local configuration in order to trade off optimality for a shorter run time, which would allow more rounds of negotiation to be performed. Spending more time on negotiation may be preferable, for example, when there are many boundary tasks compared to internal tasks. In fact, the DPC could make this decision for each round in the negotiation process. This would allow a fast estimate of the optimal local configuration

Table 13.1
GeMEC reasoning loop for Netrads

1.	Extract task
2.	Use performance profile database to generate meta-alt task structure
3.	Send meta-alt task structure to DPC
4.	Convert meta-alt task structure to a MDP
5.	Derive optimal policy and recommend best action choice

to begin negotiation and then switch to a better optimization in later rounds or perhaps to begin with the current brute force optimization and switch to other methods after negotiating for a while.

Toward Formalizing the Multiagent Metalevel Control Process

Our approach to the DPC involves formalizing the agent's metalevel control problem using an MDP (Raja & Lesser, 2007; Alexander, Raja, & Musliner, 2008). The advantage of using an MDP to model the metalevel control problem is twofold: the MDP supports sequential decision making allowing for nonmyopic decision making, and metalevel reasoning will be inexpensive as it will involve only MDP policy lookup. Several researchers (Peshkin et al., 2000; Nair et al., 2003, 2003) have studied multiagent MDPs, but most have assumed full (individual) observability. However, as shown by Becker et al. (2003) the Netrads application involves agents having partial and different views of the global state. The decentralized Markov decision process (DEC-MDP) (Bernstein, Zilberstein, & Immerman, 2000) is a suitable framework for these types of problems. A DEC-MDP is a DEC-POMDP that is jointly fully observable (i.e., the combination of both agents' observations determines the global state of the system). The complexity of DEC-MDPs has been shown to be NEXP-complete for finite horizon problems and undecidable for infinite-horizon problems (Bernstein, Zilberstein, & Immerman, 2000). The complexity is mainly the result of the explosion in states, action choices, and observations due to agent interactions.

One way to overcome this complexity is to approximate the solution. An approximation of particular interest (Goldman & Zilberstein, 2008) leverages the idea that a lot of decentralized problems have some structure with influence on the level of decentralization. The key idea is that a feasible approximation can be found by decomposing the global reward function into local and temporal problems. A communication policy is then used to synchronize the single-agent MDPs occasionally. This would allow agents to exchange information at certain times to obtain a global state (Xuan, Lesser, & Zilberstein, 2001). When not communicating, the agents will act independently of each other and not necessarily follow the optimal policy. This local policy of an agent can be viewed as Sutton's options (Sutton, Precup, & Singh, 1999). The options will have terminal actions, specifically communication actions. In this model, it is also assumed that all options are terminated whenever at least one of the agents initiates communications. It is also assumed that when the agents exchange information, the global state of the system is revealed.

This model is known to be equivalent to a multiagent Markov decision process (MMDP) (Goldman & Zilberstein, 2008). The optimal policy would involve searching over all possible pairs of local single-agent policies and communication policies. For example, each agent needs to ensure that it enters into a negotiation mode only upon agreement of the partner agent to enter into a similar mode. If the other agent refuses to negotiate, the requesting agent should make sure that it does not enter into a negotiation mode. This behavior will be manifested by an appropriate definition of the reward function and will enforce *coordinated metalevel control*. The reward function for each state s will have two components and can be defined as: $R(s) = R_{\text{local}} + R_{\text{coord}}$ where R_{local} is the reward obtained from executing local actions and R_{coord} is the reward obtained from actions requiring coordination. This reward function has to capture the fact that an agent should not consider negotiating as an action choice for a particular time frame unless the other agent is choosing the negotiation action for an overlapping time frame.

In addition to agreeing to negotiate, the agents must agree on negotiation parameters. Each agent also needs to determine how much time and resources to allocate to the negotiation process. The motivation for longer durations would be to improve the success rate of negotiation. The agent can also choose to interleave the negotiation with a local domain action execution so that the negotiation has more end-to-end time, thus accounting for uncertainty in outcome, which improves the success probability of the negotiation.

We now describe a simple example of the DPC's decision-making process. Consider a scenario where there are two agents, A1 and A2, with an interdependency requiring negotiation. Figure 13.3 describes the metalevel MDP for agent A1. State *S21* is a state where the agent has to communicate with agent A2 and determine whether A2 is willing to negotiate in the next time period. This is represented by action *a11*, which has a duration of 2 units. Agent A2 can respond with one of two responses: agree to negotiate (outcome *o1*) or refuse to negotiate (outcome *o2*). The states reached and action choices available to agent A1 vary depending on the outcome of action *a11*. The actions available from state *S22* allow agent A1 to allocate different amounts of time to negotiation where the entire processor is allocated to negotiation only (duration 3 for action *a12* representing the 2-cycle negotiation option and duration 6 for action *a13* representing the 5-cycle negotiation option), or the agent can choose to interleave the negotiation with a domain action (method *M2*) for a duration of 10 units (action *a14*). If outcome *o2* occurs, agent A1 will not move into a negotiation phase and instead will try to ensure that it uses its resources efficiently by choosing one of its local domain actions (actions *a15* and *a16*).

Empirical Study

We have developed a set of experiments based on a heuristic method to determine whether metalevel control is indeed useful in the Netrads application. Specifically, we study the usefulness of changing heartbeats of the MCC in order to handle dynamic weather patterns. Our goal, if we can successfully show the need for metalevel control,

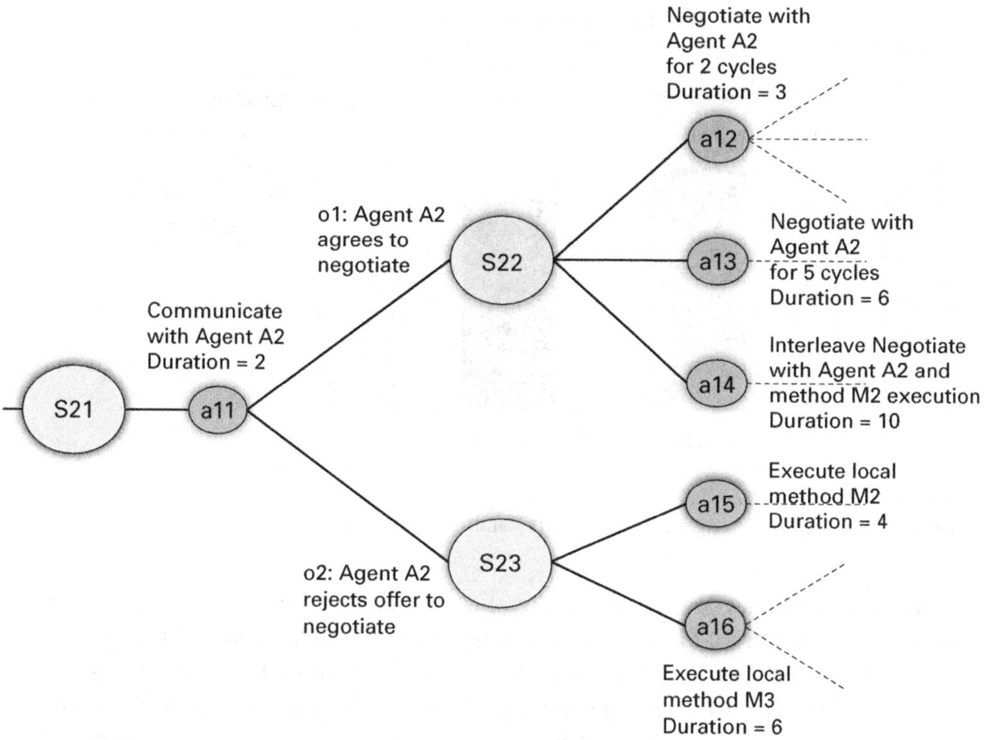

Figure 13.3
Snapshot of decision process for determining negotiation actions.

is to use the parameters obtained from the heuristic approach to define the DEC-MDP state and action space in our future work.

The Netrads simulator implements four different categories of weather tasks called Storm, Rotation, Velocity, and Reflectivity. For our experiments, we focused on Storms and Rotations. The differences between these tasks are the size (Storms occupy a much larger area than Rotations) and the elevations at which a radar must scan the task to obtain useful information (Storms must be scanned at the lowest four elevations, but Rotations must be scanned at the lowest six). We used two kinds of weather scenarios: "Storm scenarios" and "Rotation scenarios." Storm scenarios contained eighty storm tasks as well as one task each of the other three types, and Rotation scenarios contained eighty rotation tasks as well as one task each of the other three types.

For each of these scenarios, we compared the effectiveness of a 30-second MCC Heartbeat to a 60-second MCC Heartbeat, while varying the added value we assigned to more up-to-date information. Radar scans with a 60-second heartbeat received a

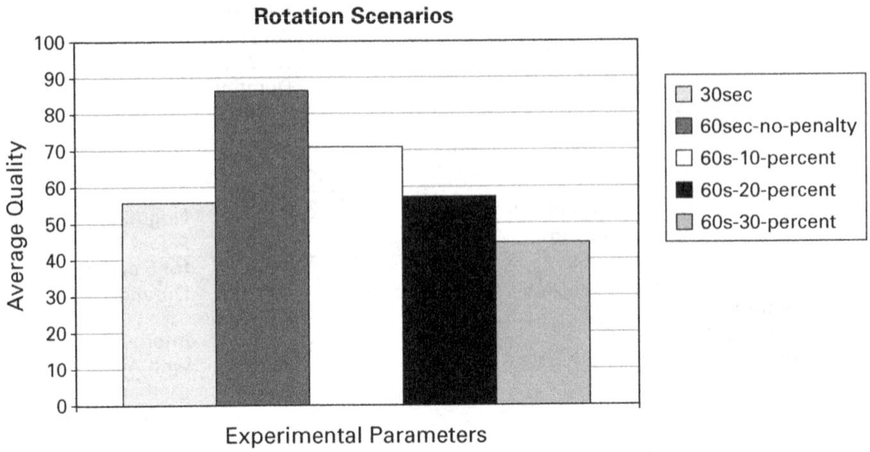

Figure 13.4
Quality obtained by changing heartbeats in Rotation scenarios.

penalty, because they are not up to date; that is, they were assigned just a percentage of the value they would otherwise have achieved, while radar scans from runs where the heartbeat was set to 30 seconds received the full value. Four different penalty values (no penalty, 10 percent penalty, 20 percent penalty, and 30 percent penalty) plus the 30-second heartbeat (with no penalty) were used in 200 runs each for a total of 1,000 data points per weather scenario that we examined. The mean results are shown in figures 13.4 and 13.5.

When no penalty was assessed, a 60-second heartbeat was better in both scenarios; but when too great a penalty (30 percent) was assessed, the 30-second heartbeat was better in both scenarios. Thus, for these cases, there is no need for online metalevel control—a single heartbeat value dominates regardless of task type. However, when the penalty was set at 10 percent or 20 percent, the optimal choice of heartbeat depends on the task type: 60 seconds is better for rotations due to the need for more scanned elevations, and 30 seconds is better for storms. Note that, for rotation tasks, the average value with a 30-second heartbeat is not much less than the average value achieved by a 60-second heartbeat with 20 percent penalty, and for storm tasks, the average value with a 30-second heartbeat is not very much greater than the average value achieved by a 60-second heartbeat with a 10 percent penalty. These results indicate that metalevel control is useful if the late penalty assessed for 60-second heartbeats lies within a critical range of roughly 10–20 percent. If the penalty is too low, the increased amount of scanning performed in a 60-second interval dominates, but a 30-second heartbeat dominates when the penalty is too high to be overcome, even for the more scanning-intensive rotation tasks.

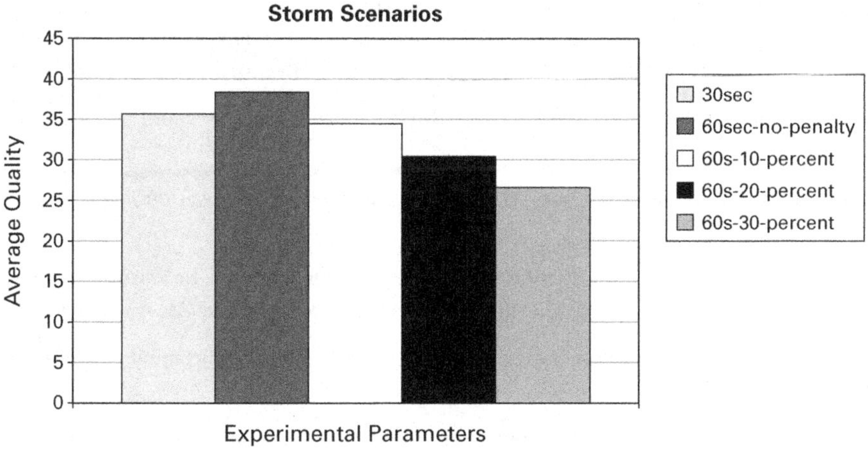

Figure 13.5
Quality obtained by changing heartbeats in Storm scenarios.

Conclusion

In this chapter, we map the various multiagent metalevel questions to a single generalized formalization of metalevel control. We then elaborate how these issues will be addressed in a real tornado tracking application. And finally, we describe a methodology to construct a class of MDPs with the ability to model interactions among multiple metalevel decision process components and provide some initial experimental results that identify the scenarios where metalevel control could potentially be useful in the Netrads tornado-tracking application.

References

Alexander, G., Raja, A., & Musliner, D. (2008). Controlling deliberation in a Markov decision process-based agent. In L. Padgham, D. Parkes, J. Müller, & S. Parsons (Eds.), *Proceedings of the Seventh International Joint Conference on Autonomous Agents and Multi-Agent Systems* (pp. 61–468). Richland, SC: IFAAMAS.

Becker, R., Zilberstein, S., Lesser, V., & Goldman, C. V. (2003). Transition-independent decentralized Markov decision processes. In *Proceedings of the Second International Joint Conference on Autonomous Agents and Multi Agent Systems* (pp. 41–48). Richland, SC: IFAAMAS.

Bent, R., & Hentenryck, P. V. (2004). Regrets only! Online stochastic optimization under time constraints. In D. McGuiness & G. Ferguson (Eds.), *Proceedings of the Nineteenth National Conference on Artificial Intelligence* (pp. 501–506). Menlo Park, CA: AAAI Press.

Bernstein, D., Zilberstein, S., & Immerman, N. (2000). The complexity of decentralized control of Markov decision processes. In C. Boutilier & M. Goldszmidt (Eds.), *Proceedings of the Sixteenth Conference on Uncertainty in Artificial Intelligence* (pp. 32–37). San Francisco, CA: Morgan Kaufmann.

Bertsekas, D. P., & Tsitsiklis, J. N. (1996). *Neuro-dynamic programming.* Belmont, MA: Athena Scientific.

Cox, M. T. (2005). Metacognition in computation: A selected research review. *Artificial Intelligence, 169*(2), 104–141.

Dean, T., & Boddy, M. (1988). An analysis of time-dependent planning. In *Proceedings of the Seventh National Conference on Artificial Intelligence* (pp. 49–54). Menlo Park, CA: AAAI Press.

Doyle, J. (1983). What is rational psychology? Toward a modern mental philosophy. *AI Magazine, 4*(3), 50–53.

Goldman, C., & Zilberstein, S. (2008). Communication-based decomposition mechanisms for decentralized MDPs. *Journal of Artificial Intelligence Research, 32,* 169–202.

Horvitz, E. J. (1988). Reasoning under varying and uncertain resource constraints. In *Proceedings of the Seventh National Conference on Artificial Intelligence* (pp. 111–116). Menlo Park, CA: AAAI Press.

Krainin, M., An, B., & Lesser, V. (2007). An application of automated negotiation to distributed task allocation. In *Proceedings of the 2007 IEEE/WIC/ACM International Conference on Intelligent Agent Technology* (pp. 138–145). Los Alamitos, CA: IEEE Computer Society.

Musliner, D., Goldman, R., Durfee, E., Wu, J., Dolgov, D., & Boddy, M. (2007). Coordination of highly contingent plans. In *Proceedings of the International Conference on Integration of Knowledge Intensive Multi-Agent Systems* (pp. 418–422). KIMAS-07. Los Alamitos, CA: IEEE Computer Society. http://www.musliner.com/david/papers/ksco07.pdf.

Nair, R., Tambe, M., Yokoo, M., Pynadath, D., & Marsella, S. (2003). Taming decentralized POMDPs: Towards efficient policy computation for multiagent settings. In G. Gottlob & T. Walsh (Eds.), *Proceedings of the Eighteenth International Joint Conference on Artificial Intelligence* (pp. 705–711). San Francisco, CA: Morgan Kaufmann.

Peshkin, L., Kim, K. E., Meuleau, N., & Kaelbling, L. P. (2000). Learning to cooperate via policy search. In C. Boutilier & M. Goldszmidt (Eds.), *Proceedings of the Sixteenth Conference on Uncertainty in Artificial Intelligence* (pp. 307–314). San Francisco, CA: Morgan Kaufmann.

Raja, A., & Lesser, V. (2007). A framework for meta-level control in multi-agent systems. *Autonomous Agents and Multi-Agent Systems, 15*(2), 147–196.

Russell, S. J., Subramanian, D., & Parr, R. (1993). Provably bounded optimal agents. In *Proceedings of the Thirteenth International Joint Conference on Artificial Intelligence* (pp. 338–344). San Francisco, CA: Morgan Kaufmann.

Simon, H., & Kadane, J. (1974) Optimal problem solving search: All-or-nothing solutions. *Computer Science Technical Report CMU-CS-74-41,* Carnegie Mellon University.

Simon, H. A. (1976). From substantive to procedural rationality. In S. J. Latsis (Ed.), *Method and appraisal in economics* (pp. 129–148). Cambridge: Cambridge University Press.

Simon, H. (1982). *Models of bounded rationality* (vol. 1). Cambridge, MA: MIT Press.

Smith, S., Gallagher, A., Zimmerman, T., & Barbulescu, L. (2006). Multi-agent management of joint schedules. In E. Durfee & D. Musliner (Eds.), *Working Notes of the 2006 AAAI Spring Symposium on Distributed Plan and Schedule Management* (pp. 128–135). Technical Report SS-06-04. Menlo Park, CA: AAAI Press.

Stefik, M. (1981). Planning and meta-planning. *Artificial Intelligence*, *16*(2), 141–170.

Sutton, R. S., Precup, D., & Singh, S. P. (1999). Between MDPs and semi-MDPs: A framework for temporal abstraction in reinforcement learning. *Artificial Intelligence*, *112*(1–2), 181–211.

Wagner, T., Garvey, A., & Lesser, V. (1997). Criteria-directed heuristic task scheduling. Technical Report TR-97-16. UMASS Department of Computer Science.

Xuan, P., Lesser, V., & Zilberstein, S. (2001). Communication decisions in multi-agent cooperation: model and experiments. In *Proceedings of the Fifth International Conference on Autonomous Agents* (pp. 616–623). Richland, SC: IFAAMAS.

Zink, M., Westbrook, D., Abdallah, S., Horling, B., Lyons, E., Lakamraju, V., et al. (2005). Meteorological command and control: An end-to-end architecture for a hazardous weather detection sensor network. In *Proceedings of the 2005 ACM Workshop on End-to-End, Sense-and-Respond Systems, Applications, and Services* (pp. 37–42). Berkeley, CA: USENIX Association.

14 The Role of Metareasoning in Achieving Effective Multiagent Coordination

Zachary B. Rubinstein, Stephen F. Smith, and Terry L. Zimmerman

The ability to dynamically manage internal computational activity is important in many agent-based systems. We focus in this chapter on a system of scheduling agents, which are engaged in managing and executing a joint plan in an uncertain environment. Such agents have limited time to take correcting actions in response to unexpected execution results, placing a premium on the need for bounded rationality (Zilberstein, this vol., chap. 3; Simon, 1957). The agent must balance the time it spends locally revising its schedule (actions slated to restore feasibility and/or capitalize on detected opportunities for local schedule improvement) with the time it spends coordinating with other agents (actions taken to identify and exploit opportunities to boost global schedule quality through joint change). The former is necessary to keep execution going but may be prone to myopic, suboptimal decisions, given its local incomplete view of the overall problem and solution. The latter can lead to better joint scheduling decisions, but the computation and communication costs in obtaining them may render them obsolete before they can be acted on. Given these tradeoffs, it makes sense to try to exploit aspects of the current control state (e.g., the tempo of execution and level of dynamics in the environment) to dynamically configure appropriate sorts of computational actions.

The role of metareasoning in this work is to modify agent control during plan execution in response to a changing environment. Conceptually we have precompiled the metareasoning decisions into the object-level reasoning process as discussed by Zilberstein (this vol., chap. 3) rather than introducing an explicit metalevel as depicted in figure 14.6. In our application, we employ a set of rules that we inferred based on operational experience to govern this behavior. As noted in the discussion of results, a more principled approach based on learning, such as that of the GeMEC framework presented by Raja, Alexander, Lesser, and Krainin (this vol., chap. 13) may be warranted. Unlike the research presented by Kennedy (this vol., chap. 15) on distributed metamanagement for self-protection and self-explanation and the chapters in Part V of this volume, our work, with its emphasis on operational performance improvement, does not make any epistemological inferences about the mental state of the individual agent or about the states of other agents, nor does it make any claim about the nature of cognition. Rather, an agent monitors its activity and seeks to reconfigure responses based on its ability to process and analyze information in a timely manner. In our architecture, agents reconfigure solely based on the computational and messaging load on the agent and not on the predicted behavior of other agents, as Borghetti and Gini describe in their work on weighted prediction divergence for metareasoning (this vol., chap. 16).

The specific system of interest in our research is the "CMU agent" (Smith, Gallagher, Zimmerman, Barbulescu, & Rubinstein, 2007), one of three competing approaches developed within the DARPA Coordinators Program for solving the distributed schedule management problem. In brief, this problem requires a set of agents to jointly execute a schedule so as to maximize the quality obtained by all executed activities. These "scenarios" provide each agent with the portion of the initial schedule that it is responsible for, a set of alternative (substitutable) activities, and associated outcome and duration probabilities for all assigned activities. Each agent is also given limited visibility of interdependent activities that have been assigned to other agents, but no agent has a global view of either the problem or solution. The CMU agent design takes a scheduler-centric perspective to solving the Coordinators problem. An incremental, flexible times scheduler sits at its core and is used to drive the agent's two core processes: (1) it is invoked to perform local scheduling in response to external feedback, and (2) it is invoked hypothetically to generate and evaluate "non-local" options—opportunities that entail interagent coordination in order to boost global solution quality.

In the sections below, we consider the control problem that the CMU agent faces in allocating cycles to each of these core processes. In operation, our multiagent system must interact with a simulated environment in near real time, and hence only limited computational cycles are available for allocation to either of these processes. We examine the hypothesis that dynamic management of control parameters related to this division of computational effort between local scheduling and interagent coordination can lead to improved performance over any fixed configuration of these parameters.

Before discussing the control parameters of interest and settling on a specific subset for experimental analysis, we briefly summarize the CMU agent.

Overview of the CMU Agent

The CMU agent architecture is schematically depicted in figure 14.1. In its most basic form, an agent comprises four principal components—the Executor, the Scheduler, the Distributed State Manager (DSM), and the Options Manager—all of which share a common model of the current scenario and solution state. This common model

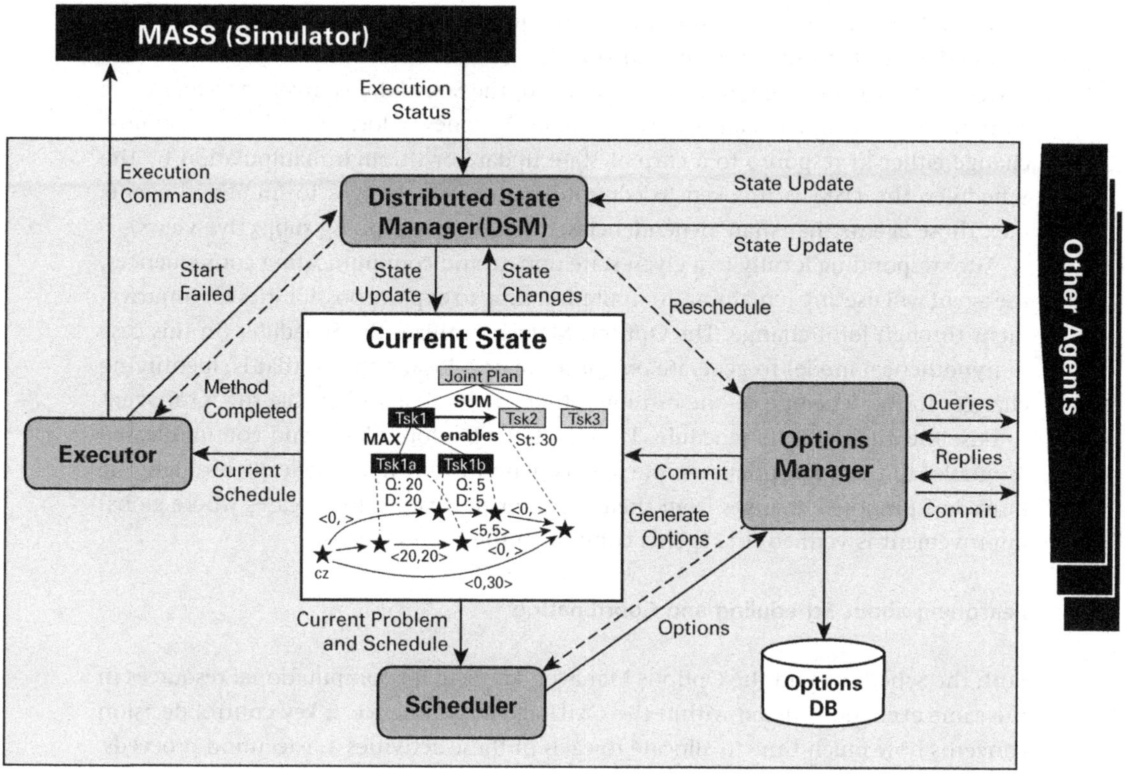

Figure 14.1
CMU agent architecture.

couples a domain-level representation of the agent's local (subjective) view of the overall scenario (encoded as a c-taems [Boddy et al., 2005] task structure) to an underlying simple temporal network (STN) (Dechter, Meiri, & Pearl, 1991). At any point during operation, the currently installed schedule dictates the timing and sequence of domain-level activities that will be initiated by the agent. The Executor, running in its own thread, continually monitors the enabling conditions of various pending activities and activates the next pending activity as soon as all of its causal and temporal constraints are satisfied. The other three components run on a separate thread in a blackboard-based control regime and are responsible for coordinating with other agents and managing the current schedule over time.

When execution results are received back from the environment (shown in figure 14.1 as the MASS simulator, i.e., the execution simulator provided by the Coordinators program) and/or changes to assumed external constraints are received from other agents, the agent's model of current state is updated. An incremental propagator based on Cesta & Oddi, 1996, is used to infer consequences within the STN. In cases where this update leads to inconsistency in the STN or it is otherwise recognized that the current local schedule might now be improved, the Scheduler is invoked to revise the current solution and install a new schedule. Whenever local schedule constraints change either in response to a current state update or through manipulation by the Scheduler, the DSM is invoked to communicate these changes to interested agents (i.e., those agents that share dependencies and have overlapping subjective views).

After responding locally to a given state update and communicating consequences, the agent will use any remaining computation time to explore possibilities for improvement through joint change. The Options Manager utilizes the Scheduler (in this case in hypothetical mode) to generate one or more non-local options, that is, identifying changes to the schedule of one or more other agents that will enable the local agent to raise the quality of its schedule. These options are formulated and communicated as queries to the appropriate remote agents, who in turn hypothetically evaluate the impact of proposed changes from their local perspective. In those cases where global improvement is verified, the agents commit to the joint changes.

Reasoning about Scheduling and Coordinating

Both the Scheduler and the Options Manager compete for computational resources in the same execution thread within the CMU agent, and hence, a key control decision concerns how much time to allocate to each of these activities as execution proceeds. By default assumption, explicit coordination actions (issuing queries to other agents, generating options in response to queries, etc.) are given lower priority than local model updating and schedule revision actions. However, within this default structure there are still many degrees of freedom in controlling and interleaving scheduling and coordination processes. The Options Manager can be constrained in its frequency of use, in the type and number of options that it generates, and in the duration of the "freeze" period where options can change activities on the schedule only after that period. Likewise, the Scheduler's operation can also be constrained by limiting how frequently it is called and the amount of search performed. Ideally, the setting of parameters relevant to these different Scheduler and Option Manager "configurations" should be driven dynamically by characteristics of the current control state.

In this section, we describe the various control parameters associated with the Scheduler and the Options Manager in more detail and hypothesize desirable settings as a function of current control circumstances. Then, in the section discussing experimental design, we identify a specific subset of parameters of interest and describe a series of experiments aimed at demonstrating the benefit of dynamically managing these parameter settings as a function of the agent's current control state.

Managing the Execution of the Scheduler

The Scheduler component of the CMU agent is designed to incrementally maintain a high-quality local schedule as the dynamics of execution unfold. In brief, it operates through iterative application of two subprocedures: a quality propagator and an activity allocator. Upon invocation, the quality propagator is first applied to compute the set of activities that (if scheduled) would maximize overall quality from the agent's local viewpoint. The activity allocator then takes this set of contributors, unschedules all activities in the current schedule that are not in this set, and then attempts to incrementally insert all currently unscheduled contributors into the current schedule. If at any point during this last step, the activity allocator is unable to feasibly add an unscheduled contributor activity into the schedule, this activity is marked as "nogood" (i.e., it is "unschedulable" together with the set of activities already in the schedule). It is removed from consideration and the quality propagator is reinvoked to compute a new set of contributors, and the process continues. The Scheduler terminates when the set of unscheduled contributors becomes empty (i.e., either all have been inserted into the schedule, or some subset has been ruled out and the set of substitutable activities has been exhausted). (The reader is referred to Smith et al., 2007, for further details.)

There are several basic options for controlling the amount of search performed by the above procedure:

• Satisfaction of soft constraints when placing unscheduled contributor activities (*explore-facilitated-choices*): The operation of inserting a new activity into the current agent schedule consists of finding a feasible "slot" (position) in the current scheduled sequence. In the absence of soft constraints (which in this context act to boost the quality of a given activity if appropriate precedence relations can be established with one or more other facilitator activities), all feasible slots are equally good and hence search can be streamlined by simply taking the first slot found. This in fact is the default mode of operation, wherein satisfaction of soft constraints is only achieved serendipitously. However, in scenarios rich with facilitated possibilities, better-quality solutions can be found by enumerating and selecting from among all feasible slots.
• Resetting of previously established "nogoods" (*reset-nogoods*): By default, an activity that fails in all attempts to place it on the timeline is tagged a "nogood" and will remain nogood across calls to the Scheduler. Since the schedule is changing incrementally, it is likely that the set of activities in the schedule for which a potential contributor activity that has been determined to be nogood is likely to persist over time, and hence, the added computational expense of redetermining that these potential contributors are nogood on each call can be avoided. However, in circumstances of high local schedule volatility, perhaps due to forced changes in interdependent decisions in other agents' schedules or to the introduction of new higher-priority tasks with

high impact on the set of contributors, failing to reconsider the set of nogood activities can be quite suboptimal (since they were determined heuristically in the first place).

• Rescheduling conditions (*reschedule-strategy*): A basic assumption of the CMU agent design is that its underlying "flexible times" representation of the schedule provides a hedge against uncertainty. Accordingly, the agent operates with a default policy wherein the Scheduler is invoked to revise the schedule only when the results of execution take the agent outside of the set of feasible evolutions of the future delineated by the current schedule. Of course, this policy can be conservative and miss opportunities for optimization (e.g., when activities finish early). In circumstances where scheduled activities have high uncertainty, a more aggressive rescheduling strategy that invokes the Scheduler whenever execution results deviate from expectations by more than an established threshold can provide a better option.

Managing the Execution of the Options Manager

The Options Manager is designed to identify and evaluate opportunities for improving the quality of the current schedule through joint change by two or more agents. At present, improvement opportunities center around the establishment of new "enablement" chains, which, in essence, establish preconditions that allow a currently unscheduled local activity to be scheduled. When invoked, the Options Manager uses the Scheduler in hypothetical mode to compute the maximum quality local schedule(s) that could be achieved if various remote enabler activities were assumed to be scheduled (rather than remaining in their current unscheduled state). The output of the Scheduler in this mode is a set of non-local options, each of which indicates the new expected quality and the set of enabler activities of other agents that must be scheduled for this option to be taken. From this set, the Options Manager determines if there is an option with the highest-quality gain, and, if so, issues a query to each agent owning an enabler activity identified in this option. The query requests the maximum quality that the remote agent could attain, given that the enabler activity must be included in its new schedule. Upon receiving responses to the issued queries and determining that the non-local option does indeed boost overall quality, the Options Manager issues messages to all parties to commit to this option.

Similar to the scheduling process, there are several parameters for controlling this explicit coordination process:

• Frequency of use (*coordination-frequency*): One basic parameter specifies how frequently to trigger the non-local option generation process. Within the blackboard control framework, nonlocal option-generation actions are generally given lower priority than model-updating or rescheduling actions. However, there is still an issue of how frequently to attempt to generate non-local options, since once such an action is initiated it cannot be preempted. *coordination-frequency* = *n* simply specifies that a non-local option-generation action will be queued for execution once every *n* ticks. In situations of high dynamics (demanding frequent updating, rescheduling, and DSM communication among agents), it makes intuitive sense to dial down (decrease) coordination-frequency. Alternatively, in situations of low dynamics, it makes sense to accelerate the search for productive multiagent change.

• "On demand" triggering delay period (*quiescence period*): A second mode in which the Option Manager and explicit coordination can be triggered is "on demand," that is, in response to some specific event. The receipt of a new task structure is a good example of this sort of event, as the integration into the agent's schedule of high-value local activities introduced by this structure may require another agent to schedule an enabling activity. In this case, integration of the new task, discovery of all interdependencies with activities of other agents, and establishment of a new local schedule that reflects this new task may take a few simulator ticks. To initiate non-local option generation prior to this point is not likely to be productive. The *quiescence period* parameter provides a knob for calibrating the timing of an "on demand" response.

• Number of options generated (*nbr-non-locals*): The number of options that are generated on any given call to the Options Manager is a third parameter. By default, the system currently generates only a single non-local option at a time. However, in situations where dynamics are low and the computational load is relatively low, increasing the number of non-local options generated can broaden the search for productive multiagent change.

• Freeze period for generating non-local changes (*non-local-freeze-period*): This parameter on the non-local option-generation process stipulates a time window relative to current time within which agents involved in the non-local option are precluded from either altering existing scheduled activities or allocating new ones. Since it takes time to coordinate with other agents, the viability of negotiated scheduling changes depends on advance planning that accounts for time likely to be consumed in communicating and committing to them. Through experience with the agent, we have established a nominal default value for this non-local-freeze-period. However, in situations of high dynamics and high communication overhead, we expect that it may be advantageous to increase this horizon.

• Response priority (*response-priority*): When an agent receives a query from an agent pursuing an explicit coordination session, it has to determine when to allot processing time to generate the response. While the response is being generated, processing of updates and scheduling may be delayed. The default policy is to make the *response-priority* low, which means that, while there are update calls and scheduling calls on the control agenda, they are processed before the response is generated. While this policy allows the agent to keep up to date with critical updates, the trade-off is an increased likelihood of failed coordination sessions, as query responses may be delayed

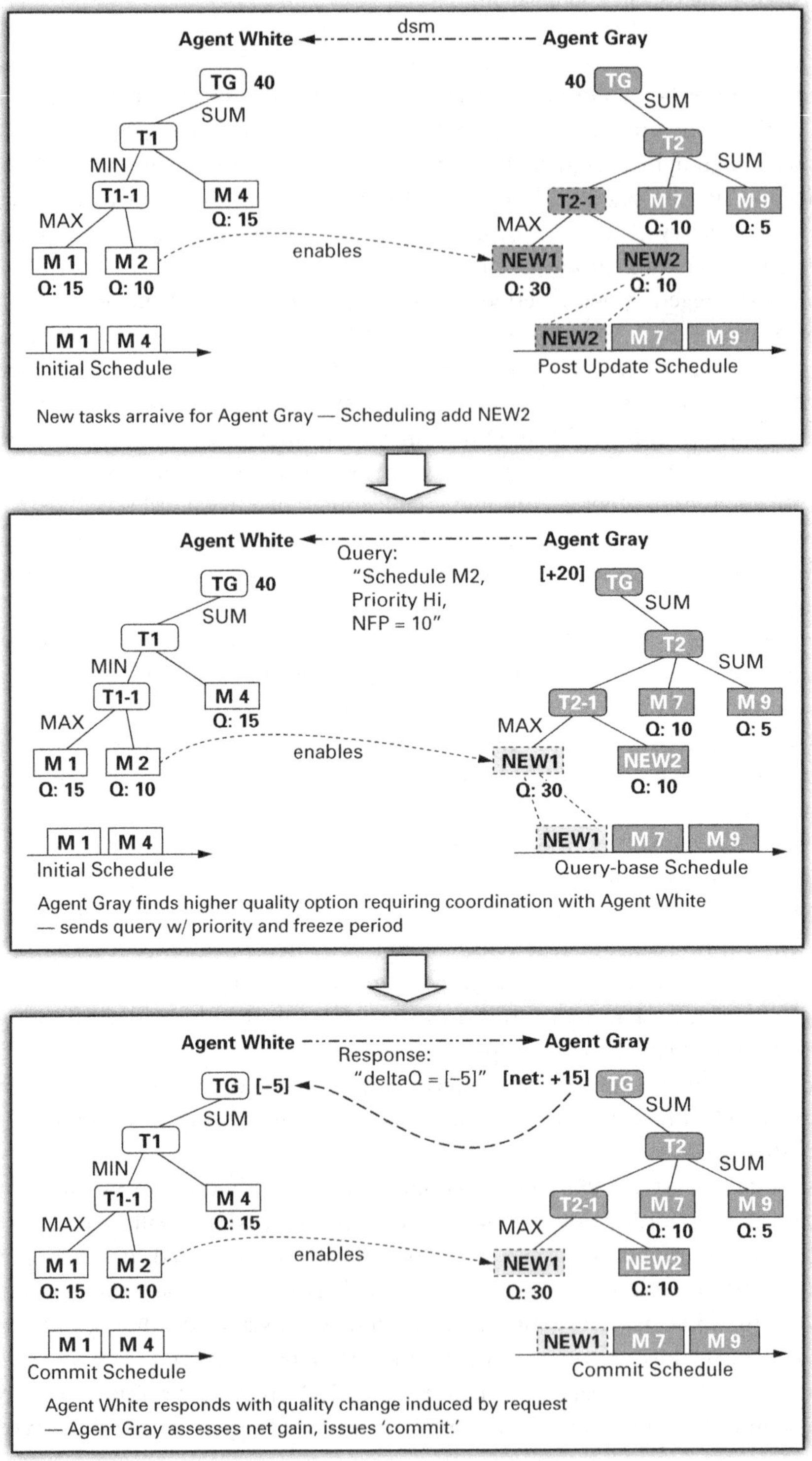
Agent White
dsm
Agent Gray
TG 40
SUM
T1
MIN
T1-1
M 4
Q: 15
MAX
M 1
M 2
Q: 15
Q: 10
enables
40 TG
SUM
T2
SUM
T2-1
M 7
M 9
MAX
Q: 10
Q: 5
NEW1
NEW2
Q: 30
Q: 10
M 1
M 4
Initial Schedule
NEW2
M 7
M 9
Post Update Schedule
New tasks arraive for Agent Gray — Scheduling add NEW2
Agent White
Agent Gray
Query:
"Schedule M2,
Priority Hi,
NFP = 10"
[+20]
TG 40
NEW1
Q: 30
NEW2
Q: 10
Initial Schedule
NEW1
M 7
M 9
Query-base Schedule
Agent Gray finds higher quality option requiring coordination with Agent White
— sends query w/ priority and freeze period
Agent White
Agent Gray
Response:
"deltaQ = [–5]"
[net: +15]
TG [–5]
Commit Schedule
NEW1
M 7
M 9
Commit Schedule
Agent White responds with quality change induced by request
— Agent Gray assesses net gain, issues 'commit.'

such that the initiating agent cannot secure a joint commit in time for the earliest necessary activities to start. Thus, in some situations, it may be beneficial to raise the priority of the responses so that they may be completed in a timely manner.

Control Parameters

Table 14.1 summarizes the metalevel control parameters available for managing the interplay between local scheduling and non-local coordination in the CMU agent. For purposes of reasoning about the setting of these parameters, we make qualitative value assumptions. In the next section, we identify and focus on a specific subset of parameters with the goal of demonstrating the leverage to be gained by managing them dynamically over the course of a given problem-solving run as a function of the evolving control state.

An Empirical Analysis of the Benefit of Metareasoning

We focus here on the above defined metalevel control parameters that are most effective in boosting quality via explicit coordination between agents. The sequence in which such coordination might unfold is illustrated for a simple two-agent example in figure 14.2. The three frames show the subjective views of the two agents and their respective schedules as they respond to the arrival of a new task structure (the T2-1 subtree) for Agent Gray. The representation here reflects the c-taems formalism of specifying quality for leaf nodes (along with other attributes such as activity duration and probability distributions, not shown) and a quality-accumulation function (QAF) that specifies how the qualities of scheduled children are aggregated. Communications

Table 14.1
Control parameters in the CMU Agent

Control Parameter	Possible Values
coordination-frequency	low, high
quiescence period	low, high
nbr-non-locals	1. . . n
non-local-freeze-period	normal, extended
response-priority	low, high
reschedule-strategy	lazy, aggressive
explore-facilitated-choices	t, nil
reset-nogoods	t, nil

◀ **Figure 14.2**
Explicit coordination example.

between agents, such as the messages from an agent's DSM in transmitting assessed quality for a task, are depicted with dashed lines between the agent names at the top of each pane in the figure.

The snapshot in the first frame shows Agent Gray's schedule shortly after the new T2-1 task subtree (with a new *enables* constraint) is added to its subjective view. As a result of local scheduling, Agent Gray has boosted local quality by adding the NEW2 activity to its timeline. It is not useful for Gray to schedule the higher quality NEW1 activity since Agent White has not scheduled the required enabler activity, M2. For its part, Agent White does not modify its schedule upon arrival of T2-1 since its quality assessment over its subjective view does not perceive a quality boost in scheduling M2 so that NEW1 can be scheduled.

In the second frame, Agent Gray's Option Manager has requested a scheduling pass for non-local options and it identifies an opportunity to boost local assessed quality if Agent White cooperates. Gray then issues a query requesting Agent White to schedule the *enables source activity M2* with a latest finish time consistent with the NEW1 allocation. (Not shown is the unrolling that each agent does after these hypothetical scheduling operations.) In the third frame, Agent White responds to the query by sending back that scheduling the *enables source* reduces its local quality by 5. Agent Gray determines that there is a net gain of 15, issues a commit directive to Agent White, and reinserts NEW1 on its timeline per the option that generated the query.

Experimental Design

Ultimately, as our understanding and refinement of the explicit coordination component mature, this study will be extended to characterize the first four parameters of table 14.1, which shape key aspects of explicit coordination. This will entail extensive runs over the large, randomly generated problem sets typical of the Coordinators competitive evaluations. For this scoping study we restrict our analysis to a few hand-generated scenarios that illustrate the impact of dynamically modulating one of the explicit coordination control parameters on option generation and selection. Here we isolate the impact of the control parameter *non-local-freeze-period* used by the initiating agent to select the best option to pursue, that is, the one that will have both the best chance to be coordinated successfully and the most additional quality.

As defined above, *non-local-freeze-period* specifies the time window from the current time within which an agent is prohibited from modifying its existing schedule. Intuitively, the smaller that window is, the more options that may be potentially discovered but the less time is available for an explicit coordination session to complete. Our hypothesis is that the best setting for *non-local-freeze-period* is context dependent and that no single setting is best for all contexts. Our intuition is that the processing stress on an agent over a suitable recent time window (henceforth, referred to as the "process load") will be a good predictor of the current context and, consequently, of the appro-

Table 14.2
Two-term model of metacognition for pursuing explicit coordination

non-local-freeze-period	response-priority	process load	quality gain?
normal	low	low	no
normal	low	high	yes
extended	low	low	yes
extended	low	high	yes
. . .	. . . .	. . . .	. . . .

priate setting. We suspect that the heavier an agent's process load is, the longer the *non-local-freeze-period* should be, since both its own negotiation response time and that of other involved agents are likely to lag due to many competing updates.

To measure an agent's process load, we measure the average latency of jobs on the control agenda from when they arrive until they are processed. Such jobs include updates from the simulator, updates and queries from other agents, scheduling invocations, as well as calls for generation of non-local options, which the agent imposes on itself. Specifically, this latency corresponds to the average time that a job sits on the blackboard control agenda until it is selected and processed. The longer the latency is, the busier the agent is.

For the purpose of this experiment, we have simplified the set of possible values for both the control parameter settings and the process-load measure. The *non-local-freeze-period* parameter can be either normal or extended, and an agent's process load can be either low or high. The effect of an agent's process load on the control parameter settings is assessed according to the quality gain accumulated at the end of the run relative to the agent running in a baseline explicit coordination configuration. This baseline configuration is described later in this section.

A longer-term goal of this study is to learn the model for these settings using a training set of problems. Table 14.2 shows an example portion of such a learned model for two of the four parameters directly involved in explicit coordination: *non-local-freeze-period* and response priority. However, we defer further discussion of this effort to learn the best setting to the discussion in the final section, and focus here on a set of model values that is based on logged experience working with the agent. We next discuss how such a model is used during scenario execution.

Suppose an agent receives an update of new activities that present the possibility of a non-local coordination. All agents owning or having visibility of portions of the new task structures first enter a brief "quiescent period" during which they exchange certain information they need to effectively coordinate over the new tasks (Smith et al., 2007). Once they exit this quiescent period, each agent adopts an anytime scheduling policy in that it first seeks improvements to its existing schedule based only on local changes it can implement and then later may initiate an explicit coordination session if it has the potential to boost quality. The behavior of the agent subsequent to the local scheduling pass is the focus here. The baseline configuration of the agent can be summarized as follows:

- Trigger non-local options search after five time ticks following the quiescent period.
- All agents use a default *non-local-freeze-period* of two ticks and a default response priority of low.
- Sort options by quality and pursue the highest-quality option (by transmitting it as one or more queries) if it improves current quality as estimated by the initiating agent.
- Commit to option if net gain is positive when all involved agents respond.

We propose a three-phase metalevel control mechanism for explicit coordination (given the arrival of new activities with opportunity for non-local coordination):

1. Configure the non-local scheduling pass: The current value of the process load is used to set *non-local-freeze-period* for a scheduling call to find non-local options. If both normal and extended settings indicate a quality gain according to the model, then the normal setting is used to avoid missing opportunities.
2. Select a returned option: When/if the Scheduler returns non-local options, sort the options by quality and tag each option with the number of remote agents involved. Then choose the highest-quality option with positive quality gain, breaking ties for options with the same quality by choosing the one involving fewer agents.
3. Given a feasible, quality-boosting, non-local option, configure it as one or more queries, and transmit to relevant agents along with the *non-local-freeze-period* setting.

Each agent that receives such a query must then enforce the *non-local-freeze-period* when conducting its scheduling pass as it attempts to schedule the requested enabler activity(ies) while respecting near-term activities and restricted space on the agent's timeline.

The chosen metacognition dynamics were examined over twelve problems generated across two problems classes that can be characterized as:

1. Overall low-stress conditions in which agents receive a new task with a near-term deadline that requires rapid explicit coordination to achieve maximum quality.
2. Overall high-stress conditions in which too much and/or too early explicit coordination activity can potentially interfere with the more urgent need to respond to a flurry of updates coming from environmental dynamics.

The stress level on agents for these scenarios was induced by modulating the number of dynamic events affecting each agent around the approximate arrival time of new tasks. These newly arriving tasks offer the opportunity for highest-quality gains if explicit coordination is successful but does not interfere with the agent's ability to keep pace with execution. These dynamic events are reflected in the process load of the agents which, in turn, selects for a normal (2 ticks) or extended (5 ticks) setting of the *non-local-freeze-period* parameter.

Results

Initial experimentation to characterize process load revealed that it fluctuated rapidly within highly dynamic scenarios, in some cases backing up more than fifty updates and activities on an agent's control agenda, but at times processing the entire agenda within a tick. As a result, low-stress scenarios representative of the first class were relatively easy to generate (they could be kept small in size) and tended to produce predictable and reproducible results:

- The normal *non-local-freeze-period* value of two ticks provided ample time for agents involved in explicit coordination to complete negotiations and successfully accrue the associated quality boost.
- All observed coordination episodes in low-stress scenarios required less than one tick from initiation of the search for non-local options to a final commitment of agents' schedules.
- Fixing the *non-local-freeze-period* value to *extended* for these scenarios never improved performance and degraded it in terms of overall quality for three of the six scenarios.

We experienced considerably greater difficulty in definitively characterizing metacognition performance for the high-stress scenarios. Even for low-dynamics scenarios involving many agents, the vagaries of execution are such that final accrued quality can be quite sensitive to such things as small communication delays across platforms/machines. As a result, identical performance is often difficult to reproduce across multiple runs of the same scenarios. This effect is compounded for high-stress scenarios as they depend on inducing agent congestion via injecting concentrations of many cascading dynamic changes during the scenario run. Such scenarios require much larger task structures, and the impact of any one attribute such as *non-local-freeze-period* on overall quality accumulation can be masked by myriad other uncertainties of communication and execution. Here is our experience with the six high-stress scenarios:

- When running under a *non-local-freeze-period* value of *extended* during the interval surrounding arrival of new tasks, 1 of 6 scenarios resulted in significantly higher quality compared with running with a *non-local-freeze-period* fixed at *normal*.
- Running with a *non-local-freeze-period* of *normal* in high-stress intervals never produced higher quality than the *extended* setting.
- Explicit coordination logs revealed that often agents burdened with overambitious explicit coordination attempts during high-stress situations correctly addressed the

most pressing updates first due to the default low priority of explicit coordination (*response-priority*).

- Run-to-run variations in quality of 5–10 percent were noted even with the same parameter settings.

These scoping results suggest that we may not have yet adequately simulated a sufficiently high dynamic stress level to observe the impact, if any, of an extended setting of *non-local-freeze-period*. Moreover, the problem sets need to be expanded considerably in order to determine whether there is a statistical benefit to the extension of *non-local-freeze-period* for these high-stress situations.

Discussion and Conclusions

This chapter reports the results of an investigation into the application of metareasoning to improve the performance of an agent involved in distributed problem solving in a dynamic execution environment. In this initial phase, we focus on the impact of modulating just one parameter of a diverse set that collectively influences the agent's scheduling response to execution dynamics. The target parameter has a role in constraining the set of possibilities an agent can consider in response to interagent coordination queries, and we posit that an agent capable of modulating the parameter based on the process load it is facing will outperform an agent with a static setting.

The empirical evidence to date indeed suggests that the implemented metareasoning mechanism effectively reconfigures the agent's scheduling apparatus to boost performance across a range of process load conditions. However, the experiments also emphasize the difficulty of isolating and demonstrating a consistent impact for such metacontrol in complex agents where there are many, often interacting, mechanisms that influence problem-solving performance. Even when a parameter setting is suboptimal, different mechanisms in the agent have been observed to compensate so as to mask any negative impact. Moreover, we have encountered a challenging problem of reproducing a consistent target level of high-stress load in the simulation environment, in part because the load depends in complex ways on the induced agent-to-agent communication levels themselves.

This experience suggests that full characterization of the impact of single-parameter metacontrol in such a complex agent may require a significantly larger test suite. In addition, extending the metareasoning to modulate multiple parameters may boost performance across a wider range of environment dynamics, if an appropriate model for such a parameter set can be developed. In the presented experiment, we engineered a control model for the configuration switching based on our observations of the agents' performances over a large number of problems. Though engineering the model is feasible in specific, easily identifiable situations, it does not represent a general solution. The complexities of the interactions among the control parameters and the features of the environment make it difficult to generate models for a number of control parameters operating in a varied environment. A more robust solution would entail having agents learn control models for the appropriate actions for different contexts by classifying the performance of different configurations of the agent over those contexts.

To support this learning, we are investigating using MetaMod, a metareasoning component based on Raja & Lesser, 2007. Using a classification algorithm, such as the naive Bayes classifier algorithm provided by MetaMod, the agent will learn the model by being trained over a set of problems, where each contains specific events that exercise the control parameters being trained and the overall set presents a variety of values for the selected environment features. All problems will be run with all combinations of the control parameter settings (a portion of which appears in table 14.2), while measuring selected features of the environment and of the agent's state. The metareasoning component will then apply the learned model in the same manner as is described in the experimental design section above.

We note by comparison that the role of metareasoning in the FORR learning and problem-solving architecture (Epstein and Petrovic, this vol., chap. 4) is to modulate the learning component itself to improve problem-solving performance (including scheduling cast as a CSP). It does so by choosing which of a learned set of heuristics to apply and in what order. While that may eventually also prove useful in our distributed environment, we will first aim to have the architecture learn a single more general "heuristic" and employ the metareasoning mechanism to effectively apply it.

Acknowledgments

This work is supported by the Department of Defense Advanced Research Projects Agency (DARPA) under Contract FA8750-05-C-0033. Any opinions, findings and conclusions, or recommendations expressed in this chapter are those of the authors and do not necessarily reflect the views of DARPA.

References

Boddy, M., Horling, B., Phelps, J., Goldman, R., Vincent, R., Long, A., & Kohout, B. (2005). *C-taems language specification v. 1.06.* Unpublished.

Cesta, A., & Oddi, A. (1996). Gaining efficiency and flexibility in the simple temporal problem. In *Proceedings of the Third International Workshop on Temporal Representation and Reasoning* (pp. 45–50), TIME'96. Los Alamitos, CA: IEEE Computer Society Press.

Dechter, R., Meiri, I., & Pearl, J. (1991). Temporal constraint networks. *Artificial Intelligence, 49,* 61–95.

Raja, A., & Lesser, V. (2007). A framework for meta-level control in multi-agent systems. *Autonomous Agents and Multi-Agent Systems, 15*(2), 147–196.

Simon, H. (1957). A behavioral model of rational choice. In *Models of man, social and rational: Mathematical essays on rational human behavior in a social setting*. New York: Wiley.

Smith, S. F., Gallagher, A., Zimmerman, T., Barbulescu, L., & Rubinstein, Z. (2007). Distributed management of flexible times schedules. In *Proceedings of the 2007 International Conference on Autonomous Agents and Multiagent Systems* (pp. 484–491), AAMAS-07. Honolulu, HI: The International Foundation for Autonomous Agents and Multiagent Systems (IFAAMAS), Research Publishing Services. Available at http://www.ifaamas.org/Proceedings/aamas07.

15 Distributed Metamanagement for Self-Protection and Self-Explanation

Catriona M. Kennedy

In autonomic computing (Ganek & Corbi, 2003), "self-protection" is one of the "self*" properties enabling an autonomous system to recover from faults and intrusions. Such a system requires a metalevel to recognize and correct problems in its own operation without external intervention. The simplest design for an autonomous self-protecting system is hierarchical with a metalevel ensuring that the system operates according to requirements. However, a single metalevel cannot critically evaluate its own operation and state of knowledge.

In earlier work (Kennedy, 2003; Kennedy & Sloman, 2002, 2003) we developed some implementations in which distributed metalevels monitor and repair each other to overcome the vulnerabilities of a hierarchical system. In this chapter, we show how distributed metalevels can be integrated into a full cognitive architecture required for human-like cognition. In particular, we argue that distributed metalevel architectures are also capable of self-explanation as emphasized by Cox (this vol., chap. 9).

A Cognitive Agent with Metamanagement

As a starting point for distributed metamanagement, we define a cognitive agent with a single metalevel, based on the H-Cogaff architecture of Sloman (2001). H-Cogaff has three layers: a reactive layer, which responds rapidly to events in the environment but with very little thought; a deliberative layer, which uses its knowledge of the environment to reason about hypothetical scenarios and to plan ahead; and a metamanagement layer, which critically evaluates the deliberative layer and interrupts it if necessary (e.g., if it is not making progress). The metamanagement concept is related to that of Beaudoin (1994), Hansen and Zilberstein (2001), Cardon et al. (2001) and Singh (2005).

Our simplified version of H-Cogaff is shown in figure 15.1. This shows an agent as a two-layer structure containing an object level O1 and a metalevel M1, respectively.

KE represents object-level knowledge of the external world to allow deliberative reasoning. Some of this can be a predictive model (e.g., involving rules about expected behavior of objects), which can be internally simulated (Minsky, 1968). O1 also includes a reactive layer, which involves immediate reactions to the external world. The dotted vertical arrows within boxes are translations between levels of abstraction. "Perception" is a translation from sensor readings to high-level knowledge. Similarly, "control" is a translation from the selected options on the knowledge level into motor sequences.

Our object level in figure 15.1 (containing both reactive and deliberative layers) corresponds to the object level in figure 1.2 in chapter 1, and the environment in figure 15.1 corresponds to the ground level in figure 1.2.

Metalevel

The metalevel in figure 15.1 monitors and critically evaluates the *information states and processes* that the object level is *relying on* (its knowledge and algorithms). For example, the deliberative layer in O1 could enable the agent to predict the effect of

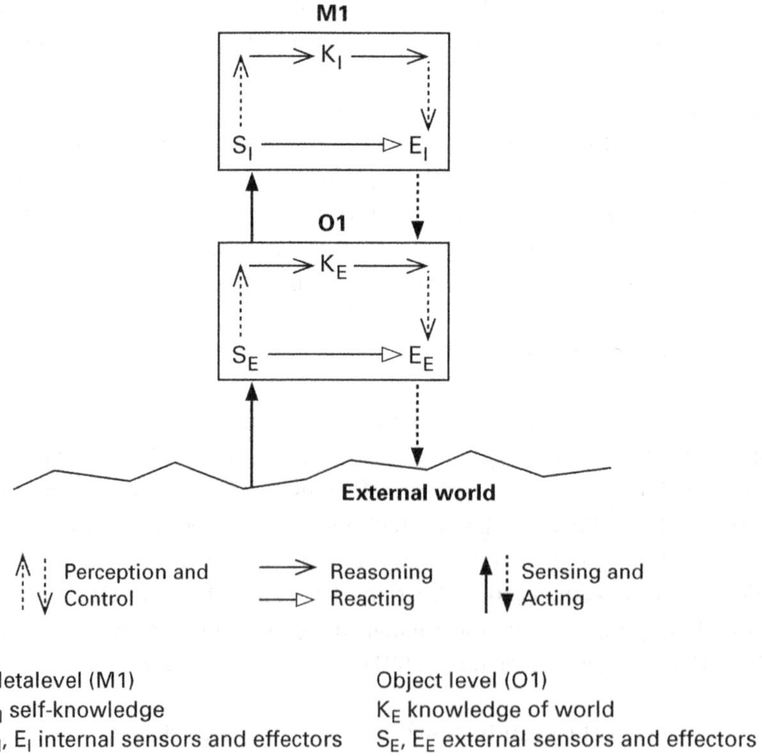

Figure 15.1
A cognitive agent with metamanagement.

its actions using its knowledge KE ("if I move the red block onto the blue block, then the blue block will be covered"). In contrast, the metalevel does not rely on KE but can question it. For example, it might predict problems due to limited understanding of blocks ("my knowledge of 'blocks' and 'surfaces' is limited and I might get confused"). Therefore the metalevel requires "knowledge about knowledge" or metaknowledge—part of KI ("internal knowledge") in the diagram.

Self-Model KI can be regarded as a partial "self-model" and contains the following:

1. *A map of object-level components*, along with their *current and recent states* (traces) and *a model of their normal behavior* in the form of expected trace patterns. A "component" might be a software component or executing process, or it can be an abstract concept (such as "focus of attention") used within an ontology of mental states (an agent may detect that its attention is being distracted). See, for example, Gordon, Hobbs, and Cox (this vol., chap. 19). The model of normal behavior can be learned through self-familiarization, which is a process of generalizing from self-observation in different circumstances. Simple examples are given in Kennedy, 2003. This normal behavior model is similar to the model of "self" learned by an artificial immune system (Hofmeyr & Forrest, 2000; Mitchell 2005).
2. *Knowledge of the agent's goals and motivations*. In autonomic computing, these can be a specification of correct operation (where this differs from normal operation). Some goals may be externally specified as "policies," while others may be secondary goals developed by the agent itself.
3. *Knowledge about the agent's knowledge* (metaknowledge), including known failures or knowledge gaps that it wants to correct. In our single-agent approach, metaknowledge is a part of self-knowledge. In a multiagent system, metaknowledge may include beliefs about other agent's knowledge. In the single metalevel of figure 15.1, the agent's metaknowledge is its knowledge of KE. This is called W** in the taxonomy of Minsky (1968).

Metalevel Control of the Object Level

Internal sensors and effectors (SI and EI) are software components used by the metalevel to sense and modify object-level states and processes. Internal sensors read object-level traces (such as recent rule-firing or memory access history). Internal effectors adjust object-level processes to correct any problems and to make improvements as defined by the agent's goals. Examples of effector action include interrupting a reasoning process that is not making progress, replacing a flawed component with an alternative, or initiating a new learning process. Additionally, the scheduling of different object-level processes may be adjusted according to changing circumstances and estimated cost see, e.g., Russell & Wefald, 1991; Etzioni, 1991).

Evaluating Object-Level Performance

The metalevel detects and corrects "anomalies" in the object level's performance. This is similar to the metacognitive loop of Schmill, Anderson, Fults, Josyula, Oates, Perlis, Shahri, Wilson, and Wright (this vol., chap. 12). An "anomaly" is an unexpected occurrence that may indicate a problem. In figure 15.1, KI contains self-knowledge acquired through earlier self-familiarization and allows the metalevel to predict the pattern of reasoning of the object level, given a known environmental event. Effectively the agent anticipates its own mental state. Similar models of reasoning processes have been applied in case-based planning (see, e.g., Fox & Leake, 1995).

One kind of anomaly (type 1) occurs when the object-level reasoning does not follow a desirable pattern. It may be distracted by irrelevant details or it may violate a requirement, for example, one involving temporal constraints (Rubenstein, Smith, & Zimmermann, this vol., chap. 14, use temporal constraints to control schedules, but they may also be applied to an agent's reasoning priorities).

Another kind of anomaly (type 2) occurs when the model in KE predicts a state that does not correspond to the reality. Although this kind of anomaly may be detected partly by the object level (e.g., measurements may be out of range), the recognition of the "strange" nature of the new situation is an introspective (hence metalevel) function because it involves questioning whether the *agent's current knowledge is sufficient* for the situation (see also Goel & Jones, this vol., chap. 10). The diagnosis process should determine whether any new learning is required or whether the anomaly is due to other factors such as the failure of a sensor interpretation component.

Metareasoning and Self-Familiarization

Any new learning process resulting from a metalevel decision might include further self-familiarization (in addition to object-level learning processes). For example, the agent may decide to learn more about why it gets confused in some situations. The kind of learning involved in self-familiarization is itself a form of metareasoning, since the agent is constructing a general hypothesis (that a rule exists) by observing its own reasoning, including its learning.

In contrast, we would not define a purely reactive adaptation process (e.g., a neural network) as metareasoning, even if its inputs are reasoning traces. We are assuming that metareasoning involves the ability to explain and critique the object-level reasoning or learning (see also Cox, this vol., chap. 9).

Ground-Level Interaction with the Metalevel

To detect lack of knowledge, the metalevel must reason about informational entities that *refer to entities in the external world* (e.g., its concept of "block"). This means that the metalevel also needs to know the state of the world. Ground-level information is an additional requirement for type 2 failures (lack of knowledge) that is not necessarily required for general metamanagement such as detecting oscillations in object-level reasoning (type 1). However, even with type 1 anomalies, undesirable outcomes in the environment often need to be taken into account when evaluating the object-level reasoning (e.g., if there is imminent danger due to its focusing on a minor problem).

In our architecture, the metalevel interacts only indirectly with the ground level, by cautious and exploratory use of object-level components that it is only partially trusting. For example, a robot expects to find an office at the end of a corridor, but instead finds a cupboard. Without metalevel reasoning, it may still detect an anomalous measurement, but it would just assume that the cupboard is a very small office. With metalevel reasoning, it can consider two possibilities: (a) the object level has made an error (such as in navigation or in feature recognition) or (b) the object-level knowledge of the building is incomplete, which led to a wrong expectation about this particular corridor. To rule out (a), it can explore the area using alternative object-level methods (for route planning, sensing, and perception). If they all give the same anomalous result, the robot may conclude instead that its knowledge is incomplete. At each point in its exploration, different object-level components are being trusted, while others are being critically questioned. The *role* of the metalevel is to have the capability to do this questioning. It would not in this case question all components simultaneously, since it needs to rely on some components to deliver the ground-level information.

Note that a "self-protection" scenario is not significantly different from an "accidental" one. For example, a hostile agent may deliberately confuse the robot by causing an error, or it may exploit the robot's lack of knowledge by deliberately inserting anomalous components in the terrain.

An Example Implementation

In previous work (Kennedy, 2003), we designed a virtual world called "Treasure," implemented in SimAgent (Sloman & Poli, 1995), in which an autonomous vehicle collects treasure while avoiding ditches and ensuring that its energy supply is regularly recharged. Components of the agent controlling the vehicle can fail or be subverted by an enemy. For example, the perception of the agent can fail so that it interprets the environment incorrectly.

In SimAgent, each agent is implemented as a set of "condition-action" rules, which is divided up into modules (rule sets). Each module is concerned with sensing, perception, acting, or other functions such as metareasoning. In the Treasure implementation, the metalevel's model of expected internal processing (corresponding to KI) is a set of patterns of rule-firing traces associated with different activities that were learned during a self-observation phase.

During operation in a hostile environment, this model can be used as a guideline for the correct behavior of object-level components. The agent can access a trace of recently fired rules, which is comparable to the episodic memory required by Cox (this vol., chap. 9). If the actual rule-firing pattern does not fit the model-predicted pattern, and is accompanied by an unexpected worsening of the external world, the metalevel decides that a failure in the affected set of rules has occurred.

Distributed Metamanagement

In the self-protection context, a hostile environment can attack *any* part of the system, including the failure detection and recovery components of the metalevel. For example, the metalevel failure-detection code may be illegally modified or some of its reasoning components may be prevented from executing. They may also fail due to an error.

A more complex kind of failure is a lack of knowledge or inaccurate knowledge to detect problems in the object level. The metalevel relies on its knowledge (KI) of the object level in the same way as the object level relies on its knowledge (KE) of the world.

In order to question the metalevel (and the knowledge it is relying on), the agent requires an additional metalevel. To avoid an infinite regress of monitoring levels ("homunculus" problem), the metalevels may be distributed so that they mutually monitor each other. One particular configuration of this is shown in figure 15.2.

In this case, two metalevels (M1 and M2) monitor each other, and both monitor the same object level. The two metalevels represent different metareasoning methods. For example, they may use different measures to evaluate object-level performance. The relation between M2 and M1 has the same nature as that between M1 and O1. The main difference is that the interaction between M2 and M1 is two-way (since M1 also monitors M2). The actions, however, need to be coordinated so that metalevels do not interfere with each other. This is indicated by dashed arrows pointing away from the boxes, meaning that the actions are not always executed (or not immediately). Some examples of mutual metalevels were implemented in the Treasure Scenario (Kennedy, 2003).

In chapter 1 of this volume, figure 1.5 defines a form of distributed metareasoning as a multiagent architecture in which the metalevels of the respective agents exchange information in order to coordinate their actions. Our approach is different from this multiagent architecture, because we are aiming for distributed metalevel control *of one agent*, where the inter-metalevel relationship is mutual; in other words, metalevels are also each other's "object level."

Since the metalevels are distributed, the agent also has a distributed self-model. In figure 15.2 the different kinds of self-knowledge (versions of KI) held by M1 and M2 represent two perspectives from which the self-model is viewed. Note that the self-

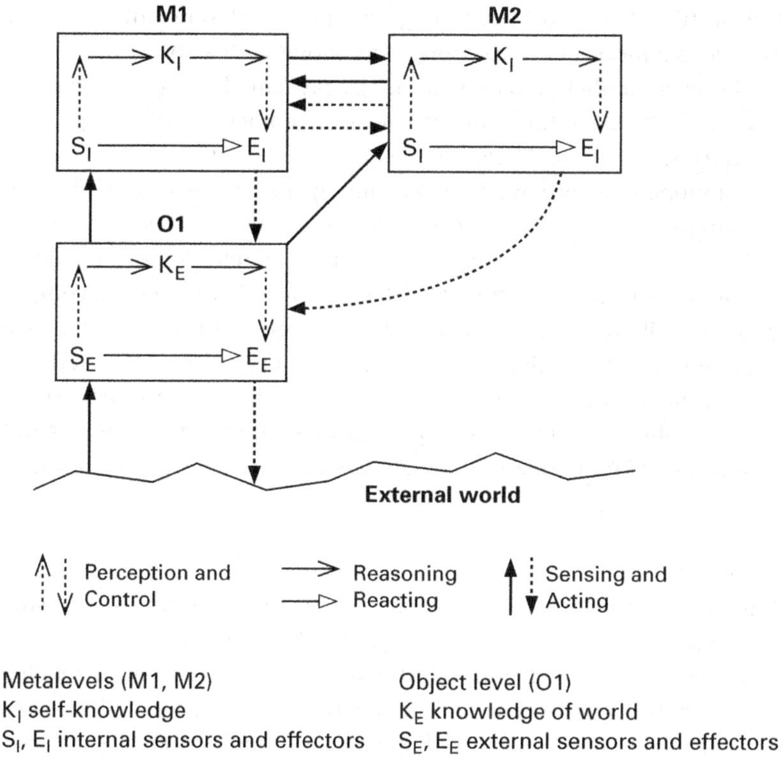

Figure 15.2
Distributed metamanagement.

model of M1 includes M2 and vice versa. The figure may be generalized to produce networks of meta- and object levels in which each metalevel controls a subset of the network. The aim is that all metalevels are monitored and evaluated by at least one remaining metalevel to provide full self-protective coverage.

Action Coordination in Distributed Metamanagement

For self-protection, all levels are active concurrently. M2 should be able to dynamically adjust its monitoring of M1 in response to any problems it finds. The same is true for M1's monitoring of M2 (as well as its monitoring of the object level). If an anomaly is detected, the metalevel requires more processing resources (e.g., for more detailed monitoring) to enable timely intervention.

Different metalevels may detect different kinds of failure. In our implementation, the first metalevel to make a decision on how to act inhibits all others by broadcasting that it has made a decision. The remaining metalevels cannot evaluate the "winning" metalevel's action until it has made some progress; they must wait until the new metalevel has produced a meaningful reasoning trace along with associated environmental states. In this way, conflicts and oscillations are prevented. (Longer-term oscillation may of course still occur, but for complex real-world problems, human cognition is also subject to indecisiveness and "false starts").

However, the components may have to agree among themselves before allowing any action, such as in metalevel cost evaluations. In a hostile environment, any metalevel may contain hostile code and cause rapid damage. A classic fault-tolerance approach is to use a majority voting system to determine whether to allow a component to take action. Distributed agreement has been addressed in the fault-tolerance literature (see, e.g., Verissimo & Rodrigues, 2001). Multiagent systems are also addressing these challenges, but they assume that the agents are cooperative (not hostile). See, for example, this volume, chapters 13 (Raja, Alexander, Lesser, and Krainin) and 14 (Rubinstein, Smith, and Zimmerman), to which we will return after elaboration of distributed metamanagement below.

Accurate Models of "Self"

The agent's self-model must be *sufficiently accurate* to allow it to survive in a hostile environment in which any component may be attacked. The aim is to ensure that all metalevels are themselves monitored, and that the monitoring is sufficiently detailed for the situations the agent must survive in. The distributed self-model (all versions of KI) should represent the normal behavior of *all* metalevels and object levels so that anomalies can be detected when compared with observations. The nature of the environment dictates the required level of detail in the model and monitoring (as with natural evolution).

Closed metalevel networks If all metalevels are monitored, the network is "closed" in the sense that no external "agent" is monitoring or controlling any part of the system (it is fully self-protective). Since it also monitors its self-monitoring (with some time delay), it has some aspects of "loopiness" (Perlis, this vol., chap. 2) in a weak sense. However, practical engineering considerations prevent it from being fully "loopy," since it must have object levels with externally defined functionality (they are not self-referring). A related idea to "loopiness" is that of "organizational closure" in biological systems (Maturana & Varela, 1980) in which living systems are defined as "self-producing" (autopoietic) and have no externally defined functionality—they only refer to and produce themselves. Autopoiesis has been applied to social systems (Luhmann, 1982). From a psychology perspective, Antaki and Lewis (1986) also point out the "loopiness" of social metacognition: for example, "A believes that (B believes that (A believes that (B . . .)))."

Minimizing additional complexity In figure 15.2 the "horizontal" inter-metalevel relation has the same form as the vertical relation between metalevel and object level (the same kind of arrows are used). The goal is to minimize the additional features required for distributed metalevel processing by *reusing the same mechanisms* already used in the meta-object-level relation. These same mechanisms (which may be rules or sections of code) are concurrently playing different roles. They are "talking about" different things, but using the same concepts and methods. This is similar to the software engineering practice of component reuse in multiple contexts. See, for example, Northrop (2002).

It is also necessary to limit metalevel complexity in order for the system to become familiar with the correct operation of its metalevels, which is required for detecting their failure. Otherwise, there will be large gaps in the self-model. We have shown that this kind of self-familiarization is possible in the proof-of-concept implementation in Kennedy (2003). In that implementation, the architecture was "multiagent." The model of expected behavior was "bootstrapped" by discovering classes of activity in rule-firing traces. For an architecture with two metalevels, we divided the training into three phases:

Phase 1 Both metalevels learn about object-level processing: Each M*i* (where *i* is 1 or 2) learns about the normal operation of the object level in a protected environment and builds its initial model KI. The object level interacts with the environment in situations it has learned previously.
Phase 2 Both metalevels take turns observing each other detecting and responding to attacks against an object level in an environment permitting object-level attacks only. For a metalevel M*j* learning about M*i*, this looks as follows:
(a) M*j* detects failure in the object level and takes corrective action using KI.
(b) M*i* observes the trace of M*j*'s reasoning and activity during its error detection and repair of the object level and uses these traces to build its model of M*j* (part of its KI).
Phase 3 Operational phase with no restriction on hostile attacks, where a metalevel M*i* is repaired by M*j* and coordination of action is necessary.

In the above, we assume that the reasoning processes and actions of metalevel M*j* when detecting a failure in M*i* will be approximately the same as M*j*'s processing when detecting a failure in the object level (which M*i* has learned). Component reuse should make this assumption reasonable. This is also similar to the kind of assumption made about training scenarios in general; they should be a good enough approximation of reality to be useful. More details are in Kennedy (2003).

Reducing the Cost of Distributed Metamanagement

From the above, it is clear that distributed metamanagement has potential disadvantages due to its added complexity. However, the additional costs may be offset by opportunities for adaptation and self-optimization that would not be possible in a centralized metalevel system.

Metareasoning is already used to evaluate the cost of object-level reasoning options (Raja, Alexander, Lesser, and Krainin, this vol., chap. 13). The same principle can be applied on the metalevel, where one metalevel monitors another. For example, if M2 (in figure 15.2) believes that M1's metareasoning is using excessive processing resources in a low-risk situation, it may interrupt M1's analysis and restore control to any suspended object-level processes. Therefore, an agent with distributed metamanagement has the potential to recognize and reduce the cost of its own metareasoning. The conflict between M1 and M2 is not very disruptive in this case; it just means there was insufficient consensus to continue with any metalevel processing. Some related work on reasoning about the cost of monitoring includes Zilberstein (1993), within the context of algorithm compilation.

Figure 15.2 may be generalized to include *n* object levels and *m* metalevels, each able to monitor and change the other. Even if there is some partitioning of the network, only those connections that are the most useful should be preserved. For example, unproductive connections between meta- and object levels may be disabled if a sufficient number of metalevels agree that a connection has been unproductive or detrimental to the object-level task. No additional complexity is required here, other than the mechanisms already in place for agreement about metalevel interventions. The system may eventually stabilize into a configuration that counteracts the overheads of a single metalevel system, where disruptive operations are not corrected.

Comparison with Multiagent Metareasoning

A multiagent system is constrained by the metaphor of individuals in a society. In contrast, distributed metalevels within a single agent may have many configurations, including those that resemble "multiagent" systems but where the "agents" can share memory workspaces and directly reconfigure other "agents." An example "multiagent" configuration is where each metalevel controls its own object level (as well as its subset of metalevels) in figure 15.3. The object levels may interact with and reason about the world in different ways. Similarly, they may have different partial views of the current state of the world. The simplest architecture is where one object level is the "primary" (in control of action) while the other is the "backup" ready to take control if the primary fails.

The *monitoring* aspect of distributed metamanagement may be applied to multiagent architectures if they form a self-protective coalition. The agents would need to make available their reasoning traces for critical evaluation by other agents. Effectively, the agents would form a community with compatible goals ("values"), where their mental state is broadcast to a subset of other agents. The actual metamanagement (the

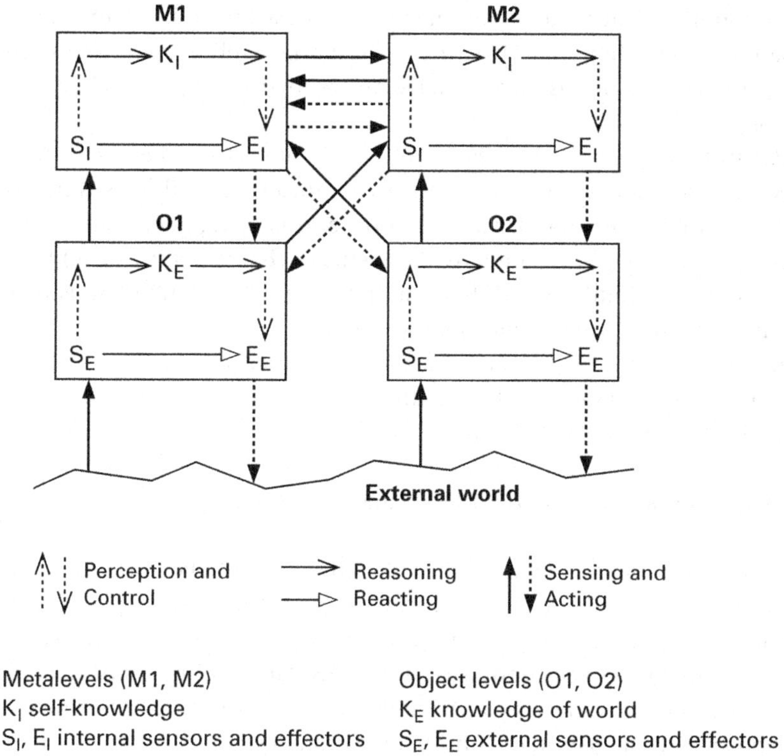

Figure 15.3
Distributed metamanagement with multiple object levels.

control aspect) would not normally apply, since autonomous agents do not activate or reconfigure each other. However, exceptions may occur if multiple agents agree about the "hostility" of another agent and the need to interrupt it (as happens in distributed metamanagement). The agent community can develop a collective "self-model" if the agents build models of each other and agree on similar goals. On the individual level the difference between "self" and "other agent" would still exist, however.

There are also many challenges in distributed metamanagement that are being addressed by multiagent architectures. We list three of them below.

1. *Coordination of action* Agreement between metalevels is similar to agreement among agents, except that the multiagent metalevels are not critically evaluating other metalevels. For example, metalevel agreement between agents about object-level options (such as when to negotiate and when to act) is addressed in the GeMEC project (Raja, Alexander, Lesser, and Krainin, this vol., chap. 13). Metalevel agreements about

joint plan execution in an uncertain environment is addressed by Rubinstein, Smith, and Zimmerman (this vol., chap. 14). These methods may be applicable to distributed metamanagement if the metalevels have to agree on whether an object-level process is problematic or not.

2. *Network connectivity and partial viewpoints* Since full connectivity between meta- and object levels is not practical, splitting the network into neighborhoods is necessary. This is also a problem for multiagent networks and is being addressed by the GeMEC project (this vol., chap. 13). Similarly the agents of chapter 14 (this vol.) have partial viewpoints of their joint task. Multiagent approaches to neighborhoods may therefore be applicable to distributed metamanagement.

3. *Self-familiarization* Many of the same principles of mutual observation are being addressed in agents that build models of each other (Borghetti & Gini, this vol., chap. 16; Gordon, Hobbs, & Cox, this vol., chap. 19).

Toward Self-Explanation in a Distributed Metamanagement System

Self-explanation has been defined by Cox (this vol., chap. 9) and plays an important role in the "episodic logic" system of Morbini and Schubert (this vol., chap. 17). Self-explanation is also important for self-protection. The agent needs to explain the cause of a failure and to plan corrective actions accordingly. Explanations by a single metalevel about one or more object levels can be added to our earlier example where a robot finds a cupboard (it can give an ongoing explanation of what its current hypotheses are, and what it will try out next). However, explanations by a distributed metamanagement system are more challenging. We present some examples below. We will refer to figure 15.2, although the examples should also apply to other configurations. We assume sensors and effectors of both metalevels can access the same object level (shown in figure 15.2).

M2 explaining a failure of M1

Example 1 "M1 failed to detect the error in O1's reasoning at step *S* (because of an error in M1's execution of step *T* in its own processing)." In this case M1 is "fail-silent" (fails to operate). Note that M2 monitors two different levels and may be able to explain failures on both levels.

Example 2 "M1 wrongly detected an error in O1 at step *S*; the problem is in step *U*." This introduces the additional problem of disagreement between two metalevels, since M1 is also reporting a problem. Furthermore, because of the mutual relationship, M1 may also claim to have detected an error in M2. Coordination methods required for consistent action can also be used for coherent explanations.

Example 3 "M1's knowledge of O1 needs to be corrected or extended." The same problem of disagreement may also occur here.

Distributed metalevels can also have an equivalent in human-like metacognition. Example 1 might be expressed as: "How did I fail to notice my mistake at step *S*? I am not being cautious enough." This is a criticism of one's own metamanagement, due to its failure to do anything at all ("fail-silence").

Example 2 is more complex, but might have the following form: "I suspect I made a mistake during step *S* as it does not seem to have gone correctly (this is M1's hypothesis because the trace of step *S* appears unusual), but I have to keep open the possibility that it is something different; maybe step *S* was correct but actually step *U* is wrong and I'm just thinking incorrectly that *S* was wrong (M2's critical questioning of M1's interpretation)." Here, the meaning of the term "I" changes from M1 to O1 and then to M2 in the course of the sentence. The relationship between the different levels and the linguistic self-explanation is made clearer in table 15.1. In this example, a disagreement between two metalevels can result in indecision.

Example 3 is similar and may have the following form: "I suspect I'm not understanding this because I don't know very much about concept *C*, but it is also possible that my knowledge about *C* is correct and I'm just thinking wrongly that I'm not understanding it." M2's hypothesis is that M1's understanding of what O1 needs to know is wrong. In this case, it may be possible to explore both competing hypotheses.

In the examples above (particularly example 3), M2 needs a different kind of model of O1 than the one used by M1. Otherwise, it has no grounds for questioning M1's knowledge (since they would both use the same knowledge and methods). For example, M1 may use rule-firing traces while M2 monitors memory-retrieval patterns (see, e.g., Gordon, Hobbs, & Cox, this vol., chap. 19).

Human-like self-explanation can provide a global and summarized overview of the agent's experience such as in "global workspace" theory (Baars, 1988). In our system, more than one metalevel may participate in constructing such a narrative by observing other metalevels. As with action coordination, the first metalevel to construct an atomic part of an explanation (such as a sentence) can broadcast its readiness to act and inhibit all others. Subsequent sentences can then be constructed by other metalevels. This means that the content of the "global workspace" may be changing during the course of an explanation.

Table 15.1
Changing meaning of "I" during self-explanation

Part of sentence	Meaning of "I"
"I suspect that . . ."	M1
"I made a mistake . . ."	O1
"but I have to keep open . . ."	M2

To satisfy the requirement of closed metalevels (where all metalevels are monitored), a metalevel constructing an explanation must itself be subject to critical evaluation in the same way as other metalevels. This would be analogous to human metacognition, where it is possible to doubt one's own self-explanation and interrupt it. As with all boxes in the diagrams used here, such a metalevel does not have to be a static component in the architecture, but could instead be an emergent stable coalition of participating components, as in some neuroscience models (see, e.g., Koch, 2004).

Conclusions and Future Work

In the context of autonomic computing or robotics, the capability of the system to protect itself against faults and intrusions requires a nonhierarchical distributed architecture. However, self-explanation is also important, not only for the system itself but also to enable humans interacting with it to understand the reasons for its actions. Reconciling these two requirements is possible, but requires an integrated, cross-disciplinary approach to cognitive systems. In addition to AI methods, research in distributed fault-tolerance, software engineering, and cognitive neuroscience can make a valuable contribution.

References

Antaki, C., & Lewis, A. (Eds.) (1986). *Mental mirrors: Metacognition in social knowledge and communication*. London: Sage Publications.

Baars, B. J. (1988). *A cognitive theory of consciousness*. New York: Cambridge University Press.

Beaudoin, L. P. (1994). *Goal processing in autonomous agents*. Doctoral dissertation, School of Computer Science, University of Birmingham, UK.

Cardon, S., Mouaddib, A., Zilberstein, S., & Washington, R. (2001). Adaptive control of acyclic progressive processing task structures. In *Proceedings of the Seventeenth International Joint Conference on Artificial Intelligence* (pp. 701–706), IJCAI-01. San Francisco: Morgan Kaufmann.

Etzioni, O. (1991). Embedding decision-analytic control in a learning architecture. *Artificial Intelligence, 49*, 129–159.

Fox, S., & Leake, D. (1995). Modeling case-based planning for repairing reasoning failures. In M. T. Cox and M. Freed (Eds.), *Proceedings of the 1995 AAAI Spring Symposium on Representing Mental States and Mechanisms* (pp. 31–38). Menlo Park, CA: AAAI Press.

Ganek, A. G., & Corbi, T. A. (2003). The dawning of the autonomic computing era. *IBM Systems Journal, 42*(1), 5–18.

Hansen, E., & Zilberstein, S. (2001). Monitoring and control of anytime algorithms: A dynamic programming approach. *Artificial Intelligence, 126*(1–2), 139–157.

Hofmeyr, S. A., & Forrest, S. (2000). Architecture for an artificial immune system. *Evolutionary Computation, 8*(4), 443–473.

Kennedy, C. M. (2003). *Distributed reflective architectures for anomaly detection and autonomous recovery*. Doctoral dissertation, School of Computer Science, University of Birmingham, UK.

Kennedy, C. M., & Sloman, A. (2002). Acquiring a self-model to enable autonomous recovery from faults and intrusions. *Journal of Intelligent Systems, 12*(1), 1–40.

Kennedy, C. M., & Sloman, A. (2003). Autonomous recovery from hostile code insertion using distributed reflection. *Journal of Cognitive Systems Research, 4*(2), 89–117.

Koch, C. (2004). *The quest for consciousness: A neurobiological approach*. Englewood, CO: Roberts.

Luhmann, N. (1982). The world society as a social system. *International Journal of General Systems, 8*(3), 131–138.

Maturana, H., & Varela, F. (1980). *Autopoiesis and cognition: The realization of the living*. Dordrecht, the Netherlands: D. Reidel.

Minsky, M. (1968). Matter, mind, and models. In M. Minsky (Ed.), *Semantic information processing* (pp. 425–432). Cambridge, MA: MIT Press.

Mitchell, M. (2005). Self-awareness and control in decentralized systems. In *Working Papers of the AAAI 2005 Spring Symposium on Metacognition in Computation* (pp. 80–85). Menlo Park, CA: AAAI Press.

Northrop, L. M. (2002). SEI's software product line tenets. *IEEE Software, 19*(4), 32–40.

Russell, S. J., & Wefald, E. (1991). *Do the right thing: Studies in limited rationality*. Cambridge, MA: MIT Press.

Singh, P. (2005). *EM-ONE: An architecture for reflective commonsense thinking*. Doctoral dissertation, Artificial Intelligence Lab, Massachusetts Institute of Technology, Cambridge, Massachusetts.

Sloman, A., & Poli, R. (1995) SimAgent: A toolkit for exploring agent designs. In M. Wooldridge, J. Miller & M. Tambe (Eds.), *Intelligent Agents*, vol. II, *Workshop on Agent Theories, Architectures, and Languages* (pp. 392–407), IJCAI-95. Berlin: Springer-Verlag.

Sloman, A. (2001). Varieties of affect and the CogAff architecture schema. In *Symposium on Emotion, Cognition, and Affective Computing* at the AISB-01 Convention (pp. 39–48). Society for the Study of Artificial Intelligence and Simulation of Behaviour. York, UK: AISB.

Verissimo, P., & Rodrigues, L. (2001). *Distributed systems for system architects*. Dordrecht, the Netherlands: Kluwer Academic.

Zilberstein, S. (1993). *Operational rationality through compilation of anytime algorithms*. Doctoral dissertation, University of California at Berkeley.

16 Weighted Prediction Divergence for Metareasoning

Brett J. Borghetti and Maria Gini

One of the most important elements of agent performance in multiagent systems is the ability of an agent to predict how other agents will behave. In many domains there are often different modeling systems already available that one could use to make behavior predictions, but the choice of the best one for a particular domain and a specific set of agents is often unclear. To find the best available prediction, we would like to know which model(s) would perform best in each possible world state of the domain. However, when we have limited resources and each prediction query has a cost, we may need to decide which queries to pursue using only estimates of their benefit and cost: metareasoning. To estimate the benefit of the computation, a metareasoner needs a robust measurement of performance quality. In this chapter we present a metareasoning system that relies on a prediction performance measurement, and we propose a novel model performance measurement that fulfills this need: weighted prediction divergence.

Agent models are internal representations of other agents in an environment. Agent modeling separates the characteristics of an agent from its environment. When an agent models another, the modeler's goal is to either *predict* future behavior or *explain* past behavior by identifying the beliefs of the modeled agent. In this work, we focus specifically on measuring the ability of models to make predictions, in an attempt to answer the following important metareasoning question: Given a world state and a collection of candidate models, how can we *a priori* select the one model (or a weighted distribution over models) that is most likely to perform the best in that state? When computational cost is an issue, the answer to this question lies within the answers to several related questions:

- How do we automatically abstract the world state space into a set of contexts to reduce the computational cost?
- How can we estimate a model's general prediction quality in a specific context without measuring quality at every possible world state within that context?
- How do we compare the relative performance of several heterogeneous models' predictive capabilities in a specific context?

While the ability to characterize relative performance of heterogeneous models is important for a wide collection of metareasoning strategies, and is thus the main thrust of this chapter, we must first examine a specific metareasoning strategy to derive the desiderata for the relative performance measurement. In the next section, we propose a metareasoning system coupled with a robust measurement of model-prediction performance to yield a powerful new method of model selection for an agent. After reviewing some of the existing methods used for performance measurement, we present a new method for characterizing model prediction performance. We then introduce one target domain for our empirical testing of this prediction-performance measurement. We discuss empirical results using this method and conclude with a description of future work required to realize the overall metareasoning system.

Context-Aware Metareasoning for Prediction-Model Selection

Consider an agent trying to choose actions to take in some world where the utility of an action is partially dependent on the behavior of the other agents in the world. We describe the behaviors of the agents (and the way those behaviors affect and are affected by the world) using an extensive-form game tree where nodes describe world states and edges describe actions taken by specific agents. The value of a world state can be estimated by summing the values of its branches, weighted by the likelihood of the branch (action) being chosen. This process can be used at each sub-branch to find the value of the sub-branches recursively. The recursion bottoms out when a branch is terminated at a leaf node that contains a real-world value. Each node in the tree may also have an intrinsic value that can be included in the calculation.

The well-known minimax algorithm (as discussed in Russell & Norvig, 2003) describes this process when there are two agents and the game is zero-sum (in every outcome, one player gains exactly the value the other player loses) and the agents are assumed to have perfect (not bounded) rationality. Many extensions to minimax have been developed that allow the assumption of perfect rationality to be relaxed (e.g., Carmel & Markovitch, 1996; Luckhardt & Irani, 1986; Stone, Riley, & Veloso, 2000; Sturtevant, Zinkevich, & Bowling, 2006). By replacing the minimizer with an algorithm that predicts the opponent's behavior at a given node (as in Carmel & Markovitch, 1996) we obtain an algorithm that selects actions with the highest value when playing against a specific modeled opponent. When the model is estimating the other agent's probability distribution over actions, then the quality of the value calculation is dependent upon how similar the predicted behavior distribution is to the actual behavior distribution.

If we want to have a metareasoner that makes decisions about which calculations to carry out using the utility of a calculation as a criterion, we need to know the cost of the calculation and the value of the calculation (Russell & Wefald, 1991). In this

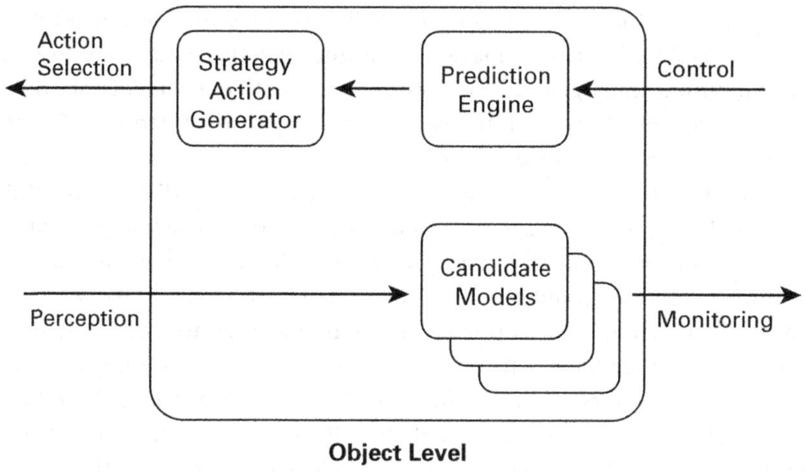

Figure 16.1
Object level: The object's candidate models observe the action of other agents and provide predictions to a prediction engine. The prediction engine is controlled by metareasoning, based on the metalevel monitoring of the performance of the candidate models.

book, part II ("Metalevel Control") and part III ("Introspective Monitoring") discuss other examples of these concepts in further detail.

In the setting described above, the relative value of several candidate calculations (queries of different predictive models) can be estimated by the quality of their predictions at the specified world state. Unfortunately, measuring the predictive quality of every model at every possible world state in a branch of the game tree is at least as expensive as obtaining all the predictions in the first place—thus, computing prediction quality for every node in a branch would not yield any resource savings. In order for our metareasoner to be useful, it must be able to *estimate* the prediction quality for each node without fully calculating prediction quality.

We now define the architecture of a metareasoning agent designed to act within the multiagent environment. At the highest level, the system is one in which the metalevel device is monitoring the performance of the object-level reasoner and computing the utility of reasoning methods, as depicted in figure 16.2.

The inside of the reasoning object is shown in figure 16.1. There are a number of candidate models that receive input from the environment (and observe the actions of the other agent[1]). We assume that each candidate model has inputs and produces

1. For the sake of linguistic clarity, we will refer to only one agent being modeled, to avoid confusion between the agent and the multiple candidate models used to predict the actions of that agent. Though not discussed further in this work, the metareasoning arrangement proposed here can be used to model multiple target agents.

a prediction output in the form of a probability distribution over the possible actions the modeled agent could take. Furthermore, we assume that the models are input-heterogeneous but output-homogenous: each model is trying to predict a distribution of what the modeled agent will do next, but each model may be considering different information from which to make predictions.

At the object level, the strategy action generator is attempting to discover fruitful strategies for future behavior of the agent. In order for the strategy action generator to choose a high-value future strategy, it may need to consider many "what if" predictions about various events that could occur in the future in order to evaluate different possible strategies. Depending on the context (collection of world states) of the desired prediction, some models may have better prediction performance than others. Thus, the selection of a predictive model (or weighted distribution over models) should be *context-aware* for *each* prediction. For each prediction-in-context that must be made, it is the prediction engine's job to generate the overall prediction using the set of available candidate models.

The prediction engine's selection of model(s) is influenced by the modules in the metareasoning level, as shown in figure 16.2. The context abstraction module determines the appropriate abstract context from a given world state. It provides this context as a tag for the activity repository for every prediction and observation event. The model generates a prediction event whenever it is queried for a prediction. Prediction events contain the predicted distribution over modeled agent actions and the

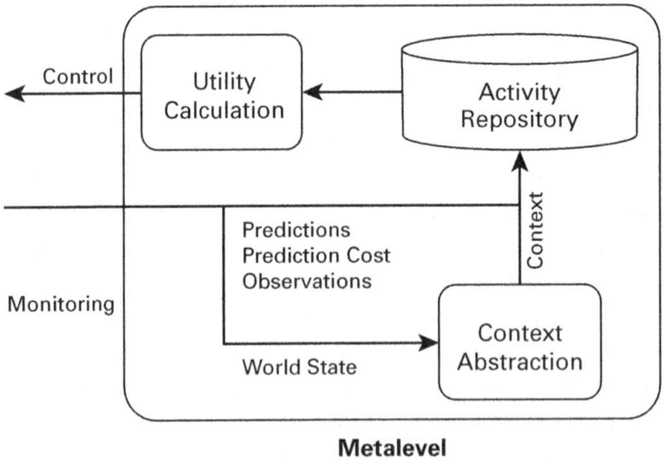

Figure 16.2
Metalevel: The metareasoner reviews past predictions, prediction costs, and observations to yield a utility measurement for each context. The utility calculation advises the prediction engine by providing an expected performance profile for each model in each context.

cost incurred by that model to generate the prediction. Observation events include the observed behavior of the modeled agent. The utility calculation first computes the distribution of agent behavior in each tagged context. Then it calculates a prediction-quality measurement from the predictions and observations seen within the context. Finally, it computes the utility for each model in each context from the prediction quality and the prediction cost. The latest performance profiles are passed to the prediction engine prior to each prediction.

The remainder of this chapter presents and explores one of the important facets of this metareasoning architecture: measuring the prediction performance of a model in a context. Before we discuss our novel and theoretically grounded measurement concept, we review the related research in the area.

Related Work

Agent modeling is often used in computational analysis of an environment to help an agent make decisions. Researchers have examined many domains where agent modeling can be useful: competitive economics, national security, politics, and, of course, games (Kott & McEneaney, 2007).

Computer science is rich with research on different techniques for how to represent an agent in a model, how to obtain the information to populate the model, how to use the model, and how to evaluate the model based on overall performance in the domain. While actual performance within the domain is ultimately the goal for an agent, there are many other factors affecting overall agent performance besides how accurate the agent model is. The structure of the environment, the prior biases in the behavior of the modeling agent, and the way it uses the information from the model are a few examples. If we want to determine *how well a model works* in order to decide which of several models is better, we need to measure the accuracy of the models *directly*.

Though many researchers have provided empirical studies that compare the overall domain performance of their methods with other modeling methods or different approaches (such as Monte-Carlo simulation, game-theoretic equilibrium play, or rules-based strategy), few have quantified how well their models predict the other agents' behavior directly.

There are several exceptions in which researchers do examine the accuracy of the model, not just the performance of the overall system. Carmel and Markovitch (1996) examine the model size and average error versus sample size while running their domain independent modeling US-$L*$ algorithm, showing that model-size growth slows with more examples while average error drops. Rogowski (2004) expands on this work, providing an algorithm *it-us-l** and presenting its domain-independent model-quality measure (i.e., average hold-out-set prediction accuracy) in several experiments.

In robot soccer games in RoboCup, Riley and Veloso (2002) use the probability of correctly recognizing which play an agent is about to make to measure their learning algorithm, but they do not provide any other direct model quality measures. In the plan recognition field, researchers have also employed the measurements of precision and recall (Blaylock & Allen, 2005; Cox & Kerkez, 2006) when comparing performance of candidate recognition algorithms.

The majority of the model prediction-quality measures in these efforts rely on extensions to error measurements intended for binary classification (1 point for correct prediction, 0 points for incorrect prediction). Though this information does provide a basic quality measure, its value diminishes as the number of possible agent actions per state grows.

In the world described in the previous section, there are no restrictions on uniformity of the number of actions leading from a node. Some nodes may have few actions leading away while others may have many. Under this condition, the value of a function comprised of binary-based prediction-quality measurements from multiple heterogeneous nodes is unclear. For the function to be meaningful, the underlying quality measure must be more general.

A more detailed representation of general classification performance (which is applicable to the performance measurement of a model that predicts which action an opponent will take) is the confusion matrix. A confusion matrix is an M-by-M matrix that represents a classifier's distribution of classification labels provided to M different classes. Column headings hold the model's predictions and row headings indicate the true class. Thus, the cells along the diagonal represent correct classifications and the cells on the off-diagonal represent incorrect classifications. In addition to providing accuracy or error rate (computed from the main diagonal of the matrix), the matrix reveals the number (or probability) of each type of mistake (off-diagonal cells). This additional information can be valuable when different predictive mistakes have different costs. Several agent-modeling efforts use the confusion matrix to characterize their model's prediction quality. Davidson uses a confusion matrix to quantify a neural-network agent model's ability to predict whether the opponent will fold, call, or raise under many different circumstances in poker (Davidson, Billings, Schaeffer, & Szafron, 2000). Sukthankar and Sycara use a confusion matrix to characterize their prediction of which type of breach-and-enter maneuver the opposing force is about to perform in a simulated military tactical engagement (Sukthankar & Sycara, 2006).

While confusion matrices are a step in the right direction, they can quickly become unwieldy if the space of possible options M is large (or continuous) or there are multiple stages of predictions that must be made during the course of an engagement (such as in chess, poker, and military endeavors). In multiple-stage prediction encounters (which can often be characterized as extensive form games and depicted with game trees) there would need to be a confusion matrix for every possible agent prediction node. Sometimes the act of getting to a prediction node is not certain—the probability depends on which events occurred over the history of the encounter (the path taken through the game tree). The probabilities might be codependent (depending on the probabilities of all the agents in the environment). In these circumstances there may be no clear way in which to generate a single confusion matrix quantifying the goodness of a model.

A New Approach for Evaluating Prediction Performance in Agent Models

Given the difficulty of the problem and the lack of its treatment in the field, we now present a flexible method for characterizing relative prediction quality that is independent of the agent in which it resides. This quality measurement does not consider total performance of the agent—only the model's ability to predict another agent's behavior. Before we present the measurement, let us first take a moment to list the desiderata of a predictive performance measurement that is to be used in a metareasoning role.

Given a *context* (an abstraction of the world state), an actual behavior distribution (a probability distribution over a finite number of possible actions,[2] which describes the behavioral choices of the agent in that context), and a prediction of the target's behavior distribution in the context (as provided by a predictive model, given the context), we characterize *prediction divergence* $PD(P,Q)$. Prediction divergence is the scalar measure of the distance between the actual distribution P and the predicted distribution Q such that $PD(P,Q)$ has the following properties:

1. $\forall P,Q : PD(P,Q) = 0 \Leftrightarrow P \equiv Q$ The function value should be zero if and only if two distributions are the same.
2. $\forall P,Q : PD(P,Q) > 0 \Leftrightarrow P \neq Q$ The function value is nonnegative and only positive when the distributions are different.
3. $\forall P,Q : PD(P,Q) = PD(Q,P)$ The function is symmetric.
4. $\forall P,Q,R : PD(P,Q) + PD(Q,R) \leq PD(P,R)$ The function obeys the triangle inequality. When combined with the previous three properties, this property completes the characterization of the function as a metric.
5. $\forall P,Q,R,S : (PD(P,S) > PD(P,R)) \wedge (PD(P,R) > PD(P,Q)) \Rightarrow PD(P,S) > PD(P,Q)$ The function values obey the transitive property.

2. While we describe a finite number of actions here, the functions presented later are applicable to continuous distributions as well.

6. Given any *extreme*[3] distribution P and any of its distributional complements[4] P^{-1} $PD(P,P^{-1}) = C$ where C is a positive constant. The function values should be bounded by a fixed constant such that any two distributions that are maximally far apart[5] are bounded. This enables the function to be scaled by dividing by C such that the function values lie on the interval [0,1].
7. $\forall$ extreme P,Q, and their respective complements P^{-1},Q^{-1} $PD(P,P^{-1}) = PD(Q,Q^{-1})$. All function bounds are equal regardless of the width of the underlying distributions. This is a minor extension of the previous property, which allows heterogeneous nodes to be weighted and summed in mathematically meaningful ways.

Comparing Behavior Models with Real Agent Behavior

We now develop the measurement function characterized by the desired properties described above. Information theory provides tools for comparing distributions. Its tools have been in use for well over half a century. Relative entropy (also known as the Kullback–Leibler distance) between two probability mass functions (Cover & Thomas, 2006) is a very widely used similarity measure. Given two distributions p and q, *relative entropy* is defined as:

$$D(p \,||\, q) = \sum_{x \in X} p(x) \log \frac{p(x)}{q(x)} \tag{1}$$

While relative entropy is characterized by certain desirable properties such as equality, nonnegativity, and transitivity, unfortunately it is not symmetric (property 3) or bounded (property 6). We instead choose a related, but lesser-known similarity measure that is symmetric and bounded as discussed by Fuglede and Topsoe (Fuglede & Topsoe, 2004; Topsoe, 2000). This measure, Jensen–Shannon divergence (*JSD*) is sometimes referred to as capacitory discrimination. *JSD* is calculated between two distributions p and q as:

$$JSD(p,q) = D\left(p \,||\, \frac{(p+q)}{2}\right) + D\left(q \,||\, \frac{(p+q)}{2}\right) \tag{2}$$

One can think of *JSD* as the average relative entropy from each distribution (p and q) to the distribution that is midway between them. In addition to keeping the desired properties from relative entropy, the square root of *JSD* is a metric (Topsoe, 2000),

3. An extreme distribution is one in which one of the elements contains all of the probability mass and the other elements all contain no probability mass.
4. We define a distributional complement for an extreme distribution as another extreme distribution where all of the probability mass is located at a different point than in the original distribution.
5. A loaded coin with P(heads) = 0, P(tails) = 1 is maximally far from a loaded coin with P(heads) = 1, P(tails) = 0.

meaning that it covers the first four properties above and provides additional validity for its use as a distance measurement. For the remainder of this work we will use the term *Root-JSD* to represent the square root of the value calculated in equation (2). By letting one of the distributions represent the predicted behavior distribution produced by the model and letting the other distribution represent the observed behavior distribution of the target agent, we can measure the predictive quality of our model using *Root-JSD*.

For any given interaction between agents, we may have many contexts. Each context consists of many pairs of predicted and observed actual behavior distributions that need to be compared using *Root-JSD*. For example, in extensive form games such as poker, a model might be based on a portion of the game tree that contains a set of the opponent's decision nodes (N). At each node ($n \in N$) where the opponent has an opportunity to decide his next action, there exists a distribution over his possible actions. Some nodes may occur more frequently or may be worth more (in terms of risked utility). When developing a prediction quality measurement we would like to weight the prediction quality at each decision node by its importance in our decision making and then combine the weighted prediction quality for all the nodes of interest.

In order to measure the overall similarity between the set of predicted conditional probability distributions (P) and the set of observed conditional probability distributions (Q) in an interaction, we define a function that combines all of the individual *Root-JSD* measurements at each agent-decision node in the set, using a weighting function for each node. Given a set of opponent decision nodes (N), associated sets of predicted and true probability distributions $\forall k \in N, P_k, Q_k$, and a weighting function for each node $\forall k \in N, W(k)$, we define *weighted prediction divergence* (*WPD*) as:

$$WPD(N) = \frac{\sum_{k \in N} W(k)\sqrt{JSD(P_k, Q_k)}}{\sum_{k \in N} W(k)} \tag{3}$$

Equation (3) yields a value in [0,1], making it very useful for comparing overall prediction quality of multiple models for entire histories of agent interactions. We can also weight the individual decision nodes within a context group according to some function of their *importance* with respect to the decision problem. Some possible weighting functions and their rationale for use include:

- Uniform weighting: all nodes are weighed equally.
- Frequency weighting: weight the nodes by their frequency of occurrence, giving more importance to decisions that have to be made more often.
- Utility weighting: weight the nodes by a function of the possible utility outcomes (e.g., $U_{\max} - U_{\min}$) so that the outcome of a valuable decision leads to more increase or decrease in utility for the modeling agent.
- Risk (reward) weighting: multiply probability of occurrence by utility weight.

In the next section, we use a tailored frequency-weighting scheme to compare the performance of two black-box predictive models (fixed and learning) in the Texas Hold'em poker domain.

Experiments

We now show how the predictive performance measure can be used to differentiate model performance in different contexts. These experiments demonstrate the validity of the technique described previously for determining which model is better at making predictions within each of several contexts. In the remainder of this section we introduce our target domain and describe the models that we are comparing and the protocol for the measurement. We then show the results of the experiments and discuss the implications for the feasibility of metareasoning using an automated version of this technique.

Texas Hold'em Domain Characteristics

Texas Hold'em poker is a well-known zero-sum imperfect information game. It is a poker variant in which players attempt to make the best set of cards from their private (hole) cards and several fully visible community cards that are usable by every player. Each hand consists of multiple rounds of dealing and betting where players try to win the pot: the hand ends when either all but one player has folded (uncontested win) or several players have stayed in the game until all betting is complete (the showdown).

There are four rounds in which players can bet chips based on the strength of their cards: the *preflop*, *flop*, *turn*, and *river*. If any player decides to fold before all four betting rounds have been completed, he forfeits any claim on the pot and must sit out the remainder of the hand while the other players finish. If all but one of the players have folded prior to the completion of the river betting round then the remaining player wins the pot uncontested and the hand is terminated without further betting rounds.

In a heads-up (two-player) limit (fixed increment bet) Texas Hold'em match, we can express each round of betting in terms of an extensive form game. In this version of Texas Hold'em there are over 10^{17} (Billings et al., 2003) possible game outcomes—making even this simplistic variant of Texas Hold'em very rich in strategic opportunity.

Opponent Modeling in Poker

There are two types of opponent models for the poker domain: fixed and learning. A fixed model is usually based on either general poker knowledge or an off-line trained program that reviews previously documented matches and builds a model from them. The fixed model does not change its function over time during an encounter with an adversary. A learning model is different from a fixed model in that it can change its strategy over time as it observes the behavior of its current adversary during an encounter.

For these experiments we compare the performance of two black-box models: a fixed-strategy opponent model and a learning opponent model. Each of these models was part of a larger modeling system in our entry for the 2007 Computer Poker Competition: PokeMinnLimit1. The fixed-strategy model was based on general poker knowledge for playing limit poker. It uses static parameters for a pot-value function that predicts the likelihood of the opponent's folding, calling, or raising. In competition, our agent uses the fixed model to provide predictions of opponent behavior before there are sufficient observations to use the learning model.

In contrast, the learning model has no predefined probability distribution over opponent behavior. Instead, it attempts to make predictions of the opponent's behavior based solely on past observations in the current match once at least one observation has been made at that decision node. At each node in the game tree where the opponent makes a decision, the learning model records the frequencies of the actions. Then it computes the probability that the opponent will fold, call, or raise in the future based on the accumulated frequencies of each action, conditional on the game tree node where the agent made the decision. This particular model makes several assumptions in order to reduce the number of nodes in the game tree that it must compute: the model does not consider what cards the opponent may have; each betting round is considered independent; all data are gathered and weighted equally for the entire course of the encounter. This particular style of model is biased toward learning a stationary policy opponent well, at the possible expense of being misled by a nonstationary adversary.

Comparing Model Quality

We now show how *WPD* can be used to compare performance between two candidate agent models. We focus on the models' ability to predict the behavior of the top performer in the 2007 Computer Poker "Limit Equilibrium" Competition: Hyperborean07LimitEq1.

The modified frequency-weighting function $W(n)$ we use in these experiments to compute *WPD* weights each node by how *relevant* it is in the poker game tree. We calculate this relevance recursively: the root-node of a tree has a relevance of 1. Each child of the root-node has a relevance of $\frac{1}{|C_r|}$ where C_r is the number of the root-node's children. Each child of the root-node's children C_c has a relevance of $\frac{1}{|C_r||C_c|}$ and so forth.

We compared the performance of the fixed model to the learning model. To compare the prediction quality of these models we needed data about the true behavior of our desired opponent. For the test-data set, we retrieved all 660 matches (1.98M hands) from the 2007 Computer Poker Competition (Zinkevich, 2007) played by Hyperborean07LimitEq1. We felt these data were representative of the true behavior of Hyperborean07LimitEq1 because it was the largest set of data available to the public, and the data document Hyperborean07LimitEq1's behavior against many different opponents. We scanned all of the test data to determine the frequency counts for each action at each game tree node in each round. We declared the resulting probability distributions for each node in the game tree as behavioral truth for Hyperborean07LimitEq1.

To determine the learning model's ability to learn the opponent's distribution of behavior, we isolated a training set of 20 matches played between PokeMinnLimit1 and Hyperborean07LimitEq1. We trained the learning model using only observations that it could have made during these 20 matches. We then gathered predictions from the trained model on the hands from the test set and calculated the *WPD* between the learning model's predictions of Hyperborean07LimitEq1's behavior and Hyperborean07LimitEq1's actual behavior. A similar procedure (without a training phase) was used to obtain the *WPD* for the fixed-strategy model. The aggregate results for 3,000 hands for both models are shown in figure 16.3. Because of the heterogeneous nature of Texas Hold'em poker's four betting rounds, we chose to separate the opponent decisions into four context groups: preflop, flop, turn, and river. While we made this decision based on our expertise of the domain, we expect that there may be better divisions of contexts that could be made (by pot size, for example) that might yield even further separation between the different models. The automation of context determination is a key area for future research in order to make further progress with the metareasoning system described in this chapter.

Discussion

Though the learning model quickly becomes better at predicting behavior than the fixed-strategy model during the preflop and flop rounds, the learning model's prediction quality in the turn and river rounds grow worse over the course of the game. After approximately 380 iterations on the turn (and after approximately 740 iterations on the river) the fixed-strategy model would have better predictive performance than the learning model.

While the learning model appears to be very useful for predicting the true opponent's behavior on the preflop and possibly the flop (at least when compared to the fixed model we used), its utility is questionable during the turn and river, where the

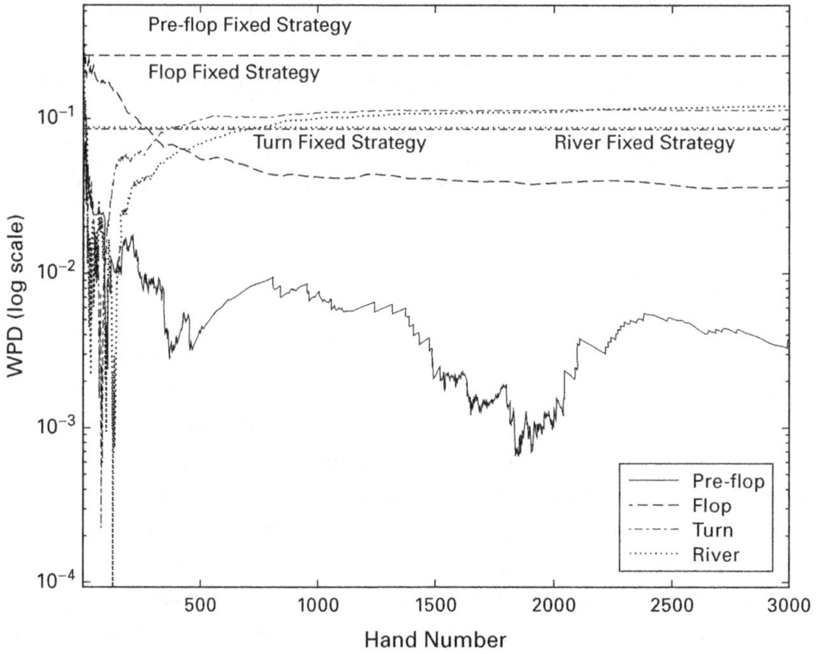

Figure 16.3
Comparing learning versus fixed-strategy models in each of the four betting rounds in a 3000-hand limit poker game: The horizontal lines represent the fixed-strategy model *WPD*. The darker fluctuating lines represent the learning model's *WPD* values, which are better (lower) than the fixed strategy for the preflop and flop, but worse than the fixed strategy for the turn and river.

fixed model's predictions might be preferred. Although finding the cause of the reduced accuracy of the learning model during the turn and the river is beyond the scope of this work, it is important to note that this analysis reveals the flaws in the learning model even when other performance-based methods fail to do so. For example, in a separate experiment with 100 matches (300,000 hands) we examined relative performance between two agents in terms of number of small bet increments won per hand (sb/h). We noticed that the learning strategy model achieves an average 0.04 sb/h greater win rate than the fixed strategy model from hands 500 through 3,000 when each played against Hyperborean07LimitEq1. If we had relied on just the earnings performance measure as the method of determining the better model (as much of the other research in the field does), we might not have realized that subcomponents of the learning model were not performing as well as the same subcomponents in the fixed model.

If the metalevel reasoning system described earlier had been available at the time of competition and could have seen the prediction-quality difference between the learning and fixed models in these contexts, it might have been possible for the recommender to advise the agent to switch to using the fixed model instead of the learning model in the turn and river betting rounds. This may have improved the performance of the agent in the competition. Testing this hypothesis is reserved for future work.

Conclusion and Future Work

We have shown that prediction-quality assessments can be used to point out strengths and weaknesses in opponent models that remain hidden under domain-based performance measurements. We identified the desiderata of a strong measure of model quality necessary for metalevel reasoning in the multimodel agent prediction setting. By borrowing a concept from information theory (Jensen–Shannon divergence), we have developed a weighted prediction divergence metric and characterized several tailored weighting schemes. Weighted prediction divergence incorporates all desired properties of our performance measure allowing us to determine the relative prediction quality between models. We have shown empirically how weighted prediction divergence values for several models could be used to select the best model for the current context. These techniques form one of the foundations of metareasoning, empowering a metalevel reasoner to make real-time decisions about which models to use in certain contexts.

There is at least one additional effort that must be completed before the metareasoner described in the introduction can be realized. We must choose a state abstraction method which can automatically cluster world states into contexts such that the prediction-quality estimation system described in this work can assess models with fewer computational resources. Though we have shown a meaningful context for poker in this work, the contexts for the collection of nodes we used were generated manually. Automating this process would enable multidomain applicability for the metareasoning technique we present.

In general, when one considers the relationship between learning and metareasoning, the two may be hard to differentiate. In our work, the goal of the metareasoning level is to determine which of several models will perform the best in a given situation. The context generator is responsible for abstracting the state to discover similar situations to those seen previously. The activity repository (which contains the contexts and the models' performance within those contexts) is merely a collection of context-sensitive observations. The utility calculation is a math equation based on the past performance of the models in similar contexts. Our metareasoning level has the ability to remember situations from the past and how well each of the opponent models would have performed in the situation. In effect, the metareasoner, by controlling model selection, can enable the agent to improve its performance in repeated situations. This is learning.

References

Billings, D., Burch, N., Davidson, A., Holte, R., Schaeffer, J., Schauenbert, T., et al. (2003). Approximating game-theoretic optimal strategies for full-scale poker. In *International Joint Conference on Artificial Intelligence* (pp. 661–668). St. Louis, MO: Academic Press.

Blaylock, N., & Allen, J. (2005). Recognizing instantiated goals using statistical methods. In Gal Kaminka (Ed.), *IJCAI Workshop Modeling on Others from Observation (MOO-2005)* (pp. 79–86). Menlo Park, CA: IJCAI.

Carmel, D., & Markovitch, S. (1996). Incorporating opponent models into adversary search. In *Thirteenth National Conference on Artificial Intelligence* (pp. 120–125). Menlo, Park, CA: AAAI Press.

Cover, T. M., & Thomas, J. A. (2006). *Elements of information theory*. New York: John Wiley & Sons.

Cox, M. T., & Kerkez, B. (2006). Case-based plan recognition with novel input. *Control and Intelligent Systems, 34*(2), 96–104.

Davidson, A., Billings, D., Schaeffer, J., & Szafron, D. (2000). Improved opponent modeling in poker. In *International Conference on Artificial Intelligence* (pp. 1467–1473). Las Vegas: CSREA Press.

Fuglede, B., & Topsoe, F. (2004). Jensen–Shannon divergence and Hilbert space embedding. In *Proceedings of the International Symposium on Information Theory, 2004 (ISIT 2004)* (p. 31). Piscataway, NJ: IEEE Computer Society.

Kott, A., & McEneaney, W. M. (2007). *Adversarial reasoning: Computational approaches to reading the opponent's mind*. Boca Raton, FL: Chapman & Hall/CRC.

Luckhardt, C. A., & Irani, K. B. (1986). An algorithmic solution of *n*-person games. In *Fifth National Conference on Artificial Intelligence (AAAI)* (pp. 158–162). Menlo, Park, CA: AAAI Press.

Riley, P., & Veloso, M. (2002). Planning for distributed execution through use of probabilistic opponent models. In *Sixth International Conference on AI Planning and Scheduling (AIPS-2002)* (pp. 72–81). Menlo, Park, CA: AAAI Press.

Rogowski, C. (2004). Model-based opponent-modelling in domains beyond the prisoner's dilemma. In *Workshop on modeling other agents from observations at AAMAS* (pp. 41–48). Piscataway, NJ: IEEE Computer Society.

Russell, S. J., & Norvig, P. (2003). *Artificial intelligence: A modern approach* (2nd ed.). Upper Saddle River, NJ: Prentice-Hall.

Russell, S. J., & Wefald, E. (1991). Principles of metareasoning. *Artificial Intelligence, 49*(1–3), 361–395.

Stone, P., Riley, P., & Veloso, M. M. (2000). Defining and using ideal teammate and opponent agent models. In *Twelfth Innovative Applications of AI Conference (IAAI-2000)* (pp. 1040–1045). Menlo, Park, CA: AAAI Press.

Sturtevant, N., Zinkevich, M., & Bowling, M. (2006). Prob-max-*n*: playing *n*-player games with opponent models. In *National Conference on Artificial Intelligence (AAAI)* (pp. 1057–1063). Menlo Park, CA: AAAI Press.

Sukthankar, G., & Sycara, K. (2006). Robust recognition of physical team behaviors using spatio-temporal models. In *Fifth International Conference on Autonomous Agents and Multiagent Systems (AAMAS)*. Piscataway, NJ: IEEE Computer Society.

Topsoe, F. (2000). Some inequalities for information divergence and related measures of discrimination. *IEEE Transactions on Information Theory, 46*(4), 1602–1609.

Zinkevich, M. (2007). Data files from the 2007 computer poker competition. Retrieved from http://www.cs.ualberta.ca/~pokert/2007/data.html.

V Models of Self

17 Metareasoning as an Integral Part of Commonsense and Autocognitive Reasoning

Fabrizio Morbini and Lenhart Schubert

In this chapter we summarize our progress toward building a self-aware agent based on the notion of explicit self-awareness[1] (Schubert, 2005). An explicitly self-aware agent is characterized by (1) being based on extensive, human-like knowledge about the world and itself and the ability to reason with that knowledge, (2) relying on a transparent (easily understood, and semantically well-defined) knowledge representation, and (3) being able to explain itself and display its self-awareness through natural language dialogues. The second point is not strictly related to self-awareness, but it facilitates implementation of some aspects, such as answer explanation, and simplifies testing and debugging of the agent. In addition, we emphasize the importance of metalevel reasoning in commonsense reasoning and self-awareness, while questioning the common view of agent control structure in terms of separate object-level and metalevel strata. Instead, we suggest a "continual planning" (and execution) control structure wherein the agent's metalevel and object-level reasoning steps mingle seamlessly.

We first review the requirements imposed by explicit self-awareness and by this intermingling of object-level and metalevel reasoning on the knowledge representation and reasoning system and then describe how these have been realized in the new version of the EPILOG[2] system. Then we demonstrate our agent by looking at a few questions, each related to some aspects of self-awareness. Finally, we conclude with a discussion of our long-term plans.

1. Conditions 1 and 3 for explicit self-awareness, by requiring human-like abilities, are intended to set aside weaker notions of self-awareness such as monitoring and regulation of internal parameters (as in operating systems or thermostats), internal event-logging (for example, of function calls and their local environments), or goal-directed behavior (as in heat-seeking missiles or ant colonies). Certainly the conditions are not intended to be *necessary* for all reasonable notions of self-awareness.

2. EPILOG is a reasoning system for Episodic Logic (see Schubert & Hwang, 2000). Its main components are a general inference engine based on backward and forward chaining and a set of specialists to aid the general inference engine in particular types of inferences (e.g., temporal, introspective).

Metareasoning

Schubert (2005) lists a series of requirements on a knowledge representation and reasoning system to enable explicit self-awareness as defined in the previous section. We first summarize these requirements, and then describe in some detail how two of these requirements have been implemented in EPILOG.

1. *Logic framework*: we require an explicit, transparent[3] representation for the agent's commonsense knowledge and metaknowledge that allows for easy browsing/editing/debugging and manipulation by general inference methods. We chose Episodic Logic (EL) as an extension of first-order logic (FOL) that is more fully adapted to the expressive devices of natural language (NL) (e.g., see Schubert and Hwang, 2000).
2. *Events and situations*: the agent must be able to refer to events described by complex sentences (e.g., the event described by EPILOG's failure to answer a question). This capability has always been an integral part of EL and therefore of EPILOG.
3. *Generic knowledge*: much of everyday knowledge is expressed using generic or probabilistic adverbs such as *usually* or *probably*. In EPILOG generics are expressed using probabilities, though this support is very limited and in need of further development.
4. *Attitudes and autoepistemic inference*: the ability to reason about one's own knowledge and to represent one's beliefs is fundamental to self-awareness. Our commitment is to a formal computational notion of knowing as described by Kaplan (2000) and Kaplan and Schubert (2000). We describe below how the basic machinery needed for this has been implemented in EPILOG.
5. *Metasyntactic devices*: a self-aware agent needs to be able to refer in its logical language to the syntax of that language itself. How some of these devices have been implemented in EPILOG will be described later in this section.

The following subsections focus on how the last two requirements, those most central to self-awareness and metareasoning, have been implemented in EPILOG. As a notational alert, we should mention that EL uses infix notation for predication and prefix notation for function application; e.g., (*EL* (*very Expressive*)) states that *EL* is very expressive; the predicate (*very Expressive*) is infixed, while the predicate modifier *very* (a function that maps monadic predicates to monadic predicates) is prefixed.

Substitutional Quantification and Quasi-Quotation

As motivated and exemplified by Schubert (2005) and Morbini and Schubert (2007), it is important to be able to refer to syntactic elements of EL in an EL formula itself.

3. An example of knowledge that is not explicit and transparent would be the matrices of numbers learned by a machine-learning technique.

For instance, this allows a formal treatment of axiom schemas, enables EPILOG to classify its own predicates and formulas, and allows EPILOG to choose executable procedures for solving certain kinds of problems deliberately, based on axioms about their effects.

To enable this kind of "syntactic self-awareness," EPILOG currently supports two devices: substitutional quantifiers and quasi-quotation. Their implementation is straightforward and posed no major problems. The two main modifications required concerned the following components:

1. *EL-Parser*: we added substitutional quantifiers and metavariables. A metavariable is a particular type of variable that is bound by a substitutional quantifier. A substitutional quantifier is much like a normal quantifier except that it quantifies over substitutions of expressions of a particular category for the metavariable. For example, $(\forall_{wff}\ w\ (w \Rightarrow (me\ Know\ (that\ w))))$[4] quantifies over substitutions of EL well-formed formulas for the variable w. The truth conditions of the formula are that all instances of the formula are true under the object-level semantics, when EL well-formed formulas (not containing metavariables) are substituted for w.
2. *Quasi-quotation*: written with a quote sign (apostrophe), quasi-quotation accepts as argument an expression that may contain metavariables; substitution for such metavariables treats quasi-quotes as transparent. As an example of the use of quasi-quotation, we can express in EL that the "=" predicate is commutative by writing ('= (*Commutative ELpredicate*)) where *Commutative* is a predicate modifier and *ELpredicate* is a predicate (true of certain syntactic objects). Other examples that will be seen later are the use of *AppearancePred* and *AppearanceFactAbout* to describe internal predicates and formulas.
3. *Unification routines*: since we have provided for metavariables, unification should be able to unify not only variables with terms but also metavariables with EL expressions of the appropriate categories. For example, we can unify $(me\ Know\ (that\ w))$ with $(me\ Know\ (that\ (?x\ Foo)))$, yielding unifier $\{(?x\ Foo)/w\}$.

Recursive QA

Morbini and Schubert (2007) described the basic properties that a computational notion of knowing should have. In that work, we indicated why *knowing* is very different from *being able to infer*, and we referred to Kaplan and Schubert's algorithmic ASK mechanism as a basis for *knowing*. As was shown by Kaplan and Schubert (2000), certain axiomatic constraints on ASK can assure soundness of simulative inference, and we can also assure compliance with certain natural requirements on knowing, such as that (ϕ *and* ψ) is known iff ϕ is known and ψ is known. Here we describe how ASK is supported in EPILOG. The intuitive way to implement ASK (and thus to answer

4. Of course, the omniscience claim expressed by this formula is absurd.

questions that involve predicates like *Know* or *Believe*) is to allow for question-asking within a question-answering (QA) process, where the subordinate QA process is guaranteed to terminate relatively quickly. If a question requires prolonged reasoning, the answer is by definition not known. Answering questions about nested beliefs thus involves further nesting of QA processes. That is the basic idea behind recursive QA.

Again, implementing this is straightforward in any system with a clean and modular implementation of the QA process. What is needed is that the QA process must work only on local variables, and the same must be true for all systems on which QA depends (e.g., knowledge base, unification, inference and normalization).

In addition to having a modular system, one needs a way to connect inference with the QA process so that this process can be started whenever it is required by some inference. In EPILOG this is achieved by using the metasyntactic devices described in the previous subsection and by providing a single special-purpose function, called "*Apply*," that the QA process knows how to evaluate whenever its arguments are quoted and metavariable-free. It executes a Lisp function of the same name for the given arguments. In particular, to implement the ASK mechanism we added the following axiom to EPILOG's standard knowledge base; this defines knowing that *w*, for a formula *w* containing no free variables, as being true just in case the *knownbyme?* Lisp function returns *yes* for argument *w*:

$$(\forall_{wff}\ w\ ('w\ WithoutFreeVars)\ ((me\ Know\ (that\ w)) \Leftrightarrow \\ ((Apply\ 'knownbyme?\ 'w) = 'yes))$$

In effect, *knownbyme?* implements the ASK mechanism as a recursive QA-process. Note that EL allows for an optional restrictor in quantified statements, and here a restrictor (*'w WithoutFreeVars*) is present. *WithoutFreeVars* is a predicate with one argument denoting an expression, typically specified using quotation, that is true whenever the argument contains no free variables. To evaluate this predicate EPILOG will have another axiom in its knowledge base:

$$(\forall_{wff}\ w\ ('w\ WithoutFreeVars) \Leftrightarrow \\ ((Apply\ 'withoutfreevars?\ 'w) = 'yes))$$

Where *withoutfreevars?* is the Lisp function that detects whether or not an EL expression contains free variables. An alternative to this approach would be to leave the attachment of procedures to EL predicates or functions implicit; however, by using explicit attachment axioms like the above, EPILOG is able to make its own reflective decisions about when to employ particular procedures.

Whenever the QA process encounters a subgoal that contains an equality in which one of the two equated terms is an *Apply*-term, where its arguments are quoted and metavariable-free, EPILOG evaluates it by executing the Lisp function specified as the first argument of *Apply*, with the arguments provided for it. The result, which must be a quoted EL term, will be substituted for the *Apply* term in the original equality.

Inference in EPILOG

In this section we will describe other characteristics of EPILOG's inference machinery indirectly related to metareasoning and important to EPILOG's overall functioning.

Normalization

Because EL uses nonstandard constructs (e.g., substitutional quantification, quotation, lambda abstraction, and modifiers), the standard FOL normalization to clause form cannot be used. Besides, clause form can be exponentially larger than the original form, for example, for a disjunction of conjunctions. Normalization in EPILOG is based on a term-rewriting system that currently employs a total of fourteen rules. They perform such transformations as moving negations inward, Skolemizing top-level existentials, ordering the arguments of ANDs and ORs, eliminating simple tautologies, and moving quantifiers inward.

As in other reasoning systems, normalization contributes greatly to reasoning efficiency by collapsing classes of "obviously" equivalent formulas into unique (sets of) formulas. As an example, consider the unnormalized form of the statement, "One email in my inbox contains no message":

(∃ *e*0 (*e*0 *AtAbout Now*)
  ((∃ *x* ((*x Email*) *and* (*x In MyInbox*))
    (*No y* (*y Message*) (*x Contains y*))) ** *e*0))

where we have reduced "my inbox" to a constant for simplicity. If this is provided to EPILOG as a fact, then normalization introduces Skolem constants for the existentials *e*0 and *x*, narrows the scope of the episode-characterization operator "**" to exclude atemporal conjuncts, separates implicit conjunctions, and (if we choose to include a rule mandating this) replaces (*No y phi psi*) with (∀ *y phi* (*not psi*)):

(*SK*1 *AtAbout Now*), (*SK*2 *Email*), (*SK*2 *In MyInbox*),
((∀ *z* (*z Message*) (*not* (*SK*2 *Contain z*))) ** *SK*1)

Note that normalization of a goal, unlike normalization of a fact, does not Skolemize existentials, because these serve as matchable variables. In proving a goal with a top-level universal, the universal quantifier may be eliminated and the variable given a unique new name. This step can thus be thought of as the dual of Skolemization.

Inference Graph Handling

EPILOG's QA is in its simplest form a natural deduction back-chaining system. It starts with the initial question and then generates a proof subgoal and a disproof subgoal (i.e., the negation of the initial question). The QA process maintains an agenda of subgoals based on a binary tree that decides which subgoal to process first. We have not finalized the method of sorting subgoals on the agenda; candidate criteria include: subgoal complexity, their probability, and their level (i.e., the number of inference steps taken to produce a subgoal from the initial question). More testing is required to decide which combination of criteria is effective in the majority of situations.

Each subgoal is first checked to see if it can be simplified:

1. Conjunctions are split into their conjuncts, and each conjunct is handled independently of its siblings until it is solved. When a solution to a conjunct is obtained, it is properly combined with the solutions of the siblings.
2. Disjunctions are split for each disjunct by assuming the negation of the remaining disjuncts. Here we make use of another feature, namely, knowledge base inheritance. Each question is associated with a knowledge base that defines what knowledge can be used to answer the question. When assumptions are made, they are loaded into a new knowledge base (to be discarded at the end of the QA process) that inherits the contents of the knowledge base used before the addition of the assumptions. Currently the consistency of the assumptions is not checked, but problems will be detected from the contradictory answers produced.
3. Implications, $A \Rightarrow B$, are converted into two alternative subgoals: (*not* A), and B assuming A.
4. Equivalences are split into conjunctions.
5. Universally quantified goals are simplified by generating a new constant and unifying the universal variable with it. If the universal quantifier has a restrictor, the restrictor is assumed.

When no more simplifications can be applied, goal-chaining inference is attempted. From each subgoal, one or more keys are extracted and used to retrieve knowledge. These keys are the minimal well-formed formulas embedded entirely by extensional operators such as quantifiers and truth-functional connectives. Each subgoal maintains another agenda that decides which key to use first for retrieval. As in the case of subgoal ordering, we have not yet finalized the sorting criterion. Possibilities are preferring keys that contain more variables, or ones with the least amount of associated knowledge (so as to focus on a quick proof, if one exists).

Naturally, if a retrieved fact exactly matches a goal, then goal-chaining terminates for that goal. In the general case, goal-chaining inferences can be thought of as being resolution-like, except that the literals being resolved may be arbitrarily embedded by extensional operators. As a simple example, suppose that we have a known fact ($\forall$ x (x P) ((x Q) *and* (x R))), that is, every P is a Q and an R. If we use this fact in pursuing a goal of form ((C Q) *and phi*) (where C is a constant and *phi* is some well-formed formula), then the derived goal will be ((C P) *and phi*). The extensionally embedded literals that were unified were (*C Q*) in the goal and (*x Q*) in the given fact. If one of these were intensionally embedded, for instance by the reification operator "*that*" (e.g., forming an object of an attitudinal predicate), the unification and hence the goal-chaining inference would not be attempted. (For details, see Schubert & Hwang, 2000.) For each successful inference performed for a subgoal together with a retrieved formula, a child subgoal is attached to this subgoal and the process is repeated (with termination if the derived subgoal is a trivial subgoal: truth or falsity).

The two processes just described (i.e., simplification and inference) construct an inference tree. However, loops and repetitions can occur, worsening performance or preventing success altogether (in case the subgoal selection proceeds depth-first). Therefore, we added two optimizations, the second of which transforms the inference tree into an inference graph:

1. Loop detection: a loop is created when the same subgoal appears twice along an inference branch. In saying that a new subgoal is the "same" as a previous one, we mean that it is expressed by the same EL formula and is associated with the same knowledge base.
2. To avoid doing the same reasoning multiple times, we detect when a new node is generated with a subgoal identical to a previous one on a different branch (thus not forming a loop). If the knowledge base associated with the previous node contains formulas not available at the new node, we treat the new node as unrelated to the previous one. But if the knowledge base associated with the new node is identical with that of the previous one, we connect the two nodes and completely stop further processing of the new node; and if the knowledge base of the new node properly contains that of the previous node, we again connect the two nodes but then continue to process the new node as if the old didn't exist. In case the old node is answered, the answer is propagated to the new node as well, using the inserted connection.

Term Evaluation

Sometimes the answer may contain complex terms, such as functions, instead of a simple result in the form expected by whoever asked the question.

For example, to the question "How old are you?" the system could answer with "The difference in years between 1st of January 1991 and now" instead of actually computing the difference. To deal with this issue, we augment the question with type constraints that define the desired type of the answers. In addition, we employ axioms that describe how to obtain a particular type from another.

For example, the above question in EL becomes:

(*Wh x* (∃ *y* ('*x RoundsDown* '*y*)
  (∃ *z* ('*y Expresses z* (*K* (*Plur Year*)))
    (∃ *e* (*e AtAbout Now*) ((*z AgeOf Epi2Me*) ** *e*))))

The QA process will then use axioms in its knowledge base that describe how to use the predicate *Expresses* to compute the *x* that expresses *y* as a number of rounded down years.

Examples

In this section we describe some of the examples used to test the features of this system. We will point out how metareasoning plays a (major or minor) role in these examples.

Morbini and Schubert (2007) provided a preliminary discussion of the questions "Do pigs have wings?" and "Did the phone ring (during some particular episode E1)?" Previously, such examples could only be handled "Socratically," leading EPILOG through the proofs step by step, whereas now the questions are solved autonomously, as projected in that paper. We will not repeat the details here, but we should reiterate the claim the examples are intended to illustrate: much of our commonsense question-answering, even if not explicitly concerned with metalevel concepts, tacitly relies on metaknowledge about our own cognitive functioning. In the case of the question whether pigs have wings, we claimed that a negative answer depends on the metabelief that our "pig knowledge" is complete with respect to pigs' major body parts (especially very visible ones; for contrast, consider the question "Do pigs have tonsils?"). This autocognitive approach (as we termed it in Morbini and Schubert, 2007) is not only more realistic than the usual default inference approaches, but also more efficient, because it substitutes fast ASK (self-query) checks for potentially unbounded consistency checks. Similarly, the question whether the phone rang, in the case of a negative answer, depends on metabeliefs about how, and under what conditions, we acquire and retain knowledge about audible events in our environment.

One of the most interesting new questions we have tried so far is the question "How old are you?" Though one can easily imagine simple shortcut methods for answering such a question, doing so in a principled, knowledge-based fashion can be nontrivial. Table 17.1 shows a selection of the knowledge used for this question.

The "@ e" construct in the third axiom means "characterizes an episode that is at the same time as *e*." The reason for introducing axioms for *AtAbout* is that this predicate appears in our interpretation of English present-tense sentences.

Expressed in EL, the question "How old are you?" as previously mentioned becomes:

$$(Wh\ x\ (\exists\ y\ ('x\ RoundsDown\ 'y)$$
$$(\exists\ z\ ('y\ Expresses\ z\ (K\ (Plur\ Year)))$$
$$(\exists\ e\ (e\ AtAbout\ Now)\ ((z\ AgeOf\ Epi2Me)\ **\ e)))),$$

Table 17.1
Most significant knowledge used to answer the question "How old are you (now)?"

EPILOG's birth date is Jan. 1, 1991:

((\$ *'date* 1991 1 1) *BirthDateOf Epi2Me*)

If an event happens at the same time as another then it happens at about the same time as the other:

(∀ *x* (∀ *y* (*x SameTime y*) (*x AtAbout y*)))

Meaning postulate relating ** and @:

($\forall_{wff}$ *w* (∀ *e* ((*w* @ *e*) ⇔ (∃ e1 (e1 *SameTime e*) (*w* ** e1)))))

The age of a physical object during an arbitrary episode is the difference between the date of the episode and the date of birth of that object:

(∀ *y* (*y PhysicalObj*) (∀ *x* (*x* (*be* (*BirthDateOf y*)))
        (∀ *e* (((*TimeElapsedBetween* (*DateOf e*) *x*) *AgeOf y*) @ *e*))))

Defines how to evaluate the function *TimeElapsedBetween* and to express the result as an amount in a given unit of measure (i.e. *type*, such as "year" or "second"):

(∀ *x* (*x ELDate*)
  (∀ *y* (*y ELDate*)
    ($\forall_{pred}$ *type* (*'type* ELTimePred)
      (∀ *r* (*'r* = (*Apply* 'DiffOfDates? *'x 'y 'type*))
        (*'r Expresses* (*TimeElapsedBetween x y*) (*K* (*Plur type*)))))))

Defines how to compute the floor of a given numeric amount:

(∀ *x* (∀ *y* ((*'y NumericAmount*) *And* (*'x* = (*Apply* 'RoundsDown? *'y*)))
  (*'x RoundsDown 'y*)))

after the addition of implicit conventional constraints on the form of the answer. The answer found is that the age of EPILOG is (*amt* 18 (*K* (*Plur Year*))). This answer is the unifier found for the variable *x* while the unifier found for the variable *z* is (– (*DateOf Now*) (\$ *'date* 1991 1 1)). Metareasoning is used to find the expression that represents the same amount of time but is expressed as a number of years. During this process the QA process applies the appropriate conversion and evaluation functions based on the syntactic form of the formulas involved.

This application of metareasoning can be seen as making EPILOG aware of the procedures at its disposal and what they accomplish, leaving to EPILOG's own deliberate decision making the choice of what procedural knowledge to use at what times. This also opens the door to future work on learning by self-programming (see Robertson and Laddaga's work in this vol., chap. 7): the creation and purposeful use of new programs (or plans) aimed at solving specific problems.

The next question considered here is "What is your name (now)?" Metareasoning enters the process only incidentally here (we'll point out where), but to the extent

Table 17.2
Knowledge used to answer the question "What is your name (now)?"

EpilogName is a name:

(*EpilogName Name*)

A name is a thing:
(∀ *x* (*x Name*) (*x Thing*))

Now is during event *E*2:

(*Now During E*2)

The event *E*2 is characterized by EPILOG having name *EpilogName*:
((EPILOG *Have EpilogName*) ** *E*2)

Have is a continuous property: if *x* has *y* in *e* then *x* has *y* at all times during *e*:

(∀ *x* (∀ *y* (∀ *e* ((*x Have y*) ** *e*)
    (∀ *z* (*z During e*) ((*x Have y*) @ *z*)))))

Meaning postulate relating ** and @:

($\forall_{wff}$ *w* (∀ *e* ((*w* @ *e*) ⇔ (∃ *e*1 (*e*1 *SameTime e*) (*w* ** *e*1)))))

For every time *e* at the same time of *e1* if *e* is during an event *x* then also *e1* is:

(∀ *x* (∀ *e* (*e During x*) (∀ *e*1 (*e*1 *SameTime e*) (*e*1 *During x*))))

---

that an agent's knowledge makes reference to itself (here, through the self-referring term EPILOG), it indicates its potential for reflective cognition. Table 17.2 lists the knowledge used to answer this question.

The question in EL is represented as

(∃ *e*0 (*e*0 *AtAbout Now*)
  ((∃ *z* ((*z Name*) *and* (*EPILOG Have z*))
    (∃ *y* (*y Thing*) (*y* (*Be* (*L x* (*x* = *z*)))))) ** *e*0))

The apparently convoluted form is due to the fact that this question is automatically generated from the NL input. ("What" is interpreted as "what thing," and the verb phrase "is your name" becomes "is (at about now) identical with a name that you have.") After normalization we obtain the simpler question

(∃ *e*0 (*e*0 *AtAbout Now*)
  (∃ *z* ((*z Name*) *and* (*z Thing*)) ((*EPILOG Have z*) ** *e*0)))

The normalization procedure moves inward the "**" operator using the knowledge that "*Name*" and "*Thing*" are atemporal predicates. This knowledge, used by the normalization procedure, is asserted explicitly in EL. This is the incidental use of metaknowledge referred to at the beginning of this example.

Table 17.3
Knowledge used to answer the question "What do you know about the appearance of pigs?"

Pigs are thick-bodied:

((*K* (*Plur Pig*)) *ThickBodied*)

ThickBodied is a predicate about the appearance of something:

(*'ThickBodied AppearancePred*)

Every formula with structure (*x P*) in which *P* is an appearance predicate is a fact about the appearance of *x*:

($\forall_{pred}$ *p* (*'p AppearancePred*)
  ($\forall$ *x* (*x p*) ((*that* (*x p*)) *AppearanceFactAbout x*)))

In the current reasoning we manually add the fact that EPILOG's name is valid in an interval of time that includes the *Now* point. However, in future we would like this property to be automatically generated by a module in charge of maintaining the self-model of the system.

The last example shows how the metasyntactic devices could be used to answer topical questions. The question is "What do you know about the appearance of pigs?" Table 17.3 contains the knowledge used to answer this question.

The question in EL becomes

($\exists$ *x* (*x AppearanceFactAbout* (*K* (*Plur Pig*)))) .

The answer found is (*that* ((*K* (*Plur Pig*)) *ThickBodied*)). Note that this answer depends on the metainference from the second and third axioms that the answer well-formed formula is indeed an appearance-fact about pigs. We are not aware of any other system capable of deductive topical reasoning of this sort, in support of descriptive question-answering. However, to retrieve more complex knowledge about pigs, for example, that pigs have curly tails, more complex knowledge would have to be used.

Discussion

The traditional conception of the role of metareasoning in an intelligent agent is diagrammed in figure 1.2 (this vol., chap. 1). The emphasis in this conception is on control and monitoring of object-level reasoning by higher-level reasoning processes, and in turn, the control of action in the world by object-level reasoning (see, e.g., Cox, 2005).

The distinction we have made between procedural knowledge, world knowledge, and metaknowledge might be thought to correspond respectively to the ground-level, object-level, and metalevel modules in figure 1.2. However, this is not so, because as our examples showed, even question-answering can make simultaneous use of procedures, object-level knowledge, and metaknowledge.

The deployment of these kinds of knowledge is not stratified, but instead tightly intertwined: any subgoal in the QA-process might draw upon procedural, object-level, or metalevel knowledge for its achievement.

It might be thought that this mingling of knowledge and reasoning levels in our system is attributable to our focus on question-answering instead of autonomous, motivated behavior. However, the kind of purposive agent we envisage (and are actively working toward) will still intertwine the various kinds of knowledge and reasoning in the manner of our QA system, rather than using cascaded levels of decision making. It will be based on continual modification, evaluation, and partial execution of a "lifelong" plan, as diagrammed in figure 17.1.

The lifelong plan will contain hierarchically structured goals and actions, and the agent will perpetually try to improve the expected long-term net utility of the plan, while at the same time executing steps that do not require further planning and are currently due. The steps themselves could be reasoning steps (e.g., try to determine the truth or falsity of some proposition) just as easily as they could be communicative or physical actions; so, in terms of the structure and execution of the life plan, there is not a clear separation between thinking and acting. Furthermore, the expansion of goals or high-level steps into executable actions in general will depend on reasoning similar to the reasoning currently carried out by our QA mechanism; that is, this

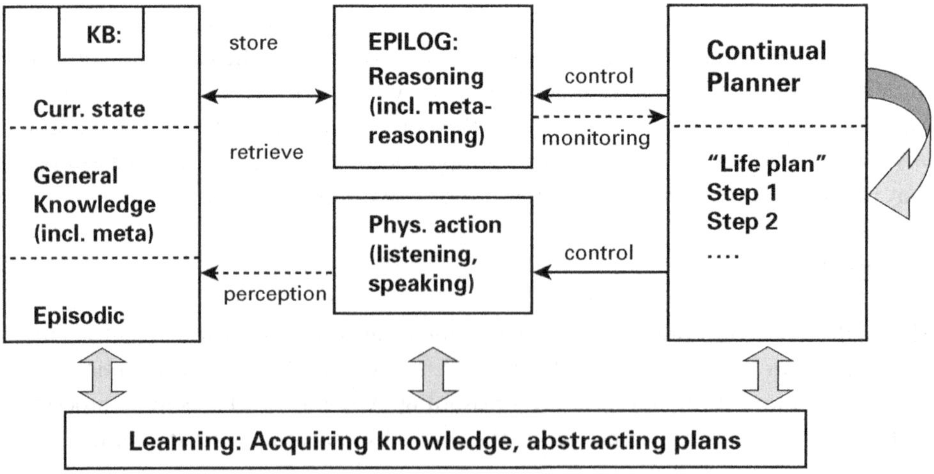

Figure 17.1
Reasoning (including reasoning based on metaknowledge) in a continually planning, self-motivated agent. (No uniform metacontrol.)

reasoning will draw on procedural knowledge, world knowledge, and metaknowledge as needed.

In short, the role played in the standard model of figure 1.2 by metalevel reasoning is played in our conceptual architecture by a continual reward-seeking planner, as in figure 17.1. Though hierarchical planning involves multiple levels of plan structure, the distinction between these levels is orthogonal to that between ground-level, object-level, and metalevel knowledge and activity. Of course, in any behavioral system (as in a human organization), the buck has to stop somewhere; at some root level, there have to be fixed mechanisms that actually make the system run. For us, that mechanism will be a carefully designed continual-planning plus execution algorithm, but exactly what it does will depend on the special-purpose procedures, world knowledge, and metaknowledge that it accesses. Note that this does not mean that all decision making takes place at a single level. The planner may well schedule subplans and procedures that already incorporate decision-making steps. However, the general planner will integrate expected utilities globally, in order to make globally rewarding decisions.

How does this outlook on metareasoning and agent architecture relate to some of the other perspectives found in this book? First, Cox and Raja's manifesto (this vol., chap. 1), along with contributions like those of Costantini, Dell'Acqua, and Pereira (2008), and several others, adhere at least roughly to the schema in figure 1.2, the emphasis being on metalevel control and self-improvement through self-monitoring. As may be inferred from our remarks above on planner-based agency, we suppose that self-improvement is primarily a matter of learning to plan better. These improvements would be a by-product of the processes employed by the fixed planning-and-execution system, including ones for synthesizing, abstracting, and storing subplans, for using available knowledge to predict consequences of contemplated actions and their net future utility, and for using the episodic record of the agent's experiences to debug, improve, and augment the available knowledge about the world, about the agent itself, about the consequences of actions, and about their utilities to the agent.

These activities aimed at self-improvement certainly will involve metalevel reasoning as well as object-level reasoning; but we have not yet explored them in detail, because they seem to us highly dependent on the fundamental knowledge representations and reasoning abilities of the agent, indicating that the latter need to be more fully developed first. For example, planning involves reasoning about the conditions before, during, and after an action is performed, and hence failure analysis is heavily dependent on the expressiveness of the action and state representations used, and on the available reasoning methods. Similarly, the problem of detecting inconsistencies or gaps in an agent's declarative knowledge depends very much on the kinds of representations and reasoning methods employed. This motivates our current focus on the issues of developing representations and reasoning methods that allow for human-like commonsense knowledge and reasoning, including reasoning about the self and about syntactic objects internal or external to the system.

Unlike Hart and Scassellati (this vol., chap. 18), we are not directly concerned with gaining insight into phenomena associated with self-awareness in humans (or higher mammals), such as self-recognition in a mirror. Our quest is for explicit self-awareness in machines that are knowledgeable and capable of reasoning, though certainly we would like to make use of findings about human self-awareness where possible. The work of Gordon, Hobbs, and Cox (this vol., chap. 19) is closest in spirit to our own, in the emphasis it places on developing a rich, human-like self-model in machines, and on formulating representations adequate for this task, rather than focusing primarily on process. However (and this may just be a terminological difference), they regard metareasoning as concerned chiefly with monitoring and control, whereas we regard the process of drawing conclusions about one's own mental contents and attributes, even in the service of settling such issues as whether pigs have wings, as bona fide instances of metareasoning.

Summary and Future Work

The examples given show the ability of the current system to handle basic forms of metareasoning, in support of commonsense question-answering about the world and about itself. This ability is based on a systematic implementation of an ASK mechanism for self-query, and of a general syntax and mechanism for handling quasi-quotation and substitutional quantification. These enhancements are layered on top of a capacity for inference in a very rich natural logic (EL) that can deal with events characterized by complex sentences, predicate modification, and various forms or reification and modality.

As we showed, the new mechanisms enable well-founded question-answering for such questions as "How old are you?" (using the birth date, and assuring an answer expressed in a syntactically appropriate way), and "What do pigs look like?" (based on syntactic inference about which internal formulas express appearance knowledge about pigs). In addition, the new mechanisms enable deliberate reasoning about special-purpose procedures available to the system and about their goal-directed invocation. We also showed previously how autocognitive reasoning can enable effective negative inferences (e.g., that pigs don't have wings, or that the phone didn't ring in the last fifteen minutes) and inferences about the system's autobiography and recent discourse events (Schubert, 2005; Morbini & Schubert, 2007). Though we have not addressed self-improvement based on metareasoning (the classical goal of metareasoning), we regard the kinds of introspective abilities we have implemented as crucial to such self-improvement. In principle, they enable reasoning about the system's own knowledge and procedures, including their shortcomings.

However, much remains to be done, and the following are some of the more pressing items:

1. So far we have implemented only an exhaustive retrieval mechanism to allow testing of the reasoning system. We will need a much more selective retrieval scheme in order to be able to scale up to a large knowledge base, as needed for commonsense applications. The original version of EPILOG had an efficient content-based indexing scheme, but it was not designed to handle the metasyntactic devices we have added, suffered from certain retrieval gaps (in proving existential goals), and depended on hand-coded type hierarchies rather than forming these automatically. We are working to overcome these limitations, and plan to test the scalability of the resulting system using some large knowledge base (e.g., the FOL version of OpenCyc; see Ramachandran, Reagan, & Goolsbey, 2005).
2. The previous version of EPILOG employed reasoning "specialists" to efficiently perform taxonomic, temporal, partonomic, and other important kinds of specialized reasoning. The specialists were invoked "unconsciously" for predicates and functions they were designed to reason about, but in the new version, we would like to make the inference engine aware of its specialists and their capabilities, using explicit attachment axioms involving the *Apply* function.
3. Another front that needs work is the refinement of the ASK mechanism for knowledge introspection. Currently the mechanism is made time-bounded by a hard limit on depth of reasoning. (However, the limit can be computed, so that several desirable properties of knowing are maintained; e.g., given that EPILOG knows *A* it also knows (*A or B*)).

Acknowledgments

This work was supported by NSF grants IIS-0328849 and IIS-0535105 and by a gift from Robert Bosch Corporation. We also thank the anonymous referees for their helpful comments.

References

Costantini, S., Dell'Acqua, P., & Pereira, L. M. (2008). A multi-layer framework for evolving and learning agents. In M. T. Cox & A. Raja (Eds.), *Metareasoning: Thinking About Thinking, Papers from the AAAI Workshop* (pp. 121–128). Tech. Rep. No. WS-08-07. Menlo Park, CA: AAAI Press.

Cox, M. (2005). Metacognition in computation: A selected research review. *Artificial Intelligence, 169*(2), 104–141.

Kaplan, A. (2000). *A computational model of belief.* Ph.D. dissertation, University of Rochester. Department of Computer Science.

Kaplan, A. N., & Schubert, L. K. (2000). A computational model of belief. *Artificial Intelligence, 120*(1), 119–160.

Morbini, F., & Schubert, L. K. (2007). Towards realistic autocognitive inference. In E. Amir, V. Lifschitz, and R. Miller (Eds.), *Papers from the 2007 AAAI Spring Symposium on Logical Formalizations of Commonsense Reasoning* (pp. 114–118). Menlo Park, CA: AAAI Press.

Ramachandran, D., Reagan, P., & Goolsbey, K. (2005). First-orderized ResearchCyc: Expressivity and efficiency in a common-sense ontology. In P. Shvaiko, J. Euzenat, A. Leger, D. L. McGuinness, and H. Wache (Eds.), *Papers from the 2005 AAAI Workshop on Contexts and Ontologies: Theory, Practice, and Applications* (pp. 33–40). Menlo Park, CA: AAAI Press.

Schubert, L. K. (2005). Some knowledge representation and reasoning requirements for self-awareness. In M. Anderson & T. Oates (Eds.), *Proceedings of the AAAI Spring Symposium on Metacognition in Computation* (pp. 106–113). Tech. Rep. No. SS-05-04. Menlo Park, CA: AAAI Press.

Schubert, L., & Hwang, C. (2000). Episodic logic meets Little Red Riding Hood: A comprehensive, natural representation for language understanding. In L. Iwanska & S. Shapiro (Eds.), *Natural language processing and knowledge representation: Language for knowledge and knowledge for language* (pp. 111–174). Menlo Park, CA: AAAI Press.

18 Robotic Models of Self

Justin Hart and Brian Scassellati

Why do puppies chase their tails? Folk wisdom would tell us that a puppy is being playful or is seeking attention. Veterinarians would say that the puppy chases, and sometimes even bites, its own tail because it does not realize that this fascinatingly evasive object is actually part of its own body. While this behavior in a puppy is nothing to be concerned with, tail chasing in an older dog is often a sign of dementia, skin irritation, or anxiety. Whereas an older dog is expected to understand that its own tail is not an object that should be chased or bitten, a young puppy is still coming to understand the boundaries of its own body. We assume that through its experiences, a puppy is able to learn that its tail does belong to itself, perhaps by observing that its tail is a constant companion or that catching and biting its tail results in pain.

Like puppies, human infants are not born with a complete sense of themselves. During the first few months of life, infants must learn to discriminate between their own bodies, the movements of parents and others who are responsive to the child, and the movement of objects on television or of wind-blown leaves, that is, items that are unresponsive to the child's actions (Rochat, 2003). They must come to understand that the flailing fingers and arms that they often see in their cribs are part of themselves, that they will be able to control the movements of these strange-looking appendages, and eventually be able to effect desired changes in the world using them.

Traditionally, robots have had no sense of self, nor did they need it. In factory automation, or even in traditional task-based robotic systems, the robot carried out a specific goal by selecting between appropriate behaviors or by tuning the parameters of a fixed behavioral repertoire. These robots could not perceive their own mechanical bodies and did not need to discriminate between different types of activity within their environment. As robots become more complex (involving richer sensing and more degrees of freedom) and as they move out of the factory and into environments like our homes, schools, and hospitals, the need for these machines to be more aware of their own limits, their own capabilities, and the results of their own actions becomes critical. Robots should not chase their own mechanical tails.

To highlight this point, consider two robotic applications. First, consider a robot operating in a factory that constructs automobiles. This robot consists of a camera system that looks down onto a conveyor belt, a mechanical arm that can maneuver parts from one position on the belt to another, and the computational resources to recognize defects in these parts. As parts slide into view on the belt, the robot must decide if the part is defective. The robot must orient itself to defective parts, grasp them, and remove them from the line. In this case, distinguishing the robot's arm from other objects in the field of view can be accomplished simply in multiple ways. One solution would be to paint the arm and gripper a distinctive color that is not used elsewhere in the vicinity of the robot, allowing the robot to spot the gripper and the part by identifying the unique color. Another would be to preprogram the kinematics (the body structure and motion capabilities) of the robot. The kinematic equations could then be solved algebraically to identify how to move the arm to grasp particular parts. When wear and tear on the robot's parts slowly degrade the accuracy of these precoded equations, trained technicians can be on hand to recalibrate or reprogram the equations as needed. Faults can be detected simply by establishing boundaries on the robot's behavior. If the gripper moves too far away from the assembly line, or parts are not picked up as frequently as expected, a fault can be signaled. The system could then be stopped until a technician repairs the equipment.

Now compare this factory automation system to a robot designed to aid elderly homeowners carrying groceries or other supplies from their car to their kitchens. Perhaps with two arms and a wheeled base, this robot would need to perform grasping, lifting, and carrying of arbitrary packages under the direction of its owner. This home assistant robot requires many of the same behavioral capabilities as the factory robot; it too must recognize important components in the environment, grasp them, and maneuver them into appropriate positions. However, none of the easy-to-construct systems that were used in the factory robot are likely to be successful in the home assistance robot. We cannot count on selecting a unique color for the robot that completely distinguishes it from all homes and from all shopping packages. We also cannot rely on maintaining a perfect kinematic model to predict the locations of the robot's limbs—without the constant supervision of trained technicians, these equations are likely to be useful for only a short time. Instead, our robot requires some more flexible way of identifying itself, identifying when faults occur, and adapting to new configurations (such as when it is carrying a large shopping bag).

The real-world requirements of robotics add a dimension to the self-model not directly considered in other chapters of this book. To our formalism, this chapter will add the capability to reason about the robot's physical presence in the world, its construction, its sensory capabilities, and its interactions with its environment. As adaptive and self-trained kinematic and sensory self-models are introduced, we will also observe that lower-level processes, traditionally hard-coded into the system and buried beneath convenient abstractions, will become first-class cognitive models accessible directly to the system (as discussed in this vol., chap. 1).

Self-Identification

In ethology, the traditional test of self-awareness in animals is the mirror rouge test (Gallup, 1970). Figure 18.1 shows a chimpanzee participating in this test. First, a mirror is placed into the habitat of an animal and the animal is given time to acclimate to its presence. During this phase, many animals will engage their own reflection with either social or aggressive behaviors, as they do not recognize the reflection as themselves. After acclimating to the mirror, some animals, such as chimpanzees, will begin to use the mirror to groom themselves, in a recognizable self-directed behavior. The animal is then anesthetized, and a section of the body that can only be seen in the mirror (such as the forehead) is dyed. If the animal inspects the mark through use of the mirror, it is considered to have recognized its own appearance in the mirror.

Gallup's (1982) model supposes that the animal must have a self-concept, typically in the form of an image that resembles the animal. This supposition leads to a model of how to perform self-recognition based on similarity of appearance. An appearance-based model stores an explicit representation of appearance that is then matched against a current sensory state to determine if the animal (or robot) currently perceives itself. Though this technique has a simplicity that is appealing, there are many difficulties in implementing this solution. First, the perspective of the image is often seen as third person (as one would appear in a photograph), though this is clearly not easily

Figure 18.1
A chimpanzee subject of the mark test. (Photo used by permission of Daniel Povinelli.)

matched to a first-person perspective (as the animal might observe itself). Second, the complexity of the matching process makes a complete implementation of this strategy infeasible. To identify the difficulty inherent in this process, imagine looking down at your hand and attempting to catalog all of the possible shapes that your hand might form. The range of possible appearances from a fist to an open palm to a peace sign provides an endless variety of physical appearances.

A second methodology focuses not on visual appearance matching but rather on some matching process between the movement of the body and the visual scene. Mitchell (1997) supports the idea of kinesthetic-visual matching in which the only knowledge required to recognize oneself in the mirror is the relationship between the visual scene and proprioception. In our own research, we have demonstrated the effectiveness of this alternative explanation by constructing a robot that can distinguish between self and other. An early version of this system (Michel, Gold, & Scassellati, 2004) used temporal contingency to learn timing parameters that distinguished the movement of the robot's own arm (seen in the camera's field of view) from the movement of people in the environment. The robot estimated the delay between sending a motor command and observing a visual change. Though this approach had some advantages, it was limited in its extensibility and by sensor noise.

A more recent version of this system (Gold & Scassellati, 2007) uses a Bayesian kinesthetic-visual matching model to allow a humanoid robot to perform self–other discrimination and mirror self-recognition without social understanding and without an explicit kinematic model. A humanoid robot named Nico learned the relationship between its own motor activity and perceived motion by observing the movements of its arm for four minutes. Each new observation was used to update three models for each object in its visual field. The first model is that of random noise, generated with no structure over time. The second model consists of an observed internal state of motor activity that generates the external feedback of motion; thus, the consistency of the match between motor activity and motion dictates the likelihood of this model. The third model is that of motion generated by somebody else; it is identical to its own self-motion model, only the motor state is hidden and must be reasoned about probabilistically. Presented with a mirror, the robot then judged its mirror image to match its "self" model, while people were judged to be "animate others." Figure 18.2 shows the scene through Nico's cameras during this test. In this picture, we can see Kevin Gold in front of Nico, a mirror that Nico can see himself in, and to the right we see Nico's finger. In figure 18.3, we see that Nico has segmented out Kevin as an animate other, marking him in purple. Nico has marked himself both in the mirror and directly in his visual field in green. Other moving objects determined to be noise are marked in red.

Why pursue such research for a robotic system? What advantage does the ability to recognize oneself provide to a robot? One answer is that the modeling effort itself

Figure 18.2
Nico looking at himself in the mirror, with experimenter Kevin Gold behind it (Gold & Scassellati, 2007).

Figure 18.3
Nico's software segmenting himself and an animate other, Kevin Gold, from the scene (Gold & Scassellati, 2007).

has value, as it provides insight into potential methodologies and algorithms that may be occurring in biological systems. Though the fact that a robot performs a task in a certain way is never proof that a biological system also necessarily utilizes the same solution, the computational model can both provide a proof-of-concept for a particular solution and potentially provide insights into the nature of the problem itself (Webb, 2001). In this case, the fact that a kinesthetic-visual matching algorithm can successfully solve the self-identification problem leads us to question the necessity of purely visual appearance-based methods.

A second answer is that these self-identification algorithms are the first step toward a more comprehensive robotic model of self. Current research in our lab focuses on developing robotic self-models that integrate the kinematic and sensory systems of the robot (Hart, Scassellati, & Zucker, 2008). Kinematic self-models such as ours and others (Hersch, Sauser, & Billard, 2008) enable robots to learn through experience the structure of their bodies and how they move through space. We will argue that a robot that had a more comprehensive model of its body schema and of its own capabilities would provide connections to other areas that have been traditionally disparate areas of research in robotics: fault recognition and recovery, causal learning, and tool use.

Fault Detection and Recovery

Though the majority of robotic systems operate with no fault-detection mechanism, the detection, identification, and diagnosis of faults in machinery is an active area of interest in both research and industry. Systems used to perform this in an automatic fashion offer both the capability to assist human technicians in diagnostic tasks as well as to allow machinery to automatically diagnose and recover from faults.

In industry, the dominant method to accomplish this task is rule-based diagnosis (Darwiche, 2000). These systems use hand-crafted sets of rules written by domain experts that are checked against the system's status. More popular in research is model-based diagnosis, in which a model of the system is developed using symbolic logic (de Kleer & Williams, 1987, 1989; Darwiche, 2000; Hofbaur & Williams, 2002). An automated theorem prover then uses this model along with status reports from devices in the system in order to perform diagnosis.

Rule-based diagnosis systems are favored in industry because they have a lower computational overhead and do not require a background in symbolic logic and artificial intelligence to understand (Darwiche, 2000). Model-based diagnosis systems offer a number of advantages including being easier to update and modify and allowing developers to mathematically prove properties of the model.

Perhaps the most intriguing use of model-based diagnosis to date has been the Livingstone system, which was employed in the Remote Agent software aboard NASA's *Deep Space One* probe (Muscettola, Nayak, Pell, & Williams, 1998). *Deep Space One* was the first spacecraft to be controlled by artificial intelligence without human supervision. Though *Deep Space One*'s self-model was built by scientists and engineers on the ground, it did use a logical model of itself while operating in space in order to adapt its control policy to systems reporting faults.

Fault detection as it is currently envisioned follows either rule-based or model-based techniques, both of which require a constant detection and recovery system to be preconstructed by the programmers when the system is initially deployed. These techniques cannot adapt to online changes in the system's hardware configuration, nor can they adapt to changes in the control architecture. For a robot that can construct its own model of its physical extent, its kinematic structure, and its capabilities, fault detection takes on a somewhat different role; fault detection becomes an ongoing process of comparing current short-term models of the robot's self with a more stable longer-term model of the robot's self. An adaptive model thus allows for a more flexible recognition process that is based on the perception of the robot's current capabilities that also allows for long-term modifications.

Causal Learning

Causal learning is a research area concerned with the sequences of events that link causes with effects. Often modeled by the forward algorithm (Rabiner, 1989), which asserts that prior time steps have a causal relationship to future ones, causal learning often operates over symbolic descriptions of the world (which at times makes it difficult to apply in robotic systems). These symbols are linked together in either predetermined or statistically salient sequences to create causal chains that indicate the prevalence at which a particular event (the cause) results in the production of a secondary event (the effect). Though this learning is often symbolic in nature, there have been many attempts to ground these symbols in perceptually salient cues (Yoshikawa, Hosoda, & Asada, 2004; Yoshikawa, Tsuji, Hosoda, & Asada, 2004).

Notice that this process, by which a causal learning system searches for pairings of events separated in time, is very similar to the process of kinesthetic-visual matching described above for self-identification. Rather than seeking a visual stimulus to match an earlier motor command from the robot, we instead initially match any motor command from the robot with a later-occurring event. If these two events recur under similar actions and situations, we can imagine that the robot could learn to produce particular actions (causes) to create a certain desired result (the effect). While this process by itself may provide interesting evidence and goal-directed behavior to the robot system, the most common application for this type of learning is tool use, which we discuss as a special case below. Causal learning has also been studied in the context of fault detection and diagnosis, as implemented in the OCCAM system (Pazzani, 1990a,b).

Tool Use

When a person uses a tool, that tool becomes causally tied to him or her. An interesting example of this incorporation into the self-model comes from Yamamoto, Moizumi, and Kitazawa (2005), in which it is demonstrated that when a person touches something with the tip of a tool, the sensory experience attached to that action is the sensation of feeling the tip of the tool contacting the object being touched rather than the feeling of the tool providing increased tactile resistance in the hand in response to the touch. In other words, while the person is using that tool, they perceive it as an extension of his- or herself.

Experiments to allow robots to build better models of this boundary between themselves and the rest of the world also mark the crucial difference between a robot that must be programmed to grip an object in its gripper and one that can learn to grip an object on its own. The current state-of-the-art is to preprogram robots with such capabilities. A robot with a causal model, however, can learn its own optimal gripping strategies. By modeling the relationship of objects in the environment to the self, rather than programming in grasping behaviors, future robotic systems may be able learn things such as tool use without needing to be programmed to use individual tools.

Conclusion

We often think of metareasoning as a high-level component that can be added to existing agent architectures to oversee or monitor typical activity. This internal critic offers suggestions, monitors progress, or infers higher-level information from the mundane activities of the agent. Perhaps the most salient lesson from our work on self-modeling in robotic systems is that metareasoning can be built into some of the most basic components of these systems in order to solve real-world problems. This may include basic components that are often considered to be complete and beyond need for revision (such as low-level control algorithms and kinematic models). As part of the basic construction of an agent, metareasoning and self-modeling systems can serve to unify a range of problem domains under a single system-wide design. This integration also allows for problems (like self-recognition) that on the surface appear to be high-level cognitive tasks to become part of the moment-to-moment operation that is critical to agent behavior. Perhaps we should not consider metareasoning systems as an additional module that can be added late in the design process but rather as central guiding principles to self-governed behavior.

In this chapter, we have promoted a viewpoint that unifies a few subfields of robotics that until now were studied in isolation. By recasting the primary questions of these fields as part of the continual process for constructing an accurate model of self,

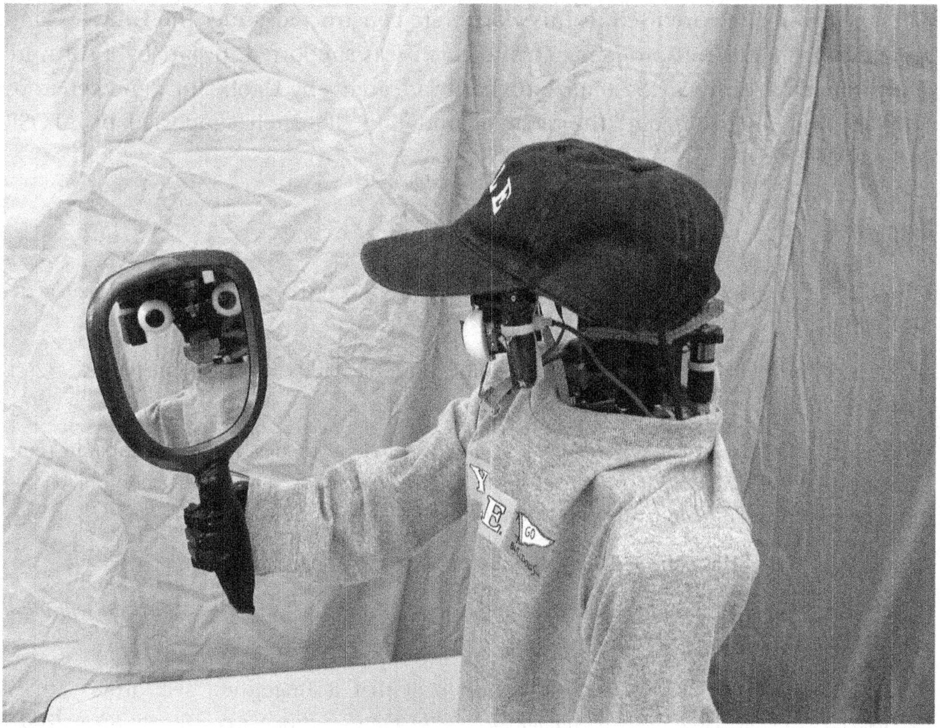

Figure 18.4
Nico, the humanoid robot, used by the authors in robotic self-modeling experiments.

we demonstrate that each of these questions can be characterized as part of a larger domain. Adaptive, self-taught models of self provide a framework for studying causal learning, tool use, kinematic analysis, and fault detection and recovery. While the study of these fields independently will continue to advance the state of the art, it is our belief that the study of these as part of an integrated self-model will allow for even more fundamental insights into how to build useful, adaptive, and practical robotic systems and may cast light onto the underlying processes of self-identification that biological systems must also solve.

Acknowledgments

Support for this work was provided by National Science Foundation awards 0534610 (Quantitative Measures of Social Response in Autism), 0835767 (Understanding Regulation of Visual Attention in Autism through Computational and Robotic Modeling), and CAREER award 0238334 (Social Robots and Human Social Development). Some parts of the architecture used in this work were constructed under the DARPA Computer Science Futures II program. This research was supported in part by a software grant from QNX Software Systems Ltd., hardware grants by Ugobe Inc., and generous support from Microsoft and the Sloan Foundation. Research supported by AFOSR and NGA.

References

Darwiche, A. (2000). Model-based diagnosis under real-world constraints. *AI Magazine, 21,* 57–73.

de Kleer, J., & Williams, B. (1987). Diagnosing multiple faults. *Artificial Intelligence, 32*(1), 97–130.

de Kleer, J., & Williams, B. (1989). Diagnosis with behavioral modes. In N. S. Sridharan (Ed.), *Proceedings of the Eleventh International Joint Conference on Artificial Intelligence (IJCAI '89)* (pp. 124–130). San Francisco: Morgan Kaufmann.

Gallup, G. (1970). Chimpanzees: Self-recognition. *Science, 67*(3914), 86–87.

Gallup, G. (1982). Self-awareness and the emergence of mind in primates. *American Journal of Primatology, 2,* 237–248.

Gold, K., & Scassellati, B. (2007). A Bayesian robot that distinguishes "self" from "other." In *Proceedings of the Twenty-Ninth Annual Meeting of the Cognitive Science Society (CogSci2007)* (pp. 384–392). Mahwah, NJ: Lawrence Erlbaum.

Hart, J., Scassellati, B., & Zucker, S. W. (2008, May). Epipolar geometry for humanoid robotic heads. In B. Caputo & M. Vincze (Eds.), *Proceedings of the 4th International Cognitive Vision Workshop (ICVW 2008)* (pp. 24–36). Berlin: Springer.

Hersch, M., Sauser, E., & Billard, A. (2008). Online learning of the body schema. *International Journal of Humanoid Robotics, 5,* 161–181.

Hofbaur, M., & Williams, B. C. (2002). Mode estimation of probabilistic hybrid systems. In C.J. Tomlin & M.R. Greenstreet (Eds.), *Proceedings of the International Conference on Hybrid Systems, Computation, and Control.* Lecture Notes in Computer Science 2289 (pp. 253–266). Berlin: Springer.

Michel, P., Gold, K., & Scassellati, B. (2004, September). Motion-based Robotic self-recognition. In *Proceedings of the IEEE/RSJ International Conference on Intelligent Robots and Systems (IROS).* Piscataway, NJ: IEEE Press.

Mitchell, R. (1997). Kinesthetic-visual matching and the self-concept as explanations of mirror self-recognition. *Journal for the Theory of Social Behaviour, 27*(1), 17–39.

Muscettola, N., Nayak, P., Pell, B., & Williams, B. (1998). Remote agent: To boldly go where no AI system has gone before. *Artificial Intelligence, 103*(1–2), 5–47.

Pazzani, M. (1990a). *Creating a memory of causal relationships: An integration of empirical and explanation-based learning methods*. Hillsdale, NJ: Lawrence Erlbaum.

Pazzani, M. (1990b). Learning fault diagnosis heuristics from device descriptions. In Y. Kodratoff & R. S. Michalski (Eds.), *Machine learning III: An artificial intelligence approach* (pp. 214–234). San Mateo, CA: Morgan Kaufmann.

Rabiner, L. R. (1989). A tutorial on hidden Markov models and selected applications in speech recognition. *Proceedings of the IEEE, 77*(2), 257–296.

Rochat, P. (2003). Five levels of self-awareness as they unfold early in life. *Consciousness and Cognition, 12*, 717–731.

Webb, B. (2001). Can robots make good models of biological behaviour? *Behavioral and Brain Sciences, 24*(6), 1033–1050.

Yamamoto, S., Moizumi, S., & Kitazawa, S. (2005). Referral of tactile sensation to the tips of L-shaped sticks. *Journal of Neurophysiology, 93*(5), 2856–2863.

Yoshikawa, Y., Hosoda, K., & Asada, M. (2004). Cross-anchoring for binding tactile and visual sensations via unique association through self-perception. In *Proceedings of the Fourth International Conference on Learning and Development*. Piscataway, NJ: IEEE Press.

Yoshikawa, Y., Tsuji, K., Hosoda, K., & Asada, M. (2004, October). Is it my body? Body extraction from uninterpreted sensory data based on the invariance of multiple sensory attributes. In *Proceedings of the IEEE/RSJ International Conference on Intelligent Robotics and Systems*. Piscataway, NJ: IEEE Press.

19 Anthropomorphic Self-Models for Metareasoning Agents

Andrew S. Gordon, Jerry R. Hobbs, and Michael T. Cox

One of the hallmarks of human intelligence is the ability to predict and explain states and events in the external environment in service of the selection of plans and policies in goal-directed behavior. This ability requires some capacity for mental representation of environmental states and events in a manner that facilitates reasoning. The manifesto introduced by Cox and Raja (this vol., chap. 1) defines reasoning as a decision cycle within an action-perception loop between the ground level (doing) and the object level (reasoning). With respect to this model, the task of the object level is to produce a mental model of the environment and use these representations in the selection of appropriate actions at the ground level. As social creatures, the mental models that humans manipulate include representations of other people—their thoughts, plans, goals, and emotions—that are used to predict and explain their behavior. As people are part of their environments, the mental models that people manipulate must also include some representation of the self, which may be the subject of object-level inference as well. However, the model of metareasoning presented by Cox and Raja suggests a more functional model of the self that includes representations of one's own object-level reasoning behavior, monitored by a metareasoning component that can directly intervene to control these reasoning processes.

One of the central concerns in the model of metareasoning as defined in chapter 1 is the character of the information that is passed between the object-level and the metalevel reasoning modules to enable monitoring and control. Cast as a representation problem, the question becomes: How should an agent's own reasoning be represented to itself as it monitors and controls this reasoning? The manifesto describes these representations as *models of self,* which serve to control an agent's reasoning choices, represent the product of monitoring, and coordinate the self in social contexts.

Self-models have been periodically explored in previous artificial intelligence (AI) research since Minsky (1968), and explicit self-models have been articulated for a diverse set of reasoning processes that include threat detection (Birnbaum, Collins,

Freed, & Krulwich, 1990), case retrieval (Fox & Leake, 1995), and expectation management (Cox, 1997). Typically built to demonstrate a limited metareasoning capacity, these self-models have lacked several qualities that should be sought in future research in this area, including:

1. *Broad coverage* Self-models should allow an agent to reason about and control the full breadth of its object-level reasoning processes.
2. *Integrated* Self-models of different reasoning processes should be compatible with one another, allowing an agent to reason about and control the interaction between different reasoning subsystems.
3. *Reusable* The formulation of self-models across different agents and agent architectures should have some commonalities that allow developers to apply previous research findings when building new systems.

Despite continuing interest in metareasoning over the last two decades (see Anderson & Oates, 2007; Cox, 2005), there has been only modest progress toward the development of self-models that achieve these desirable qualities. We speculate that this is due, in part, to an emphasis on process rather than representation in the development of metareasoning systems. That is, researchers have tended to make only the representational commitments necessary to demonstrate the algorithmic approach that they advocate. As a predictable result, the collective set of representations across this field of research is modular, narrowly scoped, and specifically tied to particular agent architectures.

As in other areas of AI, a more balanced view of the relative contributions of process and representation may lead to new opportunities in this field that are currently obscured. Instead of avoiding representational commitments, we should encourage the development of systems that make these commitments in a principled manner. This chapter describes an approach to representation in metareasoning, advocating principles to guide progress toward integrated, broad-coverage, reusable self-models.

Anthropomorphic Self-Models

One approach for achieving integrated, broad-coverage, reusable self-models for metareasoning is to try to mirror the sorts of representations that are used by people. To understand this approach, it is first necessary to recognize that people, too, employ representational models of mental states and processes as part of everyday commonsense reasoning. In the field of psychology, the model that people have of their own reasoning states and processes (as well as those of others) is commonly referred to as a *theory of mind*. The study of this model began in earnest with Heider (1958) and has received an enormous amount of theoretical attention over the last half century (cf. Smedslund 1997), particularly in the areas of developmental psychology (Wellman,

Cross, & Watson, 2001), cognitive anthropology (Lillard, 1998), and primate studies (Call & Tomasello, 1999). Although some philosophers have argued that a representational theory of mind is neither necessary (Goldman, 2006) nor beneficial (Churchland, 1986), process-oriented cognitive models of human first-person mind-reading (introspection) and third-person mind-reading (perspective-taking) have generally included a prominent role for explicit representations of mental state (e.g., Nichols & Stich, 2003).

The *anthropomorphism* approach to metareasoning representations is to formalize the self-model that people have of themselves and others and to utilize these representations to support monitoring and control in AI agents. In other words, rather than devising a new representational framework based on the functionality of the AI agents, we should identify and utilize a representational framework that is already successfully employed by billions of existing intelligent people.

Why Anthropomorphism?

The argument for pursuing an anthropomorphic approach to the representation of AI self-models is that people will be controlling, collaborating with, and designing these systems, and each of these activities will be facilitated if there are parallels that can be drawn between these AI self-models and the models that people use to think about themselves and others.

Parallelism between AI and human self-models is critical to enabling people to control these systems. As a strategy for managing the complexity of AI agents, the natural tendency of people will be to anthropomorphize these systems—seeing them as if they were people whose behavior is governed by a logic that parallels their own. Although unavoidable, adopting this intentional stance (Dennett, 1987) toward AI agents will only be fruitful if the constituents of this logic are grounded in the operation of the agent in some meaningful way. For example, consider the specific problem of interpreting natural language imperatives that a person might deliver to influence the metareasoning behavior of an AI agent: "Focus on what you are doing, Mr. Robot, and quit worrying about tomorrow's work!" People have specific expectations about how this directive should be executed by the AI agent, expectations that can only be met if there is something that parallels the concept of a *focus of attention*, among others, in the self-model of the AI agent.

The necessity of anthropomorphism in AI self-models is even more apparent when multiagent systems consist of a heterogeneous mix of AI agents and people. The manifesto defines *distributed metareasoning* as the coordination of problem-solving contexts among agents in a multiagent system, where the metacontrol component of each agent should operate according to a multiagent policy. Strategies for coordinating these problem-solving contexts are likely to be complex even if the agents (and their self-models) were homogeneous. If these systems are a heterogeneous mix of people and AI agents, then each participant will need to be able to reason about the problem-solving contexts of the others. Without a shared self-model, or at least one that is compatible at a high level, the AI agents are faced with a much more difficult reasoning problem, and the humans are faced with an impossible one. If people in multiagent collaborations are required to reason about the self-models of AI agents that are *different* from their own, then only the developers themselves will be able to participate.

For practical purposes, anthropomorphism also makes good engineering sense. Progress in the development of AI agents will continue to require the cooperative effort of large teams of researchers and developers. If these agents employ representational models of themselves that resemble those of their developers, then time and costs needed to understand and constructively contribute to these systems can be substantially reduced.

Formalizing Commonsense Psychology

Watt (1998) explored the relationship between anthropomorphism and theory of mind reasoning as it pertains to AI systems and argued for the central importance of commonsense psychology to understanding this type of reasoning. In AI, commonsense psychology has generally been approached in the same terms as commonsense (naive) physics (Hayes, 1978), that is, as a representational model (a set of logical axioms) that enables commonsense inference. However, instead of supporting commonsense inference about liquids, flow, and physical force, this representational model attempts to reproduce the predictions and explanations that people make regarding the behavior of people based on their beliefs, goals, and plans. In this view, human anthropomorphic reasoning can be understood as the adoption of this representational model for predicting and explaining the behavior of nonhuman beings.

Commonsense reasoning about human psychology is *not* the same thing as metareasoning. Whereas commonsense reasoning about psychology serves the express purposes of prediction and explanation, metareasoning is specifically concerned with monitoring and control. The most successful optimization policies employed by an agent's metareasoning capabilities may be the product of calculations that are extremely different from those employed for logical inference. However, the anthropomorphism approach to metareasoning representations argues that the formalisms used for these two disparate functions should be roughly identical. That is, the *model of self* that is passed between reasoning and metareasoning modules in an agent should be expressed in the same vocabulary that drives commonsense psychological inference.

Hobbs and Gordon (2005) describe a large-scale effort to describe a model of commonsense psychology as a set of thirty content theories expressed in first-order logic. Aiming to achieve greater coverage over commonsense psychological concepts than in previous formalization projects, this work employed a novel methodology where the breadth of commonsense psychology concepts were first identified through a large-scale analysis of planning strategies, elaborated by an analysis of English words and phrases, and then formalized as axiomatic theories in which all of the identified concepts could be adequately defined.

Gordon and Hobbs (2003) present one of the thirty content theories produced using this methodology, a commonsense theory of human memory. In the commonsense view, human memory concerns memories in the minds of people, which are operated upon by memory processes of storage, retrieval, memorization, reminding, and repression, among others. The formal theory of commonsense human memory presented by Gordon and Hobbs supports inferences about these processes with encodings of roughly three dozen memory axioms in first-order logic. Key aspects of this theory can be characterized as follows:

1. *Concepts in memory* People have minds with at least two parts, one where concepts are stored in memory and a second where concepts can be in the focus of one's attention. Storage and retrieval involve moving concepts from one part to the other.
2. *Accessibility* Concepts that are in memory have varying degrees of accessibility, and there is some threshold of accessibility for concepts beyond which they cannot be retrieved into the focus of attention.
3. *Associations* Concepts that are in memory may be associated with one another, and having a concept in the focus of attention increases the accessibility of the concepts with which it is associated.
4. *Trying and succeeding* People can attempt mental actions (e.g., retrieving), but these actions may fail or be successful.
5. *Remembering and forgetting* Remembering can be defined as succeeding in retrieving a concept from memory, while forgetting is when a concept becomes inaccessible.
6. *Remembering to do* A precondition for executing actions in a plan at a particular time is that a person remembers to do it, retrieving the action from memory before its execution.
7. *Repressing* People repress concepts that they find unpleasant, causing these concepts to become inaccessible.

Applied to the problem of representation in metareasoning, the formal commonsense theory of human memory provided by Gordon and Hobbs (2003) argues for representations of memory storage, retrieval, reminding, and repression, among other concepts. Although feasible, few argue that an agent's metareasoning functionality should be implemented as a logical theorem prover. Neither does the anthropomorphism approach to metareasoning representation take this route. Instead, the aim is to ensure that the representations used for monitoring and control of reasoning processes have some direct correspondence to the sorts of relations that appear in commonsense psychological theories. Specifically, the predicate relations that define mental states and processes in the theories should correspond to functionality that enable monitoring and control of reasoning processes.

Metareasoning about Memory in Agents

One of the characteristics of human memory is that it is fallible; few among us can consistently remember everyone's birthday, where we parked the car, or how many meters there are in a mile. This fallibility is the reason that it is useful for people to engage in metareasoning about memory, which leads us to tie strings around our fingers, leave notes for ourselves, and schedule appointments using datebooks, among other memory-supporting strategies. It would be unfortunate if the hardware memory chips inside our computers were as problematic. However, when considering the utility of metareasoning about memory in software agents, these memory chips are not the central concern. Instead, it is useful to consider the broad set of agent functionality that can be viewed as analogous to human memory; anthropomorphically, if an agent had a set of memory functions, what would they be?

Standard database actions are perhaps the most straightforward analogues to human memory functions, in the commonsense view. Memory storage and retrieval can easily be viewed as the insertion and querying of records in database tables. Other commonsense memory concepts are analogous to the functionality of full-text search engines, where memory storage is accomplished through text indexing and remindings are analogous to ranking of documents based on their similarity to a text query. Conceivably, monitoring and control of these functions through metareasoning may optimize the performance of these software systems. However, the utility of anthropomorphic self-models in agent systems is most evident when these software systems employ the sorts of artificial intelligence reasoning techniques that are inspired by human cognitive function, for example, planning, scheduling, prediction, explanation, monitoring, and execution.

From this perspective, the AI techniques that most directly align with commonsense models of human memory are those used to support case-based reasoning (Aamodt & Plaza, 1994; Kolodner, 1993; Lopez de Mántaras et al., 2006). In this view, the case base is itself the agent's memory, the cases are its memories, case indexing is memory storage, and case retrieval is reminding (see also this vol., chaps. 9 and 11). The use of commonsense concepts about human memory is one of the notable characteristics of the Meta-AQUA system (Cox & Ram, 1999), an implementation of a metareasoning agent that performs case-based explanation in a story-understanding task. Within the context of this research effort, explicit representations have been formulated for the majority of commonsense memory concepts that appear in Gordon and Hobbs's (2003) theory. In the following section, we describe how these representations are implemented in support of metareasoning within this type of case-based reasoning architecture.

Expectation-based Metareasoning

The Meta-AQUA system (Cox & Ram, 1999) demonstrated the utility of anthropomorphic self-models in an AI system that includes a metareasoning functionality. This system operated in the domain of automated story understanding, developed to explore issues of introspective multistrategy learning around a previous story-understanding system, AQUA (Ram, 1994). The original AQUA system viewed story understanding as question-driven process, involving the identification of both the questions raised by a story and the questions that it answers, supported by applying case-based reasoning techniques over a case library of explanation patterns. If we view the AQUA system as the object-level reasoning task, then Meta-AQUA can be viewed as a metacognitive layer that monitors and controls this case-based reasoning process in order to improve its performance. By employing an explicit representational model of the object-level story-understanding reasoning process to identify learning goals, Cox and Ram (1999) were able to demonstrate object-level performance improvements over experimental conditions involving the random selection of learning goals or without learning.

The specific problem that is addressed in Meta-AQUA system is to determine, given a failure of some performance of the system, a strategy to repair the problem that underlies such failures. The approach is to first explain why the failure occurred, then decide what the system needs to learn in order to avoid the failure in the future, and finally develop and execute a plan to achieve this learning goal. In the context of a question-based story-understanding system, this requires a capacity for recognizing when explanations generated through object-level reasoning were erroneous, but also the ability to reason about why a particular explanation was proposed in the first place. To perform such metalevel reasoning, the system needs a declarative representation and explicit trace of the execution of object-level reasoning. That is, a trace of *what* happened helps to explain *why* it happened.

In Meta-AQUA, explanations of reasoning failures are generated by comparing expectations with observations. Specifically, Meta-AQUA explicitly represents the expected reasoning behavior of various components of the overall system as a causal graph, and then compares these representations with the actual trace of the execution of object-level reasoning. This "mental check" aids in the diagnosis of reasoning failures; by identifying where the expected and observed diverge, the system can follow the causal links in order to assign blame.

Importantly, the causal representations of expected object-level reasoning behavior (as well as representations of observed behavior) in Meta-AQUA are described in terms of commonsense psychology. For example, Meta-AQUA employs an explicit model of *memory retrieval* and *forgetting* in order to diagnose failures of the case-retrieval functionality of system. Here the expected object-level reasoning is described as a successful memory-retrieval episode, where a retrieval goal, contextual cues, and an index cause the successful retrieval of an appropriate memory item. The causal model helps explain how this process could fail by hypothesizing a number of possible memory failures: failure due to a missing index, failure due to a missing object in memory, failure due to a missing retrieval goal, or failure due to not attending to the proper contextual cues. By comparing this causal model to the reasoning trace in the face of a reasoning failure, Meta-AQUA can select the most appropriate learning goals to pursue to improve the future performance of the system.

Discussion

Research toward the development of an effective metareasoning component for agents and agent systems has been slow, producing a modest number of prototype systems designed to demonstrate the utility of a particular metareasoning approach. Much of this work has been successful by focusing on process rather than representation, by making only the representational commitments necessary to support metareasoning within the context of a given agent architecture and task. As a consequence, the collective set of representations used in these systems has none of the characteristics that are needed to enable this technology to move forward: representations that have broad coverage, are integrated across object-level reasoning subsystems, and are reusable across different agents and agent architectures. In this chapter we have argued for making representational commitments in metareasoning systems in a principled manner, that is, through the development of anthropomorphic self-models.

The representational approach that we describe in this chapter involves two distinct research activities. First, formal theories of commonsense psychology are developed using a combination of empirical, analytical, and traditional knowledge engineering techniques. Our efforts in this task (Hobbs & Gordon, 2005) have aimed to develop theories that have both broad coverage of commonsense psychology concepts (breadth) and the competency to draw commonsense inferences in support of automated prediction and explanation (depth). Second, the commonsense concepts that appear in these theories are explicitly represented for use in metareasoning in agent systems. Our efforts in this task (Cox, 2007, 1997) have advanced a comparison-based approach, where the expected outcome of object-level reasoning behavior is compared with the actual reasoning outcomes that are observed.

In this chapter, we describe how these two research activities relate to each other in support of metareasoning about memory. The formalization of commonsense concepts of memory help us identify the breadth of concepts that will be passed between object-level and metalevel reasoning components in support of monitoring and control. The comparison-based implementation of metareasoning demonstrates that representations at this level of abstraction can be effectively grounded for use in real agent systems. Although these two research activities were pursued completely independently by the coauthors of this chapter, we see that closer coordination of these efforts in the future offer a principled approach to developing integrated, reusable, broad-coverage representations for metareasoning systems.

First, anthropomorphic self-models can achieve broad coverage by hitting the right level of representational abstraction. Commonsense psychological concepts like *reminding* and *forgetting* are general enough that they can be easily aligned with a large number of disparate object-level software functions when agents are viewed from an anthropomorphic perspective. Conversely, these concepts are specific enough to provide the metalevel reasoning component of an agent enough information and control to diagnose and correct problems as they arise.

Second, anthropomorphic self-models can achieve the goal of integrated representations by working to mirror the integrated coherence of human commonsense psychological models. Although not without its inconsistencies, commonsense psychology is remarkable in that it allows people to predict and explain behavior by drawing coherent connections between a wide variety of mental states and processes. It allows us, for example, to tell a coherent story about how forgetting something can result in an incorrect prediction about a world state during the execution of a plan, and how the failure to achieve the goal of the plan subsequently leads to emotional feelings of guilt. The ease in which people effortlessly reason *about* memory, prediction, execution, goal management, and emotion in an integrated manner should serve as inspiration for the representations used in metareasoning agents. By deriving their representational commitments from commonsense psychology, anthropomorphic self-models aim to enable this level of integration as more and more of these object-level reasoning functions are included in AI-based agent systems in the future.

Third, anthropomorphic self-models can achieve the goal of reusable representations, where the content of these representations is not inextricably tied to one particular agent implementation. Representational commitments are made not at the level of software, but rather to the conceptual framework that is used to characterize an agent's reasoning functions. By standardizing the representations used in metareasoning systems around this framework, we can begin to conceptualize metareasoning systems that are interchangeable across agent architectures and tasks. This would, in turn, enable some form of comparison and competition between different approaches, and would allow developers to apply validated research findings when building new metareasoning systems.

Acknowledgments

The project or effort described here has been sponsored, in part, by the U.S. Army Research, Development, and Engineering Command (RDECOM). The views, opinions, and findings contained in this article are those of the author and should not be interpreted as representing the official views or policies, either expressed or implied, of the Defense Advanced Research Projects Agency, of the Department of Defense, or of the United States Government. This document has been approved for public release by DARPA for unlimited distribution.

References

Aamodt, A., & Plaza, E. (1994). Case-based reasoning: Foundational issues, methodological variations, and system approaches. *AI Communications, 7,* 39–59.

Anderson, M., & Oates, T. (2007). A review of recent research in metareasoning and metalearning. *AI Magazine, 28,* 7–16.

Birnbaum, L., Collins, G., Freed, M., & Krulwich, B. (1990). Model-based diagnosis of planning failures. In *Proceedings of the Eighth National Conference on Artificial Intelligence* (pp. 318–323). Cambridge, MA: MIT Press.

Call, J., & Tomasello, M. (1999). A nonverbal false belief task: The performance of children and great apes. *Child Development, 70,* 381–395.

Churchland, P. (1986). *Neurophilosophy.* Cambridge, MA: MIT Press.

Cox, M. T. (1997). An explicit representation of reasoning failures. In D. Leake & E. Plaza (Eds.), *Case-based reasoning research and development: Second International Conference on Case-Based Reasoning* (pp. 211–222). Berlin: Springer.

Cox, M. T. (2005). Metacognition in computation: A selected research review. *Artificial Intelligence, 169,* 104–141.

Cox, M. T. (2007). Perpetual self-aware cognitive agents. *AI Magazine, 28,* 32–45.

Cox, M. T., & Ram, A. (1999). Introspective multistrategy learning: On the construction of learning strategies. *Artificial Intelligence, 112,* 1–55.

Dennett, D. (1987). *The intentional stance.* Cambridge, MA: MIT Press.

Fox, S., & Leake, D. (1995). Using introspective reasoning to refine indexing. In *Proceedings of the Thirteenth International Joint Conference on Artificial Intelligence.* Menlo Park, CA: International Joint Conferences on Artificial Intelligence.

Goldman, A. (2006). *Simulating minds: The philosophy psychology, and neuroscience of mindreading.* Oxford: Oxford University Press.

Gordon, A., & Hobbs, J. (2003). Coverage and competency in formal theories: A commonsense theory of memory. In P. Doherty, J. McCarthy, & M. Williams (Eds.) *Proceedings of Logical Formalizations of Commonsense Reasoning: Papers from the 2003 AAAI Spring Symposium* (pp. 64–73). Technical Report SS-03-05. Menlo Park, CA: AAAI Press.

Hayes, P. (1978). The naive physics manifesto. In D. Michie (Ed.), *Expert systems in the microelectronic age* (pp. 242–270). Edinburgh, Scotland: Edinburgh University Press.

Heider, F. (1958). *The psychology of interpersonal relations*. New York: Wiley.

Hobbs, J., & Gordon, A. (2005). Encoding knowledge of commonsense psychology. Paper presented at the Seventh International Symposium on Logical Formalizations of Commonsense Reasoning, Corfu, Greece. Available at http://www.iccl.tu-dresden.de/announce/CommonSense-2005/.

Kolodner, J. L. (1993). *Case-based reasoning*. San Mateo, CA: Morgan Kaufmann.

Lillard, A. (1998). Enthopsychologies: Cultural variations in theories of mind. *Psychological Bulletin, 123*, 3–32.

Lopez de Mántaras, R., McSherry, D., Bridge, D., Leake, D., Smyth, B., Craw, S., et al. (2006). Retrieval, reuse and retention in case-based reasoning. *Knowledge Engineering Review, 20*, 215–240.

Minsky, M. (1968). Matter, mind, and models. In M. Minsky (Ed.), *Semantic information processing* (pp. 425–432). Cambridge, MA: MIT Press.

Nichols, S., & Stich, S. (2003). *Mindreading: An integrated account of pretence, self-awareness, and understanding other minds*. Oxford: Clarendon Press.

Ram, A. (1994). AQUA: Questions that drive the understanding process. In R. Schank, A. Kass, & C. Riesbeck (Eds.), *Inside case-based explanation* (pp. 207–261). Hillsdale, NJ: Lawrence Erlbaum.

Smedslund, J. (1997). *The structure of psychological common sense*. Mahwah, NJ: Lawrence Erlbaum.

Watt, S. (1998). *Seeing this as people: Anthropomorphism and common-sense psychology*. Unpublished doctoral dissertation, The Open University, Milton Keynes, UK.

Wellman, H., Cross, D., & Watson, J. (2001). Meta-analysis of theory of mind development: The truth about false-belief. *Child Development, 72*, 655–684.

20 Varieties of Metacognition in Natural and Artificial Systems

Aaron Sloman

Some AI researchers aim to make useful machines, including robots. Others aim to understand general principles of information-processing machines with various kinds of intelligence, whether natural or artificial, including humans and human-like systems. They primarily address scientific and philosophical questions rather than practical goals. However, the tasks required to pursue scientific and engineering goals overlap, since both involve building working systems to test ideas and demonstrate results, and the conceptual frameworks and development tools needed for both overlap. This chapter, partly based on philosophical analysis of requirements for robots in complex 3D environments, surveys varieties of metacognition, drawing attention to requirements that drove biological evolution and which are also relevant to ambitious engineering goals.

Varieties of Requirements and Designs

AI has always included the study of metacognition for both scientific and engineering purposes (Minsky, 1968; Cox, 2005). That includes study of various kinds of self-monitoring, self-control, and self-discovery, including development of new concepts for self-description. My interest in AI started (around 1969) with philosophical and scientific concerns, aiming for designs expressing scientific theories (e.g., Sloman, 1978, chaps. 6–10), rather than useful artifacts (e.g., Russell & Wefald, 1991). This study overlaps with philosophy of mind and evolutionary biology: Evolution produced organisms with many different designs, shaped by many different sets of requirements; and we cannot expect to understand all the trade-offs in humans unless we compare alternatives, including nonhuman animals and possible robots. That involves studying both the space of sets of requirements (*niche* space) and the space of designs that can be compared and assessed against those requirements (*design* space). Such comparisons, instead of using only numerical fitness measures, should (as noted in Minsky, 1963) include structured descriptions of strengths and weaknesses in various conditions and in relation to various functions, like consumer reports on multifunctional products. A partial analysis is in Sloman (2003).

Simply simulating evolution will not yield such comparisons. Another approach, illustrated in Sloman (2007a), attempts analytically to retrace steps of biological evolution, especially identifying important discontinuities. Philosophy, especially conceptual analysis, will inevitably be involved in the process. This chapter attempts to identify issues to be addressed in an analytical comparative study. It overlaps with other chapters, but emphasizes biological needs and the physical environment.

Requirements for Organisms and Human-like Robots

In waking animals, sensors and effectors interact continuously with the environment, and do not need to share a CPU with more central processes. So internal processes, including planning, deciding, self-monitoring, reflecting, and learning, run *concurrently* with sensing and acting, using dedicated machinery, e.g., different parts of brains. This removes the problem of how much CPU time to allocate to metareasoning, investigated by many AI researchers (e.g., Russell & Wefald, 1991), though other constraints can produce similar problems, e.g., if acting and reasoning about what to do require the agent to be in different locations, or looking in different directions (Sloman, 1978, chap. 10). The nontrivial problem of how much dedicated computing power to allocate to each type of function is mostly settled for organisms by evolution.

With dedicated hardware for different tasks, the assumption that intelligent individuals must cycle through "sense→think→act" substates, possibly with metareasoning added, can be jettisoned, since architectures include interacting *concurrent* processes of many kinds. (However, some implementations use a single powerful CPU, as argued in Sloman (2008b), supporting multiple concurrently active *virtual* machines with different roles.) So arrows in architecture diagrams, such as figures 20.1 and 20.2, unlike flowcharts, can represent flow of information and control between *enduring*, functionally varied subsystems, operating at different levels of abstraction, on different time-scales, some changing continuously, others discretely. This has deep implications for forms of representation, algorithms, possible interactions, and conflicts between subsystems, and for trade-offs between design options. Such concurrency was impossible in the early days of AI, as computers had miniscule memories and were far too slow.

The environment (or "ground level") may include arbitrarily complex, partially understood, physical structures and processes, and also other information-users. Intelligent machines, like animals, may start with some "innate" information about the environment, but in many cases will have to develop theories about what sorts of structures and processes can occur in the environment, and how they work. This may

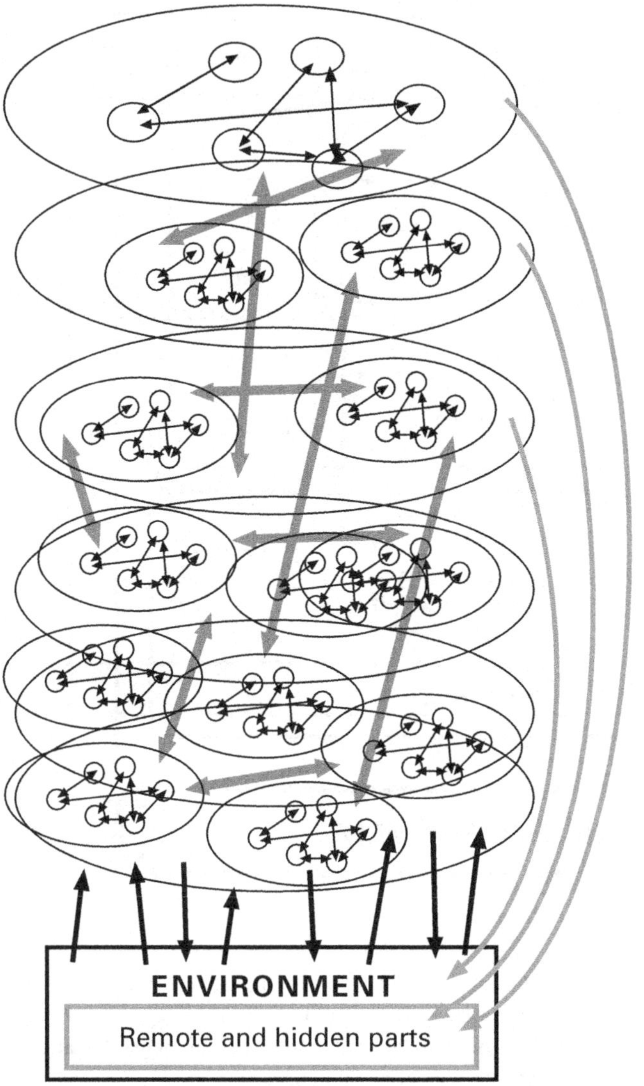

Figure 20.1
In animals and robots, concurrently active dynamical subsystems may vary in many ways, including degree of environmental coupling, speed of change, whether continuous or discrete, what is represented, etc. The longest arrows represent reference from high-level subsystems to remote and hidden entities and processes in the environment. Intermediate gray arrows represent information flow between subsystems. Short black arrows represent substate transitions.

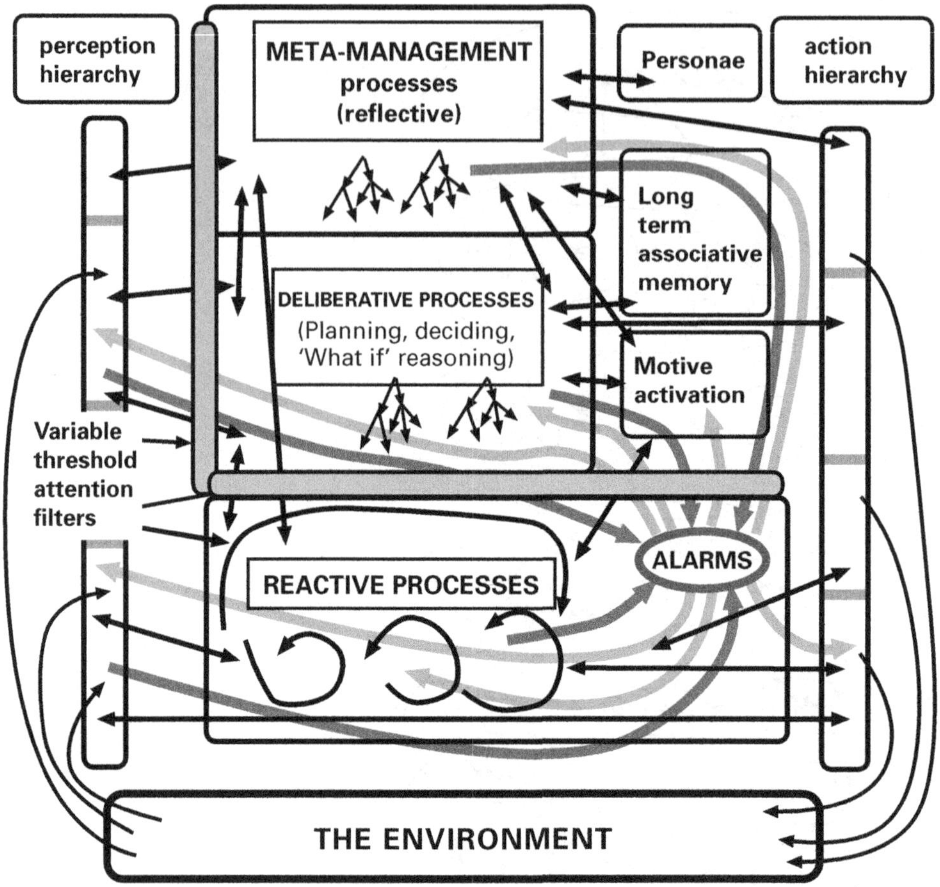

Figure 20.2
A sketchy representation of a human-like architecture specification, H-CogAff, developed within the CogAff project (Sloman, 2003). Alarm mechanisms mostly monitor passively, but can produce rapid control transfer when needed, sometimes generating emotions. The architecture grows itself while interacting with the environment. This is a special case of the CogAff schema. So far only simpler cases have been implemented. (See Kennedy, this vol., chap. 15.)

involve extending the architecture. Current AI learning mechanisms still lag far behind what animals can achieve.

Control Hierarchies

Much AI research on metareasoning aims to address problems of bounded rationality (see Zilberstein, this vol., chap. 3). However, there is a much older, more general requirement, namely the requirement for hierarchical control. That requirement was "discovered" millions of years ago by evolution and addressed in a wide variety of organisms. Instead of designing a control mechanism that deals with all possible circumstances at a low level of detail, it is often better to provide distinct mechanisms that monitor different things and propose appropriate changes on the basis of what is detected. The changes might modify behavior immediately, e.g., by changing process parameters or subgoals (e.g., causing gaze redirection), or in the long term by altering submodules—as happens in learning and self-debugging systems. Subsumption architectures do the former, using concurrent control at different levels of abstraction (Brooks, 1986). An example of metacognition producing long-term change was HACKER (Sussman, 1975).

Multiple controllers can sometimes reach conflicting decisions. It is impossible for either evolution or human designers to anticipate all such cases for a complex system functioning in a complex and partly unknown environment. So additional meta-metalevel control subsystems can be useful, monitoring other controllers and taking action when conflicts are detected. In simple cases, they may modify numerical weights to maximize expected utility (Russell & Wefald, 1991). In more sophisticated designs, dedicated meta-metalevel modules may be able to improve specific modules separately, so as to reduce unwanted interactions, e.g., adding preconditions to rules or metarules, as in Sussman (1975). They may also detect situations requiring new modules, with their own applicability conditions, and create them by copying and editing portions of older modules or by using planning mechanisms to create a new complex module for the new context, as in SOAR (Laird, Newell, & Rosenbloom, 1987). For most species this creation of new competences is done only by evolution during phylogeny, though some do it during ontogeny (Chappell & Sloman, 2007).

Metalevel decisions may themselves involve arbitrarily complex problems and the control systems involved may also be monitored and modulated by higher-level controllers. In principle, such a control philosophy can involve arbitrarily many layers of metacontrol, but in practice there will be limits (Minsky, 1968). Catriona Kennedy's chapter in this book illustrates "mutual meta-management" by a collection of subsystems each guarding a main system and also other guards. Such systems have not been found in nature, though such a design could be useful in some artificial systems. If telepathy were possible, humans might find mutual meta-management useful!

Meta-management and Meta-semantic Competence

Following Beaudoin (1994), we use the label "meta-management" (figure 20.2) to emphasize the heterogeneity of "meta-" level functioning, including control as well as monitoring, reasoning, learning, etc. Different meta-management functions can support different types of mental state (Sloman, 2002). Although many researchers regard architectures as unchangeable, in humans, higher-level layers develop over several years, including multiple switchable high-level control-regimes labeled "Personae" in figure 20.2.

Meta-management may use deliberation and reasoning along with reactive mechanisms, e.g., an "alarm" subsystem (figure 20.2) that normally only monitors processes, but can detect situations that need rapid control actions, possibly modifying the behavior of large numbers of other modules, for instance freezing (in order to avoid detection), fleeing, feeding, fighting, or mating. Other options include: slowing down, changing direction, invoking special perceptual capabilities, doing more exhaustive analysis of options, etc. Some alarm mechanisms performing these functions need to act very quickly, so they will need fast pattern recognition rather than reasoning, and may produce errors. Different effects of such alarm mechanisms in a layered control hierarchy correspond to different types of "emotion" (Sloman, 2001; Wright, Sloman, & Beaudoin, 1996). Different architectures support different affective phenomena (Sloman, Chrisley, & Scheutz, 2005). Acquiring "emotional intelligence" includes learning not to react in some frightening situations, and learning how to modulate "disruptive" control mechanisms to reduce risks, e.g., when controlling a dangerous vehicle. Running alarm mechanisms continuously removes the problem of how often to pause to decide whether to reconsider the situation.

Systems that acquire and use information have *semantic competences*, whether (like neural nets) they use information expressed in scalar parameters or (like symbolic AI systems) they use structural information about states of affairs and processes with more or less complex objects, with changing parts, features, and relationships. In contrast, using information about information, or information about things that acquire, derive, use, contain, or express information, requires *meta-semantic* competences, including the ability to represent things that represent and what they represent. This includes *representing* having or rejecting (as opposed to merely having or rejecting) beliefs, goals, and plans of both oneself and other individuals.

An individual *A* with meta-semantic competence may need to represent information *I* in another individual *B* where *I* has presuppositions that *A* knows are false, but *B* does not. For example, *B* may think there are fairies in his garden and have the goal of keeping them happy. *A* must be able to represent the content of *B*'s beliefs and goals even though *A* does not believe the presuppositions. Further, *A* may know that a description *D1* refers to the same thing as description *D2*, and therefore substitutes *D2* for *D1* in various representing contexts. But if *B* does not know the equivalence, such substitutions may lead *A* to mistaken conclusions about *B*'s mental states. Dealing with such "referentially opaque" information is more difficult than handling "referentially transparent" forms of representation. Some theorists explore adding new logical operators to standard logic, producing modal belief logics, for example. Instead of using *notational* extensions, we can provide *architectural* extensions that allow information to be represented in special "encapsulated" modes that prevent "normal" uses of the information. Such an encapsulation mechanism can be used for various meta-semantic purposes, such as representing mental states or information contents of other things, counterfactual reasoning and metaphorical reasoning. An example of such a mechanism is the ATT-Meta system of Barnden.[1]

Important research questions include: which animals have which sorts of meta-semantic competence, how and why they evolved, when and how such competences develop in young children, and what brain mechanisms are required to support them. More research is needed on what sorts of meta-semantic competence are required for the meta-management architectural layer in figure 20.2, and for the higher-level visual capabilities required for seeing someone as happy, sad, puzzled, looking for something, etc., or for intentionally performing communicative actions. Construction of AI models can help us identify requirements and trade-offs, but powerful tools are needed. The SimAgent toolkit (Sloman & Logan, 1999), used in Kennedy's work, was designed to support (among other things) architecture-based meta-semantic competences.

Meta-management and Consciousness

It is often suggested that consciousness depends on the existence of something like a meta-management layer in an architecture, though details differ (Minsky, 1968; Sloman, 1978; Johnson-Laird, 1988; Baars, 1988; Shanahan, 2006). However, the concept of "consciousness" (like "emotion" and "self") is riddled with confusion and muddle. For serious science it is best replaced with a collection of precisely defined labels for special cases, e.g., notions of self-knowledge (McCarthy, 1995). Some self-knowledge based on introspection includes trivial, transient cases such as a program checking the contents of a register or a sensor reading, and nontrivial cases, e.g., architectures with self-observation subsystems running concurrently with others and using a meta-semantic ontology referring to relatively high-level (e.g., representational) states, events, and processes in the system, expressed in nontransient reusable information structures (Sloman, 2007b).

A system with an architecture allowing introspection to acquire information about its internal states and processes, including intermediate data-structures in perceptual and motor subsystems, could be said to be self-aware. This subsumes cases discussed

1. See http://www.cs.bham.ac.uk/~jab/ATT-Meta/.

in McCarthy (1995), and also much of what philosophers say about "qualia" and "phenomenal consciousness." Introspection is a kind of perception and therefore has the potential for error, notwithstanding arguments that knowledge of how things seem to you is infallible (Schwitzgebel, 2007). That claim "I cannot be mistaken about how things *seem* to me" or "I cannot be mistaken about the contents of my own experience" is a trivial but confusing tautology, like "a voltmeter cannot be mistaken about what voltage it reports." What seems to you to be going on inside you cannot be different from what seems to you to be going on inside you, but it may be different from what is actually going on inside you. Intelligent reflective robots may fall into the same confusion.

Pre-configured and Meta-configured Competences

Intelligent systems may start with the ontologies they need for categorizing things (as in *precocial* biological species), or, as in some altricial species (Sloman & Chappell, 2005), may develop their own ontologies through exploration and experiment using mechanisms that evolved to support self-extension, through interaction with a complex, richly structured, changing environment. A distinction can be made between "pre-configured" competences, which are largely genetically determined, and "meta-configured" competences, produced by a succession of acquired competences (Chappell & Sloman, 2007).

Layered development processes can start by learning from the environment how to learn more in that environment, e.g., learning what one can do and what sorts of new information may result—"epistemic affordances" in the environment. Meta-configured learning can include *substantive* ontology development: creation of new concepts not definable in terms of previous concepts. This clearly happens in science (Sloman, 1978, chap. 2) and is also needed in children and intelligent robots. The widely believed theory that all symbols have to be "grounded" in sensorimotor signals is a version of the erroneous philosophical theory of "concept empiricism."[2]

One function of meta-management is discovering the need to modify current theories about the environment, e.g., because predictions have failed. Sometimes abduction can be used to produce a new theory using old concepts, e.g., a theory explaining why a beam of varying thickness does not balance at its midpoint. However, some new theories need new concepts referring to the unobserved but hypothesized properties that explain observations, e.g., magnetism. Unfortunately, the search space for abduction of new theories is explosively expanded if additional undefined symbols can be introduced. So learners may need meta-management capabilities to guide the creation of substantially new concepts.

2. See http://www.cs.bham.ac.uk/research/projects/cogaff/talks/#models.

Ontology development is needed not only for coping with the environment, but also for internal meta-management uses, extending the individual's meta-semantic competences, e.g., noticing how one's experience of a rectangular object changes as one views it from different directions or noticing that going without liquid for a long time produces an introspectable state.

Meta-semantic ontology extension may result from self-organizing capabilities of self-monitoring mechanisms, e.g., using something like a Kohonen net to develop an ontology for intermediate states in perceptual processing, such as tastes, color sensations, shape experiences, etc. Such concepts of sensory contents may be in principle uncommunicable to other individuals because the concepts are "causally indexical," i.e., they implicitly refer to the classification mechanism (as suggested in Sloman & Chrisley, 2003). This may produce philosophical confusions in some future robots.

The space of theories of metacognition is vast and unconstrained, except for specific applications. An unexplored constraint, suggested in Sloman (2007b), is that the theory should explain how different individuals with *the same* initial architecture can reach *divergent* beliefs on many philosophical problems, e.g., about the nature of human consciousness, free will, emotional states.

Affordances, Proto-affordances, and Mathematical Metacognition

Many researchers assume that the function of vision is to provide information about geometrical and physical properties and relations of objects in the environment. Gibson (1979) argued that organisms need, instead, information about which actions are available to them in particular situations and which ones will produce desired results: perception provides information about positive and negative action affordances for the perceiver. This revolutionary proposal was the first step along a major road, though we still have a long way to go (Sloman, 2009). Perception of affordances related to possible actions depends on more fundamental perception of "proto-affordances," namely possible processes and constraints on processes involving motion of 3D objects and object fragments, whether or not the processes can be produced by the perceiver, and whether or not they are relevant to the perceiver's goals, e.g., seeing how a branch can move in the breeze and how other branches constrain its motion.

Humans can also *reason* about interactions between proto-affordances of different objects, e.g., working out possible behaviors of a machine made of levers, pulleys, ropes, and gear wheels (Sloman, 1971). If one end of a long, straight, rigid object is moved down while the center is fixed, the other end *must* move up. A learner might discover such facts initially as statistical correlations. Later, reflection on what is understood by "rigidity," namely that some feature of the internal structure of the material prevents change of shape, can lead to the realization that the effect has a kind of *necessity* that is characteristic of mathematical discoveries. If objects are not only rigid but also impenetrable, many other examples of structural causation can be discovered: for example, if two centrally pivoted rigid and impenetrable adjacent gear wheels have their teeth meshed and one moves clockwise, the other must move counterclockwise.

Many truths about geometry and topology can be discovered by reflection on empirically discovered interactions between proto-affordances. Some of the consequences may be predictable even in situations never previously encountered. Sauvy and Suavy (1974) present examples of topological discoveries that can be made by children, and, I suggest, future playful and reflective robots, playing with various spatial structures, strings, pins, buttons, elastic bands, pencil and paper, etc.

Robots with appropriate metacognitive reflective capabilities could, like human children, notice invariant features in some of the structures and processes produced when they interact with the environment, for example noticing that containment is transitive. I have suggested (in Sloman 1971; 1978, chap. 8; 2008a) that this lends support to Kant's (1781/1929) philosophical claim that mathematical knowledge is both synthetic and nonempirical.[3]

Some discoveries are primarily about properties of static structures, such as that angles of a triangle must add up to a straight line. But a child learning to count through counting games and experiments may notice recurring patterns and realize that they too are not merely statistical correlations but *necessary* consequences of features of the processes. For example, if a set of objects is counted in one order the result of counting *must* be the same for any other order of counting (subject to the normal conditions of counting).

Developing a more detailed analysis of architectural and representational requirements for systems capable of making such discoveries is research in progress. The discoveries depend on the fact that an individual can first learn to do something (e.g., produce or perceive a type of process) and then later notice that the process has some inevitable features—inevitable in the sense that if certain core features of the process are preserved, altering other features, e.g., the location, altitude, temperature, colors, materials, etc. of the process *cannot* affect the result.

This makes it possible for a Kantian *structure-based* notion of causation to be used alongside Humean (or Bayesian) *correlation-based* notions of causation. It is possible that some other animals, e.g., some nest-building birds and hunting mammals, also develop Kantian causal reasoning abilities.[4]

Similarly, reflection on invariant patterns in sets of sentences could lead to logical discoveries made centuries ago by Aristotle and then later extended by Boole and Frege, among others, regarding patterns of inference that are valid in virtue of their

3. See http://www.cs.bham.ac.uk/research/projects/cogaff/talks/#toddlers for examples.

4. See http://www.cs.bham.ac.uk/research/projects/cogaff/talks/wonac for detailed rationale.

logical form alone. Bertrand Russell tried to reduce all mathematical knowledge to logical knowledge (thought of as a collection of tautologies). I suggest that logical knowledge, like mathematical knowledge, arises from use of metacognitive mechanisms reflecting on empirical discoveries, a process not yet modeled in AI.

Reflecting on Epistemic Affordances

Action affordances are the possibilities for and constraints on possible actions that can be performed, whereas positive and negative *epistemic affordances* in a situation are the varieties of information available to or hidden from the perceiver. They are linked because an agent can discover that some physical actions change epistemic affordances. Moving toward an open doorway makes more information available about what is beyond the door, whereas moving sideways both adds and removes information about the contents of the next room. As you move round a house you discover things about the external walls, doors, and windows of the house, including their sequential order. You can then use that information to *work out* the epistemic affordances available by going round in the opposite direction (as Kant noticed)—an essentially mathematical competence at work in a familiar nonmathematical context.

In the first few years of life children acquire not only hundreds of facts about actions that alter *action affordances*, but also myriad facts about actions that alter *epistemic affordances*. Every slight movement forward, backward, turning, looking down, moving an object, etc. will immediately alter the information available. Infants do not know these things are being learned: the meta-semantic competence to reflect on what is going on has not yet developed. How it develops, and what changes occur in forms of representation, mechanisms, or architectures, are questions for future research. This may have profound importance for educational policies, especially as children with disabilities (including congenital blindness, deafness, or physical deformity) can reach similar end states via different routes, and that may be true also of future robots.

Epistemic Affordances and Uncertainty

In a large, complex, partly inaccessible environment neither animals nor machines can achieve complete or certain information. In AI, psychology, and neuroscience it is generally assumed that reasoning about probabilities is required for coping with uncertainty and partial information. But in some cases there are simpler and more powerful alternatives, namely, (a) using information about which actions alter epistemic affordances, and (b) using more abstract ontologies that do not require great precision of measurement or control.

Illustrating (a): an agent who notices that there is some uncertainty about a matter of importance, e.g., because of noise or imprecise sensors, can avoid reasoning with probabilities, by detecting an action affordance that alters epistemic affordances, reducing or removing the uncertainty, so that simple reasoning or planning suffices. Examples are moving some object, or changing one's viewpoint, in order to see more of a partially hidden object or region of space. Often second-order epistemic information is available, indicating that certain actions can be performed to produce new epistemic affordances.

Illustrating (b): instead of using only geometrical descriptions it often suffices to use topological or functional descriptions, or to shift from subcategories to supercategories. For example, even if you cannot tell the precise distance between two surfaces you can sometimes see that the gap is too small for a nearby armchair to pass through, and sometimes when you cannot tell whether the thing in the distance is a male or a female, you can be sure it's a person, avoiding the need to handle the disjunction and associated probabilities, provided that the person's sex is irrelevant in that context.

Figure 20.3 indicates possible configurations of a pencil and a mug, and possible translations or rotations, with uncertain consequences. In some cases there are good

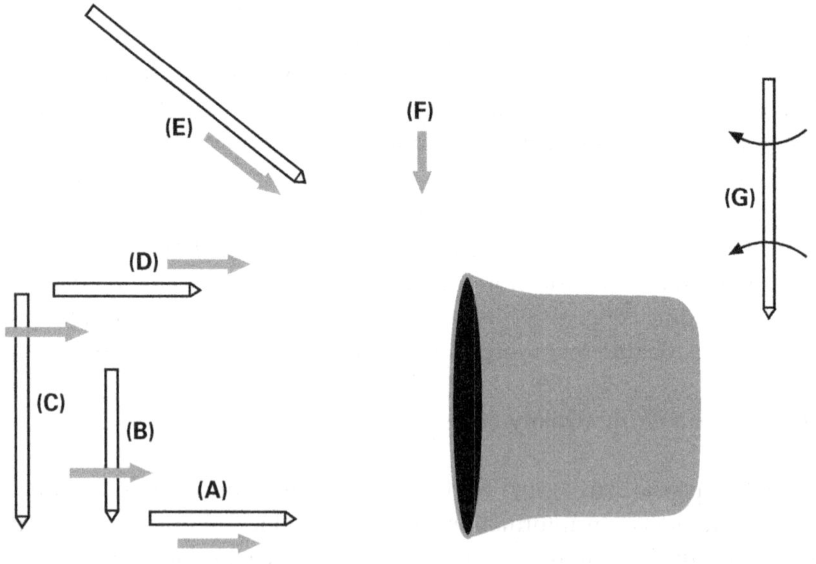

Figure 20.3
A mug on its side, with possible locations for a pencil, and possible translations or rotations of the pencil indicated by arrows. If pencil A moves horizontally to the right, will it enter the mug? If pencil G is rotated in the vertical plane about its top end, will it hit the mug? In both cases moving the pencil vertically upward removes the uncertainty. The other pencil locations also have associated uncertainty that can be removed by small changes. Different initial moves will extend epistemic affordances for different cases.

epistemic affordances, providing clear "yes/no" answers. Between those situations are "phase boundaries," where epistemic affordances are reduced. A meta-management system can learn about, or discover by reasoning, that some actions improve epistemic affordances because the configuration moves away from the phase boundary to a region of certainty. A thirsty individual may see that a mug on the table is within reach, without knowing whether it contains liquid. Reasoning with probabilities can be avoided by noticing possible actions that increase epistemic affordances: e.g., standing up to look into the mug or reaching out to bring it closer.[5]

Sometimes manipulation of probability distributions can be avoided by using the metaknowledge that there are "regions of certainty" (ROCs), definitely-yes and definitely-no regions, with a fuzzy boundary that is a "region of uncertainty" (ROU). An important type of metacognitive learning is discovering when and how it is possible to move from a ROU into a ROC, by performing some action, e.g., by changing direction of gaze, changing viewpoint, rotating an object, altering direction of movement, changing size of grip, or moving something out of the way. When you cannot tell whether you are on a course to collide with the right edge of a doorway, you may be able to tell that aiming further to the right will definitely cause a collision and aiming a bit to the left will definitely avoid the collision without having to reason with probabilities.

Conclusion

I have tried to show how designs produced by evolution, especially designs involving dedicated processors with different functions, escape some of the problems faced by AI researchers considering metareasoning in systems based on general computers. But the biological examples produce new problems and opportunities for AI. The CogAff schema presented in Sloman (2003), which subsumes figure 20.2, provides a framework for exploring, describing, and comparing alternative designs with various sorts of metacognition, including varieties that do and do not require meta-semantic competences, a requirement met in humans and other biological organisms, but very few current AI systems.

I have also tried to indicate ways in which detailed studies of the very complex environments in which animals evolved or future robots may have to perform can lead to new requirements and new opportunities for metacognition, especially requirements for making use of more varieties of affordance than Gibson identified, including first-order and second-order epistemic affordances. This can sometimes provide good nonprobabilistic ways of dealing with uncertainty.

Gibson's work has been extended, including design ideas about metacognition that have not yet been explored except in very simple situations. Further research on this

5. More examples are in http://www.cs.bham.ac.uk/research/projects/cosy/papers/#dp0702.

may contribute significantly to making machines more human-like. It may also enable us to understand humans better.

There is far more still to be done—provided that we can understand the architectural and representational requirements and the myriad positive and negative action affordances and epistemic affordances in different environments. This may lead not only to more advanced machines, but also to a deeper understanding of what humans and other animals do and how they do it. A better understanding of normal competences could lead to better diagnoses and treatments of genetic or trauma-induced abnormalities. Understanding how young animals learn about first- and second-order action affordances and epistemic affordances could give us new insights into human mathematical capability and help dedicated teachers to support mathematical learning more effectively.

Acknowledgments

I have learned from many people over many years. Recent ideas came from discussions with Jackie Chappell about nonhuman organisms and nature–nurture trade-offs, and members of the EU-Funded CoSy and CogX robotics projects: http://www.cognitivesystems.org, http://cogx.eu. I thank the editors for their patience and understanding.

References

Baars, B. J. (1988). *A cognitive theory of consciousness*. Cambridge: Cambridge University Press.

Beaudoin, L. (1994). *Goal processing in autonomous agents*. Unpublished doctoral dissertation, School of Computer Science, The University of Birmingham, Birmingham, UK.

Brooks, R. (1986). A robust layered control system for a mobile robot. *IEEE Journal on Robotics and Automation, RA-2*, 14–23.

Chappell, J., & Sloman, A. (2007). Natural and artificial meta-configured altricial information-processing systems. *International Journal of Unconventional Computing, 3*(3), 211–239.

Cox, M. T. (2005). Metacognition in computation: A selected research review. *Artificial Intelligence, 169*(2), 104–141.

Gibson, J. J. (1979). *The ecological approach to visual perception*. Boston: Houghton Mifflin.

Johnson-Laird, P. (1988). *The computer and the mind: An introduction to cognitive science*. London: Fontana Press.

Kant, I. [1781] (1929). *Critique of pure reason*. Trans. Norman Kemp Smith. London: Macmillan.

Laird, J. E., Newell, A., & Rosenbloom, P. S. (1987). SOAR: An architecture for general intelligence. *Artificial Intelligence, 33*, 1–64.

McCarthy, J. (1995). Making robots conscious of their mental states. In M. T. Cox & M. Freed (Eds.), *AAAI Spring Symposium on Representing Mental States and Mechanisms*. Palo Alto, CA: AAAI.

Minsky, M. L. (1963). Steps towards artificial intelligence. In E. Feigenbaum & J. Feldman (Eds.), *Computers and thought* (pp. 406–450). New York: McGraw-Hill.

Minsky, M. L. (1968). Matter, mind, and models. In M. L. Minsky (Ed.), *Semantic information processing*. Cambridge, MA: MIT Press.

Russell, S. J., & Wefald, E. H. (1991). *Do the right thing: Studies in limited rationality*. Cambridge, MA: MIT Press.

Sauvy, J., & Suavy, S. (1974). *The child's discovery of space: From hopscotch to mazes—an introduction to intuitive topology. Trans. Pam Wells*. Harmondsworth: Penguin Education.

Schwitzgebel, E. (2007). No unchallengeable epistemic authority, of any sort, regarding our own conscious experience—Contra Dennett? *Phenomenology and the Cognitive Sciences, 6*, 107–112.

Shanahan, M. (2006). A cognitive architecture that combines internal simulation with a global workspace. *Consciousness and Cognition, 15*, 157–176.

Sloman, A. (1971). Interactions between philosophy and AI: The role of intuition and non-logical reasoning in intelligence. In *Proceedings 2nd IJCAI* (pp. 209–226). London: William Kaufmann. http://www.cs.bham.ac.uk/research/cogaff/04.html#200407.

Sloman, A. (1978). *The computer revolution in philosophy*. Hassocks, Sussex: Harvester Press (and Humanities Press). http://www.cs.bham.ac.uk/research/cogaff/crp.

Sloman, A. (2001). Beyond shallow models of emotion. *Cognitive Processing: International Quarterly of Cognitive Science, 2*(1), 177–198.

Sloman, A. (2002). Architecture-based conceptions of mind. In P. Gärdenfors, J. Wolenski, & K. Kijania-Placek (Eds.), *In the Scope of Logic, Methodology, and Philosophy of Science* (Vol. II, pp. 403–427). Dordrecht: Kluwer.

Sloman, A. (2003). *The cognition and affect project: Architectures, architecture-schemas, and the new science of mind. (Tech. Rep.)*. Birmingham: School of Computer Science, University of Birmingham.

Sloman, A. (2007a). Diversity of developmental trajectories in natural and artificial intelligence. In C. T. Morrison & T. T. Oates (Eds.), *Computational Approaches to Representation Change during Learning and Development: AAAI Fall Symposium 2007, Technical Report FS-07-03* (pp. 70–79). Menlo Park, CA: AAAI Press.

Sloman, A. (2007b). Why some machines may need qualia and how they can have them: Including a demanding new Turing test for robot philosophers. In A. Chella & R. Manzotti (Eds.), *AI and Consciousness: Theoretical Foundations and Current Approaches: AAAI Fall Symposium 2007, Technical Report FS-07-01* (pp. 9–16). Menlo Park, CA: AAAI Press.

Sloman, A. (2008a, July). Kantian philosophy of mathematics and young robots. In S. Autexier, J. Campbell, J. Rubio, V. Sorge, M. Suzuki, & F. Wiedijk (Eds.), *Intelligent Computer Mathematics* (pp. 558–573). Berlin, Heidelberg: Springer.

Sloman, A. (2008b). The well-designed young mathematician. *Artificial Intelligence, 172*(18), 2015–2034.

Sloman, A. (2009). Architectural and representational requirements for seeing processes and affordances. In D. Heinke & E. Mavritsaki (Eds.), *Computational modelling in behavioural neuroscience: Closing the gap between neurophysiology and behaviour.* London: Psychology Press.

Sloman, A., & Chappell, J. (2005). The altricial-precocial spectrum for robots. In *Proceedings IJCAI'05* (pp. 1187–1192). Edinburgh: IJCAI.

Sloman, A., & Chrisley, R. (2003). Virtual machines and consciousness. *Journal of Consciousness Studies, 10*(4–5), 113–172.

Sloman, A., Chrisley, R., & Scheutz, M. (2005). The architectural basis of affective states and processes. In M. Arbib & J.-M. Fellous (Eds.), *Who needs emotions? The brain meets the robot* (pp. 203–244). New York: Oxford University Press.

Sloman, A., & Logan, B. (1999). Building cognitively rich agents using the Sim_agent toolkit. *Communications of the ACM, 42*(3), 71–77.

Sussman, G. (1975). *A computational model of skill acquisition.* New York: American Elsevier.

Wright, I., Sloman, A., & Beaudoin, L. (1996). Towards a design-based analysis of emotional episodes. *Philosophy, Psychiatry, & Psychology, 3*(2), 101–126.

Contributors

George Alexander is a fourth-year doctoral student in the College of Computing at University of North Carolina at Charlotte (UNCC), working in the Game Intelligence Group. He received a B.S. in computer science and mathematics (summa cum laude) from UNCC in 2006. His research interests include artificial intelligence, machine learning, and natural language. (gralexan@uncc.edu)

Michael L. Anderson is Assistant Professor in the Department of Psychology at Franklin & Marshall College, and Visiting Assistant Professor at the Institute for Advanced Computer Studies at the University of Maryland, College Park, where he is also a member of the Graduate Faculty of the Neuroscience and Cognitive Science Program. Dr. Anderson is author or coauthor of over fifty scholarly and scientific publications in artificial intelligence, cognitive science, and philosophy of mind. Primary areas of research include an account of the evolution of the cortex via exaptation of existing neural circuitry (the "massive redeployment hypothesis"); the role of behavior, and of the brain's motor-control areas, in supporting higher-order cognitive functions; the foundations of intentionality (the connection between objects of thought and things in the world); and the role of self-monitoring and self-control in maintaining robust real-world agency. (www.agcognition.org; anderson@cs.umd.edu)

Josep Lluís Arcos is a Research Scientist at the Artificial Intelligence Institute of the Spanish National Research Council (IIIA-CSIC). Dr. Arcos received an M.S. in musical creation and sound technology from Pompeu Fabra University in 1996 and a Ph.D. in computer science from the Universitat Politècnica de Catalunya in 1997. He is the corecipient of several awards at case-based reasoning conferences and computer music conferences. Currently he is working on case-based reasoning and learning, on self-organization and self-adaptation mechanisms, and on artificial intelligence applications to music. (www.iiia.csic.es/~arcos; arcos@iiia.csic.es)

Brett J. Borghetti earned a Doctorate of Philosophy in computer science in 2008 from the University of Minnesota, Twin Cities, Minnesota; a Master of Science degree in computer systems in 1996 from the United States Air Force Institute of Technology

(AFIT) Dayton, Ohio; and a Bachelor of Science in electrical engineering in 1992 from Worcester Polytechnic Institute, Worcester, Massachusetts. He is a Lieutenant Colonel in the U.S. Air Force and is an Assistant Professor of Computer Science at AFIT at Wright-Patterson Air Force Base. He has worked at the Air Intelligence Agency (AIA) in San Antonio, the National Air and Space Intelligence Center (NASIC) in Dayton, the United States Strategic Command (USSTRATCOM) in Omaha, and the Training Systems Product Group in Dayton. (brett.borghetti@afit.edu)

Vincent Conitzer is an Assistant Professor of Computer Science and Economics at Duke University. He received Ph.D. (2006) and M.S. (2003) degrees in computer science from Carnegie Mellon University and an A.B. (2001) degree in applied mathematics from Harvard University. His research focuses on computational aspects of microeconomics, such as game theory, mechanism design, voting/social choice, and auctions. This work uses techniques from, and includes applications to, artificial intelligence and multiagent systems. (www.cs.duke.edu/~conitzer/; conitzer@cs.duke.edu)

Michael T. Cox is a Program Manager in the Information Processing Techniques Office of the Defense Advanced Research Projects Agency. He received Ph.D. (1996) and B.S. (1986, summa cum laude) degrees in computer science from the Georgia Institute of Technology in Atlanta, Georgia. Previously he was senior scientist at BBN Technologies, Cambridge, Massachusetts, Assistant Professor of Computer Science and Engineering at Wright State University, Dayton, Ohio, and postdoctoral fellow in Computer Science at Carnegie Mellon University, Pittsburgh, Pennsylvania. Dr. Cox's research foci include case-based reasoning, mixed-initiative planning, multistrategy learning, and computational introspection. In particular, he is interested in how goals affect intelligent behavior across all these processes. (mcox.org; Michael.Cox@DARPA.mil)

Susan L. Epstein is Professor of Computer Science at Hunter College and the Graduate Center of the City University of New York. Her work in artificial intelligence is directed toward knowledge representation and machine learning for the automated development of expertise. She is known for her work in constraint satisfaction, game playing, path finding, and two-dimensional layout design. A past Chair of the Cognitive Science Society, she is particularly interested in multiple representations, multiple learning methods, and the integration of visual perception with high-level reasoning. Dr. Epstein's collaborators have included linguists, microbiologists, evolutionary biologists, psychologists, chemists, mathematicians, and geographers. She holds a B.S. in mathematics from Smith College, an M.S. in mathematics from New York University, and M.S. and Ph.D. degrees in computer science from Rutgers, the State University of New Jersey. (www.cs.hunter.cuny.edu/~epstein/; susan.epstein@hunter.cuny.edu)

Scott Fults currently has a postdoctoral position with Don Perlis in the Computer Science Department at the University of Maryland, College Park. He received his Ph.D.

in linguistics from University of Maryland, College Park, in 2006. He has been using his linguistics skills to build a dialogue agent to explore ideas about metacognition and language processing. His dissertation discusses the syntax and semantics of positive and comparative adjectives, focusing on how morpho-syntactic structure affects meaning. He also works on vagueness, number cognition, and the online semantic processing of quantifiers and negation. (www.active.cs.umd.edu; scott@cs.umd.edu)

Melinda Gervasio is currently a senior computer scientist at SRI International with interests in mixed-initiative learning, machine learning for planning and scheduling, and end-user programming. Prior to joining SRI in 2003, Dr. Gervasio was a research scientist at the Institute for the Study of Learning and Expertise, where she conducted research in the areas of personalization and mixed-initiative planning and scheduling. She received her Ph.D. in computer science from the University of Illinois at Urbana-Champaign in 1996 for her dissertation on explanation-based learning for planning. (www.ai.sri.com/people/gervasio/; melinda.gervasio@sri.com)

Yolanda Gil received her Ph. D. in computer science from Carnegie Mellon University in 1992. Her research interests include intelligent user interfaces, knowledge-rich problem solving, distributed computing, and the semantic web. An area of recent interest is the use of knowledge-rich computational workflows for large-scale scientific data analysis and discovery. She is currently an Associate Division Director at the Information Sciences Institute of the University of Southern California, Marina del Rey, California, and a Research Associate Professor in the Computer Science Department. (www.isi.edu/~gil; gil@isi.edu)

Maria Gini is a Professor at the Department of Computer Science and Engineering of the University of Minnesota. Her work includes coordinated behaviors among robots and in multiagent systems, learning of opponent behaviors, and autonomous economic agents. She is the chair of the ACM Special Interest Group on Artificial Intelligence (SIGART). She is on the editorial board of numerous journals, including *Autonomous Agents & Multi-Agent Systems, Electronic Commerce Research and Applications, Web Intelligence and Agent Systems, Autonomous Robots*, and *Integrated Computer-Aided Engineering*. She is a Fellow of the Association for the Advancement of Artificial Intelligence. (www-users.cs.umn.edu/~gini/; gini@cs.umn.edu)

Ashok K. Goel is an Associate Professor of Computer Science and Cognitive Science in the School of Interactive Computing at Georgia Institute of Technology. He is Director of the School's Design & Intelligence Laboratory, and a Co-Director of Georgia Tech's Center for Biologically Inspired Design. He is an Associate Editor of *IEEE Intelligent Systems* and *ASME Journal of Computing and Information Science in Engineering*. His research on knowledge-based artificial intelligence has been supported by NSF, DARPA, ONR, DHS, and IES, and he has been a consultant to NEC and NCR. His research on self-adaptive intelligent agents described in this volume is supported by an NSF (Science of Design) Grant (0613744) on "Teleological Reasoning in Adaptive Software Design." (www.cc.gatech.edu/directory/ashok-goel; goel@cc.gatech.edu)

Andrew S. Gordon is a Research Associate Professor of Computer Science at the Institute for Creative Technologies at the University of Southern California. He received his Ph.D. from Northwestern University in 1999, and a B.A. in cognitive science from Northwestern University in 1993. He conducts interdisciplinary research in artificial intelligence, computational linguistics, knowledge management, and training technologies. He is the author of the book *Strategy Representation: An Analysis of Planning Knowledge*. (www.ict.usc.edu/~gordon/; gordon@ict.usc.edu)

Justin Hart is a Ph.D. candidate in the Computer Science Department at Yale University, where he is advised by Brian Scassellati. He received his M.Eng. in computer science from Cornell University in 2006, and his B.S. in computer science from West Virginia University in 2001. His research focuses on constructing computational models of the process by which children learn about their sensory and physical capabilities and how they can interact with their environment. (pantheon.yale.edu/~jwh42/; justin.hart@yale.edu)

Jerry R. Hobbs is a prominent researcher in the fields of computational linguistics, discourse analysis, and artificial intelligence. Dr. Hobbs earned his Ph.D. from New York University in 1974 in computer science. He has taught at Yale University and the City University of New York. From 1977 to 2002 he was with the Artificial Intelligence Center at SRI International, where he was a principal scientist and program director of the Natural Language Program. He has written numerous papers in the areas of parsing, syntax, semantic interpretation, information extraction, knowledge representation, encoding commonsense knowledge, discourse analysis, the structure of conversation, and the semantic web. In September 2002 he took a position as Research Professor and ISI Fellow at the Information Sciences Institute, University of Southern California. He is a past president of the Association for Computational Linguistics and is a Fellow of the American Association for Artificial Intelligence. In January 2003 he was awarded an honorary Doctorate of Philosophy from the University of Uppsala, Sweden. (www.isi.edu/~hobbs; hobbs@isi.edu)

Eric Horvitz is a Distinguished Scientist at Microsoft Research. His research interests span theoretical and practical challenges with developing computational systems that sense, learn, and reason. He has pursued principles of bounded rationality and metareasoning under limited computational resources. His research introduced and explored several core concepts in metareasoning, including the use of flexible computational procedures under uncertain and varying computational resources, decision-theoretic metareasoning, expected value of computation, continual computation, and the pursuit of bounded optimality. Eric has been elected a Fellow of the Association for the Advancement of Artificial Intelligence (AAAI) and of the American Association for the Advancement of Science (AAAS). He has served as President of the AAAI, and on the advisory boards of the NSF Computer and Information Science and Engineering (CISE) Directorate and the Computing Community Consortium (CCC). He received his PhD and MD degrees at Stanford University. (http://research.microsoft.com/~horvitz; horvitz@microsoft.com)

Joshua Jones is a Ph.D. candidate in computer science in the School of Interactive Computing at Georgia Institute of Technology and a member of the School's Design & Intelligence Laboratory. His research interests lie at the intersection of knowledge-based AI and machine learning. In particular, his Ph.D. work investigates the use of metareasoning for diagnosing and repairing classification knowledge when a classifier makes an incorrect prediction. After graduation in 2009, he plans to work at University of Maryland, Baltimore County, as a postdoctoral research scientist. He received his B.S. in computer science from the University of New Hampshire in 1999. (www.cc.gatech.edu/~jkj; jkj@umbc.edu)

Darsana Josyula is an Assistant Professor of Computer Science at Bowie State University, Bowie, Maryland and is a member of the ALMECOM group at the Institute of Advanced Computer Studies, University of Maryland. Her research interests include commonsense reasoning, resource-bounded reasoning, knowledge acquisition, metacognitive computing, and natural language understanding in artificial agents. She received her Ph.D. in computer science at the University of Maryland, College Park, in 2005. Her dissertation work developed a model of metacognition that uses a time-sensitive and contradiction-tolerant reasoning mechanism on explicit representations of beliefs, desires, intentions, expectations, and observations, to monitor and correct actions of an agent operating in a setting where concurrent actions are allowed. The model was implemented in a natural language interfacing agent to monitor and fix problems in natural language understanding as well as task execution. (www.cs.umd.edu/~darsana; darsana@cs.umd.edu)

Catriona M. Kennedy has a B.Sc. in computer science from Stirling University Scotland (1982). After extensive experience as a software developer she returned to academia to pursue a Ph.D. (2003) at the University of Birmingham in the area of reflective agents under Aaron Sloman. Since then she has worked as a research fellow at Birmingham University, specializing in software architectures for autonomic computing and intelligent scientific assistance. She is currently a visiting scientist at the MIT Computer Science and AI Lab. (www.cs.bham.ac.uk/~cmk/; C.M.Kennedy@cs.bham.ac.uk)

Jihie Kim is a Research Assistant Professor in Computer Science at the University of Southern California, a Computer Scientist at the USC/Information Sciences Institute. Dr. Kim received a Ph.D. from the University of Southern California and a master's and a bachelor's degree from the Seoul National University. Her current interests include pedagogical tools for online discussions, knowledge-based approaches to developing workflow systems, and intelligent user interfaces. (www.isi.edu/~jihie; jihie@isi.edu)

Michael Krainin is currently a graduate student in computer science at the University of Washington. Michael received his bachelor's degree in computer science from the University of Massachusetts Amherst, where he worked as an undergraduate researcher in the Multi-Agent Systems Lab. In cooperation with the Collaborative Adaptive Sensing of the Atmosphere (CASA) Engineering Research Center, he has conducted research in distributed control mechanisms for adaptive sensor networks. His achievements include an honorable mention in the 2007 CRA's Outstanding Undergraduate Award, a 2008 Goldwater Scholarship, and the Overall Undergraduate Achievement Award given by the UMass Computer Science Department. (mkrainin@gmail.com)

Robert Laddaga is a Senior Scientist at BBN Technologies, where he has been working on symbolic learning systems, self-adaptive vision systems, and self-adaptive networking. Dr. Laddaga is the PI of BBN's self-adaptive networking software effort, PI of BBN's Enhanced Bootstrapping effort, and Project Director of BBN's Integrated Learning project. Dr. Laddaga was a research scientist at the MIT Computer Science and Artificial Intelligence Laboratory (CSAIL) for over nine years. He served as Director of Software Development at Symbolics Inc., and was the President of Dynamic Object Language Labs and of Artelligence. He was an Assistant Professor of Computer Science at the University of South Carolina. His past research accomplishments included work in intelligent tutoring of symbolic logic and probability; work in cognitive science including eye-tracking and speech generation; work in software and AI development environments; development of DARPA research programs in Self-Adaptive Software and Autonomous Negotiating Agents; and research on AI, self-adaptive software, adaptive networking, vision, sensor networks, pervasive and perceptually enabled environments, and information survivability. (openmap.bbn.com/~laddaga/; rladdaga@bbn.com)

David B. Leake is a Professor of Computer Science and Associate Dean of the School of Informatics at Indiana University. He is also a member of the faculty of the university's Cognitive Science and Human–Computer Interaction programs. He received his Ph.D. in computer science from Yale University in 1990. His research interests include case-based reasoning, context, explanation, human-centered computing, intelligent user interfaces, introspective reasoning, and knowledge capture and management. He has over 100 publications in these areas. He is the Editor in Chief of *AI Magazine*, the official magazine of the Association for the Advancement of Artificial Intelligence. (www.cs.indiana.edu/~leake/; leake@cs.indiana.edu)

Victor R. Lesser received his B.A. in mathematics from Cornell University in 1966 and the Ph.D. degree in computer science from Stanford University in 1973. He then was a research computer scientist at Carnegie-Mellon University, working on the Hearsay-II speech understanding system. Since 1977 he is has been on the faculty of the Department of Computer Science at the University of Massachusetts, Amherst, where he is a distinguished professor. He is an internationally recognized researcher in the areas of multiagent/distributed AI and blackboard systems. He has also made contributions in the areas of real-time AI, signal understanding, diagnostics, plan recognition, computer-supported cooperative work, and computer architecture. Professor Lesser is a Founding Fellow of the Association for the Advancement of Artificial Intelligence (AAAI), an IEEE Fellow, and recipient of the IJCAI-09 Award for Research Excellence. He was General Chair of the first international conference on Multi-Agent Systems (ICMAS) in 1995, and Founding President of the International Foundation of Autonomous Agents and Multi-Agent Systems (IFAAMAS) in 1998. To honor his contributions to the field of multiagent systems, IFAAMAS established the "Victor Lesser Distinguished Dissertation Award." (dis.cs.umass.edu/lesser.html; lesser@cs.umass.edu)

Fabrizio Morbini received a Laurea in electronic engineering from Università degli Studi di Brescia in 2002 with a thesis on extensions to the DISCOPLAN system supervised by Professor Alfonso Gerevini. He began graduate studies at the University of Rochester in the fall of 2003. Under the guidance of Lenhart Schubert, he pursued his research on the EPILOG reasoner, revising and extending it to support his work toward a self-aware agent. He received his M.S. from the University of Rochester in 2004. (www.cs.rochester.edu/~morbini/; fmorbini@gmail.com)

Oğuz Mülâyim is a Ph.D. Student at the Artificial Intelligence Institute of the Spanish National Research Council (IIIA-CSIC). His undergraduate degree is in computer science. His research is devoted to applying reactive and proactive introspective reasoning techniques to improve the performance of case-based reasoning systems. (oguz@iiia.csic.es)

David Musliner received his B.S.E. in electrical engineering and computer science from Princeton University (1988) and his Ph.D. in computer science from the University of Michigan (1993). Dr. Musliner designed and implemented the Cooperative Intelligent Real-Time Control Architecture (CIRCA), one of the first AI control architectures capable of reasoning about and interacting with dynamic, hard real-time domains. CIRCA includes active metacontrol for managing its planning processes to meet soft real-time deadlines. In 1995, Dr. Musliner joined the Automated Reasoning group at the Honeywell Technology Center, where he led research projects on real-time tasking and time-sensitive multiagent planning and scheduling systems for human coordination. In 2008, Dr. Musliner joined SIFT where he is currently investigating new concepts in high-level control of UAV teams, formal verification for spacecraft operating procedures, and planning for autonomous satellite defense (www.musliner.com/david; david.musliner@musliner.com)

Karen Myers is Director of the Intelligent Mixed-Initiative Planning and Control Technologies (IMPACT) program within the Artificial Intelligence Center at SRI International. She is also an SRI Principal Scientist. Her current interests lie with the development of mixed-initiative AI systems that enable humans and machines to solve problems cooperatively. Dr. Myers joined SRI in 1991 after completing a Ph.D. in computer science at Stanford University. (www.ai.sri.com/people/myers; myers@ai.sri.com)

Tim Oates is an associate professor in the Department of Computer Science and Electrical Engineering at the University of Maryland, Baltimore County. He received his Ph.D. from the University of Massachusetts, Amherst, and, prior to coming to UMBC in the fall of 2001, spent a year as a postdoc in the Artificial Intelligence Lab at the Massachusetts Institute of Technology. His research is in the areas of artificial intelligence, machine learning, data mining, language acquisition, and robotics. The top-level goal of his research is to develop a theoretical and algorithmic basis that will allow machines to replicate the human transition from sensors to symbols to semantics. (www.coral-lab.org/~oates; oates@cs.umbc.edu)

Don Perlis is currently a Professor of Computer Science at the University of Maryland, College Park. He received his Ph.D. in computer science at the University of Rochester in 1981, under the direction of James Allen. His research has evolved from studies in "pure" mathematical logic, then to applications of logic to formal commonsense reasoning, and more recently to the use of metacognition in commonsense behavior more generally. His efforts most recently have revolved around developing a methodology for general-purpose self-modeling and self-repairing systems. (www.active.cs.umd.edu; perlis@cs.umd.edu)

Smiljana Petrovic is an Assistant Professor of Computer Science at Iona College, New Rochelle, New York. Her research interests lie primarily in the areas of constraint satisfaction programming and machine learning. Dr. Petrovic develops problem-solving techniques that select and combine heuristics. She holds a B.S. in mathematics from the University of Belgrade and M.S. and Ph.D. degrees in computer science from the City University of New York. (www.iona.edu/faculty/spetrovic/; spetrovic@iona.edu)

Anita Raja is an Associate Professor of Software and Information Systems at the University of North Carolina at Charlotte. She received a B.S. Honors in computer science with a minor in mathematics (summa cum laude) from Temple University, Philadelphia, in 1996 and a M.S. and Ph.D. in computer science from the University of Massachusetts Amherst in 1998 and 2003, respectively. Her research focus is in the design and control of multiagent systems with particular emphasis on metacognition and bounded rationality. She has led efforts in studying the role of metalevel control in complex single-agent and multiagent systems. Professor Raja was the program co-chair of the First International Workshop on Meta Reasoning in Agent-Based Systems (MRABS) held at AAMAS 2007, the AAAI-2008 workshop on Metareasoning: Thinking about Thinking and the SASO-2009 workshop on Metareasoning in Self-adaptive Systems. (www.sis.uncc.edu/~anraja; anraja@uncc.edu)

Paul Robertson is a Senior Scientist at BBN Technologies, where he has been working on computer vision, self-adaptive software, health-care computing, computer learning, and metareasoning systems. Dr. Robertson was a Research Scientist at MIT, where he worked on robotics and autonomous systems. His projects at MIT included model-based autonomy, vision for autonomous robot navigation, self-regenerative software systems for multirobot cooperation, and learning spatial models for robot navigation. He was Chief Scientist at Dynamic Object Language Labs, where he developed advanced languages and reasoning systems for artificial intelligence. Dr Robertson was PI on an Oxford University, DARPA-funded contract to develop a Self-Adaptive Satellite Image Interpretation System that utilized metareasoning to avoid unlikely interpretations. He was manager of PC Products at Symbolics, Inc., where he led a team to develop PC-based solutions that bridged the gap between Lisp machines and the emerging PC market. He was Assistant Professor of Computing Science at the University of Texas at Dallas where he conducted research into computer learning systems. (openmap .bbn.com/~robertson/; paulr@bbn.com)

Zachary B. Rubinstein is a Systems Scientist in the Robotic Institute at Carnegie Mellon University. Dr. Rubinstein's major research focus is in effective collaboration among heterogeneous agents in dynamic environments. He has an extensive background in the areas of scheduling, planning, distributed systems, multiagent systems, blackboard systems, and case-based reasoning. Prior to his current position, he was an Assistant Professor in the Department of Computer Science at the University of New Hampshire. He received his Ph.D. in computer science from the University of Massachusetts, Amherst, and has worked in industry for more than fifteen years, building a variety of complex systems in the areas of dynamic process management, nearly autonomous systems, blackboard architectures, and assisted financial profiling. (www.cs.cmu .edu/~zbr/; zbr@cs.cmu.edu)

Brian Scassellati is an Associate Professor of Computer Science at Yale University. Dr. Scassellati received his Ph.D. in computer science from the Massachusetts Institute of

Technology in 2001 under the direction of Rodney Brooks. He also holds a Master of Engineering in computer science and electrical engineering (1995), and Bachelor's degrees in computer science and electrical engineering (1995) and brain and cognitive science (1995), all from MIT. His research focuses on building embodied computational models of the developmental progression of early social skills. He was named an Alfred P. Sloan Fellow in 2007 and received an NSF Career award in 2003. (www.cs.yale.edu/~scaz/; scaz@cs.yale.edu)

Matthew D. Schmill is a Research Assistant Professor at the University of Maryland, Baltimore County. He received his Ph.D. in computer science at the University of Massachusetts, Amherst, in 2004 for a dissertation entitled "Learning the Structure of Activity for a Mobile Robot." His current research includes improving the robustness of AI systems using metacognitive problem-solving, learning syntax for unknown terms in artificial student–teacher interactions, and applications of machine learning to computational finance. (matt.schmill.net; matt@schmill.net)

Lenhart Schubert is a Professor of Computer Science at the University of Rochester, a post he took up in 1988 after many years at the University of Alberta. His research interests center around language, knowledge representation and acquisition, inference, planning, and self-awareness. These interests are tied together by the general goal of developing agents with common sense and the ability to converse and acquire knowledge through language. Schubert is a Fellow of the AAAI and a former Alexander von Humboldt Fellow, has served as program chair of several major conferences in natural language processing and knowledge representation, has numerous publications in those areas, and has led the development of general systems for commonsense inference (EPILOG), knowledge acquisition from text (KNEXT), and invariant discovery in planning (DISCOPLAN). (www.cs.rochester.edu/~schubert/; schubert@cs.rochester.edu)

Hamid Shahri is a Ph.D. student in the Department of Computer Science, University of Maryland, and a graduate research assistant in the ALMECOM research group. His research interests include information integration, knowledge representation, and adaptive and intelligent systems. He received his B.S. from Ferdowsi University of Mashhad, Iran, and an M.S. from the University of Maryland, both in computer science. (www.cs.umd.edu/~hamid; hamid@cs.umd.edu)

Aaron Sloman took a first degree in mathematics and physics (1956, Cape Town), then was seduced by philosophy and did a DPhil on Kant's philosophy of mathematics (1962, Oxford). He later became convinced that the best way to do philosophy is to build successively larger fragments of working minds, as proposed in *The Computer Revolution in Philosophy* (1978). He has worked on vision, ontologies required for animals and robots, affective states and processes, mathematical development, nature–

nurture trade-offs, architectures, software tools for teaching and research in AI, understanding causation, and forms of representation in intelligent systems. He is a Fellow of AAAI, ECCAI and SSAISB. Hon DSc Sussex University (2006). (www.cs.bham.ac.uk/~axs/#whoiam; A.Sloman@cs.bham.ac.uk)

Stephen F. Smith is a Research Professor in the Robotics Institute at Carnegie Mellon University where he heads the Intelligent Coordination and Logistics Laboratory. He received his B.S. in mathematics from Westminster College in 1975, and his M.S. and Ph.D. degrees in computer science from the University of Pittsburgh in 1977 and 1980, respectively. Dr. Smith's research focuses broadly on the theory and practice of next-generation technologies for complex planning, scheduling, and coordination problems, and he has authored or coauthored over 215 technical articles in this area. In 2005, Dr. Smith received the Allen Newell Medal for Research Excellence, awarded annually by the Carnegie Mellon University School of Computer Science. In 2007 he was elected a Fellow of the Association for the Advancement of Artificial Intelligence. Dr. Smith's current research interests include adaptive search algorithms and heuristics, stochastic optimization frameworks, mixed-initiative and collaborative planning and scheduling tools, reconfigurable and self-organizing planning and scheduling systems, and agent-based frameworks for distributed task and resource allocation.

Shomir Wilson is a Ph.D. candidate at the University of Maryland. He earned bachelor's degrees in computer science, mathematics, and philosophy from Virginia Tech in 2005. His research interests include commonsense reasoning and natural language understanding. (www.cs.umd.edu; shomir@umd.edu)

Dean Wright is a Ph.D. candidate in computer science at the University of Maryland, Baltimore County. He has received multiple degrees from Hood College in Frederick, Maryland. He is researching ways to use metacognition to improve agent performance in the face of multiple or continuing problems. (www.csee.umbc.edu/~dean3; dean3@umbc.edu)

Shlomo Zilberstein is Professor of Computer Science and Director of the Resource-Bounded Reasoning Lab at the University of Massachusetts, Amherst. He received a B.A. in computer science (summa cum laude) from the Technion, and a Ph.D. in computer science from the University of California, Berkeley. Professor Zilberstein's research focuses on the foundations and applications of resource-bounded reasoning techniques, which allow complex systems to make decisions while coping with uncertainty, missing information, and limited computational resources. His research interests include approximate reasoning, decision theory, design of autonomous agents, heuristic search, information gathering, principles of metareasoning, planning and scheduling, multiagent systems, reinforcement learning, and reasoning under uncertainty. (rbr.cs.umass.edu/shlomo; shlomo@cs.umass.edu)

Terry L. Zimmerman is a Project Scientist at Carnegie Mellon University's Robotic Institute. His research interests lie in automated planning and scheduling, particularly methodologies for handling uncertainty, learning augmentations, and distributed and multiagent planning systems. Dr. Zimmerman has over fifteen years experience developing probabilistic risk and reliability assessment and safety analysis techniques for energy production facilities. He received his B.S. in engineering science from Iowa State University, his M.S. in nuclear science and engineering from Idaho State University, and a Ph.D. in computer science from Arizona State University in 2003. (wizim +@cs.cmu.edu)

Index

Made in the USA
Monee, IL
08 November 2026

68032038R00195